PIMLICO

600

RAGGED GLORIES

Barney Hoskyns was US Editor of *Mojo* between 1996 and 1999 and is currently Editorial Director of Rock's Backpages, the online library of rock 'n' roll (www.rocksbackpages.com).

RAGGED GLORIES

City Lights, Country Funk,
American Music

BARNEY HOSKYNS

PIMLICO

Published by Pimlico 2003

2 4 6 8 10 9 7 5 3 1

Copyright © Barney Hoskyns 2003

Barney Hoskyns has asserted his right under the Copyright, Designs
and Patents Act 1988 to be identified as the author of this work

First published in Great Britain by
Pimlico 2003

Pimlico
Random House, 20 Vauxhall Bridge Road,
London SW1V 2SA

Random House Australia (Pty) Limited
20 Alfred Street, Milsons Point, Sydney,
New South Wales 2061, Australia

Random House New Zealand Limited
18 Poland Road, Glenfield,
Auckland 10, New Zealand

Random House (Pty) Limited
Endulini, 5A Jubilee Road, Parktown 2193, South Africa

The Random House Group Limited Reg. No. 954009
www.randomhouse.co.uk

A CIP catalogue record for this book
is available from the British Library

ISBN 0-7126-0468-5

Papers used by Random House are natural,
recyclable products made from wood grown in sustainable forests;
the manufacturing processes conform to the environmental
regulations of the country of origin

Typeset by Palimpsest Book Production Limited,
Polmont, Stirlingshire

Printed and bound in Great Britain by
Makays of Chatham plc, Chatham, Kent

Contents

'Call Me Star-Struck, Uncle Sam' – A Way In

'These myths we can't undo / They lie in wait for you . . .'
Prefab Sprout, 'Hey! Manhattan' (1988)

The very idea of America captivated me from the earliest time I remember. Soaring towers, pneumatic women, comically stretched automobiles. Swamps and deserts. The sassy music of American accents.

From the day my dad came home from a business trip and presented me with a small plastic Empire State Building, it was my ambition to get out there, see this big magical land I glimpsed on screens big and small: *the You-nited States of A-mer-icah*.

I finally touched down in New York City on the night of an infamous blackout in July 1977, and still recall the shock of the humidity as I exited the air-conditioned arrivals building, like walking into a shroud of steam. Next morning in a swanky mansion on Long Island's north shore I stared at the front-page reports of looting in the *New York Times* and wondered if I'd arrived in heaven or hell. I'm still not sure which it was.

I've returned to America many times since then, and lived there twice: once in Los Angeles in the early 1980s, and more recently in Woodstock, upstate New York. Both are places that figured prominently in my work: Woodstock in *Across The Great Divide* (1993), LA in *Waiting For The Sun* (1996). I've also spent time in most other parts of the country, notably the soulful South, subject of *Say It One Time for the Brokenhearted* (1987).

American music has, I suppose, been the great fixation of my life. Even the *non*-American music I've loved most has been basically American, which is why I've always preferred the Rolling Stones to the Beatles. Is this because at some level I rejected my own culture in favour of dreams of remote wildness? Did I respond more immediately to *The Band* than to *The Village Green Appreciation Society* for the same reason Keith Richard(s) dreamed of the muddy Mississippi? Almost certainly. And definitely this had much to do with the essentially black feel of so much American music – the feel that drips from *Exile On Main St.* and from so few Lennon–McCartney songs. I hope the pieces here on Little Richard, Prince and others reflect my immersion in what Tom Waits – with Keef wailing alongside him – called 'That Feel'.

None of which explains my love of the Velvet Underground, Big Star, Todd Rundgren, Pavement – white boys all, and whiteboy-rock-crit staples to boot. Nor does it really account for the places Roy Orbison and Johnny Cash hold in my affection. In the end I think my obsession with America really comes down to the sheer sense of *possibility* the place represents.

When I lived in the Catskill Mountains in the late '90s, I felt vividly the choice I had simply to disappear into the vastness of the country – to get lost in its 'interior' and never be found again. In England you never really get away, no matter how far you travel. Nor do you ever shake off your position in the English class system: your accent fixes you wherever you roam.

What always thrilled me about America was people's movement and uprooting of themselves – the desire and the chance to change through geographical displacement. The romance of 'the road' – of what Peter Guralnick termed the 'journeys and arrivals of American musicians' – was what I heard in the best American music.

There's a price to be paid for this, of course: the gung-ho exhibitionism that's intrinsic to the American spirit, the unquestioning effusiveness that so often passes for real connection, and the paranoid xenophobia that can result from both of these. 'America has an almost obscene infatuation with itself,' notes Norman Mailer. 'America is the real religion in this country.' Never more so than now, one fears, with George W. Bush assuming the role of the world's police chief. Returning to England after four years in late 1999, I realised that we Brits are more apt to talk *to* rather than *at* each other.

Yet for all its bloated and neurotic insularity, America has unquestionably invented the future – and reinvented the world in the process. Hollywood and McDonald's and corporate globalisation notwithstanding, there's so much more that is right about the place than is wrong. From soul music to *Seinfeld*, America has shaped the way I live and feel, emotionally, intellectually and most other ways. And now I'm back in my cramped grey homeland, I realise how much of my heart I've left on the other side of the Atlantic.

When the planes went into the World Trade Center on 11 September 2001, I sat rooted in front of my television for hours and thought back to that similarly apocalyptic night when I first arrived in America twenty-five years ago. The most dwarfing towers of all had come down and 'Hey! Manhattan' would never be the same again. My heart bled, not for the lost symbols of American power but for all the decent, effusive people who'd died or had their lives shattered.

'We can be greedy, dumb and sloppy,' Ken Layne wrote in the aftermath of that ghastly day. 'But we made the nation that is the defining nation of this world. There's a reason our crappy movies and pop songs are worshipped in every corner of the world: everybody wants to be in this country, with their whole lives wide open.'

God bless y'all.

Barney Hoskyns
London, March 2003

Sources and Acknowledgements

The pieces in *Ragged Glories* were originally published, in slightly and sometimes very different form, in *New Musical Express*, *Mojo*, *Vogue*, *GQ*, *Request*, the *Guardian*, the *Observer*, the *Independent* and the *Independent on Sunday*, and on *Rock's Backpages* (www.rocksbackpages.com)

My thanks to the following editors: Neil Spencer, Tony Stewart, Mark Ellen, Paul Du Noyer, Liz Jobey, Mat Snow, Dylan Jones, Michael Hainey, Nick Coleman, Eve Macsweeney, Susan Hamre, Paul Trynka, Pat Gilbert, Danny Kelly, Jane Ferguson, Charlie English, Adrian Hamilton.

And the following writers and industry folk for their assistance: Randy Haecker, Mary Lou Arnold, Kelli Richards, Harold Bronson, Gary Petersen, Ben Edmonds, Lenny Kaye, Fred Goodman, Harvey Kubernik, Sally Grossman, Holly George-Warren, Andy Kershaw, Richard Wootton, Rob Partridge, Barbara Charone, Barbara Orbison, Steve Shelley, Robert Gordon, Tony Linkin, Laurence Bell . . . and those I've doubtless forgotten.

Not forgetting my colleagues at *Rock's Backpages*: Mark Pringle, Martin Colyer, Tony Keys, William Higham and Mat Snow.

For the terrible trio – Jake, Fred, Nat
I love you more than words than say

1

In the Grain

The Cats' Whiskers: Down Home with ZZ Top

Houston, October: the monsoon season in this blandly corporate boom-town. I descend through hot storms over a chrome metropolis built on flat sand and oil deposits, all hopes of snaring the bearded boogiemen of ZZ Top in their appropriate Texan climate rent apart by vicious cracks of lightning. Visions of boiler suits and souped-up stock cars with mad whale-tail fins against deep blue sky are washed away in the relentless rain. ZZ Top will be indoors, watching TV, thawing out frozen tacos.

Who knows what to expect of these genial loons on their home turf? I'm looking to them to subvert rock 'n' roll America, but they may just be part of Houston's boom: slick businessmen with a neat line in self-merchandising. (There must be ZZ Top *dolls* by now.) Doubtless they'll wish to be photographed in the boardroom of ZZT Enterprises.

'Lord, get me out of Houston town,' wailed soul man Ted Taylor. Everything was going wrong for Ted, but not for our good friends of the chin-blisters. ZZ Top have dwelt in the East Texan city for fifteen good years and show no signs of hotfooting it out. In many ways it's an ideal place for them, a city quite removed from the entertainment empires on the coasts and free of specific rock traditions.

Houston has grown, but grown so fast that things are still loose enough for a cartoon celebrity like Billy Gibbons to have served two years on the trustees' board of the city's Contemporary Arts Museum.

The money is new, so a generation or two can elapse before a class structure sets in hard. The latest issue of *Vanity Fair*, a kind of high-brow American *Tatler*, takes a gossipy peak at this trendy new mecca with its Philip Johnson 'scrapers, its outdoor Dubuffet sculptures and its subsidised ballet. In amongst the heiresses, the oilmen and the gallery owners is the voice of one B. Gibbons ('Rock Star'):

> Despite its size, the feeling, the thread that binds the whole of it together, is blue-collar. This is not a purely sophisticated city by any means. You've got the ship channel and the dockworkers and the refineries. The business community is firmly planted with both feet in that territory. You never really get away from an earthier kind of feeling.

The idea is to observe ZZ Top – along with Motorhead and the Blue Öyster Cult one of metal's more engaging anomalies – in their own backyard. Their album *Eliminator*, a hi-tech, rocket-ignition overhaul of their bastard hard blues, has been sitting seemingly immovable in our national Top 10 for two months. No one seems quite sure what propelled it up there; without a hit single it looks positively freakish.

It's a remarkably good record, of course, containing the mighty 'Gimme All Your Lovin'', which achieved in three minutes and fifty-nine seconds what dear old Status Quo have been striving to do for twenty whole years. Other spiffing riffs boasted by this fine disc include the video masterworks 'Legs' and 'Sharp Dressed Man', plus the mirthsome 'TV Dinners' and 'Got Me Under Pressure', with its unbeatable lines 'She likes cocaine / And flipping out with great danes'.

It's still raining the next day as I climb aboard a limo and head for the 'health spa' which ZZ Top have recently acquired in order to limber up between tours. An in-car TV box reports flooding in the north-west of the city. We glide past new housing settlements with names like Pecan Grove and White Oak Bayou on long flat roads stretching off the highway, past Pentecostal churches and cowboy surplus stores. A sign for Humble Mobile Homes comes up: humble indeed, though it was Humble Oil that later became the giant Exxon Corporation. ZZ Top's outrageously funky 'Cheap Sunglasses' booms from the tape deck. 'That dude pick the shit outta the bass,' remarks Fred, the black driver.

The ZZ Top 'spa' turns out to be fairly humble itself, though decorated in garish bordello wallpaper. A plastic imitation set of Mr T's excessive gold neckwear adorns one wall. It must be said that as we enter the spa the fellas are not exactly utilising the impressive array of Nautilus equipment on display. Nor do they exactly resemble three Arnie Schwarzeneggers. But then old Conan's pectorals would doubtless interfere with the subtle licking action which characterises Top's grooviest platters.

El primo licksman Gibbons looks about as unlike a beefy ten-gallon Texan as anyone could. In his blue pinstripe suit and white-shirted paunch he is more like a Hasidic Jew in a baseball cap; a tiny pigtail tickles the nape of his neck. Bass man and bearded double Dusty Hill is continually grinning a set of jagged little teeth and stroking his prodigious facial hair. His combination of Nike sweatpants, motorcycle boots and yellow sou'wester more than bears out his useful definition of 'sharp dressed' as 'anything I'm not wearing', and he strikes the eye as a jumble of car mechanic, hillbilly farmer and one of Snow White's seven dwarfs.

Gibbons and Hill have always struck me as the Morecambe & Wise of rock 'n' roll, or least Morecambe & Wise crossed with the false-bearded Marx Brothers of *Duck Soup*, and in the flesh this is precisely what they are. As for fresh-faced drummer Frank Beard, his little leather legs are the one thing I note about this natty, reformed-wildcat golfer person. ('Rod Stewart by way of *American Gigolo*' is how Billy Gibbons once appraised him.)

Almost immediately we repair to an almost inevitably Mexican restaurant, just two doors down on the same shopping lot, and while the culinary scene which ensues is not quite on the scale depicted in the gatefold sleeve of *Tres Hombres* – lashings of greasy cheese over guacamole and enchiladas – it's quite enough to nullify any strenuous exertions they may have managed in the spa. 'This is *purr*-fect fer Zee Zee Tarp,' drawls the laconic Beard, whose Southern acksint is simply total. 'Work out for two hours and then destroy it all.' He promptly digs into a large round of nachos.

Three iced teas are ordered for the Tops and conversation turns briefly to the subject of tolerable Mexican restaurants in London. (Café Pacifico in Covent Garden earns their highest rating.) From there it winds into more general feelings about the band's relationship with Britain. Gibbons speaks in a low, quiet voice. 'It's funny, because we waited so long to go to the UK. It was actually ten years before our first appearance. Having found a nice little cult following, it was a very warm reception in the beginning, and yet so many things had changed in music that we were very uncertain about how a ZZ Top-type band would go down in the UK, especially since the wave of new stuff in the late '70s. We were lucky to hit it just when a heavy metal thing was coming back: there was a slot we could sneak into.'

I remark that *Eliminator* is a more metallic record than *Deguello* or *Loco*. The guitars are revved up like the Corvette engine in the album cover's 1932 coupe.

'We've always been car freaks,' says Billy. 'A guy came into Houston and recommended that we go with him to California for the National Drag Racing Championships, and not having been to one in a while I really wasn't quite prepared for the magnitude and dynamics of a 2500-hp nitroburning *bomb*. It was just like a rocket with wheels, it was so *awesome*. If there was just a way to get that sound and that feeling on stage and record, well . . .'

'Hot cars and rock 'n' roll have always been synonymous,' puts in Dusty rather prosaically. 'They're already tied together . . .'

'Although Frank,' counters Billy, 'is suggesting that the next album feature the ZZ Top boat.'

Has anything changed in these three over the course of fifteen years? Were they the same merry pranksters in 1969?

'Ah'd swear they're wilder than they was tin years ago.'

Will you never grow a beard, Beard?

'Ah cain't! Ah'm jist so far behand! Ah use to say I was too yerng, but after twelve years that stopped working. Then ah said it was doo to female thigh burn, but I got married and ah cain't say *that* no more! So now I say ah'm jist too far outta the race.'

Gibbons and Hill are quick to point how much money their hirsuteness saves them tie-wise, though Billy sometimes invests regardless.

'There's a real hip little shop in Covent Garden called Robot, and they had the greatest string ties with skull and crossbones, which you just won't find in Texas. I said "I'll take ten". The guy said "*Why?*"'

Billy Gibbons' grandparents were English, which part-way explains his abiding affection for our fair isle, and his old man was Freddy Gibbons, a pianist and society orchestra leader who came to Texas from New York on account of his wife's poor health. 'I'm real glad he did because being here we've all had to figure out what it is that makes Texas such a great place to put down musical roots. I suppose one of the reasons was that up until the '70s none of this convenient modern city living was available. Growing up in Texas, there just seemed to be so much time on your hands, and that was a factor, that plus the old tradition of the Texas gunslinger. In other words, if you didn't have a six-shooter you used six strings.'

'There was also a big rhythm 'n' blues thing here and in Dallas,' says Dusty Hill, 'and you couldn't help but have that seep into you.' Dallas, three hundred miles north-west of Houston, is hometown to Dusty and Frank. Well before Billy had gotten his first Gibson Melody Maker and Fender Champ amp, a fourteen-year-old Dusty was playing some very primitive bass there with such blues heavyweights of JR-ville as Freddie King and Lightnin' Hopkins.

What first united ZZ Top, unbeknownst to each of them, was a late night blues station operating out of Mexico on which, three miles apart, they discovered the likes of Jimmy Reed, Howlin' Wolf and T-Bone Walker. 'Because he was from that high-society background,' recalls Billy, 'my dad didn't care for that jive stuff. It was the old story of the kid who wants to play rock 'n' roll, y'know, and dad says, "Why are you playin' *that* stuff." So the kid does it twice as heavy.'

In Dallas, Dusty and Frank wound up together in a dubious combo known as Lady Wild & the Warlocks, the lady in question being a Scouse siren of uncertain talents. On her ladyship's departure the Warlocks metamorphosed into the sub-psychedelic American Blues, noteworthy if only for the shocking-blue hair they sported as they gamely toured through the redneck wilds of Texas. (One of their show-stoppers was called 'Chocolate Ego'.) In Houston, meantimes, Billy Gibbons had assembled the amazing Moving Sidewalks, an acid-garage band who today rank alongside the 13th Floor Elevators in the Texan enclave of punk ancestry. The Sidewalks' '99th Floor', a collision of Them's 'Gloria' and the Elevators' 'You're Gonna Miss Me', remains a pinnacle of '60s garage punk, a stabbing riff of Vox fuzz organ and tinny, needling guitar.

It was while the Sidewalks were touring with the Jimi Hendrix Experience in 1968 that JH blessed Billy Gibbons as 'America's most promising young guitarist'. The bigger influence, of course, was Cream, the original power blues trio. The irony of Texans rediscovering their own blues heritage via a bunch of limeys reared in desperately unsoulful places like Twickenham has been remarked on before; Top have in any case taken more than two steps from the blues since then. If their first album, released in 1970, was orthodox enough, the patented humour was already sneaking through on *Rio Grande Mud* (1972), in such unbluesy odes to Americana as 'Chevrolet', 'Bar-B-Q' and 'Whiskey'n'Mama'.

The subsequent twenty years have produced a veritable cornucopia of High Trash anthems: 'Beer Drinkers and Hell Raisers', 'Nasty Dogs and Funky Kings', 'Cheap Sunglasses', 'Groovy Little Hippy Pad' and many more. Along with the Cramps and the B-52s, ZZ Top have crafted some of the wittiest pop statements ever made about America.

It's here that a curious tension develops in the conversation. For while Billy is clearly desirous of minor pontification on musical/cultural generalities, the others equally clearly aren't. When I ask (seriously) about ZZ Top's humour, Frank and Dusty get good ol' boy humorous – 'hey, humor's jist humor' – but Billy (the only really witty one) looks serious. So serious that he leaves the table. Somehow I sustain the line of inquiry.

In a way you're a kind of pop-art group, aren't you?

'You mean artsy-fartsy?? Heh heh heh!!!' bawls Frank.

'Heh heh heh!!!' concurs Dusty.

I stare long and hard at the remnants of my guacamole.

'Dusty, you goin' to that party Saturday?' inquires Frank.

'I gotta go to my mother's birthday, so I'm gon' be outta town. But I need to git a costume for Hallowe'en next week.'

'Ah wanted to go as y'all,' cackles Frank.

Mercifully, Billy Gibbons drifts back into the room. I repeat my pop-art question.

'I think that's a compliment,' he says. 'I don't think we've ever set out to present ourselves as the Talking Heads or anything, and yet there are so few bands who are aware of what American culture is about.'

'An' we're certainly not one of 'em!!' bellows Frank.

'Heh heh heh!!' Dusty bellows back.

Billy ignores them. 'There's so little regionalism. There's this kind of glaze which has made the East Coast like the West Coast and Texas like Wyoming and everywhere else. It's hard to pinpoint little segments or sections that have some oddball thing you can play off.'

I guess ZZ Top is a kind of oddball institution in itself.

'The entertainment level here in Houston is at such an ebb that we're real weirdos. Houston is not a showbiz town. I kind of enjoy the oddball attitude that is thrust on us. It keeps 'em guessing.'

It is a little-known fact that among the projects Billy Gibbons undertook during ZZ Top's three-year sabbatical of 1976–9 was a commission to compose and record some ambient electronic music for an art gallery in Paris.

A little while after Frank and Dusty have taken off in their respective automobiles, Gibbons proposes a visit to Rick's Cabaret, a 'high-class titty joint' housed in a kind of neo-Vegas Palladian villa, sort of halfway between *The Best Little Whorehouse in Texas* and the Houston 'encounter booth' where Harry Dean Stanton finds Nastassia Kinski in *Paris, Texas*. Since he is by no stretch of the imagination a priapic rock 'n' roll pig, Billy looks distinctly out of place at Rick's: at worst, framed by clusters of G-strings and nipples, he is Benny Hill rather than David Lee Roth. Feeling the acute discomfort that only a twenty-five-year-old English introvert could feel in such a temple of hedonism, I watch Gibbons being greeted by fellow Houston bigwigs, gorillas in suits and ostrich cowboy boots. I cannot decide whether to believe in this good ol' boy alter ego.

Back inside his limo, Billy turns and confesses his anger at Dusty and Frank: 'You were asking a serious question and they were being real tiresome.' Billy loves to talk, even if he loses himself in his own abstractions and has a strangely awkward way of searching out the right word. He's chuffed that people get far enough to take his humour seriously, and I think relishes the disparity between his own wide-ranging interests and the Top audience's narrower infatuation with boozy boogie. 'I hate to draw dividing lines,' he says, 'but where *does* Muddy Waters meet Brian Eno?'

By the time we've arrived at the Gibbons abode, I've stopped listening to Billy's ruminations. Instead I'm staring in disbelief at the interior decoration. The house is constructed around one outsize room overlooking the swampy-looking Buffalo Bayou River and is filled with artefacts of seriously advanced kitsch: blue neon cacti, a mannequin mummy, a pair of chrome sheep. (Yes, a pair of chrome sheep.) Everything else is merely tasteless.

Billy is reading my mind, or at least my expression. 'Americans invent things that are fun, things that go from right-field conservative to the seediest left-field expression you can dream up, and yet most of them are reactionary rather than visionary.' He is about to say more when the doorbell rings.

A lawyer friend has shown up with the rest of an Elvis-style inner echelon of pals and it's time to play good ol' boy again. The lawyer chides him for taking me to Rick's and everyone is slapping him on the back, chuckling like kids.

Time to make excuses and bid farewell, pausing only to glance back at this singularly odd fellow in his pinstripe suit, surrounded by urban cowboys.

The Benny Hill grin is a little crooked.

1984

White Boy Got The Woo-Woos: Lowell George

There aren't many of them, but Little Feat's January 1975 show at London's Rainbow Theatre was one of those legendary gigs everyone says they saw that I actually *did* see – along with Elvis Costello and most of the London pub-rock fraternity of the time.

The event is particularly etched on my mind because it marked a kind of watershed in my adolescence. Like many angst-ridden public schoolboys in the early '70s, I'd been through a major Bolan/Bowie glam infatuation, only to embark on the *de rigueur* prog-rock affair with Yes, ELP and the Mahavishnu Orchestra. By 1974, however, I'd discovered American Bands With Facial Hair, most hailing from California and the majority of them working within the idiom of country-rock. Yes, I too owned a copy of Poco's *A Good Feelin' To Know*.

Hippest by far of these groups was Little Feat, whom no one seemed to know anything about and whose album sleeves – the work of the late, great Neon Park – provided a singularly unhinged contrast to the line-up-against-a-Laurel-Canyon-sunset portraits which graced most West Coast releases. So when Warner Brothers Records put together a touring package of bands featuring Little Feat alongside Montrose, Graham Central Station and the Doobie Brothers, attendance at the Rainbow was mandatory.

As some will know or even recall, Little Feat took the stage that Sunday afternoon and wiped the floor with the Doobies, who'd enjoyed a fleeting hipness the year before but were henceforth doomed to be remembered as just another . . . well, American Band With Facial Hair. A swarthy, dumpy looking man in dungarees and floppy hat converted us to southern Californian swamp-funk, and we were never quite the same again.

Nigh on twenty years later – and fifteen years after the man's death – I'm thinking about Lowell George and asking myself just what his lasting contribution to American rock has been. Was he, in the words of his friend Martin Kibbee, 'the best-kept secret of the '70s Mellow Mafia . . . the finger in the slide on the syncopated pulse of that decade'? Or was he a booze-addled slob who never really delivered on the promise of his prodigious talent? Does his legend hinge on a mere handful of classic songs – 'Willin'', 'Sailin' Shoes', 'Dixie Chicken', 'Rock And Roll Doctor' – or is there a real *oeuvre* there to back it up?

Put it another way: just how great *were* Little Feat that January afternoon?

The first thing one needs to know about Lowell T. George is that – unlike the vast majority of LA legends – he was actually born and bred in Los Angeles. In fact, he was almost what you might call a Hollywood Brat, since his furrier-to-the-stars father lived next door to Errol Flynn and often went duck shooting with the one and only W.C. Fields.

On the sleeve of Little Feat's *The Last Record Album* (1975), with its spooky Neon Park depiction of a post-apocalyptic Hollywood Boulevard, George wrote that Hollywood was 'a giant fruit salad with a twist of cool whip like a mirage in your garage'. He was better qualified than most LA rock'n'rollers to make such solemn pronouncements.

Entering the world on 13 April 1945, little Lowell grew up in LA and went to Hollywood High, where he was a flautist in the high school band and – like Ricky Nelson before him – an enthusiastic member of the Car Club. In true showbiz-brat style, he appeared as a harmonica-playing teenager on the TV talent show *Ted Mack's Amateur Hour*, and may even have bumped into a future employer – the similarly aspirant Frank Zappa – backstage.

By 1964, however, Lowell was a junior beatnik, busy discovering folk, jazz and blues. 'I knew him at Junior College as just a charming, affable, puppy-like guy,' says Denny Bruce, an original member of Zappa's Mothers of Invention. 'We got to know each other as the oddball people on this campus, and he turned me on to a couple of coffee houses in LA where we'd listen to Howlin' Wolf on the jukebox all afternoon.' Doubtless Lowell's 'puppy-like' character was enhanced by his comparative chubbiness, which would always distinguish him from his 'elegantly wasted' peers on the LA scene. It's said that Lowell's penchant for stimulants stemmed from an early prescription for diet pills.

Nineteen sixty-five saw the formation of The Factory, whose initial claim to fame was that they played 'Hey Joe' louder than any of the countless other LA bands playing the song that year. Featuring Lowell on vocals, guitar and woodwind (primarily flute), the rest of the band consisted of childhood pal Martin Kibbee on bass, lead guitarist Warren Klein, and future Feat stalwart Richie Hayward on drums. Playing clubs such as Bido Lito's and the Brave New World, The Factory operated in a folk-psychedelic crack somewhere between Kaleidoscope and Captain Beefheart's Magic Band. Which was probably how they came to attract the attention of Frank Zappa and his manager Herbie Cohen in the fall of 1966.

Last year's Edsel compilation, *Lightning-Rod Man*, shows just how wild The Factory must have been. Consisting of demos recorded with Zappa, and unreleased UNI sessions supervised by ex-Teddy Bear Marshall Lieb, they veer between the Van Vliet-like zaniness of the title track and the more Strawberry Alarm Clock-style psych-pop of 'Candy Cane Madness' or 'Smile, Let Your Life Begin'.

Like Kaleidoscope, The Factory liked to experiment with such exotic instruments as dulcimers, piccolos and water chimes, egged on by a temporary mentor named Emil Richards. But UNI declined to issue any of The Factory recordings, so Lowell turned his attention to studying the sitar with Ravi Shankar, and the others sidled off to join Elliot Ingber – the future 'Winged Eel Fingerling', of Magic Band fame – in the ill-fated Fraternity of Man.

Despite buying into Indian mysticism big time – and studying martial arts to boot – George was ambitious enough to take over from Dick Dodd as the frontman in the Standells in 1968. It had been two years since the mighty 'Dirty Water', the Standells' Top 20 hit, and Dodd's departure had effectively spelled the end for the so-called 'garage' band.

'It was enlightening, because it was a band on a real decline,' recalled Lowell. 'The other guys in the band were bringing their hairdryers and magnifying mirrors along to gigs – they used to fluff up before the gig! I was stunned.'

George lasted barely two months as a Standell before Frank Zappa came to his rescue, bringing him on board as Ray Collins' replacement in the Mothers of Invention. 'Except that no one could replace Ray,' said Lowell later. 'He was a singer *par excellence* and had a sense of humour I couldn't hope to get near. So I really ended up playing more guitar than singing.'

It remains a matter of some contention as to exactly what George did and didn't do in the Mothers. In David Walley's Zappa book *No Commercial Potential*, Lowell griped about the lack of accreditation on *Hot Rats*, though his deranged vocals on *Weasels Ripped My Flesh* received their due acknowledgement. He also found Zappa as workaholic and unapproachable as most of the other Mothers did, which was why he quit the band in the summer of 1969. According to former groupie and bestselling author Pamela Des Barres, Zappa fired George because he smoked dope all the time, but he would almost certainly have gone anyway.

'I don't even know what Lowell was really doing in the Mothers, because it wasn't his sort of music,' Des Barres says. 'I guess he saw it as a stepping stone, which was what it turned out to be.' If nothing else, Lowell learned a lot from Zappa about band leadership.

One of the assignments George was given before he left the Mothers fold was to produce some tracks on *Permanent Damage*, the 1969 album by Des Barres and her fellow groupie superstars the GTOs. Anticipating the country-tinged songs on the first Little Feat album, 'Do Me In Once And I'll Be Sad, Do Me In Twice And I'll Know Better' was described in the sleevenotes as 'a reasonably abstruse love song with a gentle burn in it', while 'I Have A Paintbrush In My

Hand To Color A Triangle' — a song about a *ménage à trois* involving GTO member Mercy, Brian Jones and a certain Bernardo — boasted some of the hottest slide playing George ever put on tape.

Lowell actually did a lot of things on *Permanent Damage*, claims Des Barres. 'Frank worked on the theatre of the thing, but Lowell did the music. He was just a sweet-natured, angelic man. God, I just loved him, and I still have letters from him.'

Despite the parting of ways between George and the Mothers, Zappa was only too keen to sign Lowell's new band to his burgeoning Bizarre/Straight stable. Calling themselves Little Feat after a chance remark by Mothers drummer Jimmy Carl Black (apropos the size of the guitarist's shoes), the group was really the end result of 'Willin'', a truckers' ballad Lowell had demo'd with Ry Cooder and producer Russ Titelman while still a Mother. Featuring ex-Factory hand Richie Hayward on drums, ex-Mother Roy Estrada on bass, and would-be Mother Billy Payne on keyboards, Little Feat cut several demos for Bizarre/Straight in the fall of 1969, only to sign with Warner Brothers the following year.

'Lowell was rehearsing Little Feat, and he was going to sign with Herbie Cohen or with Gabriel Mekler's Lizard label,' recalls Russ Titelman. 'I said, "You don't wanna do that, why don't we go see Lenny Waronker at Warners?" So I took him and Billy Payne up to Burbank and they sang "Willin'", "Truck Stop Girl" and "Brides Of Jesus". And Lenny just said, "Make a record — it's a deal".'

Billy Payne recalls his introduction to George with great affection: 'I'd driven down to LA from Santa Barbara to meet him, and the first thing I saw was this beautiful blonde in the living room, reading Carl Sandberg and listening to Erik Satie! I was impressed! Two hours later, Lowell hops in, and right off the bat the guy was just so magnetic. He was unassuming, there was an intelligence about him, and he was intensely musical. What I liked was there wasn't any of that Hollywood shuffle about it: we just kicked some ideas around and eased into what became Little Feat.'

For Payne, four years George's junior, the guitarist was close to being a big brother: 'He was leading the way. It was like, "Here's Hollywood, Bill, and here's what we're gonna do."'

Russ Titelman says – and Billy Payne bears him out – that what the band really wanted to do with *Little Feat* (1971) was recreate the flavour of the first two Band albums, then a huge influence on the LA scene. 'We didn't manage to do it,' Titelman admits, 'and that's probably because Little Feat were much more blues-oriented than The Band. The Band were more about the white South.' Nonetheless, like The Band and Gram Parsons, Lowell George was tuning into a new-old spirit of roots Americana, revamping the blues and country music he loved.

There was Stonesy sass in 'Hamburger Midnight' and 'Snakes On Everything', Burritos balladry in 'Brides Of Jesus' and 'I've Been The One' (featuring the Burritos' pedal-steel man Sneaky Pete Kleinow), and Beefheartian Delta grunge in the Howlin' Wolf medley of 'Forty Four'/'How Many More Years'.

Part Jagger, part Dr John, and part Boz Scaggs, Lowell George came as close to White Negrohood and ersatz Dixie hip as anyone did in 1971. A large factor in this was his humming, swarming slide guitar style, developed after he'd injured his left hand building a model aeroplane. 'There is not much doubt that he was the greatest slide guitarist of his generation,' wrote Richard Williams, 'and it was his bad luck that his imagination was too subtle to capture the flavour of the masses who worshipped Eric Clapton or Duane Allman.'

Some, however, feel the idea of Lowell George as Guitar Hero has been somewhat overplayed, to the detriment of a full appreciation of his genius as a writer. 'To me, Duane Allman was a slide guitar genius,' says Billy Payne. 'Lowell was a great player, but his genius was in his lyrics and his phrasing. It was in the way he put songs together.'

Though Little Feat toured America as part of a Warners package with Captain Beefheart and Ry Cooder, the exposure did no more to sell their debut album than did Ed Ward's rave review in *Rolling Stone*. 'In their early days, it was Starvation Central,' Lowell remembered. 'Richie and his wife and kids slept in my living room, and Billy slept out in my Volkswagen van.' Only the continuing popularity of 'Willin'' – covered by everyone from the Byrds and Linda Ronstadt to Sea Train and Commander Cody – kept the name Lowell George alive on the LA scene. By the mid-'70s, this ode to 'weed, whites and wine' had become *the* truckers' anthem. (LA singer Louie Lister recalls Lowell being so enamoured of the trucking life that he was seriously considering giving up music to take to the open road.)

Even when Warners assigned the great Ted Templeman to produce *Sailin' Shoes* (1972), something seemed to jinx the band. People have conjectured that George wasn't a charismatic enough frontman to carry the band on a visual or performance level, but a more fundamental point was that he eschewed the kind of accessible Californian rock which helped the Doobies and the Eagles go platinum. There was always something gnarly and knotty about the best Little Feat songs – invariably those written by George – which ruled out the possibility of major commercial success.

With its unforgettable, Fragonard-derived Neon Park cover painting – a grotesque cake with eyes and limbs on a swing – *Sailin' Shoes* became a cult album in Britain. It still sounds pretty great in 1994. If 'Easy To Slip' wasn't so far from the LA tradition of Crosby, Stills, Nash & Young, the caustic raunch of 'Tripe Face Boogie' or 'Teenage Nervous Breakdown' (like the crunching South Side groove of 'Cold Cold Cold' or 'A Apolitical Blues') was harder than anything else coming out of California at the time. There was also a new 'n' improved 'Willin'' to savour, as well as the supremely soulful title track. These songs came closer to the glory of, say, *Exile On Main St.* than any of Little Feat's mutton-chopped contemporaries. They were also witty, sexy and vaguely surreal at a time when, as Denny Bruce puts it, most Californian song writing was about 'drinking apple juice and walking down a dusty road with your dogs'.

Not long after the album's release in March 1972, Roy Estrada split to join the Magic Band, prompting a hiatus which saw Lowell playing sessions for Etta James, Jimmy Webb and Carly Simon (to name but three), as well as attempting to put together a three-part-harmony super group with Phil Everly and John Sebastian. ('Human chemistry ruled out any chance of a workable unit,' he said later.)

It was also at this time that Jackson Browne, the ultimate '70s LA singer/songwriter, approached George with a view to forming a new band. 'I put myself in Lowell's hands for a while and made him my tutor,' he told Bill Flanagan. 'And he very good-naturedly accepted . . . he adopted that sort of big, mean approach: "OK, if you want to know what I know, you've got to do that and that . . . and when you're through we'll talk about it." He called me the student prince because I was so willing to learn.'

When Little Feat returned in 1973, it was with an expanded line-up featuring second guitarist Paul Barrere, plus Delaney & Bonnie renegades Kenny Gradney (bass) and Sam Clayton (percussion). The fact that Gradney and Clayton were both originally from New Orleans suited Lowell to a T. Increasingly smitten with the black music of that magical Crescent City, he wanted to build Little Feat into a 'sophisti-funk' powerhouse around a potent piano/slide/congas combo. The resulting *Dixie Chicken* (1973) not only boasted the pure second-line propulsion of the title track and 'Fat Man In The Bathtub', but featured an ultra-soulful rendition of Allen Toussaint's 'On Your Way Down' and a wordless hymn to Louisiana called 'Lafayette Railroad'. The whole album epitomised LA's tequila-soaked love affair with the rootsy, sensual South. With Bonnies Raitt and Bramlett on backing vocals, it was funky country chased with bayou soul – what ex-Kaleidoscope mainstay Chris Darrow called 'lizard-skin music'.

For Van Dyke Parks, the one-time Beach Boys collaborator who produced the wonderful 'Spanish Moon' on *Feats Don't Fail Me Now* (1974), George was a close friend and fascinating phenomenon: 'Lowell taught a lot of people to sing, and you can hear his style in a number of the people he worked with . . . that melisma of madness I refer to as "White Boy Got The Woo-Woos" or "Vanilla Grits".' If there were more than a few gumbo-funk moves copped from the book of Mac Rebennack – the original New Orleans 'white negro' – the essence of Little Feat was Lowell's own inspired take on the South.

The only problem was that Little Feat's expanded line-up ultimately proved George's undoing, since as time went on the swampy soul of his songs increasingly lost out to the fusion-muso noodlings of his band. The indications were already there – in the instrumental break on 'Texas Rose Cafe', in the synth work on 'Kiss It Off', for example – but it took *Feats Don't Fail Me Now* for the truth to register: that Billy Payne secretly wanted to be Joe Zawinul, and that the others felt the need to prove they could cut it with the likes of Steely Dan.

It was the old Frank Zappa hang-up about being rated for their chops, and Lowell's battle to keep things simple and soulful was harder to fight within the band's new democracy. As he said just before his death, 'the dynamics that exist within a group – who's getting to be a big shot and who isn't – can tear it apart'.

It didn't help, of course, that George was undermining his own authority as Little Feat's putative leader by indulging in sensual grat-ification on a heroic scale. 'When you look up the word "hedonism" in the dictionary, there should really be a picture of Lowell there,' says Rick Harper, who road-managed Lowell on and off from the earliest days of The Factory to the last days of Little Feat. And Three Dog Night's Danny Hutton, who provided the tired, scratchy backing vocal on Dixie Chicken's 'Roll Um Easy', recalls George as an almost permanent fixture at his Laurel Canyon 'party house', 'ingesting huge amounts of cocaine, yet somehow getting fatter and fatter'.

Nevertheless, if *Feats Don't Fail Me Now* included the dire prog of Payne's 'The Fan', it was also choc-full of marvels: the stupendously funky 'Rock And Roll Doctor', the Parks-produced 'Spanish Moon' and a red-hot medley of those old favourites 'Cold Cold Cold' and 'Tripe Face Boogie'. The energy of the album was testament to the new sense of freedom George felt working in the band's own Blue Seas studio in Maryland, built on a barge just off Route 83, north of Baltimore. The distance from the Hollywood scene was itself signif-icant, and Lowell spent hundreds of hours alone in the studio. 'The only thing that moves me is the ability to further the work I'm doing,' he told *Zigzag* at the time. 'Most recently, that turned out to be our recording studio, which moved me a great deal.'

Paul Barrere's brother Michael, who often jammed with Lowell in the early Feat days, remembers him as 'a hard-driving, possessed musi-cian, a full-on Aries', and recalls Lowell and Richie Hayward 'going nose-to-nose' about the 'busy-ness' or otherwise of Richie's drum frills. 'I don't think it was an ego thing with Lowell so much as a kind of *possession* or *obsession*,' he says. Richie Hayward himself, recently playing in London with Eric Clapton, admits that the rest of the band had an intense love-hate relationship with George: 'There were personality clashes in Little Feat that made it very uncomfortable. But they also contributed to the tension you hear on the records, so in some ways it was a positive thing. I kinda liked both Lowell's and Billy's directions, so I acted as the pressure-relief in the band. I let a lot of stuff come down on me in order to preserve the group, otherwise it would just have blown up.'

'What people sometimes discount,' says Billy Payne, 'is that Little Feat was a band. It wasn't Bruce Springsteen and the E Street guys or Bob Seger and the Silver Bullet Band, it was a band like the Stones, and that meant a situation of uncontrolled chaos. I mean, I was guilty of writing my share of fluff, but my understanding was that Little Feat was a platform for the five of us to say what we wanted to say. The fact is, we affected each other, we pushed each other, and it was that type of camaraderie that produced the music. Lowell would say, "You can't write a commercial song like that." And I'd say, "Yes, you can." And he'd say, "No, you can't." And the result of that was "Oh Atlanta".'

The first Little Feat album to crack the Top 40, *Feats Don't Fail Me Now* in due course went gold. This was principally because Bob Cavallo and Joe Ruffalo, the band's managers, went to Warners and begged MD Mo Ostin to get behind the group. By the time *The Last Record Album* was released in the fall of 1975, however, the signs were looking ominous. For the one outstanding Lowell George song on the record, the country-soulful ballad 'Long Distance Love', you had to put up with a bunch of mediocre stuff from Messrs Payne and Barrere. Even worse was *Time Loves A Hero* (1977), which included only two Lowell George songs – the dull 'Rocket In My Pocket' and inconsequential 'Keeping Up With The Joneses' – amid its smorgasbord of Doobies/Steely Dan emulations and soundtrack-style funk. The worst offender by far on this Ted Templeman-produced platter was Bill Payne's sub-Weather Report showcase 'Day At The Dog Races', during live renditions of which Lowell George would wander offstage. 'It was completely the antithesis of everything else Little Feat played,' Lowell told Bill Flanagan.

Again, the rest of the band feel unjustly maligned by rock commentators on this issue. 'When *Time Loves A Hero* came out,' says Billy Payne, 'Paul and I were lambasted by a lot of people for supposedly crowding Lowell out of the writing arena. And that just wasn't true, as anyone who looks at the credits on his solo album will see. The guy just wasn't coming up with songs.'

It didn't help that George was no longer the mentor/big brother figure he'd been eight years before. 'The drugs and drink had a lot to do with Lowell's losing his authority within the band,' says Richie Hayward. 'I mean, we all had our problems, but he was very scattered. He'd hide in the studio for days on end, not being very productive, and it made him terribly unhappy.'

Unlike Steely Dan – still capable in 1977 of the awesome *Aja* – Little Feat were slowly turning into Old Farts. Although they performed for adoring fans when they returned to the Rainbow in the summer of 1977 (the results can be heard on the intermittently exciting *Waiting For Columbus* live double), they now epitomised everything punk rockers detested about southern California. Travelling on a separate bus from the others, moreover, George had effectively ceded leadership of the band to Paul Barrere.

By this point, George's health was deteriorating fast, especially with the onset of chronic drugs-related hepatitis. Living up in Topanga Canyon with his beleaguered second wife Liz and daughter Anara, he was increasingly becoming a burden to friends and colleagues. 'I worried about him, just like everyone else did,' says Rick Harper. 'He was always putting off seeing doctors until it was almost too late.'

For his old friend Martin Kibbee, co-author of several Feat classics, 'Lowell was carrying on grandly and having a great time, unaware of how sick he was becoming.' It's said that George dreamed of putting together a Little Feat without Payne and Barrere, and that he was a little miffed when Warners saw fit to release a Lowell George solo album comprising a mixed bag of tracks recorded over a period of two and a half years.

Featuring the usual West Coast session suspects (Jim Keltner, Marty Paich, J.D. Souther et al.), *Thanks, I'll Eat It Here* was a typical LA album of the time: lots of horns and gospelly organ, backing vox galore – all very Boz Scaggs. Opening with another Allen Toussaint song, 'What Do You Want The Girl To Do?', it rounded up the Mexican ballad 'Cheek To Cheek' (penned with Van Dyke Parks), a stab at the Hi classic 'I Can't Stand The Rain', and a whimsical Jimmy Webb number called 'Himmler's Ring'.

'Easy Money', meanwhile, came from the pen of Rickie Lee Jones, whom George had heard in a Topanga bar called the Post Office; the song would lead to her Warners deal in the same way 'Willin'' had led to Lowell's. Best of all, though, was the beautiful '20 Million Things', as good as 'Willin'' or 'Long Distance Love' or any of Lowell's other great ballads.

The record never rose any higher than No. 71, but it did get George back on the road that summer of '79. 'It's much easier on the old nervous system,' he said, a few days into the tour. 'I'm not trying to keep a couple of other guys in order while trying to keep myself in order.'

Martin Kibbee believes George thought he was about to become a big star, and that he was consciously leaving his old friends behind: 'I think he was blind to the support he'd had from his friends. He was pretty callous and self-centred in those last months.'

Not long before Lowell left to go on the road, Billy Payne told him he could take no more: unlike George, he'd got his act together and pulled back from the brink of self-destruction. 'I suggested he do his little tour and let Little Feat slide for a while. I told him he should get properly into producing, since that was where he seemed the happiest. [George had produced the Grateful Dead's 1978 album *Shakedown Street*.] I told him what a miserable fucker I thought he was, and how misspent his talent was. I wasn't a boy scout and I couldn't save him, but at least I said everything I wanted to say.

'Just before he set off on his tour, he came out to my house in the Valley on his motorcycle. It was the middle of the night, and his eyes were as big and black as saucers. He came to the door and started to say something, but he just couldn't say it. His eyes started to brim with tears, and then he just walked away. That was the last time I ever saw him.'

When Bill Flanagan interviewed George on 18 June 1979, the thirty-four-year-old singer was 'overweight, overtired, and had a bad cold for which he was taking antihistamines'. He was also hoovering up absurd quantities of coke. Eleven days later, after performing at

George Washington University in Washington, DC, he keeled over from a heart attack.

Back in LA, his friends couldn't believe he'd gone. Many tears were shed at his funeral, and then again at a tribute concert in which old flame Linda Ronstadt sang 'All That You Dream'. Jackson Browne wrote about him in 'Of Missing Persons', and artist/songwriter Terry Allen (author of Little Feat's 'New Delhi Freight Train') dedicated 'Heart Of California' to his memory.

In late 1979, Warners issued the Little Feat album *Down On The Farm*, with four Lowell George tracks including a fine song from his Blue Seas days called 'Front Page News'. (The very different original appeared on the fascinating 1981 double album *Hoy-Hoy!*, along with such rarities as a mix of 'Rock And Roll Doctor' with Allen Toussaint-arranged horns and a solo Lowell George outtake called 'China White'. Martin Kibbee, who wrote the album's sleevenotes under his song-writing pen-name 'Fred Martin', says there are countless other gems in the can, including some of the best material Lowell ever wrote.) By then, Payne and Barrere were playing in Nicolette Larson's band, and continued, like the others, to play sessions through the '80s.

In 1988, the two men re-formed Little Feat with guitarist Fred Tackett and ex-Pure Prairie League singer Craig Fuller to record the modestly successful *Let It Roll. Representing The Mambo* (1990), the band's final Warner Brothers album, was a rather more tedious exercise in 'stretching out'.

'He was a sweet, sweet creature who got fucked up,' says Pamela Des Barres of her old friend. But not all fuck-ups are sweet creatures, let's face it, and Lowell George seems to have been a slightly more endearing human being than most coke freaks.

'He'd been scarred by the business and he could be distant and aloof,' says Michael Barrere, 'but he was never mean to his friends.'

Almost everyone who knew George says the same thing: that he was genuinely obsessed with music, and genuinely unimpressed by the trappings of rock stardom that came with it. When the Rolling Stones pitched up at a Little Feat show and sent some roadie over to ask if they could jam with the band, Lowell found 'the decadence of them not being one-to-one with me' so rude he decided that 'the last thing I wanted was to have the Stones sit up there and play out of tune'. Not a natural-born crony, our Lowell.

Even George's drug use had little to do with living out some fantasy of rock debauchery. 'It was just hedonism, plain and simple,' says Rick Harper. 'It wasn't to impress, or to enable him to fit in socially, because he didn't give a shit about that.'

And the records? Up to and including most of *Feats Don't Fail Me Now*, Little Feat's albums stand alongside the work of Beefheart, Young, Newman, Cooder, Mitchell, Parsons, Becker & Fagen, Raitt, Waits and Zevon as the best LA had to offer in the first half of the '70s. Lowell had funk oozing from every pore of his body, and he had a slide finger that most white blues pretenders would have died for.

'If he's considered a minor figure, it's just because Little Feat was never a Fleetwood Mac,' says Martin Kibbee. 'But the stuff holds up critically, and the chances are that in fifty years people will go, "Hey, this guy was really on the money."'

'There's a fat man in the bathtub / With the blues,' Lowell George sang on that irresistible song from *Dixie Chicken*. No doubt his portly, hirsute body is now soaking in some bathtub in the sky. And he still has the blues in spades.

1994

25 Years From Tulsa: J.J. Cale

Fifteen minutes before J.J. Cale is due to take the famous stage of Manhattan's Carnegie Hall, a wiry, hobo-ish figure can be seen shuffling across the varnished floorboards to test the guitars and amplifiers. People are still milling around the auditorium, most of them here to catch a rare show by headliners The Band, but a fair number have already taken their seats. Some of them, one assumes, must be familiar with the recorded works of Mr Cale, which at the very least inhabit the same musical hinterland as that of The Band. Yet almost nobody appears to realise that the grizzled figure on the stage is Cale himself.

It's all part of the effect, of course. For the best part of twenty-five years, Jean-Jacques Cale has assumed the role of American rock's anonymous drifter – a shadowy Everyman, a figure you might have spotted once at some roadside diner on a highway to nowhere. As he falls into a subdued, cursory version of his signature song 'After Midnight', Cale isn't giving very much more away. The famous voice that gave new depth to the '70s phrase 'laid back' is barely a parched whisper now, testimony to the diffidence that he brings to the business of live performance – or at least to the dilemma of presenting himself as any kind of star.

He becomes more animated as, one by one, his band members join him on the vast stage; but he says almost nothing, and never once mentions the fact that he is about to release a new album. And yet

Cale's very recalcitrance is mesmerising, as though the implicit distrust of overt emotion itself induced a higher level of emotional engagement. A sleepy 'Sensitive Kind', a loping 'Crazy Mama', a hushed 'Magnolia' – each Cale classic takes its place in the steady-rolling flow, each one accompanied by his fluid, opalescent guitar picking.

Seated in these improbably formal surroundings, one has a sudden and jolting sense of what Peter Guralnick once termed the 'journeys and arrivals of American musicians'. Almost forty years ago, 'Johnnie Cale' and his band the Valentines were playing the exact same honky-tonk circuit around Texas and Oklahoma as The Band's Levon Helm, who was then drumming with rockabilly renegade Ronnie Hawkins. Four decades later, both men have somehow parlayed their canny, rough-hewn Southernness into an art form that cuts the mustard in a venue whose walls commonly reverberate to the sound of Brahms and Mozart.

'The geography has something to do with my music,' Cale tells me in his hotel room on the day before the show. 'Where I grew up in Tulsa, Oklahoma, it wasn't the South-east and it wasn't the Deep South and it wasn't quite the South-west either. For many years, too, America was so migratory: people would uproot and move, and with them would come their musical culture, which they'd blend with the culture of wherever they landed. That's kinda what happened to me: I listened to jazz, country, R & B, rock 'n' roll. And when I sat down to write a song, I had all these influences comin' through.'

When Cale's smoky, seductive first album *Naturally* appeared out of nowhere in 1972, few of the people who bought it – and thus began to make up the man's considerable cult following – realised that the singer was already thirty-two years old. The swampy stew of soul, blues and downhome country funk was effectively a distillation of twenty years' immersion in the roots music he loved, and it slotted right into place alongside the nongeneric Americana of The Band and Ry Cooder – Americana with a distinctively steeped flavour, as black as it was white, as gnarled as it was emblematic.

Like so many Okies before him, Cale had headed west to the promised golden land of California, following in the tracks of such fellow Tulsans as Leon Russell and David Gates. I ask him if he remembers

Gates, who later wrote a famous song that shares its title with that of Cale's new album *Guitar Man*. 'Oh yeah, I knew David way before he went to California. He mainly played fancier gigs, school functions and the like, whereas I'd be playin' bar dives and what have you. His music was a little . . . *cleaner*.' That should be no surprise to anyone familiar with the saccharine sound of Gates' group Bread.

In the Los Angeles of the early to mid-'60s, Cale found work not only as a for-hire guitar gunslinger in the bars of the San Fernando Valley but as a studio engineer in the employ of Leon Russell's Texan boss Tommy 'Snuff' Garrett. Garrett was the mastermind behind such West Coast pop fluff as Bobby Vee and Gary Lewis & the Playboys, with Russell doing most of the hard graft in the studio. When psychedelia struck LA like a tremor, Snuff suggested Cale round up a posse of his cronies and cut an album of 'psychedelic hits of the day' – 'Eight Miles High', 'Sunshine Superman' and the like.

Released under the unforgettably dumb name the Leather-Coated Minds, the 1966 album *Trip Down Sunset Strip* inadvertently spawned the song that would later change the course of Cale's destiny. '"After Midnight",' he says, 'was originally an instrumental that was meant to go on that album. Later on, I pulled the track back out, put words to it, and overdubbed a vocal.' Released by Garrett on Liberty, the single later found its way into the possession of Eric Clapton, whose bass player Carl Radle was another of the Okies who'd made LA their home. 'If Eric hadn't cut that song,' Cale grins, 'I'd probably still be playin' bowling alleys in Tulsa.'

By a neat coincidence, the phone rings at this point in the conversation and it turns out to be Audie Ashworth, the Nashville DJ turned record producer who first suggested Cale capitalise on Clapton's cover of 'After Midnight' and 'spec' his own album. Cale and Ashworth are in the process of putting together a box set that will be released by Phonogram – tracks and outtakes from vintage masterworks like *Naturally*, *Really*, *Okie* and *Troubadour*. 'Audie picked all the hip musicians who played on those albums,' says Cale. 'They were the demo players in Nashville, and they had more of a rock 'n' roll feel about them. We hit grooves that maybe any one of us wouldn't have hit – the whole was greater than the sum of the parts.'

Ironically, Cale has spent much of the ensuing decade and a half trying to shake off the 'downhome, laid-back' tag affixed to him in the '70s. 'People would always say, y'know, "J.J.'s got a kind of *hummin' mud* sound", and I've tried to clean some of it up. Now people ask me why I don't cut one o' them *Unplugged* albums, and I go, well, that's what I did first, and I had to move on. Seems my audience preferred me as the old acoustic guy, but when I went back to LA in 1980 it was a cultural shock, and that changed the way I made my records.'

Listening to 'Death In The Wilderness', the eco-conscious opening track on *Guitar Man*, one is hard pressed to recognise the J.J. Cale of 'Call Me The Breeze' or 'Same Old Blues'. The hi-tech programming and digital feel are very far from the sound of those hip Nashville pickers of yesteryear; if anything, they're closer to the sound of latter-day Dire Straits, the band who made a stadium-packing career out of Cale's sound. 'Ever since 1972, there's always been a coupla tracks I've done by myself, and this is kind of the apex of that. I pretty much manufactured it by myself. I got rid of my analogue stuff about six or seven years ago and moved into the digital realm. My live performance is different – I don't even try to emulate anything I do in the studio. Makin' records is one art form and playin' live is another. It's like the difference between makin' a movie and doin' theatre.'

One thing that hasn't changed – and almost certainly never will – is that spooked, mumbling voice. I ask Cale where on earth it came from. 'I knew that if you wrote songs you had to sing 'em to somebody. But I didn't want to sell 'em to the public, I wanted to sell 'em to more people like Clapton. People said my records were "funky" and "muddy", but the truth is they were just demos. I figured if you polished 'em up too much, people wouldn't wanna sing 'em.'

And the famous J.J. Cale mystique?

'It just happened that way. I did not try to figure out a good marketing ploy. People said I stood over in the corner with my back to the audience, but that was because we didn't rehearse and the band didn't know the tunes. See, I've just tried to live normally. I don't jive myself. I play the guitar and write songs for a living like the maid cleans this room. If I'm original, it's by accident – it comes from not being able to do what other guys can do. I tried to sound like Chet Atkins but I couldn't pick it all out. And not doing that, it started to sound like *me*.'

1996

The Lonely Blue Dream
of Roy Orbison

'{He's} a songwriter who sings about tragedy to such a fucking degree it's almost impossible to comprehend the depth of that soul. It's so deep and dark it just keeps on goin' down – but it's not black. *It's blue, deep blue. He's just got it. The drama. There's something sad but proud about Roy's music.'*

Neil Young

He stands stock-still, or nearly so. His right hand mechanically strums a black Gretsch guitar, and his left leg slightly trembles. He could be a waxwork come weirdly to life. He is dressed head to toe in black, topped off with immovable Ray-Bans and a jet-black conk of hair that only make his skin look the more marble-white. Perhaps most extraordinary is the way his magnificent tenor voice comes through thin pursed lips, as though from outside his body. There is no emoting here, just intense concentration on the words he is singing to a stark bolero beat.

'Just running scared, each place we go / So afraid that he might show . . .'

Rows of impassive Dutch teenagers sit watching the singer like kids forced to sit through a school play. For them he is already an outmoded figure, a throwback to the quaint early '60s with no place

in the moptop-rebel world of the Stones and the Kinks. Between songs
an earnest fellow named Jos Brink springs on to the stage to ask him
questions. One exchange leads Jos to make the solemn observation
that the singer 'does not design the songs for a teenage public' –
which, come to think of it, isn't so far from the truth. Soliciting opinions from the audience, Brink learns from one gormless-looking youth
that the singer's faster numbers – 'Dream Baby', 'Mean Woman Blues',
a version of Ray Charles' 'What'd I Say' – are preferable to his slow
ballads.

Combo Concert, a recently released video of a Dutch TV performance
Roy Orbison gave on 23 March 1965, captures the man at the crest
of his '60s success – or maybe just beyond it. Behind him is the string
of great hits that starts with 'Only The Lonely' in 1960 and climaxes
with 'Oh, Pretty Woman' in late 1964; ahead of him lies decline,
tragedy, and – much later – a remarkable, phoenix-like ascent from
the ashes of stardom. But the video also preserves Orbison at his most
magnetically iconic, a monochrome statue with a voice supernatural
in its operatic sweep and drama – a man out of pop time.

Four years after the *Combo Concert* date, Bruce Springsteen saw
Roy Orbison perform live at a festival in Nashville. 'The thing that
shocked me most was that he was so still,' the Asbury Park bard
remembered. 'He had a feeling about him where it seemed like if
you went up to him and tried to touch him, your hand would go
through him. It seemed like he'd fallen from another planet. He had
that purity when he sang . . . and he always had that loneliness, and
that distance.'

Purity, loneliness, distance: are these the things that Roy Orbison
has come to embody for us? When we listen to his anguished ballads
of broken reveries and unrequited longings – to 'Crying', to 'In
Dreams', to the chilling 'It's Over' – it's as if the voice allows us to
wallow in pain, to glory in our own sorrow. Orbison is pop's great
outsider, the dumpy smalltown boy who somehow turned himself into
the charismatic personification of inconsolable loss. He is the pitiful
figure hunched over his dying wife in Guy Peellaert's morbid illus-
tration from *Rock Dreams* – in Kurt Loder's fine words 'an inscrutable
curio of faded youth, locked away in a prestigious but seldom-visited

back room of pre-Beatles rock'. Is there anything wrong with this picture?

'He was like a buddha,' says k.d. lang, who duetted with Orbison in 1988 on a movie soundtrack version of 'Crying'. 'A lot of people think he had a real tragic life, which he did, but he didn't wear it. He seemed to break through that and become very spiritual and very analytical and philosophical about it. He was very quiet and very peaceful and very solid. His music to me was this tremendously emotional, almost operatic kind of offering, but it was like he'd lived his emotional life through his music and that had left him very peaceful and calm.'

'I'd always thought he was kinda like this weird dude, with the glasses and the funny hair,' says Jim Keltner, who drummed with the Traveling Wilburys and played on Orbison's posthumous *Mystery Girl*. 'But after meeting him I became just such a huge fan. And seeing how people treated him: one of the songs I did with him, Bono came in and produced it, and all day long it was like Bono was with the President. He just worshipped Roy. Everybody was like that – Elvis Costello was like that, and everybody that was around him. Roy inspired that from people.'

'Roy always felt this way about it,' says Barbara Orbison, the singer's German-born widow who has carried the torch for him since his death in 1988. 'He would have said: I'm sitting in front of you here, you can see I have a suntan, I'm skinny, I have dogs running around, kids, I have a great-looking wife. And yet the world has given me this place in rock 'n' roll of the sad, lonely, pale, pudgy man. He would have said, I'm so sick and tired of holding that place.'

Barbara Orbison sits in a large loft-style office in the imposing four-storey building she owns in Nashville, its floor-to-ceiling windows commanding panoramic views of the city. Looking towards the downtown business district one can see the Gotham-style Bell South tower, with the old Ryman Auditorium peeping out from behind it. Looking along Broadway one can make out Music Row and the gleaming fortresses that house the new corporate record business.

Between reminiscences of her late husband, Orbison takes phone calls, some pertaining to the Roy Orbison catalogue, others to her own publishing company. 'Did we get that George Strait cut?' she asks of one caller. Another call concerns the use of Roy's 'Blue Bayou' in a new Adam Sandler movie. It quickly becomes clear that Roy Orbison's widow has become a tireless and astute businesswoman. And when you take a gander around the offices of Barbara Orbison Enterprises — their disc-bedecked walls a virtual shrine to Roy — it's hard not to stop and reflect that all this began with a runty kid's dreams in the tiny west Texas town of Wink.

Would Roy have been impressed, I ask?

'Roy always had big dreams, you know,' she smiles. 'If you're coming from Wink, Texas, you want to be No. 1 all over the world. So yes, maybe there was a touch of grandiosity there. Roy was a dreamer.'

Roy was *a dreamer*: what else, after all, was there to do in Wink? The town was so small that you could only leave it the way you came in. There was a small movie theatre and a pool hall, but that was about all the entertainment the place afforded. The prevailing culture was centred in beer and football and fighting. Roy, who'd been born three hundred miles away in Vernon on 23 April 1936, was not a natural fit. With his myopic sights set firmly on the horizons that stretched all ways in the flat, dusty, treeless oil country, he barely fitted in at home.

'When Roy went to the movies, he was so fascinated by bad guys wearing black,' says Barbara. 'And every once in a while they would have movie stars making a local appearance, and it made him realise that somewhere out there in the world was another place that you can create. So Roy lives in this little oil town where the dreams are basically to grow lots of hair under the arms and to play football. He loved football till he died, but he didn't play after he was twelve because his family couldn't get his glasses taken care of.'

What Roy did have going for him was a singing voice that made adults crowd round every time he perched himself on a high stool and crooned into a microphone. At eight he was already singing on local radio stations in Vernon and Fort Worth, performing songs he'd learned from his guitar-playing father Orbie and from listening to country singers like Ernest Tubb and Lefty Frizzell. It was a voice that sounded grown-up before its time.

'The family moved to Fort Worth as the war began,' says Barbara Orbison. 'Roy figured out really fast that it was wartime, and everybody would drop by the parents' house, and there was a flavour in the air that this might be the last night they had together – men were being drafted. All the kids had to go to bed, but as a kid, if you could play guitar and sing, you could stay up. So Roy learned how to stay up! He'd sing all these little dirty songs that were cute for a little kid to sing. He learned very early on that he was treated different playing the guitar.'

Settling in Wink after the war had ended, Orbie Lee worked as a mechanic in the local oil fields and Roy started out on the uncertain road of adolescence. All his great songs would be rooted in the emotional intensity of puberty, and in the pain he felt as a physically unprepossessing, unathletic boy. More than most pop dreamers he was determined to triumph through music, to stick it to the rednecks of Wink by becoming a star.

'He was very quiet and shy, a good person,' recalled mandolin player James Morrow, who began performing in a duo with Orbison in 1948. 'We sang at the Day Drugstore in town, and the roughnecks and roustabouts pitched quarters when we played.' Morrow remembers Roy listening avidly to the Louisiana Hayride show out of Shreveport, as well as to the R & B records Stan 'The Man' Lewis would broadcast on KWKH. With the border just a hundred miles south-west of Wink, Orbison also heard the passionate, overwrought music of balladeers on Mexican stations.

'You can hear a lot of Spanish influence in Roy's over-the-top emotion, the high emotional peaks,' says songwriter Will Jennings, a fellow Texan who wrote with Orbison in the five years before the singer's death. 'I think he just absorbed that through his skin in west Texas. He had that passionate nature. He was a shy, reserved fellow, but when he sang he let the other self emerge. It was a voice as big as Texas.'

With Morrow and three other Wink High School buddies, Orbison at the turn of the decade formed the Wink Westerners. Charlie 'Slob' Evans played upright bass, Richard West tinkled away at the piano and Billy Pat Ellis bashed at a primitive drum kit. 'They were all extraordinary guys – poetic, well-read and all different,' says Barbara. 'And I think they really supported Roy. I think if he had just had to hang out with the knuckleheads, it would have been very tough. Roy taught them all an instrument and what songs to play. And the band got really famous in the area, and Roy learned to play dances. We still have little notebooks where he would put down the band's expenses: car, gas, food. The guys all say it was basically Roy that had the vision, he would write the songs and get the gigs.'

'The rest of us were just going along for the ride,' confirms 'Slob' Evans. 'We always knew the talent was there in Roy.' Roy it was who pushed the band into becoming one of the most in-demand attractions in the Midland–Odessa area, an act not only hired for local dances in nearby Kermit and Monahans but given their own slot on an Odessa television show while they were still in high school. Customising everything from 'Moonlight In Vermont' and Glenn Miller's 'In The Mood' to fit their feisty teenage sound, they were completely in synch with the wave of greasy Southern boys who would soon be creating rockabilly.

'We were maybe countrybilly,' says Evans. 'We were trying to mesh these things together, because we didn't wanna be classified as country and western.' Among Orbison's contemporaries was Buddy Holly, who lived ninety miles away in Lubbock and would shortly become a friendly rival of Roy's at Norman Petty's little recording studio in New Mexico.

The sheer shock of seeing Elvis Presley perform in Dallas in April 1954 was all it took for Orbison to revamp the Wink Westerners as rockabilly band the Teen Kings. The band became busier than ever, and even built up their own retinue of groupies, among them a curvaceous fourteen-year-old named Claudette – a 'beautiful dish' Orbison would eventually marry. Finally it came time to cut a record.

'By the time he was seventeen, Roy was just about professional,' says Barbara. 'He always heard another way of playing. He was already different. Roy didn't want to sing country music, and he didn't want to sing big band music. He left Wink, he moved to Odessa, he found Clovis, New Mexico. He talked some couple out of eleven hundred dollars to record "Ooby Dooby", released it there and had a local Texas hit. They had a television show: I mean, people always say Roy was really shy, but obviously when he really wanted something he went for it.'

'Ooby Dooby' was a dumb rock 'n' roll dance tune penned by two fellow students at North Texas State. Recorded by Norman Petty in Clovis, it was released on Je-Wel in early 1956, with a version of Elvis' 'Tryin' To Get To You' on the flip. (This was the side Claudette played incessantly after Orbison plucked up the nerve to initiate a relationship.) Like most of the surviving recordings by the Teen Kings – versions of Little Richard, Chuck Berry and Carl Perkins classics – 'Ooby Dooby' required little vocally of Roy but proved he could sing rock 'n' roll as well as any of the redneck hepcats bobbing about in Presley's mighty wake. If anything it was the kid's let-it-rip guitar playing that most caught the attention.

One night, Johnny Cash blew through Odessa to play a gig. When Roy not only caught Cash's show but invited him to come and guest on his TV show, the original Man in Black suggested he change his name, lower his voice, and phone Sam Phillips at Sun. Cash wasn't to know that Phillips would be in a major grouch the day the bespectacled Texan called – that he would snap at Orbison and tell him Johnny Cash had no business playing record scout for his label. But as fate would have it, a record store owner in Odessa also telephoned Phillips, insisting he listen to 'Ooby Dooby' down the line.

This time the man who'd unleashed Elvis on the world proved more obliging.

'I think Sam at first thought Roy would be as big as Carl or Jerry Lee, but then after "Ooby Dooby" we worked and worked and tried to come up with something and never really did, and I think Sam gradually lost some of his enthusiasm for it.'

The speaker is 'Cowboy' Jack Clement, the man who came to work as Sam Phillips' right-hand man not long after the rerecorded 'Ooby Dooby' was released on Sun in May 1956.

'Roy liked Sam and in a way idolised him, but Sam confused him,' Clement continues. 'He wasn't as attentive to Roy as Roy thought he should be. Roy was coming from a different place musically, and I think he probably realised it.'

Looking back forty years on, it's hard to imagine anyone less like Jerry Lee Lewis (or even Johnny Cash) than Roy Orbison. How did this timid, bespectacled Texan come to join that irascible clan of post-Elvis wildcats in Memphis? Not for Roy the rampant fornication and hell-raising that characterised Sam Phillips' roster, nor – as it turns out – the raw-edged rockabilly music those wildcats were making. When the remade 'Ooby Dooby' reached No. 59 on the *Billboard* Hot 100 in July 1956, Roy Orbison was already heartily sick of the song.

'It was very cordial between him and the rest of the Sun artists,' says Jack Clement. 'But he had that thing they all have in that part of the world – I don't know if he started it or Buddy Holly started it. He was different to people who came from Mississippi and other places in the South. I thought the world of him. We were big buddies, and after I got divorced he stayed at my house for quite a few months. We were out on the town every night, and working in the studio.'

Clement soon saw that Orbison wanted to do something more ambitious than 'Ooby Dooby' or 'Go, Go, Go' or 'Rockhouse', and that the primitive Sun studio simply wasn't equipped to do justice to the elaborate music Roy was hearing in his head. Nor did it help that Sam Phillips was focused almost exclusively on the careers of Lewis and Carl Perkins.

'I spent a lot of time with Roy trying to come up with something,' says Clement. 'He was always trying to do something that sort of taxed the capabilities of the musicians, and taxed the sound that we were able to deliver at that time. He was into big production sounds, and we just didn't have the personnel or the studio to deliver that. I did tell him he'd never make it as a ballad singer, and he never let me forget that. He did surprise me. I didn't see what a great singer he would become.'

Clement can be forgiven for his lack of foresight, because even on Sun ballads like 'Devil Doll' and 'Sweet And Easy Love' it was far from clear that Orbison had the potential to become a vocal giant. What does seem obvious now is that Orbison, like the Everly Brothers, was a transitional artist, a bridge between hillbilly rock and '60s pop. Some of the demos he cut at Sun – songs like 'I Never Knew' and the minor revelation that is 'The Clown' – hint strongly at the vein of wistful melancholia he would later mine on Monument Records.

Before Monument came a stint on RCA-Victor, under the aegis of the redoubtable Chet Atkins. Unfortunately, countrypolitan maestro Atkins had little idea how to turn teen pop ballads like 'Seems To Me' and 'Sweet And Innocent' (both 1958) into anything more than insipid syrup. Boudleaux Bryant, who'd written 'Seems To Me', recalled Orbison as 'a timid, shy kid who seemed to be rather befuddled by the whole music scene' and who sang 'softly, prettily, but almost bashfully, as if someone might be disturbed by his efforts and reprimand him'. That is certainly how he sounds on 'Seems To Me'.

By this time the married Roy and Claudette had relocated to Nashville, where Roy had signed a publishing deal with Acuff-Rose and made his first real money. (The song 'Claudette', a sassy tribute to his beloved first demo'd at Sun, had wound up on the B-side of the Everlys' No. 1 smash 'All I Have To Do Is Dream'.) Real success, however, continued to evade him, even as he squandered every dime he made. Things got so bad that the couple, with newborn son Roy Jr in tow, were forced to move back to Wink and stay with Orbie Lee and Nadine.

In 1959, Roy Orbison's gross income totalled $1700.

Orbison always claimed it was a fluke that he was signed by Fred Foster's Nashville-based Monument label. In his version of events, Foster, a former promo man with Mercury and ABC-Paramount, was under the misapprehension that he was signing Sun rockabilly singer Warren Smith, of 'Rock And Roll Ruby' fame. Foster himself denies this, though the signing perhaps had more to do with the persuasiveness of Wesley Rose, Roy's publisher and manager, than with any perceived greatness in Orbison.

The first indication that Roy had found his feet on the label wasn't 'Paper Boy', a milky rerecording of a discarded Victor track released in September 1959, but 'Uptown', a song Orbison had written with fellow Texan Joe Melson. This swaggering R & B outing was the first fruit of a writing partnership that was about to produce a succession of pop masterworks, and arguably the first song on which Orbison sounded truly assured as a singer.

'I'd wanted to use violins,' Roy recalled, 'and since I'd had such a rough time at Sun trying to get what I wanted, I was really ready to fight for violins. And Fred said, "Okay, no problem". Then I think maybe it was all the flavouring and the special musical things that happen on my records came out of my hunger. I'd wanted to do that for a long time and wasn't able to.'

But it was on the next Monument 45 that Roy really hit his stride. With its unforgettable vocal introduction – the semi-whispered 'Dum-dum-dum-doo-be-doo-wah' phrase magicked up by Melson – 'Only The Lonely (Know How I Feel)' was a two and a half minute slice of perfection that instantly dwarfed the sappy teen-death discs and banal novelty songs released in that limp limbo period between rock 'n' roll and Beatlemania: songs like Mark Dinning's 'Teen Angel', Brian Hyland's 'Itsy Bitsy Teenie Weenie Yellow Polkadot Bikini', and even, for that matter, Elvis Presley's 'It's Now Or Never'.

With this one record, a No. 2 smash hit in June 1960, Orbison introduced the persona of the crestfallen, stoically heartbroken loner, explicitly reaching out to every teenager whose love had gone unreturned. Only the lonely knew how Orbison had felt, but then everyone has known loneliness at one time or another.

It is a measure of how focused Roy was that he stood up to Fred Foster's misgivings about the song's unorthodox 2/4 time signature. 'When he came to Studio B on the Row here, Harold Bradley [session bassist] tells me Roy was so organised and so headstrong,' says Barbara Orbison. 'Here comes this skinny kid, and they were all very accomplished players. Told them all what to play, and how to play it. Fred said to Roy over the switchback, "'Only The Lonely' is not gonna work like this", and Roy said, "Why not?" Fred said, "We all feel it's not in a good time because you couldn't dance to it." And Roy just said, "I never wanted to dance to any of my songs, I just want to sing it, and this is the way it goes."

'In those days I think he was really driven. I think it was a vision that he held for himself and for music, that it was much larger than himself. When you look at Roy's life, I think he came here to do two things: one of them was to sing and one of them was to perform. By the time he had the big success, he had been holding on to this vision since he was seven years old. The dream for Roy was so strong that even at Sun he and Elvis would kid each other, "You think this is gonna last another half a year?" There was no history, no map. You did it for the love of it. Who knew that a good session guitar player in Nashville would be making half a million dollars a year in 1998?'

Having been proved wrong on the matter of 'Only The Lonely', Fred Foster became the most sympathetic of producers: from there on in, he pretty much gave Orbison free rein. Roy in turn became the essence of amenability and consistency. 'He never changed in his attitude towards me,' remembered Foster. 'He had a great deal of humility – you couldn't have asked for a more pleasant person to be around.'

If anything, Foster encouraged Roy to take risks he might not have contemplated. With 1961's epic 'Running Scared', Orbison's first No. 1 hit, Foster not only suggested they change the beat to a bolero but dared Roy to sing the climactic, ascending phrase in full voice rather than falsetto. Few other singers would have been capable of such a thing, let alone have attempted it. 'With "Running Scared", Roy always said Fred embarrassed his manhood,' says Barbara. 'And Roy saw red – if you challenged him, he would be determined to let you have it.'

'Fred said, "Run it by us one more time", and I did it in full voice,' Orbison told Joe Smith. 'I didn't even know I could do that at the time. I didn't know there was a difference between full voice and falsetto. I could feel the difference, but I didn't understand the technical differences. Then the power of the voice came. It was a gradual thing, and it came with confidence.'

'Running Scared' is a brilliant mini-melodrama, a song that starts with a sombre hush and builds over two minutes to a fever pitch of intensity unparalleled till then in white pop. Who had heard such vulnerability in a male singer before? 'Roy was not afraid to let you look inside,' said Fred Foster. 'He didn't feel it diminished him.' Far more so than 'Only The Lonely', 'Running Scared' introduces a note of pure dread into the arena of teen angst: when the ending turns out to be a happy one – the girl splits with the singer and not his rival – it's even more of a shock than the scene of desolation one is anticipating.

'I think honestly the first thing I noticed about Roy was his songs,' says Raul Malo of the Mavericks. 'He wrote songs for himself – he had nobody else in mind but himself. And that's a striking thing. When you hear a song like "In Dreams", I can't imagine anybody else doing it but him. And he had a voice that afforded him the ability to be different. He wrote these songs with these incredible little changes that really hadn't been done before, and I think part of that was because of his voice, which allowed him to write stuff like that and to get away with it.'

The great hits Roy Orbison chalked up between 1960 and 1964 defied the rules, ignoring verse-chorus-verse orthodoxy and trashing the divide between pop and country. 'Roy's songwriting really ended up influencing me, because it showed a tremendous disregard for form,' says k.d. lang. 'And I love that, I like that it was really about just emotional crescendos and the movement of the song rather than sticking to a regular form.' With the Nashville Symphony Orchestra cascading behind them, the records sounded like Phil Spector's Wall of Sound transported to Nashville, with a generous dash of Tex-Mex heartache on the side.

True, Roy always ran the risk of straying into kitsch, as evidenced by lesser songs like 'Leah' and 'Mama'. But when he and Joe Melson got it right, as they did on the magnificent 'Crying' and the pining 'Blue Bayou', the records were thrillingly beautiful.

'They were story ballads,' said Fred Foster. 'Because of the way they were orchestrated and the way they were planned, they never got boring. He used such intricate, beautiful melodies. He brought a kind of baroque, classical style to pop music.'

'I didn't mean "Crying" to be taken as neurotic,' Orbison told Nick Kent, days before his death. 'I wanted to show that the act of crying, for a man – and that record came out in a real macho era when any sign of sensitivity was really frowned on – was a good thing and not some weak . . . defect, almost.'

'In Dreams', which he wrote by himself, was perhaps the supreme expression of Orbison's dream fixation – the perennial pop theme of the mismatch between reverie and reality. 'In dreams I walk with you / In dreams I talk to you,' he crooned sweetly. 'In dreams you're mine all of the time / We're together in dreams . . .' On one level, this is the innocent cry of a hopeless love seeking solace in slumber; on the other it's the slightly sinister fantasy of possession that David Lynch responded to and used to such devastatingly creepy effect in *Blue Velvet*. (Interestingly, Orbison said the scene in the film in which Dean Stockwell lip-synchs the song – one described without much exaggeration by James Wolcott as 'a necrophiliac mass' – gave him almost the same chills as seeing Elvis perform for the first time.)

It wasn't long after 'In Dreams' rose to No. 7 in the spring of 1963 that Orbison took to wearing his trademark sunglasses on stage, and at most other times of the day. It was this peculiarly cool character who became a regular fixture in Britain, where his records had all been big hits, and who – unlike so many pre-Beatles American performers – endured well into the era of the British Invasion. The Beatles themselves were ardent admirers of Orbison's: so slavish an Orbison pastiche was the original, unrecorded version of 'Please Please Me' that George Martin insisted they rework it into a more uptempo song.

Other English fans of the Big O's included the Rolling Stones, who toured Australia with him, and Marianne Faithfull, who got to know him on a British tour in February 1965. 'Keith Richards said to me after Roy died, "In life, as in death, Roy was always half a step in front of everyone else,"' remembers Barbara. 'He said, "When we toured, they called me Keith and they called Mick Mick, but they always called Roy "Mr Orbison".'

'The difference was that Roy was a grown-up, he wasn't a child in grown-up clothes,' says Faithfull, who so charmed Orbison that he let her remove his sunglasses for a famous photograph. 'He was very quiet and self-deprecating and modest – just a really nice musician. I know quite a few musicians like that, and they're often the very greatest. All I know is that he did come to see me in my room and actually took off his glasses. I don't even know what that meant. It's possible that he was making a pass. He must have liked me. He used to twinkle at me, but if he was making a pass it went right by me. With me he was an absolute perfect gentleman, and it didn't slip for one minute.'

Orbison's second British No.1, and his seventh UK Top 10 hit, may have been the greatest of all his records: this writer certainly counts it among the ten best pop singles of all time. Penned with Bill Dees, who had taken over from a disgruntled Joe Melson as Roy's principal writing partner, 'It's Over' sounds a remorseless death knell for a love affair – one the more poignant when one learns that Orbison had just learned of Claudette's infidelity with a family friend.

'Roy came in and sang Fred this new song,' says Barbara. 'Roy by now is the hottest male solo singer in the world: there are only groups, and the only one who stands up to the groups is Roy. When he finishes the song, Fred gets up and leaves and he's crying. Roy thinks, I must have written a really incredible song this time, but Fred knew that Roy's marriage was having severe problems, and as a friend didn't know whether or not to tell him.' In due course, the couple were divorced.

The fact that they managed in time to patch things up – she having inspired his final No. 1 hit, 1964's playfully lusty 'Oh, Pretty Woman' – only makes it the more tragic that two years later, on 6 June 1966, Claudette Orbison was killed while she and Roy were riding their motorcycles through Gallatin, Tennessee, not far from the home they'd built in Hendersonville.

'After the divorce, he threw himself into touring,' says Barbara. 'He always said he felt safest on stage – that's where he could keep up that part of him that wanted to crumble. He had to really figure out who he was, and what about the kids . . . where do we go now? And you can hear it in his recordings of that time. He never laid the blame, never played the victim: even in "Crawling Back", he says "I play the clown because I love you". I think Roy definitely had to come through really rough waters, and then losing Claudette must have been like the torment of torments. They had married again, but where was the relationship? He's left with three kids, one of one, one of four, one of six, and a torn heart. How can you expect a man to go slay the dragons in the charts after that?'

It didn't help that Orbison had parted ways with Fred Foster – who lacked the funds to keep him on Monument – and signed with the considerably bigger MGM. Certainly it was more than coincidence that his long run of hits dried up almost instantly with the move.

Perhaps his reign would have ended even if he *had* continued writing songs as strong as 'It's Over' and 'Oh, Pretty Woman': the dawn of psychedelia made the pop world an increasingly uncomfortable place for singers of his vintage. But with a handful of exceptions ('Crawling Back', the ambitious 'Southbound Jericho Parkway', and – from the soundtrack to *Zabriskie Point* – 'So Young') the records co-produced by Jim Vienneau and Roy's mentor Wesley Rose were markedly inferior to his Monument masterpieces.

'I remember Roy would come in off the road on Friday and say that we needed six songs by the following Thursday,' Bill Dees told Colin Escott. That was certainly no way to work with a vocal artist of genius.

'MGM was a big company, and they painted a rosy picture for me and gave me a lot of money,' Orbison told interviewer Steve Pond not long before his death. 'But the transition wasn't really that smooth. I think the records were OK, maybe, through 1968 or so. But I was having to record a lot, plus I'd had some personal problems . . . so on one hand you had a company that wasn't really viable, and then on the other you had me, with things happening around me and to me. I mean, it was a dark period for me.'

The world turned darker still with the horrific death of Orbison's two oldest sons, Roy and Tony, in a fire that gutted the Hendersonville house in September 1968. (It was Orbison's neighbour on Old Hickory Lake, Johnny Cash, who summoned the fire department.) The only brightness in this hellish period came with his courtship of eighteen-year-old *Fraulein* Barbara Wellhoener, whom he'd met in a discotheque in, of all places, Leeds. In March 1969 the couple were married, with their first son, Roy Kelton Jr, arriving the following year.

Orbison chose to keep working, but his heart had gone out of his music. As the '60s came to a close he was fast becoming what he most dreaded turning into: a 'golden oldie'. To his credit, he refused to jump aboard any rock 'n' roll revival bandwagon, just as he refused to perform undignified medleys of his hits in nightclub shows, but he had little viability as a recording artist.

'As the '60s turned into the '70s I didn't hear a whole lot I could relate to,' Orbison told Nick Kent, 'so I kind of stood there like a tree where the winds blow and the seasons change and you're still there and you bloom again. With time.'

'Was it Roy's time?' says Barbara Orbison. 'I don't know. Did Roy care? I don't think so. It wasn't that he didn't care about performing or singing well. But he never watched the charts. He was never hooked into Roy the chart guy. He designed houses, he collected cars, he bought model aeroplanes, he was a student of history, he loved to travel. His world was very complete without being a musician. You could have been on an overseas flight between New York and London for eight hours sitting next to him, and he would have talked to you about writing, about his kids, your kids, politics, football . . . he would never have said, "I'm a singer-songwriter".'

When *Crawdaddy*'s Greg Mitchell interviewed him in 1974, at the start of a brief stint on Mercury, Orbison seemed to be taking his decline badly. Constantly on the road – at one point that year he played 125 shows on 105 consecutive nights – he struck Mitchell as being 'more of a curiosity than a legend'. Even a reunion with Joe Melson failed to produce anything to rival 'Running Scared' or 'Only The Lonely'. 'If I try to write for Roy Orbison, it doesn't work,' Melson complained to *Melody Maker* in 1977; 'it takes forever and is no good anyway'.

Marginally more encouraging was the reunion with Fred Foster that produced 1977's Monument album *Regeneration*, packed with vaguely steamy songs by Southern writers like Dennis Linde ('Belinda', 'Under Suspicion') and Tony Joe White ('I'm A Southern Man').

Orbison was not only in the pop wilderness, he was in desperately poor health: in January 1978, aged forty-one, he underwent triple-bypass heart surgery. Then as soon as *he* got well, Barbara fell ill, taking up most of his attention for the next three years. 'For three years a career was not important,' she remembers. 'I mean, Roy drove the kids to carpools, he was very involved as a father. There were numerous years when he didn't *have* a recording contract. And it wasn't because people didn't want him. Jordan Harris, who went to Virgin from A&M, called us once a year for seven years. But there was no reason.' Adding to the stress of this period was a lawsuit that Roy – at Barbara's prompting – filed against Wesley Rose in 1980, alleging conflict of interest on Rose's part and claiming income from lost royalties.

Slowly, though, the tide was turning back to acknowledge Orbison's stature as a singer and as a writer. Bruce Springsteen's namechecking of Roy on *Thunder Road* had done its part to remind people of the 'Big O's importance. In 1977, Linda Ronstadt had a massive hit with 'Blue Bayou', taking it all the way to No. 3 on the Hot 100; four years later Don McLean topped the UK chart with his version of 'Crying'. Van Halen reached No. 12 with their crunching 1982 version of 'Oh, Pretty Woman', and a 1980 duet with Emmylou Harris, 'That Lovin' You Feelin' Again', gave Roy his first country hit and his first Grammy. Nineteen seventy-nine's pseudo-funky *Laminar Flow* may have been among the feeblest he ever recorded, but the world seemed to want him back. 'It was like everyone was starting up my career without me,' he later reflected. 'Eventually the parallel careers sort of merged.'

'I had the impression that this was a low period for him,' says Will Jennings, who went to Nashville to write with Orbison in the late summer of 1984. 'He was really getting it in the teeth, and he was having to tour a lot to keep the cash flow together. But he was tough, and his spirit was strong. He knew who he was, and he knew what he was capable of. I saw all that, plus I just loved the cat, y'know? He was a *good guy*. He had a royal quality, a princely quality.'

Recording the Orbison/Jennings song 'Wild Hearts' for Nic Roeg's film *Insignificance* was in itself a minor turning point. When David Lynch then used a rerecorded 'In Dreams' in *Blue Velvet*, it gave Orbison a sorely needed shot of credibility that put him right back on the pop map.

'*Blue Velvet* was so talked about because it was so different for a sweet song like 'In Dreams' to be put in a spot where you really have to look at the dark side,' says Barbara. 'Roy went and he saw the movie, and he could see that it was just confronting the dark side.' Lynch was so besotted by Orbison that he supervised the rerecording of eighteen more of the singer's classic hits for the 1987 double album *In Dreams – The Greatest Hits*. (The director's Orbison obsession was still apparent in 2001's acclaimed *Mulholland Drive*, in which a

Mexican-American diva sings a tortured Spanish version of 'Crying'.)

With the Wesley Rose suit finally settled, and with Barbara's encouragement, Orbison found the determination to give his wilting career a second shot. Symbolic of the sense of rebirth was the couple's decision to move to Malibu in California.

'In 1985, when Roy decided to go for it one more time, he was pretty much a free man,' says Barbara. 'He got his health really into shape, and really bonded with the family in a different way. I think he could see something completely different for himself. And Malibu was really good to him emotionally. It reminded him of Texas, those cold mornings and cold nights. He used the fireplace, he loved the sunsets. He loved driving a convertible every day. I think it lifted all of those old feelings about Hendersonville. I don't think anybody in Hendersonville ever saw Roy, whereas in Malibu he went everywhere – to the grocery, to have breakfast, to the beach.'

'He'd had this music room in the back of the house in Nashville, and it looked out over Old Hickory Lake, and he said something like, I've sat in this room in so many years, it's so hard,' recalls Will Jennings, who lived near Malibu at the time. 'Out here, I think he was going toward freedom, and just loosening up and broadening up. It was a wonderful change. He loved it, and he blossomed.'

Some dreams do come true after all. The last two years of Roy Orbison's life were among the happiest and most fruitful of his career, a period in which a flurry of activity led to an abundance of opportunities. A new contract was signed with Virgin Records, and he was inducted into the Rock and Roll Hall of Fame with a speech by Bruce Springsteen that brought tears to his eyes.

'There was a lot of interest in him, but also a lot of misconception,' remembered Sarah McMullen, a publicist at Virgin. 'A lot of people thought he was blind because of the dark glasses. They thought his first wife had just died. It was as if time had stood still. So we got writers out to his shows to meet him. More than anything, they came away talking about his voice. They didn't think of him as a '60s act any more.'

In September 1987, Barbara Orbison organised a wonderful tribute to Roy at LA's Coconut Grove club – a 'Black and White Night' that rounded up such stellar admirers as Springsteen, Elvis Costello, Bonnie Raitt, Tom Waits, Jackson Browne and k.d. lang.

'The Black and White Night was definitely an evening where every ounce of ego was checked at the door,' remembers k.d., recruited to sing backing vocals alongside Raitt and Browne. 'It was definitely a show of respect and love for Roy. I was pretty young, so my whole concept of that world was pretty naive, but I could definitely feel that it was about him. Even though he didn't command it, it was given to him. He would sit quietly in a room and *preside* over the energy. And it was amazing, because you had really diverse people there. We were like disciples in a way. We were very quiet and very focused on doing our jobs. I can just remember feeling like somebody who was really there working for the man.'

Most amazing for anyone watching Orbison for the first time in years was just how unaffected the voice was by the passing of time: he sounded exactly as he had in 1962.

'I never heard him sing flat or out of tune, even up until the very end,' says Raul Malo. 'And for all I know he did everything wrong that you're not supposed to do as a singer. Before he'd go onstage he'd have a Pepsi and a cigarette, which goes against everything that we know nowadays you should do as a singer.'

Suddenly everyone wanted to be Roy's friend and to pay homage. On stage at the Black and White Night, Springsteen broke through a taboo when, in a spontaneous and unrehearsed move, he mosied over to Roy's mic and sang with him on 'Dream Baby'. It was a significant and charming moment, for Orbison had only ever been seen alone at the centre of the stage.

Fittingly enough, a song called 'Not Alone Anymore' was Roy's great moment-in-the-spotlight on a busman's holiday project dubbed *The Traveling Wilburys, Vol. 1* – a group born on a whim one night in the summer of 1988 and consisting of Roy, George Harrison, Jeff Lynne, Tom Petty and none other than Bob Dylan.

'I remember showing up at Dave Stewart's house in Encino, and there was a bunch of guys sitting out on the front porch together,' says Jim Keltner, who drummed on the album. 'As I got closer, I could see who they were, and it blew my mind. And they were obviously all there because of Roy. They treated him as if he was royalty.' Roy's alias for the album was Lefty Wilbury, a nod to the great Texan singer Lefty Frizzell, who'd so influenced him.

'When he sang his parts in the studio, the others would all stand around with their mouths open,' says Keltner. 'That incredibly big, intense voice was always done with the least effort. One time we were standing in the dark, catching him from a side view. He was standing with a little light on the music stand, a pencil in his right hand, and this enormous voice was coming out with all this emotion, and yet he was standing perfectly still and it looked like maybe he was just talking to himself. It was just totally effortless for him.'

'Not Alone Anymore' was one of the highlights on the ramshackle, good-humoured collection, with Roy's pure, pellucid notes cushioned by the softly Beatle-esque harmonies of his comrades. In much the same vein was the Jeff Lynne-produced 'You Got It', the hit single from the posthumous album Orbison was working on throughout 1988. *Mystery Girl*, as the album came to be titled, was a perfect last testament, full of songs about dreams and loneliness – the Will Jennings/Richard Kerr ballad 'In The Real World' standing out a mile – but also suggesting a kind of serene resolution.

'When you say somebody sings like a bird, he really did,' says Steve Cropper, who played on 'The Only One', penned by Roy's son Wesley. 'And he was just as strong the week before he died as he was twenty-five years before.' Substantially written by his new buddies (by Lynne and Petty, by Bono and the Edge, by Elvis Costello), the record received glowing reviews when it appeared in early 1989.

'The last time I saw Roy alive was at A&M studios,' says Jim Keltner. 'Somebody brought up about how great he was looking. He had lost a bunch of weight and was looking real trim, and somebody had styled his hair in kind of a Samurai style so he had a little tiny ponytail. He just looked like some youthful martial arts guy. And so we were talking about it, and he was telling us he was on a new diet, and it was great because he could eat biscuits and gravy and all this Southern shit he loved, and of course I was laughing probably the hardest because I'm from Oklahoma. But it was obviously working for him in some kind of way because he'd lost so much weight, and we all thought, what a great thing that Roy is enjoying all this attention from the Wilburys, and his album is ready to come out and it's gonna be real good, he's looking great and everything is fantastic.

'And then the next thing I heard was that he had died of a massive heart attack.'

On Tuesday 6 December 1988, Orbison was back in Nashville visiting his mother and his son Wesley. After an afternoon spent flying remote-controlled model aeroplanes, he began to feel sharp pains in his chest. Late that night, Wesley Orbison found his father's lifeless body slumped on a bathroom floor. Rushed to the Hendersonville hospital by ambulance, Roy Orbison was pronounced dead at 11.54 p.m. He was fifty-two.

'The great tragedy of Roy's untimely death is that he was going to be the one to actually make a real comeback with all his powers intact,' says Will Jennings. 'Because the voice the day he died was as good as it ever was. And that was just thrilling to me. It broke my heart when he died, but it was even worse that here was somebody who was, you know, *right there*.'

On 15 December, Jennings served as a pallbearer at Orbison's funeral in Westwood, Los Angeles. 'It was a terrible day, raining torrentially,' he remembers. 'It was just so sad. The weather was ungodly. Then down at the Wiltern we had a Celebration of Life, and I recited Byron's "We'll Go No More A-Roving". People loved Roy. He was a decent man, and he bore his talent well.'

'You couldn't even compare Roy's death with Elvis', because Elvis' was a death in darkness and Roy was very much involved in daily living,' says Barbara Orbison. 'You know, so many people adored Elvis, but I don't think he ever could feel it. Roy was so fortunate not only that other artists loved him and that he could feel the love.'

'He was the nicest man I've ever met in show business,' says Chris Isaak, one of Orbison's most illustrious disciples. 'He passed away right when we were getting together, and it was a real drag. I mean, I *really* liked this guy. He just felt like a kindred spirit. It's like when you meet somebody and you get along with them real good and you know this guy's gonna be your best buddy. We just had the same ideas about everything. Because he was kinda partially a redneck, a hick, and partially a songwriter with a lot of ideas that he was driven by – and all those things I can relate to.'

'People say I sound like Roy, and that's a great compliment,' says Raul Malo, another of the man's disciples. 'But I think more so than just his sound, it was the effect of drama that he brought into the music. That's what really got me, and as I've got older I've really learned to appreciate that dramatic flair. Sinatra had it, Elvis had it, and Orbison definitely had it.'

Sitting in her elegant mansion in the toney Belle Mead section of Nashville, Barbara Orbison reflects on the twenty years she shared with her husband. When she talks of the friendships Roy made with Bono and Bruce Springsteen, with Jeff Lynne and George Harrison, tears form in her eyes.

'He was very different from not just the average musician but from the average man,' she says. 'That's what I knew first. I just knew there was something in Roy that was truthful and so honest – his own integrity, that you couldn't manipulate and you couldn't change. The way he lived in the world was really, really honourable.

'Right at the end of his life, Roy was asked why he was working so much. He said, I have found out in life that it's not the goal – the next Grammy or the next No. 1. It's the journey. He said, I sleep better at night, and I'm a better father, a better husband. It's not about the outcome, it's about the daily appliance to life.'

1999

The Shock of the Old:
Beck and the New Americana

'. . . to be an American (unlike English or French or whatever) is precisely to imagine a destiny rather than to inherit one; since we have always been, insofar as we are Americans at all, inhabitants of myth rather than history . . .'

Leslie A. Fiedler, quoted in Greil Marcus' *Mystery Train*

Nestled in the heart of the sonic boomtown they used to call 'Music City', gobbing distance from the new marble compounds that house Nashville's wavy-haired record moguls, is a hallowed repository known as the Country Music Hall of Fame and Museum. This collection of vintage Gibson guitars and fringed Nudie shirts is a vivid reminder of country music's credentials that mutely mocks the calculating, conveyor-belt world of Music Row: how many of today's behatted, bun-hugged bucks, one wonders, have even *heard* of the Carter Family?

But let's not be too hard on the wavy-haired moguls. This year they've made a concerted effort to pay what they're calling a 'Tribute to Tradition', doubtless aware of the flak country has taken during the decade in which it exploded into what Nick Tosches termed 'the Biggest Music in America'. With Garth Brooks' sales finally tapering off into a gratifying plateau, the industry has woken up to the need for some preservation, some credible veneration of its founding fathers and mothers. The *Tribute to Tradition* album, featuring contemporary luminaries revisiting C & W chestnuts, is a corporate-mentality way of saying, Hey, We Care.

Almost as central to the general fealty-paying is the release of *The Complete Hank Williams*, a magnificent ten-CD box which rounds up virtually every recording ever made by the doomed backwoods bard. Which is why we are gathered at the Hall of Fame tonight to hear Hank Williams Jr, ol' Bocephus himself, sing the praises of his hard-drinkin' pappy. And not just Junior, neither: also saying his piece at the podium is singer Marty Stuart, sometime linchpin of Emmylou Harris' Hot Band and a man introduced tonight by the box's scholarly English compiler Colin Escott. 'Everyone pays lip service to tradition,' says Escott, 'but Marty walks the walk.'

When mulleted Marty takes the podium he doesn't mince his words. 'Hank Williams had his finger on the pulse of human emotion,' states this avid collector of Hank memorabilia. 'That's not the case with country today. Country music today is driven by numbers.'

Muted applause greets the pronouncement, maybe because no one's too sure which wavy-haired moguls may be in attendance, maybe because the pulse of human emotion isn't something that greatly interests these folks. When Bocephus takes the stage after Stuart, he calms the rocked boat, muttering some piffle about his old man being 'the real king of rock 'n' roll'. Not long afterwards, a bodyguard hustles him out of the joint and the evening dribbles away on an outgoing tide of beer and canapés.

Here's to you, Hank.

'I started this damn country band / 'Cause punk rock was too hard to sing . . .'

(Whiskeytown, 'Faithless Street', 1996)

If anyone is going to keep the songs and sounds of Hank Williams alive into the next millennium, it's not the slick executives of Music City; it may not even be Hank Williams, Jr, who has his own hoary music to make. By an odd paradox, the people who really care about Hank today are the children of punk rock, urban nerds who for one reason or another have gone scurrying back to America's musical past for succour and perhaps comfort; who've survived punk, hardcore, goth, grunge, and industrial music and now just want to quieten down a little, get out into the country, and connect with the traditions and myths of what Greil Marcus – author of the still hugely influential *Mystery Train* and the timely *Invisible Republic: Bob Dylan's Basement Tapes* – calls 'the old, weird America'.

The heavily garlanded reissue last year of Harry Smith's remarkable 1952 *Anthology of American Folk Music* made explicit this attempt to connect. Featuring a host of scratchy, primordial recordings by everyone from Uncle Dave Macon to Blind Lemon Jefferson – almost all of them dating from the '20s – the *Anthology* kindled in a new generation the same bemused awe that Dylan himself had felt on first hearing songs such as Bascom Lamar Lunsford's 'I Wish I Was A Mole In The Ground'.

It was music, as Dylan said back in the mid-'60s, that 'comes about from legends, Bibles, plagues, and [. . .] revolves around vegetables and death', and it directly inspired the rambunctious, wilfully sloppy excavations on the 'basement tapes' he recorded with the Hawks/The Band at Big Pink in the summer of 1967.

Today's Hank Williams fans – like today's fans of the *Anthology* and *The Basement Tapes*, of Robert Johnson and Gram Parsons and Woody Guthrie, of the Dock Boggs and Stanley Brothers compilations on John Fahey's inspired Revenant label – are people who, somewhere along the way, have fallen under the spell of ancient records, old blues and bluegrass songs, mildewed murder ballads that transport them to vanished places, hill towns, mining communities, places they've never seen and can only imagine.

They're people like Greg Garing, who for the past year has hosted a Monday night hootenanny dubbed The Alphabet City Opry on New York's Lower East Side. They're people who've taken the haunted music of the past and grafted it on to the present, adapting blues and country and folk music to their own, often highly oblique purposes. Some of them are sons and daughters of the South, but many aren't, and that's not the point anyway. When the Jayhawks and Uncle Tupelo jumpstarted the 'alternative country' sound in the second half of the '80s they did it in the somewhat unlikely environment of the Midwest.

Listen to Richard Buckner's 'Lil Wallet Picture', to Palace Brothers' 'You Will Miss Me When I Burn'; to Son Volt's 'Ten Second News', Silver Jews' 'New Orleans', Smog's 'Red Apple Falls'; to the gothic ear candy of Sparklehorse's *Good Morning Spider* and Jim White's *Wrong-Eyed Jesus!*; listen and you'll hear a common steeping in the sheltered lives of a hidden, backwater America. Listen to the acts Ben Thompson describes in his highly entertaining *Seven Years of Plenty* as denizens of a 'Woodchuck Nation', a diaspora of indie cranks stretching from Manhattan to Malibu and Miami to Manitoba: people like Whiskeytown and Willard Grant Conspiracy, Wilco and Wagon and The Waco Brothers. Listen to Lambchop, whose Kurt Wagner coined the term 'Woodchuck Nation' in the first place, and to Lullaby of the Working Class.

Hell, while you're about it, why not listen to the straw-haired saviour of rock himself.

> *'Looking back at some dead world / That looks so new . . .'*
> (Beck, 'Diamond Bollocks', 1998)

'I was immersed in stuff like the *Anthology of American Folk Music* when I was growing up,' says Beck. 'Of course a certain amount of it was romantic and macabre and intriguing and fascinating. That faraway strange quality is definitely something I gravitated towards when I was younger. And I guess travelling through America, I realised that a lot of that strangeness is still out there, only it's maybe a little more frightening because it's alive here and now. It doesn't have the convenience of the remoteness of the past to make it more palatable. The boggy wasteland of the American spirit as it exists here and now is more fluorescent than ever.'

Beck Hansen is sitting in a Los Angeles photo studio wearing a pair of grey cords and a particularly skimpy pink sweater. Unkempt and unshaven, he doesn't look like someone who'd ever have heard Harry Smith's *Anthology*, or who's played Skip James songs on a dobro, and yet he is a crucial figure in the new roots explosion: a twenty-eight-year-old hybridiser who ten years ago was singing blues and folk songs in an ancient-before-his-years baritone voice, croaking Carter

Family death ballads for the amusement of indie-rock punters who were just that – amused.

'When I started doing that stuff, there weren't any indie rockers who even cared about that music,' he says. 'And I think right about the time when I stopped working in the really traditional folk vein, around 1991, was when all that stuff started coming in. It wasn't really a matter of people thinking I was for real or not, it was more that people didn't know what I was doing, period. I'd befriend certain older guys who'd been playing Blind Willie Johnson and Blind Blake tunes, but they tended to be twenty years older than me. In the '80s, nobody was really listening to that music. It was very rare to find people who knew what that was about. I never presented myself as a purist, although I tried to retain the raw approach of more traditional musicians – the original recorded musicians, anyway, because who knows what monsters of folk were happening before people were being recorded.'

Beck has just released *Mutations*, an album recorded this past spring in a two-week burst of spontaneity with Radiohead boardmeister Nigel Godrich. As made clear in advance press on the record, *Mutations* is categorically not the follow-up to 1996's amazing *Odelay* – which may only be another way of saying there were no computers or Dust Brothers involved in its making. What the album is, then, is a consciously scaled down, relatively straightforward collection of very good songs, several of which reach back into the folk/blues/country past in the way Beck did on the much more primitive *One Foot in the Grave* (1994). If anything it's a good deal more artful and arranged than we'd been led to expect, with exotic instruments like harpsichords filling out the arrangements. 'Tropicalia', the single, is a spirited bossa nova in the vein of Os Mutantes (part-inspiration for the album's title). 'We Live Again' and 'Dead Melodies' are limpid, Beatle-esque waltzes. 'O Maria' is sort of Kurt Weill via Ray Davies, and bonus track 'Diamond Bollocks' is as radically (de)constructed as anything on *Odelay*.

Still, the lasting impression left by *Mutations* is one of treated, messed-with tradition. With its Greg Leisz pedal steel, 'Cancelled Check' is the very essence of alt.country, and 'Bottle of Blues' is a rollicking, *faux*-Stones juke-joint rocker with honking harmonica and Brian Jones slide fills – not exactly the Jon Spencer Blues Explosion but on the same wavelength. 'Nobody's Fault But My Own' may boast a beguilingly Zep-ish sheen of sitar and strings – as arranged by Beck's pa, David Campbell – but under those folds it remains a deeply moving folk ballad, maybe the loveliest thing Beck's ever written. Next to *Odelay, Mutations* is like *John Wesley Harding* on the heels of *Blonde On Blonde*.

'I think I've wanted to make a record like this for at least five or six years,' says Beck. 'I tried a few times and it just wasn't the right place or time. Maybe *One Foot in the Grave* was an attempt. I mean, that record was specific, and it has its own place. Those songs are more sketches, they're more rough, unformed ideas of songs, not really fleshed out. I definitely wanted *Mutations* to be more emotional. The reason I went in and cut most of it live is that I wanted it to capture a performance – something I felt was missing from my other records.'

Why *Mutations*?

'To me, the word was representative of who I am as a songwriter,' he says. 'These aren't pure folk songs or country songs. I've been influenced by other sounds. I can play a Woody Guthrie song, but I've heard Merzbow. I'm attuned to a lotta different things, so I guess in a way I'm a bastard, I'll never have that purity the Carter Family had, that remoteness in time and place and culture. And we all are at this point, so I'm just embracing it. I think of the word as a positive word. I'm embracing all the elements that make our time interesting.'

'. . . he had seen the metal face of the age and had been so stunned by it that when he thought into the future, all he could vision was a world from which everything he counted important had been banished or had willingly fled.'

(Charles Frazier, *Cold Mountain*)

Purity and remoteness: isn't it the point of all this new-old music, this twisted Americana, that we can never recapture the 'purity' of the original mountain and Mississippi Delta musicians? Even a supposed neo-traditionalist like Gillian Welch is really remoulding the form to her own ends. (Could the Louvin Brothers conceivably have sung a song like 'My Morphine'?)

When Richard Buckner sings of his 'Lil Wallet Picture' on 1997's *Devotion + Doubt*, the song may sound like a mutant Appalachian ballad, but the picture in question dates from 1985 not 1925. On their soaring 1995 bluegrass hymn 'Gone To Stay', punk-birthed urban critters Freakwater sing irreligiously of 'the kindness of an atheist'. Even more irreverent are Ween, who hired a group of veteran Nashville sessionhounds to back them on ditties like 'Piss Up A Rope' and 'Help Me Scrape The Mucus Off My Brain'.

We owe much of this to Dylan, of course. It was he who blew the dust off America's cobwebbed folk culture, freeing it from the ingrained coffeehouse correctness of the Cambridge/Greenwich Village establishment. It was Dylan who knew that the old had to be made new if it was to have any contemporary resonance. Nearly thirty-five years after he affronted the Newport Festival crowd with his first electric set, and a little less since the scandalous touring that climaxed in the cry of 'Judas!' at Manchester's Free Trade Hall, we find ourselves suspended somewhere between past and future, between preservation and destruction, unsure of what we want to hold on to as we greet the new dawn of the twenty-first century.

Do we want to go back to the roots and 'get it together in the country' or step forward and seize our cyber-tech future? Or do we want to blend the two and find a new music that re-imagines the past while it embraces change?

One band who've managed to elude facile categorisation while operating in the slipstream between past and future is the marvellous Mercury Rev, whose new album *Deserter's Song* takes its title from Greil Marcus' chapter on The Band in *Mystery Train* – and also happens to feature guest appearances by that august group's Levon Helm and Garth Hudson.

'All the music I listen to is from the '20s and '30s,' says Rev frontman Jonathan Donahue. 'We operate on a very different time lapse, as opposed to more popular bands who say, "Well, this is what the kids'll like in six months so if we record it in three it'll get popular." Our frame of reference is, at the very least, forty-five years off. It takes a little bit of work, or just a slight acknowledgement that what went on before is valid in its own right. There were people who were very nonplussed that we were working with Levon and Garth. Well, I like people from that era. You go to the source, you don't go to somebody who says they can play like Levon. It's worth getting it from the horse's mouth.'

True, Mercury Rev are so ornery in their displacement that it's hard to use them as a gauge of any trend. The same might be said of the above-mentioned Buckner, or of Vic Chesnutt, whose album *The Salesman and Bernadette* continues his sweetly jaundiced probings of marginal smalltown existence. In fact, the misfit lugubriousness of alt.Americana troubadours like Chesnutt, Smog's Bill Callahan, and Lambchop's Kurt Wagner is precisely what makes them so appealing.

What we can say is that American rock 'n' roll has never quite managed to shake off its ties to the rural past. The influence of *The Basement Tapes* and the first two albums by The Band is almost as prevalent today as it was in the late '60s, when it persuaded Eric Clapton to abandon the pounding blues-metal bombast of Cream's *Wheels Of Fire* as a lost cause. The lasting impact of Gram Parsons and his hip-ifying of country music can be felt even more widely today than when it inadvertently propelled the Eagles into becoming one of the biggest selling bands in history.

The idea of forsaking the bravado and violence of electric rock 'n' roll for something more downhome was there long before MTV unplugged itself, and long before R.E.M. stripped down their sound for *Out Of Time* and *Automatic For The People*. It was there when Dylan holed up at Big Pink, it was there when Neil Young cut *Tonight's The Night* at Studio Instrument Rentals in Hollywood, and it was still there when Uncle Tupelo namechecked The Band after they released their first, influentially titled album *No Depression* in 1990.

With the waning of grunge in the mid-'90s, it was perhaps only a matter of time before bands began to retreat from the often spurious rage of alternative rock. When Nirvana of all people recorded an MTV-unplugged album in 1994, it strongly suggested that warmed-over punk rock had become a redundant cul-de-sac. Kurt Cobain's inclusion on the album of Leadbelly's death ballad 'In The Pines' (aka

'Where Did You Sleep Last Night?') was itself a harbinger of things to come.

Since Cobain's death, a divide of sorts has opened up between alt.country acts faithful to certain country music conventions and those hostile to the very concept of 'alt.country'. On one side is the essentially trad, Neil Young-meets-Gram Parsons country rock of the Jayhawks, Whiskeytown, Bottle Rockets, Old 97s, Golden Smog, and the post-Tupelo bands Wilco and Son Volt; on the other the murky, troubled mumblings of Smog, Silver Jews and the various editions of Kentucky-based Will Oldham (Palace Brothers, Palace, Palace Music et seq.). When the media caught the sniff of a movement, variously dubbing it Alternative Country, Insurgent Country, Y'awlternative, and (after the Tupelo-inspired fanzine) No Depression, it only made the principal protagonists the more keen to dissociate themselves from each other.

'I like old music, but it doesn't seem different to me from new music,' says Will Oldham, whose *I See A Darkness* (recorded as Bonnie Prince Billy) ranks among his best and most accessible album since 1995's Steve Albini-produced *Viva Last Blues*. 'These other bands may consider that they are traditionalists, or at least working within a tradition. I don't feel that way about myself – where would the fun be then?' (Even the Jayhawks grew tired of being viewed as preservers of pastoral tradition: when Gary Louis assumed the group's leadership after the departure of Mark Olson, he said that he would 'rather risk being silly instead of this safe, pure, timeless Midwestern prairie band'.)

Such truculence suggests a postmodern version of the Groucho Marx Syndrome: what band would want to join a club that actively sought its membership? 'It's kind of what artists always do,' says Peter Blackstock, co-editor with Grant Alden of *No Depression*, and of the recent *No Depression Compendium* anthology. 'We've tried to make it as clear as we can that the borders of what we cover in our magazine are really open. We do that by poking fun at it with the subtitle. Instead of "alternative country bimonthly", we make some wisecrack about it each issue . . . we're not trying to follow any sort of pre-prescribed alternative-country quota.'

The point is that none of the bands working in or anywhere near this field wishes to be painted with the same retro-revivalist brush. Aware of the irony of post-punk rockers playing the music of reactionary rednecks, no band – alternative, insurgent or otherwise – wants to be seen as seeking sanctuary in nostalgia. (Few of them even feel a connection with '80s 'cowpunk' bands like Rank & File or Jason & the Scorchers – 'I didn't really dig them at all', Vic Chesnutt told Ben Thompson, adding, 'I needed harsher lyrics' – and only a handful espouse any link to the country-rebel tradition that runs from Willie Nelson to Steve Earle.)

'I identify with it, but it's also a security blanket, just like it's comforting to watch an old film and see the old actors and the way people lived,' says Beck. 'I think originally I was obsessed with a lot of this music, and I was very, very interested in simulating it and recreating it exactly how they did it, just from the standpoint that I grew up hearing elements of it so bastardised in the '70s and '80s that I didn't even know I really liked that music till I heard the original stuff. But I think that wore off after a few years, and I soon realised that if Leadbelly was around today he would be rockin' an 808 and a Roland Juno 60 way before he'd be rockin' a twelve-string guitar.

'But I still think there's a thread there. I'm interested in the similarities between Memphis Minnie and Klymaxx. It puts your own time in perspective. I think being influenced by that music and drawing from it isn't retroactive, it enriches what's going on in the present and makes you realise which traditions a lot of this music comes from. Otherwise a lot of the music might seem kind of disposable. I'm interested in a lot of the disposable music of our time, but I want to try and fuse those with things that are a little more substantial and see what kind of friction happens.'

It is a measure of Beck's desire to move on, to embrace his time, that he has left the follow-up to *One Foot in the Grave* – provisionally entitled *A Tombstone Every Mile* and set to appear on K Records – unfinished. (A few of the *Tombstone* songs, like 'Cold Brains' and 'Dead Melodies', found their way on to *Mutations*.) For Beck, the real fun lies in melding traditional musical elements with the synthetic beats and textures of our hyperreal present.

After finishing *Mutations* in April, he set to work on an album which will inevitably be seen as the true 'follow-up' to *Odelay* – a record which, let's not forget, featured Delta blues slide guitars ('Hotwax') and country pedal steel ('Sissyneck') alongside Them, Schubert and Mantronix.

'I'm definitely, for the moment, a little more ambitious sonically,' he says. 'The stuff on *Mutations* is an indication of the kinds of things I would want to do with a straight, traditional song approach. I think I'll eventually go back and do something with the K songs, but I've really had to make choices because my time is so limited.

'I don't really know what the new album is going to come out to be – I'm really just getting started with it. I'm doing a lot of it myself, and I'm producing it at my house. So far it's fairly uninhibited: I guess I'm trying to make something stupid. Most of my favourite music is fairly stupid, in the sense that it's got an innocence and a simplicity to it – something that just kind of hits you. It's fairly liberating, and it's what I've been wanting to do for the last two years. Making *Mutations* was sort of taking care of some old business, and the new record is very much what I've been about for the last two years.

'As time goes on, I'm more and more interested in embracing my own time. I think there's been so much reliance on the '60s and '70s, and at this point the early '80s are looking a lot more dynamic and original than things do now, and whoever thought we'd be saying that? At least people were taking some chances and doing some new things. I don't know, it's a very safe and calculated time in music, and I want to see some danger. I want to see some mistakes. I want to see people going out and being idiots. If Jim Morrison came along now, he'd be an idiot. Same with Jagger, even James Brown.

'I just want to get excited again.'

1998

2

Soul Music or Thereabouts

Little Richard: The King and Queen of Rock 'n' Roll

You catch sight of him across the Hilton's gaudy foyer – an ordinary enough black man in tracksuit top, tuxedo pants and matted wet-look coiffure.

Then you see that he walks with a little bumpy limp, a funny clumsiness you've heard about but don't expect. With him is a pretty black boy, sort of Earth Wind & Fire's baby brother mascot, and your first thought is, Jeez, surely he's given that up for God. The kid could be his grandson.

He hobbles past and you rise to your feet, unsure whether to salute him as your emperor or greet him like your grandma. You know as you approach that he's going to call you 'chile' or 'baby', and he does. He takes your paw and peers through dark glasses, wanting to be sure you're not merely some diehard fan but deciding you're a little too young for that.

Five minutes later you're sitting with him in a suite whose view extends to the Surrey hills, doubting somehow that this is the man who started all this and gave the Word all-rutti. You flash back to film of the wild pompadour thicket swaying over pencil moustaches and silken zoot suits and it don't connect.

The King of Rock 'n' Roll a lovable old queen?

Mais oui. All Ricardo Wayne Penniman did was play rhythmic blues a tad faster and a touch gayer than the others and lo, in a powder-puff crucible, rock 'n' roll was born.

There was nothing very heroic about this. He was a weird, deformed kid who preferred to play with his ma's make-up than with his handsome bootlegger dad. He liked to do his 'no-manners' in a box and wrap it up as a present for old Miss DuCane down the lane. He didn't really want to sing the decent, masculine blues; he wanted to be naughty and frivolous.

When producer Bumps Blackwell heard 'Tutti Frutti' tinkling in the Dewdrop Inn in New Orleans, the first properly infantile music of our age was born. A single drumroll on the tongue went AWOP-BOPALOOBOP AWOPBAMBOOM and Little Richard Penniman was in show business.

At fifty-two, Little Richard is still something of a child. Twenty years of hoovering up powders and watching people copulate haven't killed that winsome smile or the endearing need to be loved. The British media are all over him this week, and he couldn't be happier. What could be more fun, after all, than promoting a book about oneself?

Charles White's *Life and Times of Little Richard* is, he says, 'one of the most important books ever written in the history of this world', and no understatement is intended.

'The book is settling everything. You know I am the quasar, which is one of the brightest stars in the universe. Um, there's so many artists have been imitated by me [sic]. You know Jimi Hendrix was mah gittar player. The Beatles, Mick Jagger, Tina Turner . . . I taught her, I was one of her teachers in voice. James Brown . . . you go down the whole line and what else could you be but the King, the founder?'

I think we do know all this, Richard.

'And I didn't say Elvis wasn't a pillar. I never said that. He's one of the greatest performers ever lived. I *never* denounced Chuck Berry, I wouldn't and I couldn't, but *I'm the architech* [sic]. *I'm the pilot light*, and I just want the world to know the truth while I'm still alive. At the age of fifty-two, I do want to be true!'

Well, I'm sure we all appreciate the honesty. Some might claim there was a contradiction between saying rock 'n' roll is demonic and at the same time needing to be thought of as the King of Rock 'n' Roll, but really . . . such pedantry . . .

'Uh uh uh uh, that's just like you once owned a jewellery store and it got burned down and torn down and you don't have it anymore, but you owned it and you're still proud of that spot although you got a new location. That's what happened in my life. I have a new location. I'm a minister of the gospel now, but that don't keep me from being the King of Rock 'n' Roll. That was a stairway that was a part of me, that's history and it will always be there.

'Demonic in music . . . music itself can't do anything, it's the lyrics. My music made people happy, my music brought the races together. Even before Dr King started teaching integration they was integratin' in mah dances! I was a forerunner even in that I wouldn't say rock 'n' roll itself was demonic. I would just take that away, period.

'I would tell Jerry Falwell this, that if a man is a Christian and say he love God, he's supposed to be so dedicated that his hands are supposed to know what to turn on and what to turn off. That's his *own* choice. God don't make you serve Him. If you don't want to hear me sing, you can turn me off, and that's the way it is. It's freedom of thinking, freedom of choice, freedom of what you want to hear and don't want to hear.'

You didn't seem very remorseful on *The South Bank Show* TV documentary.

'Well, no, I'm very happy to be alive at the age of fifty-two. Most of my contemporaries are dead, and I'm a survivor, and I'm grateful and just glad that I had a chance to read my own book!'

He flashes another toothsome cutie-pie grin and pats my knee. He remembers *NME* when it was *New Musical Express* and reviews were 'write-ups'. He thanks God that a young man like me is interested enough to prepare a detailed interview with him – says he's *deeply moved*.

Chas White, momentarily in the room, remarks that the *NME* has 'sure changed'. 'Last time I opened it,' he says in a thick Irish tongue, 'I found two pages on Nitchy!' Still, White concedes that 'Nitchy', aka Friedrich Nietzsche, might not have been immune to the Dionysiac properties of 'Lucille' or 'Ready Teddy' or 'Good Golly, Miss Molly',

nor blind to the orgiastic hysteria that Little Richard's '50s performances inspired. "They were both anarchists,' he avers.

Like one of his first devotees – Otis Redding – Richard Penniman
hailed from Macon, Georgia. (An early influence, the neighbourhood
washboard-player Bamalama, found his way into the title of Redding's
debut waxing, 'Shout Bamalama'.)

Raised as a Seventh-Day Adventist, he sang in the family Penniman
Singers at camp meetings and Battle Of The Gospels contests, but a
deformity that made one arm and leg shorter than the others led to
teasing and victimisation. He drifted away from his ten siblings into
Macon's seedy gay underworld.

By the time he was fourteen, he had already been sexually abused
by white men and whupped by his father for being effeminate, so he
ran off with a medicine show to hawk snake oil at fairs and carnivals.
Later he toured the chitlin circuit with a minstrel troupe called
Sugarfoot Sam's Traveling Show and landed up in the gay district of
Atlanta, where he was to record his first sides for RCA Camden.

'I think being born in the South gave me the feeling, the determination, and the perseverance that was needed to smash. No producer
today wants to try no new artist, he don't wanna take a chance. I had
to scream like a white lady! You had to do something to make it, and
if you can't make it, you can't make it. You've got to know it to show
it, and live it to give it! And I have learned that through the years.

'There was so much oppression in the South, so much depression,
so much racism and animosity, and rock 'n' roll brought joy. In rock
'n' roll people could forget about their sorrows, and I gave 'em that
joy that made 'em feel like a little baby boy with a toy! Rock 'n' roll
was something like a deliverer.'

It was also something like an accident. The Little Richard who
sang with The B. Brown Orchestra in 1950 was only just graduating
out of Louis Jordan songs into the sound of urban R & B stylists like
Roy Milton and Jimmy Liggins, stars of the Specialty label he was to
make famous. He was certainly no rock'n'roller.

The four RCA sides cut in 1951–2 could be any one of a hundred
Roy Brown imitators of the period. There is nothing in this suavely

operatic blues tenor of the holler that Paul McCartney would ask Richard to teach him in 1962. Not even Johnny Otis in Houston managed to coax anything very special from the Penniman larynx. What perhaps none of them suspected was that Little Richard didn't *want* to sing R & B.

'I was not a Muddy Waters, an Elmore James, a Z.Z. Hill or a Johnnie Taylor. I was rock 'n' roll, which really is nothing but rhythm 'n' blues uptempo. You got to remember that black people start trends and they create styles of dancing. White people don't do that, they do whatever they feel about the music. Black people got to get a little thing goin', a little jerk, jump, hop, and so they keep creatin' beats for that, and I wasn't into that, I did whatever *I* felt too, so me and the white kids fitted.'

What Little Richard really wanted to be was a star at any cost. Without a doubt the single most important influence on him was Atlanta singer Billy Wright, who was dolling up his hair with gel, plastering his face in Pancake 31, and shouting a hoarse gospel blues when Richard was still washing dishes back in Macon. Wright's flamboyance plus the piano technique of New Orleans wizard Esquerita equalled 'Tutti Frutti'. Rock 'n' roll, in other words, came out of gay camp.

'It was a part of show business, the glitter and all of that. I was show business. Whatever was available I used, not as a homosexual but as an entertainer, and a lotta people thought I was gay that didn't even know *what* I was. They think every entertainer is gay. They didn't know if I was a bird or snail or puppy or an ostrich, and they *still* don't know.

'And you know, I have gay friends all over the world, bisexual friends, straight friends, lesbians, and they have a right to be whatever they wanna be and that's a God-given right. People must remember that we can't be prejudiced against someone because of what their choice is in life. *All* of us got to keep God's Ten Commandments to make it in the kingdom, whatever the style is!'

It was only by chance that Richard's camp excess revealed itself at the end of a long day on his first New Orleans session. Sitting alone at a piano, the nth takes of 'Kansas City' and 'Directly From My

Heart' behind him, the madness of 'Tutti Frutti' suddenly erupted on the keys as a sort of afterthought.

Later recorded by everyone from Pat Boone to the MC5, 'Tutti' is rock's Big Bang, its generative eruption. Of course it sounds tinny and shambolic to our thirty-six-track ears today, but there's still something in Richard's crude, loose-lipped gibberish and in the crashing break by drummer Earl Palmer and tenor man Lee Allen that still zaps our sated synapses.

Used to Fats Domino's more leisurely vinyl excursions, the Crescent City cats thought Penniman was a 'kook'. 'They thought I was stoopid and crazy and that I didn't know where I was going.' And yet, as Mac Rebennack has said, 'it was the New Orleans sound that got Little Richard across, and since he left that behind he's never been successful'.

When Richard took off for LA with his own band the Upsetters, the hits did not keep on comin'. At the height of his career, he concentrated on touring, and therein lay his fall from grace.

Sex, drugs, and rock 'n' roll is one way of putting it. *The Life and Times of Little Richard* is another.

Penniman had always been a perv, but touring opened up new worlds of titillating voyeurism for our hero. A favourite pastime was watching his girlfriends being serviced by other musicians. One such was Buddy Holly — hung, according to the book, like the proverbial stallion.

'People came from everywhere, because there was a whole lot to be seen in those orgies, some things you ain't seen the like of in your life. Tree trunks, really! I met a guy, his penis was eighteen inches, and he was kinda difficult because sometimes he didn't want people to see it. I used to call him a bridge over troubled water! He used to suck himself. Couldn't no girl have sex with him, he was too big. I would call people in to see it, and we'd say, where did you *get* this from? Did you buy it, did you borrow it, or did you *rent* it?'

'Richard the Watcher', as he was fondly known, tried to mend his ways in 1957 after receiving a sign from God which was in fact the first Soviet Sputnik flying over Sydney Stadium in Australia. Rumour had it that his subsequent enrolment at a theological college in

Huntsville, Alabama, was not unconnected with the fact that ministers were exempt from income tax, but he did not play another note of rock 'n' roll until a Don Arden-promoted comeback tour of England in 1962.

The Church rejected him as a homosexual, and pitiful scenes of arrest in male lavatories followed, yet he stuck to gospel, recording haunting sides like 'Jesus Walked This Lonesome Valley' and a fine Mercury album with Quincy Jones.

After the British tour, which co-starred Sam Cooke, Little Richard went secular on record once more, cutting, from 1964 onwards, hard-rocking soul sides for Vee Jay and OKeh. He has stated that he felt uncomfortable with black labels like OKeh because he was 'not primarily a black artist', but some of his best performances were the bluesy ballads on Modern (1966–7) – an updated 'Directly From My Heart', Cooke's evergreen 'Bring It On Home To Me'.

The period 1967–76 was his lowest slump, a nightmare of self-parody and cocaine paranoia. The ongoing contest to decide who was *really* the King of Rock 'n' Roll reached tiresome All–Frazier proportions with Jerry Lee Lewis in America and Chuck Berry at the 1972 Wembley Rock 'n' Roll Jamboree, but there was little music to back it up either way.

The Bronze Liberace, as Richard sometimes billed himself, had lost hold of his God and descended to hell. Playing hippie festivals one day and Las Vegas the next, surviving on the kind of nostalgia that gave birth to Sha Na Na, and a legend based on about ten songs, the King and Queen of Rock 'n' Roll wasted away to 115 pounds and became all but schizophrenic. Larry Williams nearly shot him over a coke deal. Friends and relations started dying. Bumps Blackwell dismissed himself. Time was running out.

When his brother Tony died of a heart attack, it was enough to make Penniman put down the drugs and look again for God. 'You can't give up no alcohol and stuff without God. He's a good God.'

Penniman worked as a travelling salesman for Memorial Bibles International, becoming a fully-fledged evangelist in 1979 and 'preaching the parable of his redemption' all over America. Charles White puts it with less than total reverence: 'And so he changed to the religious and abstemious lifestyle with the ease of a chameleon changing colour.'

Why have all the great rock 'n' roll pioneers been such walking disasters, Rich?

'Because they didn't come close to God. I think I found God in time. I believe this book is sent from God, I believe God sent Charles White to America. It's like when Jesus stood before Lazarus' tomb and said, come forth . . .'

Little Richard grins again, shoots me the bug-eyed born-again look. He reaches for another copy of his book and clasps it to his breast as if it were a child.

1985

The Big Kahuna: Jerry Wexler and Atlantic Records

Get Jerry Wexler started on the big bands of the '30s and '40s and you'll never hear the back of it. Most ageing music moguls have long since sloughed off any real love for music they started out with and sunk into a torpor of cocktails and daytime television. Not Wexler. Wrapped in his enormous hooded bathrobe, with the sea lapping against the jetty at the end of his garden, Wexler seeks solace from his favourite saxophonists – Johnny Hodges, Lester Young, Ben Webster – long into the Florida night. Fifty years after first hearing them on 52nd Street he's still hero-worshipping them, still can't listen to Henry 'Red' Allen on 'Meet Me In The Moonlight' without wanting to cry.

But it wasn't jazz that put Jerry Wexler's name in the history books. It was the music for which he famously coined the term 'rhythm and blues', and the 'soul' sound that followed in its wake. In 1949, as a young reporter on the music industry magazine *Billboard*, it was Wexler who suggested to its editor Paul Ackerman that they change the label on their black music charts from 'Race Records' to 'Rhythm and Blues' – thus providing a neat tag for the new black sound that had evolved out of urban blues and big-band swing. It was his love of that music that took Wexler into a partnership at Atlantic Records, and what he achieved at Atlantic makes him one of the key figures in postwar black American music.

In the '50s, Wexler oversaw sessions by Ray Charles and the Drifters that still rank as R & B masterworks. In the early '60s he put the new gospel-based soul style on the map by signing a portly preacher-boy called Solomon Burke; then made a crucial distribution deal with the tiny Memphis label that became Stax Records, home to Otis Redding, Booker T & the MGs and so many others. By the middle of the '60s he'd produced Burke's 'If You Need Me' and Wilson Pickett's 'In the Midnight Hour'.

Finally, in 1967, Wexler turned a church-reared girl from Detroit into a superstar. Aretha Franklin was the jewel in Atlantic's soul crown, and her string of great hits, from 'Never Loved a Man (The Way I Love You)' through 'Respect', to the exquisite 'Say A Little Prayer', remain arguably the greatest songs of the soul era.

Had it not been for Wexler's fascination with the South – inspired as much by William Faulkner as by Ray Charles – the story of soul would almost certainly have been very different. It wasn't easy for a New York Jew in Tennessee or Alabama, but Wexler, more than any other out-of-towner, was responsible for opening up the South, getting away from the fussy arrangements of New York and tapping into the raw musical emotion stored up in such places as Memphis and Muscle Shoals, Alabama. It was his particular genius to grasp its essence and to bring the right people – singers and songwriters and session men – together to record it.

The phone rings often in the house on Siesta Key, in the geriatric paradise of Sarasota. Any feelings of awe at meeting Wexler are instantly dispelled by the sight of his shrunken barefoot figure scampering away to get the phone: comparisons with an elderly but admirably spry chimpanzee would not be out of place. In fact, you'd be forgiven for imagining that he hadn't retired at all: constantly making calls, pulling out old tapes, talking all the time. ('Hey, I'm a state-o'-the-art interviewee,' he chuckles).

He's spent his winters in Florida since marrying his third wife, the novelist Jean Arnold, in 1985; chronic bronchitis meant that he couldn't take the New York cold. If Sarasota, with its soporific climate and Hollywood retirees, is hardly the South he loves, the golf is good and the seafood's fresh. This is a comfortable enough place to be when you're seventy-six. 'Nobody's *from* here, you understand,' he says. 'I doubt that a single baby has ever been *born* in Sarasota.'

It was here that Wexler started work on his memoirs, published in America as *Rhythm and the Blues: A Life in American Music* and written with the help of biographer David Ritz.

'I never woulda written the book without David,' Wex says. 'Trouble is, I'm so fuckin' lazy. There's so much inertia . . .' You could have fooled me, but I take the point that there's a difference between restless activity and productive output.

The key word in Wexler's vocabulary is 'incidentally', a word that generally heralds a digression involving the gentle command to 'turn that tape off a second' and allow for the recounting of some scandalous music-biz *conte*. The book has the same ebullient tone as his conversation, pitched somewhere between Catskills comedian and Talmudic scholar. Wexler's early life reads like the synopsis for a Gotham sitcom: born in 1917, the father 'plodding through life like an animal in harness', the mother, a Jewish matriarch, 'pushing me far beyond my tolerances'. 'My saving grace,' he says now, 'was that while I was running amok in school and the neighbourhood, I was still cultivating my mind, applying myself to books, theatre, music.'

One of the book's key points is to prove it's possible to operate in the world of rock 'n' roll and still be a man of 'probity, taste, and intelligence' – hence the heavy emphasis on his culture and learning, his love of quotes and literary references, the casual film buffery, the piles of the *New York Review of Books* in his living room. I'd phoned him just before the interview and had asked if he was watching the Oscars. 'Absolutely not,' he snorted sharply. 'I'm watching a tape of Truffaut's *The Man Who Loved Women*.'

In 1940, you could watch foreign art movies at the Museum of Modern Art in New York for ten cents. The twenty-three-year-old Wexler and his friends gathered there every Sunday afternoon prior to catching Roy Eldridge or Pee Wee Russell at Jimmy Ryan's. It was a formative time in which he came under the spell of men like producer John Hammond, not only responsible for discovering and recording most of Wexler's favourite jazz musicians in the '30s, but a left-wing blueblood and nattily attired into the bargain. Later on, ironically,

Wexler would succeed with Aretha Franklin at Atlantic where Hammond, at Columbia, had failed.

In 1946, Wexler was discharged from the army. He'd taken a degree in journalism at Kansas State College before the war, and returned to New York to turn his passions for writing and music into cash. He worked initially for Broadcasting Music Inc. (BMI), and then for *Billboard*, where he got his first proper sniff of the music business by writing reviews and news stories. Among the new independent companies whose black releases he regularly reviewed was Atlantic, formed in 1947 by two Turkish brothers whose paths he'd crossed on the jazz circuit, Ahmet and Nesuhi Ertegun.

The music business held a curious appeal for a man who had hitherto dreamed only of becoming the Jewish John O'Hara – and whose fiction had been published in *Story* magazine. Dominated by Jews, it was excluded from WASP high culture. 'I was determined to use all my wit and courage to confound the Christian tormentors,' Wexler says, referring to the 'immanent anti-Semitism that existed then and exists now'. It's like Dr John says, '"I don't want no one hangin' no jacket on me."' He is, in fact, a confirmed atheist of many years' standing.

Wexler was approached by Ahmet Ertegun and asked to run the publishing arm of Atlantic Records. Ertegun, the son of a Turkish ambassador and precisely the kind of well-bred entrepreneur who so impressed Wexler, laughed when he was bold enough to demand a partnership. But a year later he was in.

'He was just what we needed,' says Ertegun today. 'A man of extreme intelligence with great feeling for all kinds of music – not just jazz and rhythm and blues but country and western, too. He had an extraordinary ear for melody and a knack for picking great songs.'

Wexler was the perfect complement to Ertegun. Where Ertegun inhabited a brownstone on New York's Upper East Side, Wexler commuted from a suburban house in Great Neck. Where Ertegun solved problems with suave diplomacy, Wexler bullied his way through them like a Bronx shop steward. 'Ahmet always had the style of the impoverished aristocrat,' says Wexler. 'He was the Hungarian cavalry officer throwing his last bag of gold to the gypsies.' Wexler, by contrast, was neurotically obsessed with money. Or at least with the fear of losing it.

From 1953 to 1959, Ahmet's and Jerry's partnership worked like a dream, to the extent that, when the original partner Herb Abramson returned from the army in 1955, the company's office wasn't big enough and he was bought out. After Wexler's arrival, Atlantic had thirty Top 10 R & B hits in two years. 'We just never seemed to miss. We had this incredible roster of repeating singers, and almost no one-hit wonders' – Ruth Brown, Chuck Willis, Big Joe Turner, Clyde McPhatter and the Drifters. For Wexler, the knack lay in 'accumulating good songs and saving them for good singers'. 'We had certain standards of *bel canto*,' he says. 'We believed in singers and not just interpreters.'

Then there was Ray Charles, the company's first and biggest star through the remainder of the '50s. Even when he was stoned on heroin and nodding out in the bathroom at 234 West 56th Street, Charles was ready to do his job in the makeshift office-turned-studio constructed by engineer Tom Dowd. In 1955, he made the most seminal record of his career, 'I've Got A Woman', a fusion of gospel and blues that paved the way not only for further slices of his own genius but for all of '60s soul.

If you stand on West 56th Street in midtown Manhattan and look up at the floor that housed Atlantic for most of the '50s, it's hard to believe such tracks as Joe Turner's 'Shake, Rattle And Roll' and Ray Charles's 'What'd I Say' were actually cut in this unassuming four-storey building.

'You couldn't get a full horn section in there,' says Wexler. 'We just got away with the line-up for "What'd I Say", which was probably four horns, three rhythm pieces, and the Raelets. The room just happened to be right acoustically. After that, it was just a matter of Tommy Dowd setting up the mics in the right places.'

The Italian restaurant Patsy's, which must have reverberated to the sounds of Big Joe and LaVern Baker, still stands there, but there's no plaque to commemorate the legendary New York label that outlasted all the other great R & B independents of that era.

Anyone who worked in the 56th Street office at that time remembers Wexler as a tyrant who drove people as mercilessly as he drove
himself. Chain-smoking from dawn to dusk, the telephone jammed
permanently against his ear, he could be heard screaming abuse all
the way up to Central Park. When I remark that pictures from this
time make him look personable enough, he replies: 'Hey, Stalin had
a big grin and a moustache.'

'I'd never had dominion over anybody before,' Wexler says. 'See, it
was based on this: I require you to be at least as diligent as I am, if
not as intelligent. In other words, if I'm willing to do this, you must
do it. There was no respect for time off or home life.' Years later,
Wexler must have asked himself if the price had been too high. When
his daughter Anita became a heroin addict, he had to wonder about
his priorities through the '50s and '60s.

'Would I live it differently?' he says. 'William James talked about
"live options", and this is not a live option, so I can't respond to it.
But since purgatory requires endless repetition of the same thing,
probably I would do the same thing again and again.' On the subject
of his daughter – and her eventual death from AIDS four years ago
– he is taciturn for the first time in our talk.

By the end of the '50s, like most of the pioneering independent
labels, Atlantic was experiencing problems. The golden age of R &
B was over; the payola scandal, which had unearthed the bribery of
disc jockeys by record companies, hit the industry hard; and the magic
was draining from the sessions.

'Entropy had set in with the way we were making black music,'
Wexler says. 'It had gotten very sluggish, to the point where you'd
be in the studio *knowing* you were stinking out the joint.'

Three things enabled Atlantic to weather the slump. First, in 1958,
came Walden Robert Cassotto, aka Bobby Darin, greatest by far of
the teen idol types who succeeded the original rock 'n' roll rebels.
Second came the brilliant songwriting duo of Jerry Leiber and Mike
Stoller, whom Ahmet's brother Nesuhi had unearthed in Los Angeles;
and third, an overweight Philadelphian by the name of Solomon Burke.
Burke sounded like a Baptist preacher in a country church, and for
Wexler he was the first and possibly the greatest of all '60s soul men.

After Solomon's success, Wexler and Ertegun seemed to head off in separate directions. While Wexler concentrated on Burke and the equally gospel-styled Wilson Pickett, Ertegun focused his attention on the pop market. He recovered from the defection of Bobby Darin (and Ray Charles) by signing Sonny & Cher, eventually moving on to the hipper rock acts of London and Los Angeles – Cream, Crosby Stills & Nash and company.

'I think we turned their label white,' Sonny Bono would remark some years later. But it wasn't just their tastes in music that divided Ahmet and Jerry. There was an increasing disparity in the two men's lifestyles, particularly after Ertegun's marriage in 1961 to Mica Banu, a Park Avenue hostess in the making, followed by a traumatic episode in 1964 in which Ertegun became convinced Wexler was plotting with Leiber and Stoller to oust him from Atlantic. To this day, Wexler dismisses the notion as laughable; Ertegun remains silent on the subject.

While Wexler made Southern-style records in New York, a clutch of new indie labels was beginning to emerge in the South itself. Among them was the Memphis label Satellite, which signed a distribution deal with Atlantic before changing its name to Stax. It wasn't long before Stax was producing classic hits by the likes of Otis Redding and Carla Thomas. Wexler decided to check Memphis out for himself. What he found there was a way of cutting records that made Atlantic's *modus operandi* look outdated and unnecessarily expensive. The session boys at Stax (Booker T & the MGs) were making records without an arranger, building up their sound organically in the studio. Wexler was as entranced by this laid-back approach as he was by the records that resulted.

'I'd go down there and watch [guitarist] Steve Cropper and [bassist] Duck Dunn come in every morning, hang up their coats, and start playing, whether they had a song to rehearse or not,' Wexler remembers. 'Compared to what we were doing in New York, it was very fresh.'

Wexler's greatest brainwave was probably to take Pickett down to Memphis, where in May 1965 the singer co-wrote 'In the Midnight Hour' with Steve Cropper, triggering a four-year run of classic hits that included '634–5789', 'Land of a Thousand Dances' and 'Funky Broadway'.

Eighteen months later, Wexler rescued Aretha Franklin from Columbia's misguided attempt to mould her into a black Barbra Streisand and 'took her back to church' – in this case, the FAME studio in Muscle Shoals. Here, using a motley crew of white musicians, Wexler produced her first single for Atlantic, 'I Never Loved a Man (The Way I Love You)'. The track was a slinky blues in semiwaltz time, a triumphant example of Wexler's stripped-down production instincts. It sold 250,000 copies in two weeks and climbed to No. 9 on the pop chart. Franklin has arguably never topped it.

Aretha never went back to the Shoals. At the session, a drunken horn player had pinched her behind and incurred the wrath of her manager-husband, Ted White. So Wexler flew his sessionmen up to New York to cut the series of spectacular hits that ensued: 'Respect', 'Natural Woman', 'Chain Of Fools' and too many more to mention.

'There was a sadness about her, and you couldn't define it,' he says of Franklin. 'It was ungraspable, like quicksilver. But it was my job to furnish the most nurturing context for the music, to get the kind of players who were alert to the little changes or improvisations that she might throw in there.'

Wexler says he's heard that Franklin is annoyed that the Muscle Shoals debacle has been dragged out for another airing in the booklet accompanying a new box set. 'I guess she's not going to be too happy when my book comes out', he adds with a mock-sheepish grin.

It was in 1969, at a convention of NATRA (National Association of Television and Radio Announcers) in Miami, that a group of militant blacks calling themselves the Fair Play Committee chose to confront the white men who'd made so much money out of black music. Many of the grievances were legitimate, but Wexler's life was threatened, and New Orleans producer Marshall Sehorn was beaten up in his hotel room.

'I remember some heavy-weight guys slappin' Jerry around,' says Dan Penn, a legendary Muscle Shoals songwriter. 'Immediately after that, white people quit signin' blacks. I mean, it wasn't only that one

time, it was during the whole time. When black people were gettin'
angry and Martin Luther King was shot. But that's when the whole
Muscle Shoals era came to a screeching halt. Didn't nobody get scared,
but it came down real fast.'

Though many whites did pull out of black music then, Atlantic
was already moving strongly into the rock market – a shift that would
culminate in Ahmet Ertegun's distribution deal with the Rolling
Stones. By the time *Sticky Fingers* was released in 1971, Wexler was
ensconced in a studio in Miami, fighting a kind of rearguard action.
'I never rejected rock 'n' roll,' he says, 'but I never liked the music
that people called rock.'

Although Aretha Franklin cut some of her best sessions at the Miami
studio, Wexler spent most of his time – both there and in Muscle
Shoals – nurturing a new breed of white musicians who fleshed out
his fantasies about 'life below the Smith & Wesson line': Duane
Allman, Dr John, Delaney & Bonnie, Tony Joe White. To the rest of
the Atlantic staff it was little more than an expensive hobby. Even
Ahmet felt that his partner had lost touch with the reality of the
music industry.

'When he moved to Florida, there was a natural void,' says Ertegun
in his most fastidious tones. 'You can't move that far from the centre
of activity and carry on the same way. See, Jerry had been a terrific
all-round record man, and after he left New York he was only interested in A & R work. He was making the music he loved, which was
great, but at a certain point you also have to make records people are
going to buy.'

Things weren't helped by the fact that it was Wexler – mostly out
of what he describes as 'ravening fear' – who had pressured his part-
ners to agree to the sale of Atlantic to Warner-Seven Arts for the
risible sum of $17.5 million. (It was worth at least twice that.)
Marooned down in Florida, Wexler couldn't seem to decide if he
wanted in or out. And by the time he returned to New York in 1973,
it was obvious that Atlantic was no longer the glorified mom-and-
pop company it had been for two decades. In the new corporate offices
in Rockefeller Plaza, Wexler didn't even recognise half the A & R
staff. As Solomon Burke said, 'It wasn't a family any more.'

'I didn't fit, and it was disturbing,' says Wexler. 'In retrospect it was clear that I'd abdicated, but it was only when I got back to New York that it really hit me. I was so used to being the Big Kahuna, the honcho, that I thought I could be any place and tell people what to do. I didn't realise that Atlantic was moving into the era of mass merchandising and I didn't know squat about any of it.' Ironically, it was Wexler and not Ertegun who'd signed the ultimate behemoth of '70s stadium rock, Led Zeppelin. In due course, Ertegun would go on to add Genesis, Foreigner and AC/DC to the Atlantic stable. Soul fans wept.

By 1974, when Ertegun proposed a merger with Elektra/Asylum that would have made him and David Geffen joint heads and Wexler a mere vice president, divergence widened into a rift. Wexler was understandably incensed. It didn't help that he detested Geffen, a whiz kid from LA. 'You'd jump in a pool of pus to come up with a nickel between your teeth,' he screamed at Geffen in an outburst at the Beverly Hills home of Warners head Joe Smith. Wexler left Atlantic the following year, only to become a vice president at Warners in New York. It was here that, along with Dire Straits and the B-52s, he brought the Sire label – plus, in the long term, Madonna – into the Warners fold. He was still a player, but an era was over.

The rest of the '70s saw Wexler's reputation consolidated by his co-production of Bob Dylan's *Slow Train Coming* (the irony of Dylan coming to Wexler 'to get the Jesus feel' was lost on neither of them), and an album by one of his R & B heroines, Etta James. In the '80s, he 'took what I could get': albums by Jose Feliciano and Carlos Santana that sounded fine but sold indifferently, and helped to produce an off-Broadway labour of love, *One Mo' Time*. After his second marriage foundered in 1982, Muscle Shoals remained one of the few constants in his life, a place of 'deep country retreat'.

In May 1988, Atlantic Records celebrated forty years in the music industry with a big bash at New York's Madison Square Garden. Everybody was there. Even Ahmet's old partner Herb Abramson had been tempted out of exile in California to take a bow. But there was one conspicuous absence. Shrugging off inquiries as to the whereabouts of his former partner, Ertegun maintained that Jerry was ill.

But Wexler wasn't ill: he was at home, disgusted by the entire charade.

'I knew it was gonna be Ahmet's show, with everyone else lined up behind him like adjuncts,' he says. 'I didn't wanna be a prop in a TV monstrosity. It wasn't a celebration of what we'd done at Atlantic, it was a huge plug for what the company was trying to accomplish then and there.'

For his part, Ertegun (to whom, incidentally, *Rhythm and the Blues* is dedicated) claims that Wexler is a melancholy figure: 'He is sad because he sees the music to which he gave his life is no longer important.' Survival is what counts, and for Ertegun it's paid off handsomely. Wexler says the only thing he's sad about is getting old. 'Mo Ostin of Warners told me, "Jerry, you missed out. You were still playing in the Babe Ruth era."'

But he isn't moaning: he plays golf, walks the beach at dawn, eats fresh shrimp and pompano in the evening. Still, there's no chauffeur, and by the time he's eighty a chauffeur might be nice.

So which of the two friends got it right? Ahmet on Park Avenue, entertaining Michael Hutchence and William F. Buckley Jr? Or Jerry on Siesta Key, alone in the night with his Red Allen reissues? The pat summation at the end of *Rhythm and the Blues* – 'to have somehow participated in the universalisation of black music . . . was the privilege of a lifetime' – doesn't fully answer the question.

Last year, Wexler went back to Muscle Shoals to cut a new album with Etta James. 'I slipped back in like I'd never missed a beat,' he smiles. *The Right Time* isn't as good as he thinks it is, but it includes 'Evening Of Love', a marvellous country-soul ballad on which Etta gives her bruised, enormous all.

'That was a song I'd kept on file for her since 1985,' says Wexler. 'When we came to do it, I had to keep after her. She wasn't singing it the way I wanted, and . . . well, let's just say it got a little bloody . . .'

1993

Inside the Enigma: Prince

'I am not a woman, I am not a man / I am something that you'll never understand . . .'

On a cold night in the spring of 1983, a cavalcade of Luxuricruiser buses pulls off Interstate 94 in northern Indiana and – to the mild consternation of the establishment's regular clientele – unloads a motley assortment of spangled, strangely becoiffed freaks into a huge truckstop diner. Members of The Time, Vanity 6 and Prince's backing band the Revolution mingle with roadies and techies and tour personnel and pour into the restaurant to replenish themselves after an exhausting show in Kalamazoo, Michigan.

I am an *NME* writer tagging along with the *1999* tour for three dates to try to make sense of the burgeoning pop phenomenon that is Prince, and I take my place in one of the booths with manager Steve Fargnoli and the lissom Dee Dee Winters, aka 'Vanity'. The general atmosphere on the tour seems to correspond loosely with Prince's much-vaunted rhetoric about a big happy freaky multiracial party, so I'm assuming that the empurpled genius will be joining us for dinner.

Rash assumption, as it turns out. Only when everybody is settled and ready to order does Prince, engulfed in the shadow of his giant bearded bodyguard 'Chick' Huntsberry, enter the restaurant, gliding silently past the row of booths and making his way over to the other side of the room – about as far away from his band members, protégés, crew and manager as is physically possible. Just Prince and Chick, then, and not much evidence of lively conversation when you dare to peer over at their booth.

Nobody at my table says anything about how odd this is, or how conspicuously it fails to synch with what Prince is singing about every night. For that matter, nobody seems to remark on how peculiar it is that Vanity, supposedly enjoying pride of place between the little chap's sheets at this time, actually kips on her own in a separate bus and scarcely exchanges a word with him throughout the three days I'm on the tour.

It all leaves me even more nonplussed about the curious creature whose career I've been following assiduously ever since 'I Wanna Be Your Lover' made the American Top 20 at the tail end of 1979. And I find myself asking a numbingly obvious, crassly stupid question that I will put to myself repeatedly over the ensuing decade: Who the hell *is* Prince?

'Why do people have to know who I am?'

That was the question Prince Rogers Nelson asked teen mag *Right On!* back in 1979, when he was still just a budding *Soul Train* contender with a giant Afro. And he had a point. One could argue that any *ad hominem* approach to the man is hopelessly reductive: in Simon Reynolds' 1988 words, 'Prince isn't so much a person as a *persona*.' Madonna may have been right when she said that, like her, The Artist 'has a chip on his shoulder, he's competitive, he's from the Midwest, from a screwed-up home, and he has something to prove'. But doesn't he defy such pat showbiz socio-psychology? Isn't his genius so much less deconstructible than that?

Then again, we're only human, and we still can't quite contain our fascination with this man. As with any genius, we long to know more: to get inside his head and 'understand' what makes him tick. And there are particular reasons for asking these questions again at this time, as pivotal a point as any in his twenty-year career. For The Artist has a) finally broken free of the Warner Brothers recording contract that he perceived as so enslaving, b) released *Emancipation*, a three-CD album that contains, at the very least, a smattering of his best work since *Lovesexy*, and c) become a husband, as well as the father of a baby that tragically died in November 1996.

He himself is only too aware of how much is at stake at this moment: can he recapture the ground he lost with indifferently received '90s albums like *Come* and *The Gold Experience*? Can he re-establish contact with the audience that has deserted him this decade? More to the point, does he have a hope in hell of doing it with a triple album that retails for upwards of $30?

To help flog *Emancipation*, The Artist has even gone so far as to open the doors to Paisley Park and allow talk-show hostess Oprah Winfrey to interview him and his wife Mayte. Broadcast back in mid-November, the Winfrey interview has been widely received as a PR triumph, revealing the man as a calm, coyly charming figure even as it yanked away a heavy layer of mystique.

Still, as might be expected, the Oprah chinwag raised more questions than it answered, teasing us with revelations that weren't quite explanations: in particular, the fact that therapy had revealed an 'alternate personality' created by Prince at the age of five, something which arguably makes a mockery of the whole question of The Artist's 'identity'.

Several former The Artist insiders I spoke to after the interview said they were hardly surprised by the news. 'I absolutely concur with him that there may be more than one personality in there,' says Owen Husney, the manager and mentor who got Prince signed to Warner Brothers in 1976. 'I was conscious of seeing that personality shift at a very early age. One was a more nurturing personality, and the other was the more hurt side. The mind is a very interesting playground when it comes to protecting itself. If you've been hurt as a child, you throw up all kinds of protections. You may not let people get close to you; your whole thing after that happens is keeping others at a distance. If you're a control freak like him, you're just trying to control your environment so you won't get hurt.'

Minneapolis writer Jon Bream, the first journalist ever to interview Prince and author of *Prince: Inside the Purple Reign* (1984), goes still further: 'I've always said he's like Sybil – I think there are multiple personalities there, and there always have been. And the nice personality that we're seeing now, I've seen it before. Not in abundance, and not for such a prolonged period of time, but it's been there.'

Even if we take the schizophrenic theory with a pinch of salt, it's clear that many of The Artist's personality traits – his isolation, his overweening need to control, an inability to trust that borders on paranoia – stem from a childhood that roughly answers to the term 'dysfunctional'. Whether or not he witnessed the domestic violence depicted in the film *Purple Rain*, he undoubtedly felt rejected by his parents. Had it not been for guitarist André Cymone's mother allowing Prince to live in her basement, the boy wonder might have been homeless.

'In some respects he was an all-American boy,' says Susan Rogers, Prince's engineer during his five-year commercial peak in the '80s. 'But there was some abuse in his childhood and he had a weird name and he was smaller than his classmates. From the start you had the makings of someone who'd grow up to be an artist – an extremely intelligent and very sensitive young man. What no one could have predicted was just how extraordinary this guy would become; how, all on his own, culturally isolated from the rest of the country, he would plan out the arc of his career.'

Focused and disciplined beyond his years, Prince's chronic introversion was already notorious by his mid-teens. Unable or unwilling to express himself through language, he worked at music with near-fanaticism, mastering several instruments in the process.

'At seventeen, Prince had the vision and astuteness of a forty-year-old man,' says Husney. 'He was the kind of guy who could sit in a room with you and absorb everything in your brain and know more than you by the time you left the room and then have no more use for you. That's not his fault, that's an ability he has, and I saw it time and time again in the early days. Prince might hang late, but it was all for music. He wasn't looking to get high with the guys.'

'It seems pretty clear that most of Prince's personality traits and eccentricities were pretty well set before his success,' says Alan Leeds, Prince's tour manager from 1982 to 1992. 'Sure, money and fame change things, but the leanings were there. Talk to people who knew him as a youngster, they'll tell you he was shy and introverted, and these things continue to be the case.'

To Leeds I volunteer the theory that Prince, in going from high school more or less straight into a record deal, missed out on the vital stage of emotional growth in which you form a peer group around you and develop the social skills that carry you through your career and family life. 'Yeah, but he was a very impatient person, and continues to be. I'm not so sure that he would have been content to go through that phase, and the fact that he was able to leapfrog over it said everything. Here was a guy who said, I don't wanna waste five years jerkin' around, let me figure out a short cut. And he did.'

The first journalists to encounter the brilliant Midwestern prodigy all tell the same story of taciturnity bordering on autism; of a strange doe-eyed youth who could barely bring himself to answer 'Yes' or 'No' to questions.

'I'd seen him around Minneapolis with Husney,' says Jon Bream. 'He seemed very aloof and he'd stand against the wall and keep to himself. When I first interviewed him, I talked to him for an hour and a half and did almost all the talking. He told me at the end that this was the longest he'd talked to anyone in his entire life. He also said that at some point he would stop doing interviews altogether. And another thing I'll tell you, I knew him for six years before he ever looked me in the eye.'

'He sort of mumbled and looked at his feet a lot,' says veteran *Rolling Stone/Creem* writer John Morthland. 'He was struck dumb by very simple questions. He would say things that were completely self-contradictory, and I'd pick him up on those things and he'd just get this sort of puzzled look on his face and glaze over. He seemed to me to be really afraid of people. I don't think there was much image-conscious smokescreening. If he was controlling things in any way, it was with what he *didn't* say – with the silences. I wasn't surprised, as he got bigger and bigger, that he went deeper and deeper into a fairly small manageable world entirely of his own making, which I think is what Paisley Park is.'

The silence and bashfulness are clearly things that haven't improved much in twenty-odd years. When Mavis Staples first met with him in 1989 to discuss recording an album for his Paisley Park label, he completely clammed up on her.

'He wouldn't talk at all,' she remembers. 'I think I must have been with him about six months before he really opened up. He was just like a little kid, you know: when they first meet you, they shy away from you . . . until they get to know you, and then everything comes out. I've seen the little boy, I've seen the kid, and I've seen the man in him. He likes to goof around, jump out from behind things and scare you – "I love to see that scared look on your face, Mavis!" He's kind of like a little animated character at times. He does things that just seem to me like they should be in a cartoon.'

Along with the silence and the mumbling came occasional shocks for early interviewers; conceivably this was evidence of an alternate personality coming to the fore. 'I remember there was this interview he did with *Record World*,' says Bob Merlis, for many years Prince's press officer at Warners. 'The girl asked him the typical boilerplate-interview questions, and then suddenly he asked her, "Does your pubic hair go all the way up to your bellybutton?" And this became known to us back here in the office, that he had kind of a different skew!!'

Perhaps the 'multiple personality' theory is the only way to reconcile the tales of Prince's crippling shyness with his onstage transformation into a lewd sex god – or with his increasingly ruthless control of the Minneapolis music scene, for that matter. 'The real mystique of Prince,' says Susan Rogers, 'is how a guy could come out of Minneapolis and not only start a new trend in soul music but have the foresight to invent his own competition. To realise that if he rose up from Minneapolis on his own it wouldn't have as much impact as it would if there was a scene around him.'

If this was another 'side' of Prince, it was certainly one that put more than a few backs up. 'You can't work with Prince unless he controls you absolutely,' grouched Alexander O'Neal, originally the lead singer of the band that became The Time. On the other hand, Time keyboardist Jimmy Jam gave Prince his dues as 'a great motivator', even after being sacked by the miniature generalissimo during the *1999* tour. 'He's a classic control freak,' says Jon Bream. 'The most honest lyric he ever wrote was "Maybe I'm just too demanding" in "Doves Cry". But then the quality wouldn't have been so high if he *hadn't* been so demanding.'

'I know that in the five years I worked for him I put in fifteen years' work,' says Susan Rogers. 'You were exhausted, because this was a guy who'd work for twenty-four hours straight, then sleep for four hours, then work for another twenty-four hours. But when you're on top like that, you have the fire underneath you. I mean, we weren't winning any prizes for engineering, we were shovelling coal into the fire, so it just depended on how motivated you were. I gave up a lot in order to do that. There were other people who were perhaps more balanced than I who wanted to have a life beyond the studio.'

Did she see Prince as a workaholic?

'Yeah, I did see it as workaholism. We worked so many Christmas Eves and New Year's Days. It was compulsion, it was ambition, but it also filled a vacancy in his life. There wasn't much else going on. We'd spend time talking, but it was always while working. He always figured, as long as I'm sitting here talking to these musicians I could just as easily be recording them.'

Others have stronger words for the man. 'I think he's almost like a vampire,' says Chris Poole, who for five years worked as The Artist's British press officer. 'He'll latch on to somebody and take what he wants from them and then, you know, move on to somebody else. I think there are some very sad cases where people built their whole lives around him . . . I saw a few people who were completely devastated. His personal assistant of twelve years, his valet who had been running around, just got dumped unceremoniously and unfairly. He's got weird expectations of people: he'll take a valet and expect him to be able to promote concerts, and then completely blow him away when they don't meet those expectations. He can be charming, but he can equally be utterly loathsome. It's almost like this incubus figure appears in front of you. I've seen him reduce people to tears.'

Alan Leeds, who worked for Prince for the best part of a decade and parted from him on amicable terms, defends his former boss against such charges. 'Too many people in pop music live through artists. The secret is, don't fool yourself about who these people are. My self-esteem wasn't dependent on Prince, just as it's never been dependent on anyone I've worked for.'

One thing that seems clear is that, over the last few years, The Artist has increasingly isolated himself within the music business, starting with the move to sever himself from Warner Brothers and culminating in his decision last year to both close Paisley Park as a rental property and let go of almost his entire staff.

'I think he's constructed a universe where nothing touches him that he does not want to,' says Alan Light, editor-in-chief of Quincy Jones' *Vibe* magazine and a journalist who has spent several hours with The Artist. 'It's all about enabling him to work. Everything else is designed that if he doesn't choose to come out of that music bubble, he doesn't have to. When he wants to, he'll reach out and bring you in, but not the other way round. When you're dealing with the raw genius of what his talents are, that's an isolation unto itself anyway.'

'You have to look at who this man is,' says Alan Leeds. 'This is, by rock 'n' roll standards, a remarkably provincial man. Someone who's had on his doorstep the opportunity to become a lot more worldly than he has chosen to be. For whatever reasons, he's eschewed that and stayed in his little cocoon.'

The battle with Warner Brothers seems to have brought out the worst of the self-cocooned The Artist's paranoia. Quite apart from the obscenely inappropriate use of the word 'Slave' – an insult to the entire African American people – the very public feud betrayed a bizarre degree of vituperation in the man.

'Something that's very typical of a person who's been hurt as a child is projected anger,' says Owen Husney. 'What happens narcissistically is that it can't be your fault – it has to be Warner Brothers' fault. I think Warners did make some mistakes, but on the other hand you cannot write "SLAVE" on your face, because you have to understand that maybe those are your own chains. The bottom line is that there were some people back there in the early days who absolutely protected that kid. I know times where [Warners CEO] Russ Thyret went to the point of putting his job on the line for Prince, and you can't fuck with that, no matter what.' For Husney, there is enormous hubris in 'slashing the faces of those who protected you'. 'When you cut those chains,' he says, 'you float free and you become real vulnerable.'

Just how vulnerable *is* The Artist in January 1997? What happens if his grand 'emancipation' backfires miserably? When one considers that *Chaos And Disorder* sold a mere 98,000 copies in America, the likelihood of a far pricier three-CD set improving on those sales seems remote.

'I think he could be successful both commercially and artistically if he accepts a role as a major international cult figure,' says *Vibe*'s Alan Light. 'The problem comes when there's a disparity between wanting to have the freedom of a cult artist and wanting to be treated as an A-list superstar. What I worry is that, while he's being more accessible for this album, if it doesn't immediately explode, he's gonna say: "See, I tried to do it your way and it didn't happen", and he's gonna close off even more.'

One American journalist who interviewed The Artist recently is *Rolling Stone*'s Anthony DeCurtis, who found him 'isolated, even if he was much friendlier than I thought he'd be'.

'There was this moment where he was negotiating with me as to whether there would be a court stenographer present during the interview,' says DeCurtis. 'He's standing there with the phone in his hand, with his assistant on the other end asking him what he wants to do . . . and it was almost touching in a certain way, but he seemed very vulnerable. I asked him what was worrying him, but I'm not sure he really knew. He seemed a little clingy as far as Mayte was concerned. He was likeable and interesting and smart, but I wondered how many people feel like they're close to him.'

'Obviously it's got to concern anyone when your records don't sell as well as they once did,' says Susan Rogers. 'There isn't a person alive in the business who hasn't hit that wall. Look at Stevie Wonder, look at Brian Wilson: everyone who was ever great gets to a point where they're past their peak. Because The Artist is highly intelligent, I think he'll be able to look at that and deal with it philosophically. He probably understands that this is inevitable, and he'll probably be able to set his sights on some further goal and at some point evolve into a musician doing creative and vital work again.'

The most reassuring words come from mama Mavis Staples, who thinks The Artist is 'as happy as a lark . . . as light as a feather' after cutting his ties to Warner Brothers. For her, at least, the total control that The Artist now has is not tantamount to the total isolation that others see him bringing on himself.

'If it all goes wrong,' she says, 'I think that this child is strong enough and bright enough to know that, well, that didn't work but I'm not gonna go under because of it. I'm gonna pick myself up, brush off and start over again. I don't think he's gonna let it take him out. He'll know what to do.'

Let's hope this is true. And for The Artist's sake, let's hope there are still enough people who *care* whether it's true.

1997

Coda

I am standing in the corridor outside a suite at London's posh Four Seasons hotel and listening to a high, whinnying cackle that's issuing from inside the room.

It is coming from the same throat that, back in 1983, urged us to party like it was 1999. And now, in 1999 itself, an American representative of Arista Records hovers anxiously beside me as she waits to usher me in to the august presence of The Artist Formerly Known As Prince.

For me there's a strong sense of *déjà vu* about the situation. Seventeen years ago, with '1999' in the Top 30 in Britain, I stood outside the door of a dressing room in Kalamazoo, Michigan, and awaited an introduction to the then Prince. Never have I forgotten the suspicious little face that eventually poked its way through the faintest of cracks, barely grunting in acknowledgement of my presence. Until now, that was the closest I'd ever got to the man.

Another loud whoop from inside the Four Seasons suite. The Arista gal looks faintly relieved. More relieved than she looked three days ago, when hundreds of disgruntled meejah folk were kept waiting at

London's Mermaid Theatre by His Artistry, all the while being enter-
tained by the sight of Arista supremo Clive Davis 'getting down'
onstage to the track-by-track playback of The Artist's tepid new
offering *Rave Un2 The Joy Fantastic* — a spectacle roughly akin to
watching Henry Kissinger do the Hustle at Studio 54.

Of course The Artist finally came on and blew us all away. And of
course it was almost as exciting as seeing the brilliant delinquent
sprite of 1982, parading his fishnet stockings before a legendarily
sparse gathering at London's Lyceum. And who should show up to
watch and worship but Beck, whose polymorphous pleasurefest *Midnite
Vultures* positively fizzes with the influence of Prince-as-was . . .

And thus it all comes around again . . .

Now I'm face-to-face with the black-clad elfin deity, right hand
extended as I approach him, not so much nervous as disbelieving that
this can really be him, the mercurial marvel I've studied and rhap-
sodised about for years.

And what he does he go and do, contrary little fucker, but stick
out his *left* hand. Is this some Indian hygiene issue, or is it The Artist
screwing with my head?

The answer comes quickly enough.

Barely has the Arista *señorita* departed the room when the man
jumps on my case. Turns out he's closely scrutinised the article I
wrote back in 1997, based on interviews with a clutch of people
who, in various capacities, had worked with him: people like Owen
Husney, his first manager, and Susan Rogers, longtime engineer at
the Paisley Park studio in Minneapolis. Also turns out that he puts
pieces like this up on his own website and corrects any factual errors
they contain . . .

'You think Susan Rogers knows me?' he asks. 'You think she knows
anything about my music?'

Shocked lump in throat, I respectfully suggest that yes, she might
know a thing or two.

'Susan Rogers, for the record, doesn't know anything about my
music. Not one thing.'

I see.

'The only person who knows anything about my music . . . is me.'
Right.
'As for Owen Husney, that's a joke.'
If you say so.
'Lemme ask you something. What you wrote about me, was that the truth or was it conjecture?'
'Erm . . .'
'Was it the truth or was it conjecture?'
'Some of it was conjectural.'
'And if conjecture is not the truth, then what is it? Isn't it just *lies*?'

Understand that all of this is said with a broad smile, and accompanied by occasional pattings of my knee. And that's just for starters. When I ask him about something Minneapolis writer and early Prince champion Jon Bream told me – that the boy wonder never once looked him in the eye in six years – The Artist rises to his feet, runs across the room and hurls himself headfirst into an armchair.

'Jon Bream didn't *know* me!' he shrieks when he's recovered from a virtual fit of squeals. 'That's where the conjecture game kicks in real deep. How you gonna write about me when life is ever-evolving? The truth is that we human beings are separate, but we become even more separate by putting labels on each other. My wife knows me. She's the one who brings me tea in the morning. She's the one I call God's queen. Jon Bream didn't know me. Maybe I appeared to be shy, but "appeared" is the key word there. If you look at it, I've only really ever given you music. I'd give cryptic little answers to questions that made no sense. I've always really been the same person.'

Jeez, whadda ya say to *that*?! I'm sitting here literally dumbfounded by a man who didn't speak a word for years and is now spouting forth this heady brew of mysticism and embitteredness.

'People think they know my music,' he continues. 'They think they know where my songs come from. But you can't speculate on a song like "The Ballad of Dorothy Parker". People pick these things up and that becomes the truth. It makes me fear for the planet. Well, not fear, because I don't believe there's any such word as "fear", but it makes me pity the planet.

'We forgot God's will at some point. God is ever-evolving and ever-revealing. Larry Graham [The Artist's bassist and former linchpin of the Family Stone] goes door to door to tell people the truth about God. That's why I told myself, I need to know a man like him. He calls me his baby brother. Do you know how wonderful it would be if you and I could respect one another? We could really do something positive. Otherwise you're gonna further confuse an already confused reader.'

Why do I have the distinct sense that this interview is turning into a covert exercise in torment?

'All these *non-singing, non-dancing, wish-I-had-me-some-clothes fools* who tell me my albums suck – why should I pay any attention to them?'

Worse is to come. When I rashly let slip the fact that I once wrote a whole book about him, he asks what it was called. *Imp of the Perverse*, I limply inform him.

Boy, does he love *that*.

'Imp, huh? That's what, a small person?'

'Well, I meant it more in terms of a sprite, a mischievous creature . . .'

'What about perverse? That's the same thing as perverted, right?'

'I meant, you know, deviating from the norm . . . like you were doing in the '80s.'

He's less than convinced.

'The book is a total celebration of your music,' I add feebly.

'Is it truth or is it conjecture?'

Oh shit, not back to that . . .

'Did you come to the source for the truth?'

'*You think I didn't try to get an interview with you?!?*'

'Yeah, but what gives you the right to write a book of conjecture about my life?'

Erm, it's a free country?

'See, what I do is I look for the truth in things. We're talking about spirit and interaction. We've got to stop this madness. Jimi Hendrix was trying to do that at the point when he passed away. You're talking about a guy who played "The Star-Spangled Banner", but he played

it in a way that showed exactly what it was about. He played it on
TV on Dick Cavett's show and Cavett said it was "unorthodox".
Hendrix said, "Well, it's beautiful to me." Dick Cavett, you just boxed
him in, and you don't have that right!'

Keen to get away from the truth/conjecture issue, I ask him if he
always knew that – like Hendrix – he was going to bridge the worlds
of R & B and rock?

'You have to understand that those terms are just language. I have
a bunch of great stars on my new album – No Doubt, Sheryl Crow,
Ani DiFranco – but it's almost like you wouldn't notice. Gwen Stefani
is just a cool sister to me. I put her on a track on the album I thought
she'd be good on, and she blends right in. The more I think about
it, the more music is all just based on colours and sounds.'

What did he learn from people like Miles Davis and Sly Stone,
artists who bridged different musical worlds?

'Yeah, but Miles wasn't thinking in terms of bridging. People
wanted to play with him because they knew he wasn't going to bow
to any rules. A strong spirit transcends rules. See, Maceo Parker and
Ani DiFranco love one another and laugh about the same things.
There's no categorising in the studio. RZA of Wu Tang said to me,
"I ain't commercial, it's y'all who tell me whether I'm commercial or
not." You'd have to be blind, deaf or a music critic not to like Larry
Graham's playing.' (Charmed, I'm sure . . .)

So why has he signed to Arista after all that hoopla about only
releasing his music through the internet? Is it part of a change that'll
bring him back into the music mainstream?

'Well, understand that Arista signed to *me*. I don't have a contract
with them. Our agreement is just for *Rave Un2 The Joy Fantastic*. Clive
Davis may not even *be* at Arista this time next year. As for the "mainstream", we have to define what that word means. It might mean
something different to me than it means to you. My mainstream is
the one that goes to my bank account! [Loud laughter.] Am I getting
my money straight away or is it TLC royalty? Mainstream is the way
Ani DiFranco is doing it. She's taking $7 an album where some rapper
is getting $1.50 and out of that he has to pay all his costs.'

Does he like contemporary hip hop?

'I like positivity, I like the truth. I like the brothers who are gonna enrich and not degrade. Why would I want to listen to music about bitches and shooting people? It's just somebody's *idea* of what "bitches" are. See, Eve [hip hop guest on *Rave Un2*] changed her groove up for me, and that says something about me and it says something about her and it says something about the record industry that will accept that. And yes, we all have to take responsibility for things we may have sung in the past. I take responsibility by changing.'

Ms Arista is hovering again, worried that The Artist will be late for a *Top of the Pops* taping of 'The Greatest Romance Ever Sold', his feeble new single. I ask him why he decided to bring 'Prince' back to life as the producer of *Rave Un2 The Joy Fantastic*.

'It's funny, when you see a picture of yourself at ten years old, why do we call it an "old" picture? Language is so confining. In fact, I might just stop talking again and not do interviews.'

You read it here first.

1999

The Trouble with James Brown

'How do you stop . . . before it's too late?' Eleven years ago, on one of the most strangely pained records of his career, James Brown asked this question – asked it of us, of himself, of R & B history. How do you stop when performing – singing, dancing, preachifying – is all you've ever known or done? How do you stop a runaway train? Written and produced by the late Dan Hartman, the song was so affecting, so resonant, that Joni Mitchell would later cover it on *Turblent Indigo.*

Few people knew in 1987 that James Brown, Godfather of Soul. Minister of Funk, Emperor of the One, was deeply entangled in something else he couldn't stop: addiction to a drug of such psychotic properties that it was shunned even by ghetto crackheads.

'PCP was such a weird drug for someone that age to start doing,' says Brooklyn-based writer Amy Linden, who has interviewed Brown several times. 'It's like giving yourself a nervous breakdown. I've never met anyone who was sane who did it. It's not a young person's drug, it's not even a *black* drug; it's a white or Latino street drug. It's weird that he would choose something that has no good side to it. You just get *out there* on it.'

In the spring of 1988, the wider world learned that James Brown was in trouble. In March, the singer's wife Adrienne filed for divorce on grounds of cruelty, claiming Brown had beaten her with an iron pipe and shot into her car as she tried to leave their sixty-two-acre home in Beech Island, South Carolina. In April, she herself was busted for possession of PCP at Augusta airport. In May, Brown accused his wife of setting fire to a hotel room in Bedford, New Hampshire.

It got worse, and also more bizarre. Adrienne's bruises were photographed for the titillation of *National Enquirer* readers. Filing charges of assault with intent to murder, together with charges of aggravated assault and battery, Adrienne later dropped all of them, claiming the *Enquirer* pictures had merely been a publicity stunt. A local sheriff in South Carolina revealed that the Godfather had been arrested seven times in eighteen months, mostly on offences relating to PCP and guns.

Then came the climax. On 24 September 1988, armed with a pistol and a shotgun, James Brown entered a building next door to his Augusta offices. An insurance seminar was being conducted in the building, and Brown was furious that someone attending it had used his bathroom without asking. When police were called to the scene, Brown took off in his truck and led them on a chase that crossed over the state line into South Carolina. Only after police shot out its tyres did Brown eventually bring the truck to a stop. Allegedly, out of his mind on dust, the Godfather stepped out of the truck and broke into the opening lines of 'Georgia On My Mind'.

Convicted of aggravated assault and failure to stop for a police officer, Brown served two years of concurrent six-year sentences in the State Park Correctional Center in Columbia, South Carolina. 'I'll tell you, it's like an omen,' Brown told *Rolling Stone*. 'As a kid in prison, I found myself. The same place I'm at right now. That was the beginning of my life, in 1950. This is the beginning of my life again. An omen.'

On the morning of 15 January 1998, almost seven years after his release from prison and exactly two since the drug-related death of his wife Adrienne, James Brown stood on the front lawn of his home clad in nothing but underpants and fired shots into the sky from a .30-calibre rifle and a .22-calibre semiautomatic handgun. He had been up for most of the night on angel dust, brooding about Adrienne.

Brown's daughter Deanna, having spoken to him on the phone, was worried sick about her father. She telephoned Vicki Anderson, one of

James Brown's great funk divas of the '60s and '70s, and begged her to give Brown a call.

'Deanna said he probably wouldn't talk to me, but he did,' says Anderson, who is married to Bobby Byrd, for many years the Godfather's right-hand man both on and offstage. 'I was trying to calm him down, and for a minute he would be calm, and then other times he was crying and just saying things like, "I'm tired".'

Anderson agreed with Deanna that Brown sounded deeply depressed and might be in danger. When Deanna said she was going to call the police, Aunt Vicki backed her up. 'We just discussed it, and I felt then and feel now that she did the right thing,' says Anderson. 'I know if he were my father, I would much rather see him put in a hospital than dead.'

Bearing a probate court order, Aiken County deputies arrived at Brown's home and conveyed him – a 'mental transport', the report said – to a hospital in Columbia. There he remained until 21 June. A press release from his office claimed that he'd become addicted to painkillers after injuring his back onstage in Florida. Six days later, on 27 June, the Godfather was charged with unlawful use of a firearm while under the influence of alcohol or a controlled substance, and with simple possession of marijuana. (Brown claimed he smoked it because he has 'bad eyes'.)

'My daughter made a mistake,' Brown told reporters. 'She should have just called me and asked if she could come over and check on me, but she called the police. Then they came and asked if I would go to the hospital, and I didn't want to say no.' Brown has not spoken to Deanna since the incident, a situation that angers Vicki Anderson: 'Deanna has to suffer with that now. Even though she saved his life, it's like she's branded or blamed for something.'

Four months after the incident, a woman named Mary Simons filed a $5 million lawsuit against Brown, claiming that for three days before his arrest he had assaulted her and held her against her will.

How did it all go so wrong for a man who was once the most potent and powerful black singer in America? A man notorious for maintaining rigid control, for turning rehearsals into boot camps. A man who throughout the '60s and early '70s barely allowed a drug or drink to pass his lips.

How could someone who'd been a musical Muhammad Ali, a surrogate Afro-American president, make such an undignified mess of things so late in his life? And why was he doing it all ass-backwards, fucking up in ways that would have shamed a twenty-year-old?

'It's a frightening thing when somebody waits till their fifties to begin experimenting with drugs,' says Alan Leeds, Brown's tour manager in the early '70s. 'I mean, these are things that a lot of us, at least of my generation, chose to do at a younger age when our bodies and minds were stronger and hopefully you were resilient enough to figure out your limits. And this is a guy who, if he had two drinks before he went to bed, it was a lot.'

Most JB acolytes agree that the Godfather's troubles started in the mid-'70s, when his record sales went into precipitous decline, his grooves were appropriated by legions of freaky funksters, his relationship with Polydor Records became severely strained, and the IRS began hounding him for millions of dollars in back taxes. (Outweighing all of these was the tragic 1973 death in a car accident of his eldest son Teddy.)

'It was around that time that he started smoking pretty heavy dope,' says Cliff White, the English writer who for years was the world's leading Brown-o-phile. 'I don't think he got on to anything harder than that till the '80s, but he was pretty strung out on it.' In Geoff Brown's astute biography *James Brown: Doin' It To Death* (part-based on research by White), former road manager Charles Bobbitt is quoted as saying that Brown was 'starting to get paranoid, and I think that's what finally led him to where he is now . . . he's always had that touch of paranoia, and I'd say since 1974/75, when he started going backwards, I think that was the turnaround'.

Many people have claimed that Brown's introduction to PCP came via Adrienne Modell 'Alfie' Rodriguez, a stylist and make-up artist he met while taping the TV show *Solid Gold* in Los Angeles in February 1982. No one disputes that Rodriguez already had a dust problem, but it now seems more likely that the pair simply bonded over their shared taste for the drug. 'He was doing that stuff before

Adrienne,' says Vicki Anderson. 'It's very easy to blame the mate.'

'I don't think she gave him the drug problem,' says Steve Bloom, who interviewed Brown several times for *High Times* during this period. 'I think he had his own problem before he met her. It was like a little secret in the band and among people around him back in the early '80s that angel dust was floating around. I remember going to a show one night at the Lone Star in New York, and he just didn't show, and all the band guys were on the bus kind of depressed, saying James was at the hotel sick. And James is never sick, never misses a gig, so obviously something was wrong . . . and that was kind of the tip-off to me.'

Looking back, it is not hard to understand how difficult it must have been for Brown to take decline in his stride. Here was a man who'd ruled the roost for longer than almost anyone in the history of black music, a man who as late as 1974 was scoring three consecutive No. 1s on the R & B chart ('The Payback', 'My Thang', 'Papa Don't Take No Mess'), but who, after the splendid one-off that was 1976's 'Get Up Offa That Thing', barely scraped the black Top 20 till the 1985 monster hit 'Living In America'.

'A lot of this, frankly, is an outgrowth of a man having a career crisis and a mid-life crisis simultaneously in the late '70s and early '80s,' says Alan Leeds. 'To suddenly find himself playing roadhouses instead of major classy venues, and struggling to keep his band on the road . . . after all, this was all he'd ever done with his life. It's an oversimplification to say he was feeling sorry for himself, but there was a void there that hadn't been there before, and that kind of void can be filled by drugs and dysfunctional relationships as easily as they can be filled by something productive.'

Talking to people like Leeds about Adrienne Brown, whom the Godfather married late in 1984, two things rapidly become clear. First is that, for all the abuse she took from her husband, Adrienne gave as good as she got. And second is that, for all the abuse Brown meted out to her, he genuinely loved her. 'There was obviously something about her that was different to his earlier wives and girlfriends,' says Leeds. 'She had influence over him that I don't think any other women ever had. He had always controlled the relationships, and this was clearly a woman he didn't 100 per cent control.'

'I met her early during the time they were together,' says Bobby Byrd, the man who'd taken Brown under his wing when they were teenagers in Augusta. 'She seemed all right, but it was very hard to get to James with her being around. A lot of us would have liked to have got together with him to get things straightened out and ask why all this was going on, but it was impossible because she blocked all of that. But he was in love with her, I do truly believe that.' Byrd adds that it 'knocked me to my knees' when he heard that Brown was doing PCP.

Brown's commercial profile had risen slightly with the release of *The Blues Brothers*, which featured his cameo role as preacher Cleophus James. 'His famous line with me was, "The day of the legends is in",' says Steve Bloom. 'I think he had felt that he was forgotten, and his ego really was kind of bruised by that. With *The Blues Brothers* he recognised that he was gonna make a comeback.'

When, in 1985, Sylvester Stallone asked Brown to record a song for *Rocky IV*, the comeback was completed by a Top 5 hit. 'Living In America' was a travesty of the funk Brown had invented, but it put him back on top for a couple of years. The day of the legends *was* in, with the whole House of Blues/Disneyfication-of-the-Delta industry just around the corner.

Unfortunately, 'Living In America' wasn't enough to stop James and Adrienne Brown descending into the chemical abyss. Like Elvis Presley, to whom he was often wont to compare himself, Brown was battling a major drug problem while supposedly acting as a member of the presidential anti-narcotics task force — a conflict of interest perhaps explicable only in terms of a certain Southern unhingedness.

'The last few times I saw him before he went to jail, James was totally out of it,' says Cliff White. 'I remember he came to London for some dance awards show at the Albert Hall, and I went with him. Before we left the hotel, he and one of his minders went for a walk. When they came back he was completely incoherent.'

However much denial Brown was in about his drug problem, it is said that after his release from prison on 27 February 1991 he managed briefly to stay away from angel dust. A relentless performing schedule – eight or nine dates a month, on average – commenced. At a birthday bash in Augusta in 1994, Sharon Stone sang 'Happy Birthday' to him. On 8 December of that year, however, Brown was arrested on charges of domestic violence, charges which – as is so often the case in incidents of spousal abuse – were later dropped.

At 4.20 a.m. on 31 October 1995, Adrienne Brown called 911 and asked for medical assistance; her husband, once again, was arrested. Freed on a $940 bond, Brown blamed the incident on Adrienne's drug abuse. 'She'll do anything to get them,' he said. On 7 November the charges were dropped.

Two months later, Adrienne Brown died after undergoing plastic surgery in Los Angeles. 'There was substance abuse revealed by her autopsy, which has been shrouded,' says Alan Leeds. 'My understanding is that she had the surgery, and then died of an overdose of a mixture of drugs including painkillers and sleeping pills. It was a combination of the anaesthesia from the surgery and the drugs she took on her own that interacted.'

Several people I spoke to felt sure that, since Adrienne's death, Brown had become intensely lonely. Having alienated so many band members and loyal henchmen over the decades, there were few people left for him to turn to, and certainly no true friends. This may be what comes of playing Chairman of the Board for so long: surround yourself with minders and sycophants all your life and there's no one left when the money's gone. The question now is, will Brown end his life as a black Sinatra or as a superannuated version of his friend Little Willie John, whose imprisonment and death he mourned on his 1968 album *Thinking About Little Willie John And A Few Nice Things*?

'One reason he's having these problems is that back when everybody was doing well, we would keep a closer eye on him,' says Bobby Byrd. 'The people that's around him now don't seem to care that much. They see their salary and that's it.'

'When Bobby went and got James out of prison when he was a boy, when he brought him to live in his home as his brother, that was something you can't buy,' adds Vicki Anderson. 'Anybody can be your friend when you have money, but when you are a nobody and have nothing, and a man takes you in and stands by you all down through the years, don't matter what you did to him, all the wrongness and evilness . . . well, if you're lonely then, so be it. Anybody should be able to recognise real love.'

Perhaps it is Brown's tragedy that he never *was* able to recognise real love. Perhaps the chronic workaholism and despotism of 'The Hardest Working Man in Show Business' were all about staying one step ahead of the need to show feelings or reveal a vulnerable humanity. Perhaps the work was itself a drug.

'I always refer to him as a sergeant or somethin', a man who can't show weakness to a lot of people who work under him,' Brown's personal hairdresser Henry Stallings told Gerri Hirshey in her classic book *Nowhere to Run*. 'I know he feels things, but he never shows it. Maybe he goes behind closed doors and breaks down, but I never seen it.'

'He's a compulsive performer, much like Sinatra,' says LA-based writer Don Waller, who has studied Brown closely over the years. 'He'll be performing until he physically can't. He's lovesick, and people do crazy shit when they're lovesick. I also think his ego won't allow him to take direction, and yet his instincts are blunted by age and lack of success. Then again, think of Jerry Lee Lewis. Think of Chuck Berry boring holes in restroom walls so he can spy on women in his restaurant. I mean, that's conduct unbecoming a major artist. It's always an ignominious end.'

'He's sort of nuts, y'know?' says Amy Linden. 'He's the Yosemite Sam of R & B. But then all those guys are nuts. They're nuts partly because of self-preservation and partly because that was their way of getting over. It's also got to be really hard to be acknowledged but never really get the money. He never really cashed in the way he should have, considering how many hits he had and how great they still sound. In the end it's that great debate: does he become any less of a great artist because he's obviously a completely ridiculous human being?'

Reached on the phone at the New York office of Universal Attractions, Jack Bart is staunchly optimistic about the star whose bookings he took over after the death in 1968 of his legendary father Ben.

'He's doing all his jobs, and we're getting nothing but good reports,' he says. 'I've been associated with James Brown for over thirty-five years, and if I had any trepidation I certainly wouldn't have spent the time and money to book him on his forthcoming European tour. There are moments with all your acts when you worry about them, whether it's problems with the law, with drugs, or domestic problems. With James Brown, it's true, his age made it less likely that something like that would come about . . . I was surprised, I'll admit that . . . but nothing shocks me in this business.'

On the afternoon of 3 June 1998, I am granted a short telephone interview with James Brown. A transcription of our conversation follows.

Hello, Mr Brown.

Hello*ohh!*

How is everything?

Everything is fine. Get on up! Get up offa that thing!

How is your back?

Well, my back was hurtin' a little bit because I wrenched it, pulled it a little too much one way, and it kinda put a little snag in it. But that's alright, I just started back walkin' and exercisin' and I feel brand new!

Did you have your annual birthday bash last month?

We didn't have it this year because a fella out in California named Steven Cooper kinda goofed it up . . . he gave us one date and couldn't deliver and didn't tell the Judge [*Judge Bradley, Brown's manager*]. It cost us about $300,000, and he owes money from bookings so we don't know what to do with him.

What else is going on, Mr Brown?

Well, we just finished doing two albums. An album on me will be out called *Back Again* on my Georgia-Lina label, and then I have one on Tomi Rae. She's a take-off on Janis Joplin. I knew Janis when she was living, and to me this is one of the most dynamic young females that I've ever seen onstage in my life. She's got this voice like Mahalia Jackson or somebody, I can't believe it. She's a white girl, that's what's so unbelievable. And she's tall, long hair, real nice-looking girl, so you know the system gonna jump all over her.

Are you happy about all the great reissues and compilations Harry Weinger has been overseeing at Polygram?

Harry Weinger's gotta be a genius, 'cause he's put all the stuff out . . . the *Funky Divas* album . . . they're all great performers and singers, they just need to be organised. Vicki and Bobby, Marva Whitney, Lynn Collins . . .

Do you stay in touch with people like Vicki and Bobby?

Um . . . I don't get a chance to talk to them . . . Martha High was working with me for a long time, but she don't work there no more. See, we're so busy, we don't get a chance to talk to 'em. And they're trying to get their lives together, I know. Bobby's doing fine, I'm glad for him.

What is your favourite era of James Brown music?

Well, I've gotta say . . . right now would probably be the most famous [sic] era I've ever had. Now, I liked it during the years when I was able to stop the riots in Boston . . . admittedly I had the right songs out there to connect. But now I like this era better because I have business people, I have a president who's a judge, and he took a hiatus from the bench just to get out here and get this straight. Because he's so deeply rooted in righteousness — a very religious man — he feels that if we set the right example then it'll rub off through the ghetto. And he's right, because the music is the only answer to our problems across the world: our spiritual problems, our systematic problems, or just our personal problems at home.

You're still living in the South after all these years. How come you never moved to, say, Beverly Hills?

Well, I was in New York for a period. But at that time my wife [*Brown's second wife Deirdre*] wanted me to come home to Georgia. She was from Baltimore, but she wanted me to come to Augusta. And she was right. Augusta and Macon is my heart . . . and then I like Greenville and Charleston in South Carolina. All the things that were plaguing the South . . . it's about the women. It's about the relationship between man and woman, that's all the South's problems ever been about. The African woman do what she wanna do and goes where she wanna, but the Caucasian woman couldn't do it. So what happened is, black people do what they wanna do, and that stops us. That's the only thing that's holding the South back, they got everything else.

How have your recent problems affected you, Mr Brown?

Well, here is the problem: the problem is I'm the last of the Mohicans. Thank God for me being around . . . I mean, you're losing people like Sinatra, Sammy Davis Jr, you're losing some of the great acts that you need to stabilise this whole thing. You don't see Chuck Berry a lot. Jerry Lee Lewis, he don't be out as much as he should. It makes it too hard for a man like me. I know what Elvis was going through now when he was No. 1 out there and everybody was shootin' at him. So if there were a lot of people out there, maybe I wouldn't be singin' out so much for nothing.

I'm very proud. I thank God that young people like you who understand and can remember Martin Luther King and the Kennedys and Emmett Till and Medgar Evers . . . can remember those situations. I remember George Wallace came across in Alabama like he's the worst man in the world, and believe it or not he wound up being one of the better people. And Lester Maddox from Atlanta . . . one of the better people. So what's happened. It's just, I'm kind of left out there being the only one they can identify with . . . for negatives. Some people just use it to get spin-offs.

Everybody's alright, they're treatin' me good, but if I got all the records going, and all of the soundtracks and all of the samples, it's gonna make people come and bother you. That's why the Judge is here to make sure that this stuff is just rhetoric and not reality. He understands people trying to get ahead on somebody else's lifestyle. And it don't bother me. I thank God for the attention. I can walk across the street and they give me a ticket for jaywalking and you might hear about it in Congress. Some cats walk across the street with a pocket full of any kind of drugs you want and two guns in their hand and they don't get bothered. So they're treatin' me like they treat the President: they come to my house and see what I'm doing.

I'm fine, I like it, I thank God for it . . . I'm glad that somebody's concerned about me. I'm glad that my life span has reached a lot of people like you and your parents and probably your kids and your kids' kids. I just wanna do everything I can to make it better for humanity. I'm very proud of this new record I got called *Funk On Ahh Roll!* and this Janis Joplin record on Tomi Rae, 'Try'. Talk to the radio stations about puttin' this stuff on, because this is what we need to bring the happiness back to the music. The music industry right now is nothing but trouble. When you see my show, you'll know I ain't playing, I'm right back doing it like I used to: 'I Feel Good', 'Papa's Bag', 'Try Me', 'I Got The Feeling', 'I Can't Stand Myself', 'Please Please', 'Night Train', 'There Was A Time' . . . I'm doin' it all!

How do you feel you've coped with the ups and downs of your career?

Let me say something to you: do you feel good every day?

No.

Then how you expect *me* to feel? The good thing about it is, people care. Like you sayin', we worried about you.

Is it hard for the Godfather to reach out for help?

Well, you reach out for help if you need it. If I needed it, I'd probably reach out for it. I can't fight rhetoric, you know what I'm sayin'?

You don't think you need help?

I can't fight rhetoric. You didn't hear what I said. If you heard what I said, you probably wouldn't have asked me that. If you're tryin' to get a story, then let's get a story, but if you really wanna be *involved* and try to do something to see what's *really* going on, then it's a different thing. So my way is to talk about show business, 'cause if we don't, you're not going to see what I'm talking about. No way, because you read the paper and you write the paper, so you believe 'em. You *have* to believe 'em, see what I'm sayin'? So I understand where you comin' from, and when you see me, look in my eyes and look at the way I act and you say, well, I see what I see. I'm sixty-five years old and I can do all my dances. I can even do the splits if I want. Most people *twenty-five* years old can't do it. I'm in good shape, and anything that I do, drugs will not allow you to do it, so that'll let you know right away whether I use drugs or not.

How do you stop?

I'm gonna stop when George Burns come back and be born again. I'm gonna stop when Bob Hope starts bug-dancin'. I'm gonna stop when Sinatra bring the Rat Pack back, and all of them gone. I'm not gonna stop. I appreciate those people for what they gave to the business. I'm just tryin' to give half of what they gave.

Well, thank you for your time, Mr Brown.

Papa's got a brand new bag, 'member? Come on down and get it on, funk on ahh *roll!*

1998

3

An Audience
with . . .

Iggy Pop: Animal God
off the Street

Back in the bleak wastes of the early '70s – when things were really no more bleak than they are now – there was one crazed and chaotic cult figure who went further than all the other camp, glam-rock, heavy-metal poseurs simply because he made it look natural.

His name was Iggy Pop, born James Osterberg, and he rose like some industrial swamp creature out of the endless American Midwest basically to get more fucked up and out-to-lunch than any rock star had ever done.

Iggy transcended not only vaudevillians like Alice Cooper and his friend David Bowie but sham shamans like Jagger and Jim Morrison because his attitude was one of pure abandon. He was the one true subhuman archangel of punk, defining it as essentially a cartoon-style death trip. This was rock's excess and exhibitionism carried over the borders of sanity.

Jimmy Osterberg was a small, bright, slightly goofy son of a Jewish soldier who grew up in a Michigan trailer park and drummed in the kind of punky, Stonesy bands that could be heard in every other garage in mid-'60s mid-America. From one called the Iguanas he obtained the moniker of 'Iggy'. Later, in 1968, he formed the Stooges from an assortment of 'the biggest pig-slobs ever born' – a pair of sub-heavy metal drongos called Ron and Scott Asheton, plus their bassist pal Dave Alexander. The Dum Dum Boys.

What Iggy Stooge picked up on was really a violent reaction to the

Love and Peace years. It came from the Velvets, from the Stones' 'Street Fighting Man', from the Doors' creepier moments, and from the incendiary energy of fellow Detroiters the MC5, but it was fed through a vision uniquely Iggy's, one which, on the Stooges' first album for Elektra, came across as a kind of deadpan nihilism. Songs like 'No Fun' (later a Sex Pistols cover), '1969', 'Not Right', 'Real Cool Time' and 'I Wanna Be Your Dog' were as minimalist as the first Ramones album, brilliant statements anchored in Ron Asheton's asinine wah-wah guitar figures. They remain magnificent for their conciseness; rarely has such intelligence been invested in something so exquisitely moronic.

By the time *Fun House* – the most thrilling and intense rock LP ever made – was recorded in 1970, Iggy already had a reputation as a demented, drug-crazed animal. The record went way beyond John Cale's production of *The Stooges*. Where '1969' had sounded bored and sullen, '1970' was jubilant, defiant, revolutionary. Swathes of guitar were piled up over explosive drums and stabbing bass, with Iggy whooping and careening across them like a surfer on STP. 'Down In The Street', 'Loose' and 'TV Eye' were instant classics; an agonised dirge called 'Dirt' made Jim Morrison look like the pseud slob he really was. Only the Stones on, say, 'Gimme Shelter', or the Velvets on 'Heroin', have come close to the evil greatness of *Fun House*.

Drugs of all kinds were already enough of a problem by 1970 for Iggy to have undergone the treatment which first introduced him to his beloved pastime of golf. Now began the nightmarish death trip downhill which lasted over five years and all but killed him. Those of us ancient enough to have read Nick Kent's occasional reports from the end-zone of Iggy's hell will recall a sense of awe at his exploits of that time.

Generally they involved a sublime disregard for professional etiquette, an extreme degree of violence against his own person, and an ingestion of chemicals on a scale unparalleled by anyone before or since. When he dyed his hair platinum in 1972 and took up with David Bowie's management in London, he made one's idols of the time look more than a little effete. With Bowie's help, the Stooges recorded the immortal *Raw Power* album, featuring another wasted

Motor City mutant in guitarist James Williamson, who co-wrote the album's eight superb songs, from the hectic buzzsaw blizzards of 'Raw Power' and 'Search And Destroy' to surprisingly melodic 'ballads' like 'Gimme Danger' and 'I Need Somebody'. This was sick music – 'Penetration', 'Your Pretty Face Is Going To Hell', plus outtakes like 'Gimme Some Skin' – but it had its own demonic beauty.

The downhill slope got steeper. In 1975, without a manager, the Stooges undertook a last desperate tour of America, winding up in hometown Detroit with a show immortalised on the sub-bootleg *Metallic K.O.* album. With its mixture of a sense of impending catastrophe and Iggy's hilariously camp rapport with the audience of sex-starved nymphets and Neanderthal bikers, the record lives on as a testament to the band's insane genius.

Iggy reached his personal nadir in Los Angeles. Here he even became desperate enough to admit himself to the psychiatric unit of ULCA, emerging one weekend to record tracks with Williamson for the criminally underrated *Kill City* album, released on Bomp two years later. At the end of 1975, Bowie came to his rescue once more and brought him along on the *Station To Station* tour.

'With Bowie,' Iggy noted in his book *I Need More* (1982), 'I didn't feel compelled to go to sleep every time something unpleasant happened.' Just as he'd pulled Lou Reed's career out of the doldrums with *Transformer*, so the Thin White Duke set about rehabilitating the World's Forgotten Boy. In the Year of Our Punk '77, the only genuine forefather of all the snot-nosed Rotten scumbags released two Bowie-produced albums that had little to do with the ninety-second thrash-in-the pan blitzkriegs of the blank generation but nonetheless chimed in perfectly with the general thrust of it all.

The Idiot was almost futuristic, somewhere between Bowie's own great *Low* and '*Heroes*' albums and the vaguely gothic punk sound to come. Great tunes – 'Tiny Girls', 'Dum Dum Boys' – combined with ghoulish synth soundscapes to conjure a strange twilight world of machines and shadows. Funtime nightclubbing music it wasn't. *Lust For Life*, as its title part-way suggests, was altogether less sinister. Like *The Idiot*, the whole sound and style was several light years from the cosmic grunge of the Stooges – Bowie's arrangements were almost orchestral, and Iggy's singing had become deep and mannered in a Bowie/Lou Reed vein – but songs like 'Success' and the Burroughs-inspired title track were far more affirmative than anything on the LP's predecessor. 'Turn Blue' looked back over the fucked years and sounded a new note of loss and regret.

For the diehard Stooges nut, Iggy had become something of an adjunct to the Bowie empire. He'd been tamed and sounded artily self-conscious in a way one had never heard before. As a grunge purist, I began to lose interest in this newly respectable figure. The next five years saw him record a series of studio albums which, to put it politely, sucked the big one. Lost in the mire of new-wave art-rock, Iggy's attempts to be witty and elliptical in songs like (to take a random selection) 'I'm Bored', 'I'm A Conservative', 'Eggs On Plate' and 'Eat Or Be Eaten' fell desperately flat.

As with Lou Reed, the musical fire, the raw power, seemed to be extinguished. Even the James Williamson-produced *New Values* (1979) featured only one decent song, the *Kill City*-style 'Don't Look Down'. Sorriest of all was 1981's *Party*, produced by some hopeless hack and sounding like the lamest LA rock music you never bothered to hear. A marginal improvement was *Zombie Birdhouse* (1982), produced by Blondie's Chris Stein for his Animal label, but the songs were still contrived and overwritten. Maybe Iggy was just past it. Or maybe he needed another bunch of Detroit slobs like the Ashetons to revive him.

Then silence, a long one. Not a note – bar a contribution to the soundtrack of *Repo Man* – until the release of the *Blah Blah Blah* album that brings Iggy back into the fold in October 1986. It's another Bowie production, this very commercial collection of pumping video-rockers, and if it didn't feature the sledgehammer guitar of Steve Jones and sound like it was produced by Moroder henchman and Billy Idol-maker Keith Forsey it could almost be a Bowie album. I don't desperately like it – the fact that the nicest song is about a new pair of sunglasses should tell you something – but it's considerably better than the last four.

I had no idea what to expect when I knocked on the door of a

rented rock 'n' roll apartment in Mayfair – would Iggy be clean, cour-
teous, coherent? – so it was a very happy surprise when an effusively
friendly, wirily healthy man in a denim jacket and white T-shirt opened
the door and bade me enter.

He sat up close on a sofa, looked me straight in the eye, and this
is what we said.

So what's been happening? Why the long silence?

Well, in the early '80s, I grew increasingly curious as to what it would
be like to be very sober . . . *really* . . . it became almost an obsession
with me. I thought, Christ, how would that feel? Could I *do* that?
What would it be like to write a song without sort of conceding that
moment of panic, when you say, Oh hell, down a couple of quick
beers and then it'll come out, or smoke this joint and my thoughts
will expand. I also found myself suspecting that my promiscuity, sexually, was getting in the way of my music, because it didn't allow me
a home life . . . and I thought that with a home life, perhaps I'd have
better foundation for harder and better work.

Another thing I wanted to change in the '80s was the fact that I'd
never been very good at engaging in the kind of communication that
you have to do to find allies. So all these things were battin' around
my head. I was fortunate in Tokyo to meet a girl who later became
my wife, and that was the beginning of some good things. I was on
tour at that time, which I had determined would be my last for some
time, and I managed to save some money from that. I also had income
from publishing on my own records and David Bowie's cover of 'China
Girl'. So I thought here's a chance, let's see what we can do. I returned
to the States, and the first steps were just very basic – let's see if we
can manage getting up in the morning, getting through the day,
starting to do the basic things to set up a small household . . . in
short, my quest was to make order out of chaos.

I did so at a steady pace in Los Angeles, and at first it wasn't easy.
At times I felt very shaky, and as my flamboyant lifestyle had become
intertwined in my mind with my work output there were often temp-
tations to revert to form. But we overcame that, and I did one piece

of work while I was out there, which was the *Repo Man* title track. I then moved in 1984 to New York, for a couple of reasons, one of which might sound a bit sappy, which is that I find great inspiration in the new Americans, the immigrants that have come in and had to learn a new language and take rough jobs. I like their music also, the Korean music, the Dominican stuff, the Russians . . .

The other reason was that I'd been recently exposed to theatre, through Sam Shepard's work. Some of the first plays of his I thought, Christ, these are some themes that are pressing a button with me, and I'd always thought this theatre stuff was a bunch of cissy words. So I thought maybe there's a place for me in this, and among other things I did with my time was join a class of young actors, which was a good opportunity to take off my armour and perform in just a bare room with a few people who had no press clippings on me. Eventually I put myself out on the street as one more actor on call. I got an agent, a good one, and they started sending me on all kinds of auditions. I didn't limit the sort of roles, I just said if it's male and in my age range – you know, anything from teachers to psychopaths, I'm fine. Ate a lotta humble pie, too, cos I auditioned for lotsa things and didn't get the parts.

The main thing was I felt like I was growing. And to be working on the natch, with no chemicals to help me, no drink, was a very exciting experience.

Listening to you, it's hard to connect you now with the Iggy of myth and legend . . .

Well, I can connect it for you. The way I got to be a bloody myth and legend is that I was out there first, on my own, doing what I thought had to be done . . . and it was an individual experience and it's the same to me now. I didn't care what anybody else thought, I just took a look and said this is what I gotta do, and so . . . I straightened up. And I ain't ashamed!

I wouldn't want you to be ashamed, though my position on Iggy Pop is a mite ambivalent. I was and am a Stooges fanatic first and foremost, and I guess

I thought you were at your greatest when most frazzled, at the same time as regretting that you were in that state.

That's the Charlie Parker syndrome that you're gettin' into. Personally I feel those were attendant things that ruined the band. When we first started, it was really about a little marijuana and a lotta alienation. That was where we started from. What was good about us was that we had a certain purity of intention that was really good. I don't think we did ever get it from the drugs, I think they killed things. Later I did use 'em to prop up my courage in tense situations. It was a way of saying to everyone, EAT THIS. The trouble is that that attitude too often careened way over in to the area of gratuitous defiance, and that wasn't so great.

I think I had the sense that you were possessed by something, and I suppose the drugs were bound up with that in a way . . . and what happened after the Stooges had burned out was that you began to grow up and for someone like me who was pretty sick himself, I wanted you either to burn out completely or just, I don't know, stumble on . . .

That might have something to do with your own fear of growing up. I was scared of it too! It's been my experience that once people get a fix on you in their minds, it's always a ball-buster to change on them.

Do the great rock 'n' roll survivors have anything left to say to the disaffected youth of today?

I think this thing about youth, youth, youth is more a pop magazine phenomenon, I've never associated it with the musical side of things at all. I can still put on my music or somebody else's and experience a quite wide range of emotional reactions, or just a good adrenal POW!, and that's pretty much been what music does for me . . . it's always been a form of transport, and it works for me quite as well at age thirty-nine as at any other age. In physical terms I've never been stronger. I have the same drives, exactly the same drives.

Is it a miracle that you're alive today?

I don't walk around feeling that way, no, it feels just very natural to me, but then once in a while it hits me like WOW, y'know. Like anyone else, I make a pretty good attempt to drive highly unwanted memories out of my brain, and to try to make room for something else. The memories do come up . . . but it's more kind of like looking back at a strange television show. It's like a screen, I can just look right off now and see myself in a bathtub with people slapping me trying to get me to wake up. But my interior cannot feel, my God, I was very near death . . . I can still remember why I did those things VERY CLEARLY, and in a real funny and silly way I'm proud of it too . . . it's like I was this kind of picaresque figure. I mean, I still get a laugh out of *Metallic K.O.*

What's your favourite Iggy music?

Well, put it like this: the stuff I'll probably be doing live will be from *Lust For Life*, *The Idiot*, *Kill City*, some of the outtakes from *Raw Power* like 'I Got A Right', 'Scene Of The Crime', 'I'm Sick Of You', 'Gimme Some Skin', some of those. I like *Fun House* very much, but when I listen to it now some of it's a little too basic for me. I particularly like the groove on 'Down In The Street', that's my own riff.

In I Need More, *there's a gap between* Fun House *and the tour you did with Bowie in 1977. Were those missing years for you?*

Yeah. It was hard to write about those years. My intention originally in writing that book, and I veered a lot off course, was . . . well, put it like this: when I saw the movie *The Rose* I was so incensed by the intimation in the script that what was important about rock 'n' roll was the helicopters and the sycophants and the adoring crowds and the limos, and I thought no, no, no, no, no, this is *not* what it's about, and I thought I would like to set this straight. In the end, the book became a kind of an autobiography, but what I wanted to show was that the most interesting things about rock 'n' roll are the homemade things, before the band ever gets its recording contract, when they gotta carry their own amps, when they're still naive and have ridiculous dreams, when they have giant holes in their thinking. That's what's really important, when something like that actually takes root and starts to grow. Suddenly these hapless youths find a voice and make waves in the society around them.

How do you and Bowie write together?

There's two ways with David. One contribution he makes is sort of conceptual and even gets to the point where he writes some of the lyrics himself. He collaborates on the lyrics with me, not on all tracks but on some of 'em, or he'll give me a concept or a title . . . 'Lust For Life', for example. For that he had a chord progression which was written on a ukulele in the TV room, and I've always been in the habit of watching my instrumentalists and seeing if they get that gleam in their eye, and seeing if they do I'm off like a shot to get the tape recorder. It wasn't even supposed to be a song, but he saw me there with my eyes on him like, come on, fucker, pull it out. 'Some Weird Sin' was a very angry poem of mine that he found in Berlin one time. 'Isolation' was 'Let's go down to the basement and play some music'.

Will the new record give you the commercial oomph that it's obviously intended to?

What I can say is that I've already gotten about triple the airplay on this album than I've had on everything I've put out in my whole career combined. It's been a giant difference. Half of America's AOR stations are playing 'Cry For Love', and the video is playing on MTV regularly, so I'm getting exposure like I've never had.

Do you see yourself making records for a long time, or will you move into fields like acting?

In 1982 after *Zombie Birdhouse*, I was definitely questioning how long I could do things, but what I've found since is that I'll probably be making better records in five or ten years. I don't see any problem with it, maybe *because* I'm not any longer trying to cling to my youth. Sinatra had a horrible slump in the late '40s, and then as he got older in the '50s he hooked up with Nelson Riddle and made some brilliant records.

Perhaps you could become the Sinatra of the '90s.

Well, he was a real big influence on me.

So you're basically happy?

Uh, basically I'm in a state of high excitation . . . very excited and quite alive.

1986

Joni Mitchell:
Our Lady of Sorrows

She almost bounds into the room, this dowager duchess of American rock, fresh from whooping it up for the photographer on the street outside manager Peter Asher's West Hollywood offices. Where lesser mortals would have been wiped out by the session, she seems to have found it positively rejuvenating.

After this exuberant entrance, however, Joni Mitchell plunks herself down at the substantial oak table and proceeds to fire up the first of the many cigarettes she will have on the go through the course of our conversation. I'd heard whisperings that she was seriously ill, possibly even dying of lung cancer; if there's any truth to them they've made little difference to her prodigious intake of nicotine.

She's just released *Turbulent Indigo*, the seventeenth album in a career that surely stands as one of the most distinguished (and diverse) in the whole rock canon. As *Mojo* reviewer Charlotte Grieg pointed out last month, it's been a long journey from *Blue* (1971) to *Indigo* – the indigo of the tormented Vincent van Gogh, a Mitchell pastiche of whose famous self-portrait *sans* ear graces the album's cover. But the woman is still making music of great authority, still writing songs of beguiling beauty and trenchant indignation. If occasionally she over-steps the mark and strays into the self-righteousness that made early champion David Crosby say she was 'as humble as Mussolini', the best of the album's songs – 'Sunny Sunday', 'Sex Kills', 'The Magdalene Laundries', 'Not To Blame', 'The Sire Of Sorrow' – rank with the most compelling (and compassionate) musical statements ever made about the things human beings do to themselves and to each other.

Recorded at her Bel Air home with her husband Larry Klein – from whom, in rather typical Mitchell style, she separated the day before the sessions for the album began – *Turbulent Indigo* was, for a moment at least, conceived as a virtual swansong to her entire career. Released on Reprise, the label to which she was first signed back in 1967, it is an even sparser affair than her last album, *Night Ride Home*. It also boasts fewer of the guests to which we became accustomed with her '80s records: only guitarist Bill Dillon, sax god Wayne Shorter and backing vocalist Seal (on a cover of James Brown's 'How Do You Stop?') got the call this time . . . The album finishes with 'The Sire Of Sorrow (Job's Sad Song)', an astonishing distillation of the Book of Job which literally raised the hairs on the back of my neck the first time I heard it . . .

'Sire Of Sorrow' must be one of the most harrowing things you've ever recorded.

Well, in a lifetime, I think everyone sinks to the pits, and without that you don't really have powers of empathy. You may have powers of sympathy, but if you've been to the bottom you have an opportunity to be a more compassionate person. I have had a difficult life, as most people have – no more difficult than anyone else's but peculiarly difficult all the same. A life of very good luck and very bad luck, with a lot of health problems and a lot of medical carelessness. But I don't think I've ever become faithless; I've never been an atheist, although I can't say what orthodoxy I belong to. Many of the themes and images on this album have been with me for a long time, but it wasn't until now that I was cheerful enough to tackle the Book of Job.

The line about spitting out bitterness made me recall things you said at the time of Blue *about realising you had a lot of hate in your heart.*

Oh yeah, you've got to cleanse yourself. Krishnamurti said an interesting thing, which was that the man who hates his boss hates his wife, and I think that's true. If you're holding dark feelings about anyone, they carry over into your relationship; you burden them with your bitterness. The '80s were very difficult for me, physically and emotionally. A lot of financial betrayal, a lot of health problems. My housekeeper sued in a version of the new palimony; simultaneously I was butchered by a dentist. I don't want to get into the 'poor me' syndrome, but the '80s for me were like being a prisoner of war, what with the physical and mental pain and general climate of mistrust.

Have the '90s been better so far?

Oh yeah. Even the yuppies seem to have noticed that goodies only make you so happy! All human relationships are so malformed at this point, especially heterosexual relationships. Every other woman is raped in her lifetime, and generally if she's raped once she's raped many times because it's by a man who has repeated access to her, either a father or a brother or a priest. And if she's raped as a child she will not be a well-formed adult woman. You have to wonder why it is that men are so frustrated that they're beating on women, and feel they have the licence to do so. Contemporary music is full of woman-hatred. Rap grew out of the pimp tradition: 'My bitch is badder than yours.'

There does seem to be a new note of compassion for your sex sounded on this record, particularly on 'Not To Blame' and 'The Magdelene Laundries'.

I've never been a feminist – I've always been a tomboy, a companion to men – but as I get older I have more women friends. Also, things between men and women have gotten so out of line in America. Wife-battering is now a national pastime. As regards 'Not To Blame', we don't know if O.J. Simpson killed his wife but we do know that he battered her frequently and was kind of smug about it, like he was above the law. So the precariousness of my gender at this particular time was something that was hard for me to sidestep. Precariousness in the office, in the streets, even in public swimming pools, which I talk about on 'Sex Kills'.

That song takes one back to the rage and despair of 'Dog Eat Dog'.

Yes, but no one was ready for that at the time. They were all into ra-ra-Ronnie Reagan, whereas I was one of twelve artists in the state who had 85 per cent of our income taxed in a kind of experimental levy. Maybe the greed of that decade was supposed to descend on me more heavily, or more irrationally, than on other people. But I did feel like Alice with the Red Queen; I felt I was in a world where irrational law was coming at me from all directions.

There's a new huskiness and vulnerability to your voice on this record.

I'm finally developing enough character in my voice, I think, to play the roles I write for myself. A song like 'Cold Blue Steel And Sweet Fire' [from *For The Roses*] should have been sung by a man, but I think I could probably sing it better now. That was a song about the seduction of heroin, which I never did but which I was around. There are other songs in which I think I was miscast, songs I performed as an *ingénue* — even 'Both Sides Now', which I wrote when I was twenty-one and which I think is better sung by a person in their fifties or sixties reflecting back on their life.

Sinatra did it, didn't he?

Poor Frank, they gave him this folk-pop arrangement that was all wrong for him. I would love for him to have been able to really stretch out and sing the song.

You sang 'Woodstock' at the Edmonton Folk Festival. What were your thoughts about Woodstock?

Oh, the whole thing was just silly.

That's it?

Uh huh.

You said before the Edmonton festival that you didn't want people to use you as 'a sentimental journey'. Have you always tried to resist the nostalgia of your fans?

I understand how people's memories – particularly of their youth and their best years – are wrapped up with the music they listened to then. They also tend to listen to music less and less as they get older. But I'm a maker of music, and I have a painter's spirit even more than a musician's, and I like to keep moving forward. I don't like to get stuck in regurgitative situations. I don't wan't to become a 'duty player', as Miles Davis would have said.

What did you feel about, say, the Eagles' so-called 'Greed' tour?

I don't know, it's hard for me to imagine a 'Greed' tour. People think we make a lot of money out there, but they forget that the artist is the last to get paid. By the time you've paid all the people who have a piece of you, there isn't a lot left. Unless you get some kind of sponsorship. And who's gonna sponsor me apart from tobacco companies, right? [*Raucous laugh.*]

John Martyn says the problem with folk was that it didn't 'swing'. When you look back on the folkie days, would you agree with that?

Yes, but you have to remember that I was born in a swing era. When I got my legs back after I had polio, I rock 'n' roll-danced my way through my teens. My music was always very rhythmic, it just had no drums. But as I began to write my first songs, they were quite intricate and classical, so they went back to my first roots, which were classical. My friends who only knew me as a party doll thought, 'What is this and where is it coming from?' My music started off as folk music because that was a good place to get in on the guitar, but then it got more Celtic when I added the piano. Only then did it really begin to swing. Sometimes it takes a long time for your influences to show up.

Do you ever look on songs such as 'The Circle Game' and think, God, how maidenly and virginal that girl sounds now?

I sang 'Circle Game' as an encore in Edmonton, but I usually try to avoid it. What I realise now is that songs like 'Circle Game' and 'Big Yellow Taxi' have almost become nursery rhymes, they've become part of the culture. I didn't write 'Circle Game' as a children's song, but I'm very pleased to see it go into the culture in that way. Anyway, I'll sing those songs, but I'm more tempted to run by the songs that no one ever seemed to notice. 'Moon At The Window' was one I did in Edmonton, and it was very well received, despite the fact no one noticed it on *Wild Things Run Fast*.

The conflict between the temptation of fame and the fear of the crowd was a preoccupation of yours through the '70s. When did it stop troubling you?

At the time of *For The Roses* I was really mad at show business. I realise now that I'd entered into show business with a bad idea of what it was about. I've always been somewhat reluctant. I liked small clubs, I am a ham and I am an enjoyer. But on the big stage you get sonic distortion, and my open tunings are a pain in the butt, so it's not very enjoyable. Yes, at a certain point I became contemptuous of my audience. Critics seemed to praise me when I felt I was poor and slam me when I felt I was at my peak, so that also fed my bad attitude to the business. I've always loved making the albums and the writing, because that's more like the painting process. The self-promotion used to be distasteful; now it's just kind of funny to me. I guess that's one of the beauties of getting older.

You've said at various points in your career that you regard yourself as painter first and foremost. Is that true?

Oh yes.

In which case, what tipped you over into becoming a songwriter and performer?

Art school. I wrote poems that I didn't show to people, and like most poets I was a bad learner. I was always very involved with music, not as a career direction but as a spirit-lifter, so the irony of my becoming a confessional poet was very great to anyone who knew me in my teens. Anyway, just before I went to art school I picked up a ukulele with the intention of accompanying dirty drinking songs at wiener roasts. It was no more than that. When I got to art college there was a coffee house there, and I went down to see if I could pick up some pin money, and it turned out they were willing to pay me $15 for a weekend. Meanwhile the art education was extremely disappointing to me, because all the professors were fans of De Kooning and Barnett Newman and the Abstractionists, and I wanted classical knowledge. Then when I went east to hear the Mariposa Folk Festival, I discovered the whole Yorkville coffee-house scene in Toronto and decided to stay. But Canada has a tendency to eat its young, and most of the coffee houses preferred to hire mediocre Americans over talented Canadians. That's the unfortunate mental sickness of my people. Once I crossed the border I began to write, and I began to find my real voice. From the first album, it was no longer really folk music. It was just a girl with a guitar, which made it look that way.

So if the profs at Calgary Art College had given you the knowledge you wanted, would you have become a singer?

Absolutely not, I would have devoted myself to painting. But then if I hadn't had polio when I was a kid I might have been an athlete! It wasn't until Dylan wrote 'Positively Fourth Street' that a light bulb went on in my head. I thought, oh my God, we can write about *anything* now. Prior to that song, anger was a kind of closeted emotion, it just never went into songs. But then, 'You gotta lotta nerve to say you are my friend . . .'

David Geffen said you were the only artist he'd ever worked with who wanted to be ordinary. Does that seem a little disingenuous now?

In New York strangers used to holler at me across the street like someone in your class at school, like, 'Hey, Joni, when you gonna do a concert?!' That's extraordinary, but it's ordinary. They didn't suck in their breath when they saw me. In the folk clubs you could finish a set and go down and have a drink with people and maybe even go listen to music at their houses. That's the kind of ordinary I'm talking about: you haven't lost your access to life. Once you're trapped in your hotel room, it's all over.

Tell me about leaving Geffen and returning to Reprise after twenty-three years.

I had the choice to give this record to Geffen and call it my swan-song, to head up into the Canadian backbush and get on with my painting. But because Geffen hadn't done much with me in the time I was with them – I was just kind of hired and forgotten, on a lot of levels – the feedback from everyone around was that that would be a shame. And Mo Ostin at Warners was very enthusiastic about having me back. See, in my entire career there hasn't been a lot of excitement about my albums coming out. There *is* excitement about this one, for some reason. People are ready to listen, they're more ready to take something a little more to heart and to mind than they have in the past. And unlike some of my peers I haven't hit a writer's block: when I hit a block I just paint, which is an old crop-rotation trick. So since I haven't lost my voice, and since I'm over the middle-age hump and at peace with becoming an elder . . . although, of course, I did ask myself whether a woman of my age could continue in this youth-oriented genre. As a painter you're just beginning to ripen at fifty, but as a musician there's a lot of scrutiny as to how you look and so forth. It's such a shallow and fickle business.

Is it true that David Crosby used to show you off to his superstar cronies – bring you out to play a few songs?

David was very enthusiastic about the music – he was twinkly about it! His instincts were correct: he was going to protect the music and pretend to produce me. So we just went for the performance, with a tiny bit of sweetening. I think perhaps without David's protection the record company might have set some kind of producer on me who'd have tried to turn an apple into an orange. And I don't think I would have survived that. The net result of that was that [engineer] Henry Lewy and I made thirteen albums together without a producer.

You were never really a hippie, were you?

I was the queen of the hippies, but in a way I wasn't really a hippie at all. I was always looking at it for its upsides and its downsides, balancing it and thinking, here's the beauty of it and here's the exploitative quality of it and here's the silliness of it. I could never buy into it totally as an orthodoxy.

Do you feel your earliest fans had you pegged as a paragon of purity and introspection and then found it hard to adjust to the chic, jazzy Joni of the '70s?

I can't speak for how you're perceived. I can only say that you write about that which you have access to. So if you go from the hippie thing to more of a Gatsby community, so what? It's not a *Zelig* thing: life is short and you have an opportunity to explore as much of it as time and fortune allow. No subject matter ever seemed barred to me, and no class ever seemed barred. In a way, there is no region for me in the way there might be for someone like Tom Waits. There are some people who want to make a documentary about me, and I don't really know how they would do that. I don't want to bring them into my homes, because you don't really want the lunatic fringe to know where you live. I feel like I belong to everything and nothing, so how could you define my environment?

Who do you regard as your real peers as writers?

Dylan, Leonard Cohen . . . that's about it as far as lyricists go. I'm influenced by Shakespeare, not so much by the reading of him as by the idea that the language should be trippingly on the tongue, and also by the concept of the dark soliloquy, with a lot of human meat in it. Obviously it has to be more economical and direct, and that's Dylan's influence on me.

Does it ever strike you as strange that Canadians such as yourself and Cohen and Neil Young and The Band have made some of the most powerful music about America?

Fresh eyes. Hockney made great paintings of LA. The Swiss photographer Frank documented America in the '50s at a time when nobody noticed how culturally peculiar it was. People sometimes don't know what's happening under their noses.

Do you find Los Angeles inspires the kind of apocalyptic ruminations that other songwriters do?

Well, 'Sex Kills' was written on the last night of the riots. To see a licence plate with 'Just Ice' on it at that time was so poignant. I mean, did you ever think of 'justice' as two words? From the rappers, maybe . . .

There was an early gangsta rapper called Just Ice, as it happens.

Maybe that was his car! Anyway, it got me writing.

Has it been strange watching your rock contemporaries turn into virtual Hollywood deities over the course of twenty-five years?

I'll tell you a funny tale, and then we'll think about whether we should print it or not. I don't like ragging on people and making 'em look bad. This makes [Don] Henley look kinda like a jerk, but shall I tell you it anyway? OK, to me this is kind of funny.

I go to see Sting because my beloved Vinnie [Colaiuta] is drumming with him, but poor Vinnie's all alone up there, there's no one with him. So it put me in kind of a bad mood, this show. I kept going out and smoking in the wings. Anyway, afterwards there was a party and I was the first to get there. By now I was real cranky. I see Henley sitting by himself in a long, long, long booth. So I walk over as if to sit down with him and I say, 'Hi, Henley', and he does this thing where he looks left and right, with a very worried look on his face. And I know exactly what that means, that he's saving the place for Sting. So I say something casual and go sit at another table with Vinnie and Bruce Springsteen and his wife.

Finally, Sting comes in and sits next to Henley and the room fills up with people. At that point, Henley sends an emissary, a woman, to my table who says, 'You can come and sit with Sting and Henley now.' So, I launch myself into the air and I yell at Henley over at the end of the room: 'Never!'

I mean, the whole idea of that kind of political lamination, frankly, gags me with a spoon. It's so tragically hip, and I think it's the enemy of art. I'm not impressed by stars, you know? I never was as a kid. I'm impressed by heart, and fun, and a lot of things, but stardom in and of itself?

How have your worldview and standpoint changed since Dog Eat Dog?

I'm more comfortable in my own skin than I've been in my entire life: I wouldn't trade my fifties for my twenties for anything in the world. No way. In fact, I probably went through most of my fear in my twenties and I'm a good deal more fearless today as a result. There are things I have to work on, like I get pugnacious and impatient. I'm impatient with human beings for being stupid assholes.

I'm an elder now! I should still be swinging at things to a certain degree, but you need to serene on down a little bit. So I would say that nothing much about the world shocks me as much as it used to. I was enraged at the time I wrote *Dog Eat Dog*, but I'm very cheerful now. I think I'm in a good place in my own spirit, even if I still get mad in traffic. But I still think you have to tackle the deeper topics.

They say that as a writer you're a lyric poet in your youth, while in your thirties epic poetry appears because you're going over changes repeatedly. In your fifties, so the theory goes, you become a tragedian. Many of the themes and images on this album have been with me for a long time, but it wasn't until now that I was cheerful enough to tackle The Book of Job.

Have you been disappointed by the sales of your albums since Mingus*? You've described yourself as a 'radio orphan'.*

I was completely out of whack with public taste throughout the late '70s and the '80s. People aren't always going through changes at the same time as me, and sometimes I get so far ahead I look like I'm behind. The warp with public taste on *Wild Things*, for instance, was twofold. I loved the band on that record, we were all in love with each other, but that was the beginning of drum machines, so no one wanted to hear live playing. Now it's just the opposite. If you put on *Hissing* [*Of Summer Lawns*] now, the playing is beautiful.

With *Dog Eat Dog*, the press went to sleep en masse: Ronnie Reagan could do no wrong. It took a few years for the press to wake up. This Japanese interviewer said to me, 'Joni, you used to be a poet and now you're a journalist.' And I said, 'That's because America is a land of ostriches and somebody's gotta be Paul Revere.' People didn't like the politics on that album. *Time* magazine called it an adolescent work, yet it contained two of their subsequent cover stories.

How did you feel when Rolling Stone *dubbed you 'Old Lady of the Year' back in 1972?*

Oh, it was a low blow, and it was unfair. I was not abnormally promiscuous, especially within the context of the free love experiment, so to be turned on by my peer group and made an example, made me aware that the whore/Madonna thing had not been abolished by that experiment. People who were legitimately on that list, like Graham Nash, were gonna call and complain, but then they figured it would fan the flame. There were people on that list like B. Mitchell Reed, whose radio show I'd done and that was all. Assumptions were made in interpreting the lyrics, as they always were, that this was about so-and-so . . . all that nonsense that destroys the ability of the listener to identify with a song. Plus they were misinterpretations. So that was painful and unnecessary, and *Rolling Stone* had a policy for years after that to get me.

Still, you have to admit the irony of a song like 'Man To Man' [Wild Things Run Fast], a song about serial monogamy which features not only your husband but two ex-lovers, James Taylor and drummer John Guerin.

Oh, I always do that, I'm terrible at that! I've got a new boyfriend now, and John played some drums on one song on the record, and Klein was the producer! And they're all looking at me like, 'You asshole', because the boyfriend and I wrote the song, and the old boyfriend who introduced me to Klein is on the drums . . . I don't know, artists are a strange lot.

But you clearly stay friends with these guys.

Whenever possible. See, my mother says things to me like, 'Ducks mate for life', but I guess I am a serial monogamist. Klein and I spent twelve years together. We were good friends in the beginning, then we were lovers, then we were husband and wife. I love Klein: there's a mutual affection there and I can't imagine what would destroy it.

Is there a fundamental frustration about creating art – a restlessness, as you've described it – which makes it hard to live with people?

My main criterion is: am I good for this man? If at a certain point I feel I'm causing him more problems than growth, then if he doesn't have the sense to get out I have to kick him out! The 'Mr Mitchell' thing, of course, is prevalent. I was in New Orleans one night and we were partying, and this Greek guy came up and asked me to dance. And he said to me, 'In Greece they say Joni Mitchell, she doesn't need a man'. I said, 'Oh, is that right? All of Greece says this?'
    I started in the business kind of ultra-feminine, but as I went along I had to handle so many tough situations for myself – had to be both male and female to myself. So it takes a specific kind of man who wants a strong and independent woman. Klein did, but at the same

time there were things about living with 'Joni Mitchell' – not with
me – that pinched on his life in a certain way that made me think
he needed a break. Our separation, I think, was wholesome – painful
and occasionally a little mean, but never nasty or ugly. There was a
certain amount of normal separation perversity – he'd spent a third
of his life with me, after all, and I'd spent a quarter of mine with him
– but for the most part it was a wonderful growth experience for both
of us. Klein would say the friction created a pearl.

*Listening to 'Free Man in Paris' again made me think of Dylan saying that
you weren't really a woman.*

Yeah, they asked him about women in the business and he said, 'Oh,
they all tart themselves up.' And the interviewer said, 'Even Joni
Mitchell?' And he said, 'I love Joni Mitchell, but she's' . . . how did
he put it? . . . 'kinda like a man', or something. It was a backhanded
compliment, I think, because I'm probably one of Bobby's best pace
runners . . . you know what I mean, as a poet? There aren't that many
good writers. There are a lot that are touted as good, but they're not
literature, they're just pretty good for a songwriter.

*What was it like singing with Dylan at the Great Music Experience in
Japan?*

Oh, he's such a little brat, you know. He really is. He's never been
very complimentary to my face – most of the boys haven't. But he
loved 'Sex Kills', and was very effusive about it. Anyway, we played
three concerts, and they kept shifting my position on the mics and
which verses of the songs I was going to sing. On the third night
they stuck Bob at the mic with me, and that's the one that went out
on tape. And if you look closely at it, you can see the little brat, he's
up in my face – and he never brushes his teeth, so his breath was like
. . . right in my face – and he's mouthing the words at me like a
prompter, and he's pushing me off the mic. It's like he's basically
dipping my pigtail in ink. The press picked up on it and said, 'Bobby
Smiles!' Yeah, sure, because he was having a go at me out there.

Talking of brats, did you ever actually work with Prince?

No. He sent me a song once called 'You Are My Emotional Pump, You Make My Body Jump'. I called him up and said, 'I can't sing this.' He's a strange little duck, but I like him.

There are far less of the guest appearances on the last two albums than we're used to seeing. Is there any reason for that?

One of the reasons for that is that I put a studio in my house. I used to drag those guys in when they were recording across the hall. Billy Idol is cast as the bully in 'Dancin' Clown' because his voice was right, although it was viewed in England as a political and opportunistic move because he was big at the time and my stock was down. Which was *so* stupid. Even Prince called me up and said, 'Who is that guy whooping and hollering all over your record?' And I said it was Billy Idol. 'Oh, that's a good idea,' he said.

What do you consider the most neglected or underrated music of your career?

I would say *Hejira*. *Court And Spark* was about as popular as it got, although with Asylum it got lost because Geffen had just signed Dylan for *Planet Waves*. Everything after that was compared unfavourably to it. *Hissing Of Summer Lawns* was felt to be too jazzy, and the drums on it were misunderstood. *Hejira* was not understood at all, but that was a really well-written album. Basically it was kinda kissed off. It's a travelling album, it was written driving from New York to Los Angeles over a period of time, and people who take it with them, especially if they're driving across America, really find it gets to them. Given the right setting, *all of* my albums have a certain power. I wouldn't recommend them for certain moods. I'd say, 'Take this pill and stay away from that one!'

How do you feel about the countless female singer-songwriters you've influenced? You are surely the template for a certain kind of soprano-voiced siren, from Rickie Lee Jones to Stina Nordenstam.

I haven't heard them all, but the one show I heard where this DJ was likening them to me unfavourably, I couldn't see it. He'd say, 'This girl has been listening to *Court And Spark*', and I could not see it. Harmonically there was no resemblance. I mean, I've had girls come up to me and say how influenced they are by me, and then they get up and play and they sound like the Indigo Girls!

Do you find it easier or harder writing songs these days?

It's no easier or harder. It's still a matter of collecting the material and having the time. It will be difficult from here till next February because I'm in the harness promoting this record. Which is unfortunate because I've got ideas. Will they go up into the ether and get lost, or will they yet emerge? I don't know. That's the trouble with the process.

Twenty years after writing 'People's Parties', are you still living on nerves and feelings?

No. I still swing by them, but I don't live there.

1994

A Dark Prince at Twilight:
Lou Reed

The day does not begin auspiciously. The first flakes of a snowstorm descend as I open the curtains in my hotel room, adding yet another layer to the mounds of white stuff already piled up on New York's streets. And then over breakfast I make the big mistake of opening the new issue of *Vanity Fair*, which features a short questionnaire with Lou Reed, the famously unfriendly former leader of the Velvet Underground. Asked what would constitute 'the lowest depth of misery' he could imagine, Reed gives this apparently unhesitating answer: '*Being interviewed by an English journalist.*' Which is fine. It's a perfectly acceptable response. It's just that I happen to be an English journalist who is about to interview Lou Reed.

Now I am sitting in Lou Reed's office on Lower Broadway and the snowflakes are floating thickly down on to people walking six storeys below. Through the door I can hear a voice I know so well from so many records, like the voice of an old adversary or tormentor. Actually, it sounds somehow whinier than it does on his records. It's got the simultaneously wheedling and drawling tone of a young Jack Nicholson, and it seems to be complaining. Why wasn't this done? Has that *English journalist* shown up yet? Is that what he's saying?

I am, I'll be straight with you, feeling sick to my stomach. I look around me at the beautifully functional office, with its computer terminals and sanded floorboards and gold records and framed reviews – all, ominously, from American magazines. The place makes me think of some snide old words of John Cale's, who once said that Reed had 'finally become the Jewish businessman we always knew he would be' (an unsavoury remark from Victor Bockris' Reed biog, any reference to which is strictly off-limits).

Given the things Cale said about Reed only three months ago (e.g. 'I can't understand how somebody who wrote such intelligent and beautiful songs could be the exact opposite as a person' – *miaow!*), it's a minor miracle that the two men have sufficiently patched up their differences to reunite with Mo Tucker for the very belated induction of the Velvet Underground at this month's Rock and Roll Hall of Fame ceremony. More to the point, it tells you just how decimated all three of them have been by the death in 1995 of Sterling Morrison, a man who – apart from being an integral component in the Velvets' sound – was universally liked and provided a kind of emotional buffer zone between the more, shall we say, volatile temperaments of Reed and Cale.

The third song on Reed's terrific new album *Set The Twilight Reeling* is called 'Finish Line', and it's dedicated to Morrison. As an oblique rumination on death it's somewhat at odds with the mood of the rest of *Twilight*, which for the most part is a singularly upbeat, affirmative affair. Coming after the trilogy of monochrome masterpieces that firmly established Reed's return to eminence in the '90s – *New York*, *Songs For Drella* (with Cale) and *Magic And Loss* – *Twilight* is a burst of colour and humour that tells us a fair amount about where Reed, fifty-four on 2 March, is at. And where's he at seems to be pretty darned contented, all things considered. Not the least of the reasons why being his two-year-old relationship with Laurie Anderson, his love and respect for whom are only too evident in at least three songs on the record.

At this point the good humour of *Set The Twilight Reeling* may be all I have going for me. To my horror, the door is opening and Lewis Allan Reed is emerging from his office. (I find for some reason that if I think of him as 'Lewis' it very slightly reduces my terror.) Dressed nondescriptly in T-shirt, jeans and trainers, he nonetheless strolls in a semi-imperious way around the room. Since I'm the only person in it he doesn't know, the fact that he studiously ignores me leads me to suppose there's some minor psyching-out going on here.

While attempting to retain control of my bowels, I surreptitiously observe him from the corner of my eye. What strikes me most about him is that he's got bigger hair than he's had since 1973 – and we're not talking *Magic And Loss* mullet either. For reference points, imagine Kim Fowley crossed with Donovan, at once vampiric and cherubic. It's a pretty unsettling combination.

After Lou's completed a slow circuit of the office, checking on various matters with his French-born PR Annie and inspecting the website being set up by his resident net nerd Struan, he moves ambiguously towards me. Seizing what initiative I can, I extend a trembling paw and introduce myself. Very reluctantly, he places a damp, heavy hand in mine.

'*Bonnie?*' he inquires with a puzzled look. It's a common mistake, since Americans are used to hearing *Barrrr-neeee* when referring to, say, Barney Rubble or Barney the purple dinosaur, or to the New York department store Barney's – which (another ill omen) has just gone into receivership.

'Barrr-nee,' I reply somewhat awkwardly

'Hmmmm,' is what he says to that. And then he strolls off again.

'Um, I saw the piece in *Vanity Fair*.'

Lou Reed and I are now sitting either side of the vast desk in his office, and I am grasping the bull by the horns. To put it another way, I am uneasily fingering *a* horn. A horrible sort of whinnying noise now emerges from the back of my throat. It would seem that I am trying to laugh the whole thing off.

'Uh-huh,' says Lou Reed. (I am alone in a room with *Lou Reed*.)

'Ha ha ha ha ha ha. Hee hee.' Is it really me making these pathetic bleating noises? 'I do hope you won't, um, prejudge me too severely.'

Lou Reed sizes me up. Am I even worth devouring as a pre-lunch snack?

'Well, you can't *possibly* be unaware of the reputation of English music journalists,' he drawls. 'It's not *conceivable*.'

'Ha ha ha. Well, of course not. Indeed, no . . .'

'Right then.'

*   *   *

What happens next is that I decide to follow the advice of several seasoned Reed insiders and become fawningly obsequious. I jump through hoops. I talk about studios, and demonstrate brow-furrowing interest in valves and compressors. Some of this stuff does genuinely interest me, but unfortunately we're not doing an interview for *Guitar World* or *Studio Scene*. (Is there a magazine called *Studio Scene*? I have absolutely no idea.)

Reed talks slowly and dryly about the recording of *Set The Twilight Reeling* at The Roof, his own downtown Manhattan studio. He talks about finally getting the sound he's always dreamed of, and about recording the prototype of 'Egg Cream', opening track on *Twilight*, for Paul Auster's film *Blue in the Face*.

'The guiding principle behind my ideas of recording is that I want you to hear what *I* heard,' he says. 'This is unlike other productions that are really constructed at the console. I think if you ask any guitarist, "Have you ever recorded your instrument and had it sound like what it really sounds like?", they'll tell you no. They get something kinda like what it sounds like, and then at the board they'll EQ it and try and get it to where it sounds right. But it isn't it.'

There's quite a lot of this stuff over the ensuing three-quarters of an hour, but I play along. When I tell him it's great to hear the fabulous bass playing of Fernando Saunders again, he jumps up excitedly and drags me off to hear 'Egg Cream' on 'a system that can *really* play back the bass end'. When we sit down again he goes into raptures over a 1973 Neve console that his engineer found 'just sitting there in a home for aged British actors'. It's odd that he seems so much keener to talk about the technical business of recording than about writing or arranging songs, but it says a lot about how clinical he's become – as if the poet actually aspired to becoming a scientist. When he says that 'the latest and best gear, of course, is all English', I venture that it's a good thing we make up in studio wizardry for what we lack in standards of music journalism. He agrees with me.

Forty-five minutes into the interview, I think I may finally have broken the ice.

Do you think you'd have written about New York in the same way if you'd actually grown up in the city?

Oh, I have no idea. I grew up close enough to come in but not actually be there. Of course, where I grew up [Freeport, Long Island] I think of as an all-time hellhole. When I wrote 'Small Town' on *Drella*, that's what that was about. That was a good song – kind of my answer to Mellencamp's song of the same name.

As with Woody Allen, one has the sense in your songs of a great romance with the city – the city of doo-wop, of Dion and Doc Pomus. But by the same token you give us the city of 'I'm Waiting For The Man' and of New York *itself.*

But they're kind of all the same. I dunno, I really do love New York. I love the fact that at one point recently we had two *Hamlet*s in town – the Ralph Fiennes one and the Robert Wilson one at the Lincoln Center. It's great to have a choice of *Hamlet*s! I love that, and I want that. And when a movie comes out, I like that it's opening here. And book tours. And all the tech guys that are here. Although now I have to go up to Portland, Maine, to see [mastering maestro] Bob Ludwig. I've worked with Bob since *Metal Machine Music*, by the way – he was the one who helped me put it into Quad, so I guess he's a co-conspirator! Anything lobbed at me about that record might as well get lobbed at Bob. He was in on it.

Has New York *improved at all since* New York *came out?*

Oh, it's much, much worse.

One keeps hearing that the crime rate has decreased.

That's only because they started stopping people on the street to see if they had guns. A lot of the dealers have stopped carrying guns on the street because they didn't wanna get nailed with the one-year-in-jail sentence for having a gun. But every day you hear about shootings.

It seemed like the whole gang phenomenon in Los Angeles took the spotlight off New York for a while.

Yeah, but they burned down half the city! How many times can you do that? I think people will tell you that Detroit, for example, never recovered economically from the riots of 1967.

Talking of street crime, you had your collection of doo-wop singles stolen from the Velvets' Lower East Side apartment in 1965. Can you remember what any of those singles were?

It was the night of our very first job at the Dom. I got robbed that very night. I can't remember too much about them: the original 'Coney Island Baby' was probably one of them. I replaced some of them. I love the sound of those old singles, although I'm certainly not a fan of all the cracks and pops.

Speaking of which, have you heard 'Wonderwall' by the Mike Flowers Pops?

Oh, isn't that fab? That is drop-dead funny. It is so dead-on that I could see a whole segment of the population taking it seriously. The arrangement is unbelievably accurate. And you know there's been a big Joe Meek revival going on here. We had a Joe Meek compressor in the studio, because Steve the engineer is a huge Meek fan.

At the time of that first Dom date, it must have been difficult to escape the influence of Bob Dylan. 'Prominent Men' on the Velvets box set almost sounds like a Dylan parody.

Yeah, that track is very folky, although I haven't heard it on the box set because I just don't wanna eavesdrop on myself thirty years ago. But I mean, when I went to college most people were listening to various kinds of folk music, whereas I was in a rock 'n' roll band. Lyrically, I don't think there was too much else apart from Dylan and the Velvets that was engaging that part of your head. That's why, in a sense, it was so easy to do. It was like uncharted waters. Which made it so absurd to be told you were doing something shocking, with 'Howl' and *Naked Lunch* and *Last Exit to Brooklyn* already out. There was such a narrow-minded view of what a song could be. And I'd have to sit there with people saying, 'Don't you feel guilty for glamourising heroin, for all the people who've shot up drugs because of you?' I get that to this day, even though I didn't notice a drop-off in the sales of narcotics when I stopped taking drugs.

I mean, it's one thing tweaking the nose of the bourgeoisie, but really . . . and then to go to Czechoslovakia and Vaclav Havel shows you a book of hand-printed Velvet Underground lyrics which would have put you in jail if you'd been caught with it. And ironically, now we have rap and stuff, people say to me, 'Oh, your stuff's not so shocking.' And I'm saying, 'I never said it *was!*' The point is, I wanted those songs really to be about something that you could go back to thirty years later. And in fact you can: they're not trapped in the '60s, they're not locked into that *Zeitgeist*.

I wanted to ask you about your voice, which has always been one of your main signatures. Who influenced your phrasing and vocal style when you started out?

Oh, that was me. Again, if I'd lopped out a lot of words I could have become very strict, but by leaving them in I had to do a lot of vocal things – things I could hear in my head but which were hard to do for real. I couldn't do an Al Green turn that takes up eight bars and makes everybody fall over dead, but I could embellish the verbal picture I was making. This is in retrospect, by the way: I could come off really smart like I planned all that, but that's essentially what went on. And when I wrote, I liked to break the rhythm a lot, because that was the way I heard it in my head.

After the Velvets broke up, did you resent being turned into that Phantom of Rock figure – by journalists, by your own record company, and by mytholo-gisers generally?

It was kinda like my own fault, up to a point. I allowed it, and it was kind of a convenient thing to duck behind and use as a shield against just about everything. I kind of liked it – the dark prince and all this shit. And it was offered to me; I didn't have to do anything to get it. In the end it was a straitjacket and it was very confining, but . . . I didn't know any better, I hadn't done this before. And once I'd left the Velvets, there wasn't any control on it – there wasn't a Maureen to say, 'Forget that one', or a John or Sterl to say, 'That's getting a little tired', or even just 'Are you having fun?' Very few people can leave a group and survive.

The trouble was, I ducked behind the image for so long that after a while there was a real danger of it becoming just a parody thing, where even if I was trying to be serious you didn't know whether to take it seriously or not. There'd been so much posturing that there was a real confusion between that life and real life. I was doing a tightrope act that was pretty scary no matter *where* you were viewing it from. It's not like I didn't know it, I just didn't know how to get out of it. And I wrote about that, too. People would say, 'Oh this is a parody' . . . oh, don't be too *sure* about that! You might have said it's not well done or that it's mannered, but a parody? Not necessarily.

How ironic was the whole Rock 'n' Roll Animal *act?*

To record songs you'd written four years earlier and have them get popular now? That was pretty interesting. And not to play guitar on them? That was very painful. But *Rock 'n' Roll Animal* is still one of the best live recordings ever done. I've got enough distance on it now that I can hear it today. Those songs were made for that. And there's also a vibe on there that's – phew! I can't listen to any of it, it's just too difficult to relate to.

Did it feel strange finally to be a star?

That never happened. I mean, I only had one hit. It's not like 'Walk On The Wild Side' even made the Top 10. I was a one-hit wonder! That one song kept me going for a real long time, but that one song could also have finished me off in the end. Odds are that if Bowie and Ronson hadn't produced it, it wouldn't have been a hit! *My* way, there wouldn't have been a string part, especially since it's a string part I didn't write. I'm enough of an egotist where I get pleasure out of playing my own lines – not someone else's. And that's just the truth. If it'd been a part *I'd* hummed and whistled, like on 'Street Hassle', then it would have been fun to do it live.

Has it been difficult surviving your own legend – outstripping it, even?

My problem was just to survive *me*! Forget about legends and all the rest of it. Just to survive as a person: if you can do that, the other stuff will come around. You can't do it the other way. This is a really rough business, and New York is a really rough place to do it in. I had some very bad people around me, and like a lot of musicians I didn't pay attention to that side of it. Although on the other hand it's quite possible that I wouldn't be here if it wasn't for that. It was pretty terrible – lawsuits for twelve years, no royalties from 'Walk On The Wild Side', some pretty astonishing shit. And way worse than that. It's a very dirty business, make no mistake about it. Young bands, if they can find an honest lawyer . . . but that's almost an oxymoron.

Is there still a gulf between the Lou Reed you are and the 'Lou Reed' you created as a, shall we say, blue mask?

I don't know any more, but I do know that all these Lou Reeds inform the one who's here now – it's an amalgam of all of them. Still it's writing, it's made of writing. Writing is a pastiche, you're putting things together and making them work. It's not real life. Characters are made up of four or five people. However, the honesty of it – what's behind it all and what I think has informed my stuff from the very first day – that has remained a constant and that's what I have to offer.

If there's any advantage to being older, it's the hard-won experience from Day One, and that's not something you can buy. If you're dealing with someone who's honest musically and lyrically, that's something that's really important. Now if that's of no value to you, you shouldn't listen to me, you should just stick with my records when I was right out of the gate and like a rocket going off. But I could be what you call a slow burn! I'm just glad I'm still making records.

Are you increasingly painstaking as a writer? How tormenting is it getting something right?

The writing thing – that I've got nailed, I think. I know what to do about that, I know how it works. It comes, I always hear it in my head, it's always going on. I heard 'Sex With My Parents' [a track on *Set The Twilight Reeling*] in my head so crystal-clear. It was the day before recording, and I was just two blocks away from home. I knew if I could just get back to my place and get to a tape recorder and a computer, I could have this down. But if I talked to anybody or answered it would be gone – and gone forever. I'm listening to it in my head and singing along with it, which happens to me constantly. And then it's like, *Voom!* Really tight and focused and intense, to the exclusion of *everything*. It's tunnel vision, it's not leisurely.

Did you find it hard to write when you first gave up drink and drugs?

Well, I've given up caffeine because I find it offensive. Caffeine put me on my back, unable to get out of bed and move. Forget about writing! I'm very sensitive. I don't need things like that, as it turns out.

As it turns out!!

Well, I just didn't know it at the time. I didn't know I was that sensitive. I didn't. How would I? As it turns out, I'm the kinda person where a couple of sips of coffee blows my head off. Also, I was so outraged that after all I've been through, I have to drink coffee? I have to have a cigarette? It offended me. That's not what I'm all about. Here I thought I was a blithe, free spirit, and in fact I have to do these things? But I'm still getting over the shock of stopping smoking. I would say nicotine is the hardest thing to quit of all – it's the perfect drug, it's your best buddy. It just happens to have a coupla bad side effects.

At this juncture, fittingly enough, Reed asks if I'd like a cup of tea – herbal, naturally. When he opens the door of his office he discovers a crew from CNN outside. We decide to put my interview on hold and grab a bite to eat. A request comes through for Lou to introduce a Max's Kansas City reunion evening the following week. 'Oh, I don't know,' he says. 'Ask me later.'

While the CNN crew sets up in his office, a curious looking curry pastie is brought over to Lou. 'Do we have a plate?' he inquires in a petulant, spoiled-child voice: like, how could anyone even *think* of giving Lou Reed a curry pastie without putting it on a plate first? This prompts the kind of nervous titters which greeted John Hurt's Caligula's every entrance in *I, Claudius*.

Between munches, Reed and I conduct an informal chat.

Heard any good music lately?

There's a radio station I like a lot called WFMU, a college station out of East Orange, New Jersey. They played a cool song the other day called 'All Kindsa Girls', and it turned out it was by this band called the Real Kids, from outta Boston in the '70s. I'd never heard of them.

They were a kind of punk-pop band on Red Star, around the same time as the first Suicide album . . .

Is that so? Well, it's a really great song. Then there's a group I like called Cul De Sac – very ambient, very cool. And there's this song by Biz Markie that's so funny.

Are there particular people you watch out for?

Oh sure. I wanted to hear the Brian Wilson–Van Dyke Parks album. I would always listen out for Brian Wilson, because where else are you gonna hear those harmonies? But then you'll read an interview where he'll say, 'Oh I'm gonna write with Mike Love again.' I find that very scary.

Do you listen to people like —

Nine Inch Nails?

How did you know I was going to say that?!

I had a great time in Australia when I did this little tour with Trent [Reznor] headlining, and he was awesome. Oh man, was he good. Onstage they were all careening about and smashing into each other. Afterwards I asked him if he'd choreographed his act and he looked at me like I was crazy. I like the Chili Peppers too — what Flea and Anthony get up to onstage. [*Gets up and demonstrates Flea's version of basketball legend Magic Johnson's 'stutter step'.*] See, rock is fun!

Is work still everything for you, like you say on 'Work' {Songs for Drella}? How do you occupy yourself when you're not working?

Well, I relax through playing.

So what do you do when you're not relaxing?!

I like snorkelling, which I just learned how to do in the Caribbean. First time out in the ocean, looking down on Mars. Really exciting. I like that, and I like motorcycles. I like to shoot basketball. We went to this place where they had a court, and I was shootin' for about forty-five minutes to an hour, and it was one of the reasons I quit smoking, 'cos I just couldn't do some of it. I said to myself, that's pathetic — you of all people! I just couldn't have an image of myself as someone who could do a fast break and take a jump shot and then be standing there unable to move, with a stitch up the side.

How much time do you spend reading? Do you ever go back to Poe or Burroughs?

I'm reading Burroughs at the moment, and I went back to Poe recently because I did this reading of 'The Tell-Tale Heart' for a Hal Willner record. It's amazing to read it aloud — you understand it much better, the motive and why he confesses. Also I've been reading Robert Palmer's *Deep Blues* and Gore Vidal's memoir *Palimpsest*.

I've just started that myself.

Oh well, it gets better and better.

He's very funny about his mother, isn't he?

Oh, it gets better – or worse, depending on how you look at it! The best is yet to come!

Do you still have your farm in New Jersey?

Uh-uh. That's gone.

Do you miss it?

Not really, although I do like getting out of the city once in awhile.

There's another interruption here, because Laurie Anderson has just dropped by the office to say hello. Spiky-haired and agelessly tomboyish, she has a friend in tow whom she proceeds to introduce to Reed. I'd heard dark whisperings that Reed had cut Anderson off from her old life and old friends, 'brainwashed' her in the way he is said to have done with several former companions, from his Velvets-era muse Shelley Albin through his transsexual '70s lover Rachel to his '80s spouse Sylvia. That's not the impression I'm getting here. Lou and Laurie – why not call them by their first names? – seem genuinely lovey-dovey together. In fact, he's boyishly proud as he shows her the artwork for the new album, while she laughs out loud when someone gives her the *Vanity Fair* Q&A to read. (Wish I could say I'd done the same.) If Lou Reed really has managed to brainwash the fiercely independent Laurie Anderson, then he's excelled himself.

Maybe this is all too good to be true. Maybe it's just wishful thinking. I guess we all want our favourite villains to show us they're human after all.

It's dark by the time we resume.

Three songs in particular seem to refer to Laurie and the effect she's had on your life. Plus she actually sings on 'Hang On To Your Emotions'. Do you mind me asking about the relationship?

Hmmm, we'll see . . . let's see what you ask! I mean, I did dedicate the album to her.

I was struck by the lines 'You're so civilized it hurts / I guess I could learn a lot' *in 'Hookywooky' {the first single from the album}. There seems to be a new note of humility and receptiveness on the record – although one hesitates to accuse you of humility!*

It's an interesting concept, isn't it! But it's a double-edged sword, that line. On one level it means just what it says, but on the other . . . I mean, it's humorous, whereas 'The Adventurer' is a major love song, a major ode. And I don't know if it's something I'll ever be able to do live, because there are so many lyrics it's hard to imagine ever memorising them. There have been instances in the past where I thought I couldn't sing a song, and so I would eliminate a bunch of words to make it easier. But when I was with the guys in the studio they'd say, 'Come on, man, you can do it!' Fernando helped me by mapping out the lyrics, and then I had a real shot at it.

What's it like being in a relationship with a fellow artist?

Well, somebody understands when you're in the studio till five in the morning, and knows exactly what you're talking about when you call to say this happened or that happened. And vice versa. It's a great relief to have that kind of compassion and back-up available, to have someone who understands what's happening and can actually help you get through it.

Have you had any feedback from anyone – let alone your parents – about the hilarious 'Sex With Your Parents'?

[*Quiet chuckle*] The only feedback I've gotten is from people who like it and think it's very funny. Which is to say friends. But I have been told that in England the album will have to have some kind of Parental Advisory sticker.

That sounds like the, uh, mother of all ironies.

Right! And I still don't know why we have to have one. I was only just told yesterday, and I'm really shocked.

I understand what the title track is about, but what exactly does Set The Twilight Reeling *mean?*

Uh, as in exploding . . . as in shattering, an explosion of birth and sun . . . shatter the twilight, explode it, shake it, make it real.

Twilight is certainly a word that's been used to describe the world of Lou Reed. Are we talking about shattering that world?

Oh, I never thought of that, but what a great idea! It's so funny, I never thought of it, but I guess I should, shouldn't I? No, I'd simply been taking pictures from my roof at twilight, and it was so beautiful. I think that's all I meant by it.

There are various references on the record to looking down at the street from your roof or your window. Perhaps the most intriguing is 'Finish Line'.

That was also the hardest one to write, and it was the only one written in the studio. See, with the first three songs, 'Egg Cream' is about the Young Man, 'New York City Man' is about the Present Man, and 'Finish Line' is . . . well, it's obvious. And then the rest of the songs fill in that mid-period. 'Finish Line' is very intense. Up until then, one of my favourite lines I ever wrote was on *The Bells*, which you can't even buy a copy of anymore. 'If I'm so great, why am I out of print?' is what I have to say when people say I'm doin' really good.

The song is on the Between Thought And Expression *box.*

Oh yeah, I rescued it. Literally. They don't even know where the master tape is. Oh yeah, when they think of you as disposable they're not kidding. They're not sitting with your tapes in some humidified, controlled environment so these things can be preserved and trans-ferred properly to digital. No, no. Your tapes are in a warehouse in New Jersey that has no heat and nothing, and they're sitting there on a dirt floor. If they in fact exist anymore. With *The Bells*, we had to buy a vinyl copy of the album and then put it through a computer programme. Anyway, on that song the favourite line is 'First came fire, then came light / Then came feeling, then came sight', and we decided to put it on the end of 'Finish Line'. And I said to myself, Boy, I really hope I'm the one who wrote that, 'cos it sounds like a quote from something. If it is, I guess I'll be hearing about it.

'Finish Line' is dedicated to Sterling Morrison. Does the world feel like a different place without him in it?

Oh yeah. Oh my God. I mean, the Velvet Underground will never play again – not *that* Velvet Underground, which is the *only* Velvet Underground. It really won't happen. I'll never play guitar with him again, which was our mode of communication. It's very, very difficult to accept and believe. I don't like talking about it too much, to tell you the truth. I mean, Sterling was really a big guy. He covered a lot of ground, he got a lot of life into his fifty-three years. He and I were the same age, for Chrissakes. We went to college together. Knew each other for a long time, and Maureen knew him longer than I did. Jesus, how is it possible? Guy worked out, never sick a day in his life. Literally. He fucking jogged. Well, see, I just get started and – not to make a thing out of it, but he was playing more and more music, he'd sat in on Luna's album, he was working with John on something . . .

It's cruelly ironic that the Velvets are finally being inducted into the Rock and Roll Hall of Fame.

Yeah. I mean, on the box set, all the outtakes and rareties were Sterl's. I never really had much, and what I had I always lost. I was kind of on the run, so I wasn't a good person to share things with. Sterling was the archivist: he always kept stuff, saved it, gave it to somebody to hold on to for him. He was the historian.

How close was he to finishing the Velvets book we'd heard about?

Oh, he's been talking about that forever.

Was it just talk, then?

Well, I don't know that it's just talk. He's always talking about, 'Hey, you know when my book comes out . . .' I mean, for the longest time Sterl was going on about, 'Oh I should go back to school and get my doctorate,' and we'd go 'Yeah yeah yeah'. And then he did.

Talking of grieving, were you disappointed that more people didn't hear the brilliant Songs For Drella *{about Andy Warhol}? Seems it got a little overlooked.*

A *little*?! I don't think anyone even bothered to overlook it! But . . . I'm used to that. *I'm used to that.* So – depressed about it? Only to a certain point. It's happened to me enough times that I go into things without having very high expectations, put it that way.

But at the same time, what you've achieved over the past decade is considerable. When you consider that ten years ago you were at the comparatively low point of Mistrial *. . .*

Well, yeah. You're supposed to get better if you keep at something, and I've tried to get better. See, it's one thing for a short haul. Most groups are around for a year to three years, and that's a long run. And then you're outta there and it doesn't matter if you knew anything, because you're already gone. But if you're in it for the long haul and you want to start controlling it to make sure you're not just doing the same thing over and over again, it's different. Certainly I could have written another drug album, the standard Lou Reed persona, but the real thing is to be able to control it.

These things really do take time, and there are no short cuts for them. I mean, there are things on *New Sensations* that I really like; there are things on *Mistrial* that I like. But it's an up-and-down thing: some of it's good, some of it isn't good. It's always the initial set-up that's wrong. It took a long time – some people might say way too long – but I finally got to a place where I could understand what I was dealing with. Yeah, things are much better than they were with *Mistrial*. But *Mistrial* also had 'Video Violence' and 'New York City Lovers', both of which I really liked. And that was me and Fernando ten years ago! And look how far we've come! Although he was always amazing. The title song on *New Sensations* has one of the great bass parts of all time.

I love those incredible Fernando fills on The Blue Mask.

Oh yeah, that too. Those singing high notes in the hole of the bottom end. We call that 'Fernandising', literally. He was playing with Marianne Faithfull at the Bottom Line once, and he took this solo that made me jump out of my seat. I couldn't stand it! I started yelling! Fucking amazing.

There's a quote from you that interests me: 'My songs are in a way the quintessence of the rock 'n' roll song, except they're not rock 'n' roll.' Have you always felt you were doing something fundamentally different from, say, the Rolling Stones or Bruce Springsteen?

Did I actually say 'the quintessence'? Oh God, here we go. It's when I say things like that . . . I don't know if I said that. OK, with my stuff I wanted to be able to listen to it later on. Also, for better or for worse, I had literary aspirations. In the Velvets – fresh outta college and all of that – it seemed like there was this huge gap between writing in a rock 'n' roll format and being a fan of certain types of writing. What could be better than putting the two things together? I mean, you don't have to listen to the words that way, but why should the words and the music cancel each other out? Does music really have to exist only below the waist? I always thought the head had a lot to do with what turned on the crotch, for that matter. Who says you can't dance to 'I'm Waiting For The Man'? And bringing it all the way up to me right now, 'Finish Line' has rock power in it – it has the spirit of it. I mean, some of the music I like just makes me feel like going out and burning down a house or attacking a politician.

I always wondered what would have happened if one of those inane pop records you were involved with at Pickwick International in the early '60s had been a hit and you'd suddenly become a teen idol. What would have happened to your literary aspirations then?

[*Laughs*] Now *there*'s a hypothesis! I'd probably have died of an OD in a week! OD'd of embarrassment somewhere in Akron, never to be seen or heard from again. See, I couldn't have been a luckier guy. I can't think of anything I'd have enjoyed more than meeting John, running into Sterl on the subway, hooking up with Maureen and being with Andy Warhol. What an unimaginably great time! I might add, by the way, that my friend Mary Woronov, who was at The Factory, has written a book called *Swimming Underground* that I think has the most accurate portrait of Andy Warhol that you will ever run into. It's hilarious and it'll give you a couple of chills.

The new album is a triumph. It's very life-affirming and yet it's also wryly self-deprecating. Songs like the title track and 'Trade In' seem to indicate that you're feeling pretty chipper.

Oh yeah. A lot of the album is about change. A lot of people don't like change, but I like change.

On 'Trade In', you talk about 'a fourteenth chance in life'. Do you feel you've literally had thirteen chances to make a decent go of it?

Oh, way more, I should have been dead a thousand times.

Is this your last *chance?*

I certainly hope not. I mean, I'm good but I'm not *that* good! I'm like a lot of people that grew up when I grew up — I should have been dead on thirty separate occasions. It's just one of those strange things that I'm not. But I think maybe in the song he's saying fourteen is pressing it. Would there be another chance? Well, maybe, but I wouldn't wanna find out if I could avoid it. You'd like to think you'd learned something from the other thirty chances. That's how I quit smoking. It took a year and a half to quit, and it was just very, very awful. I mean, I love cigarettes. I love them, *love them*, LOVE THEM!! Since I was, like, fourteen. But there was a time to quit, and this was the time.

I like the way your albums since New York *are built primarily around guitar and vocals. There's a real intimacy about the sound, even when the performance is very austere.*

Well, if you're not careful, the drums and cymbals just eat up the guitar and the voice, because they're all in the same kind of range. So many records are built around bass and drums. Rap is just bass and drums — that's what they're hitting you with. But I'm trying to do songs that have a vocal, and not a high-endy vocal either.

The only recent comparison. I can make is Neil Young's Sleeps With Angels, *although I'm not sure he works in such a meticulous way.*

I don't know if that's true. I know he's really involved in the sound. He's got his own studio, and I think he's one of the owners of a new company that has to do with high-definition CDs. Now that's pretty serious.

You've said your albums lined up chronologically comprise your version of The Great American Novel. *Have you any plans to write an actual novel?*

I keep saying that I will, and then I start writing it and it becomes a song. So I'm beginning to suspect that this is *the thing that I do*. I just get such a kick out of it. I like the guitars and the bass and the drums to kick in, it's just more fun . . . for me.

One is used to seeing you these days at awards and benefits and tribute shows. Is it fair to say that in recent years you've come in from the cold?

Well, some of the things I'm involved in are a direct result of knowing Peter Gabriel, who's a real activist. I was at the Reebok Human Rights Awards and the Witness Programme, but because I was asked to be in it by Peter. I admire him enormously and I really follow his lead. I believe in him. I think it's one of the few things celebrity is good for. It's good for getting a better table in a restaurant when it's crowded, but it's really good for these benefits, where they're raising money or they want publicity. I did the University of Peace with Peter, where we froze our asses off in a stadium in Japan. With the work the Reebok people do, it's gonna sound self-serving, but it's so humbling to see what some of these people are doing. The tortures you hear about are just so unbelievable. I don't do that much. A couple of things come up once in a while, things where somebody really smart is in charge and where the money goes where it's supposed to.

What is your most underrated album?

The Bells. I really like that album. I think it sold two copies, and probably both to me.

And the most overrated?

I've never suffered from that. I try not to read reviews if I can possibly avoid them. I've always noticed that someone will be giving you a good review of something, and in the middle of that good review they will attack something else or say something horrible. And for you to believe the good review you have to go along with this other thing that's in there like some pit bull gnawing at your groin. There are things that are really wrong with all my old records – technically wrong – and that's why I can't listen to them. People say, 'How can you not listen to the Velvet Underground?' And I say, it's easy. I don't wanna look back and review my past. On the other hand, 'Temptation Inside Your Heart' from the box set came on the radio the other day and I got a real kick out of it. It's such a fucking great track, it could've been released yesterday. So it's fun to be surprised by something.

I know with every new record I always say *this is* the one. But I really mean it. There's nothing wrong with that. It just means it's the best I could do at that time.

If *Set The Twilight Reeling* is the best Lou Reed can do at this time, then he's doing pretty fucking well. There aren't many rock 'n' roll veterans who can write songs as deliciously soulful as 'New York City Man', as bitterly funny as 'Sex With Your Parents', as searing and engulfing as 'Riptide'. If most of the album is about redemption, as it seems to be, then long may he run.

'Although Lou's been enshrined and canonised, he likes the fact that he can still piss people off,' says *Rolling Stone*'s David Fricke, who worked closely with Reed on the Velvets box *Peel Slowly And See*. 'But you also have to consider that some of the people who badmouth him, like John Cale or Bob Quine [ex-Voidoid guitarist who played on early '80s Reed albums like *The Blue Mask* and *Legendary Hearts*], are very like Lou themselves. They're fish out of water too. And when it comes to people who share the same kind of traits – like the need to control – they're bound to be on a collision course with him.'

Lou Reed – a sheep in wolf's clothing? Somehow it seems improbable. But as you listen to the *Moondance*-style horns coming in on the third verse of 'Set The Twilight Reeling', it's hard not to conclude that the Ice King has finally begun to melt, or at least that he is now capable of looking back on his past with real wisdom and insight:

> *I accept the newfound man and set the twilight reeling . . .*

1996

Busting Loose: Johnny Cash

We're passing through Andover, Kansas, scene of one of the worst tornadoes in American history – a monstrously fat twister that levelled the little town on 26 April 1991 and took thirty lives. Every building in sight looks like it was put up in the last ten minutes. Human history has been eradicated here.

Early evening sunlight is streaming through the windows of the black and silver MCI Greyhound bus, bathing the monumental features of Johnny Cash in its warm orange rays. The left side of Cash's face is painfully swollen after the countless operations he's had on his jaw, but once again he is preparing himself to perform for a gathering of the country faithful, this time in what turns out to be the absolute Middle of Nowhere – a spanking-new shopping mall standing surreally alone in the endless flat expanse of America's Great Plains. You couldn't get much closer to the heart of Heartland USA if you tried.

Appropriately, since we have just left the outskirts of Wichita, Cash begins humming, and then singing, the famous Jimmy Webb song about the county lineman – 'still on the line' like the equally famous protagonist of Cash's own 'I Walk The Line'.

From the back of the bus emerges June Carter Cash, the epitome of homely Southern graciousness with her hair up in a towel. She too is preparing for the umpteenth show in which she will duet with her husband on 'Jackson' and 'If I Were A Carpenter' and then interleave a magical medley of Carter Family classics with her hilarious comic monologues.

Sitting across from Cash at a table that folds away to become a bed, I ask whether he is likely to sing any of the songs from his superb new album, *Unchained*, tonight. My assumption is that he'll save his versions of Beck's 'Rowboat' and Soundgarden's 'Rusty Cage' for the *haute*-hip scenesters of London and Manhattan and stick to staples like 'Ring Of Fire' and 'Sunday Morning Coming Down'.

'If there's a lotta young people, I'll do "Rusty Cage",' he says in the great deep voice, a sonorous blend of John Wayne in *The Shootist* and Robert Mitchum in *The Night of the Hunter*. 'I've got to get on and feel the audience. I know how I'm gonna start off, but that's about it. College-town audiences are my favourite – that's when it feels like the '50s again. Then we go wild.'

Soon the mall emerges on the level horizon; in the fading light we start to make out cars and pick ups parked in the surrounding fields. As the bus pulls off the highway, scores of people wait to watch Cash step out of the vehicle – a thicket of Stetsons and flatland mullets. Cash draws the curtains to hide himself, but June waves on the other side to a middle-aged couple sitting in a Winnebago. 'Our own groupies,' she informs me. 'They follow us everywhere.'

It transpires that more than 10,000 people have schlepped out on this balmy, breezy Columbus Day evening to see the show. The stage sits in the middle of the mall, a miniature golf course to one side and stores with fancy neon-lit names like London Fog, Jones New York and Rue 21 to the other. At about eight o'clock, local KFDI jock Johnny Western takes the stage and breaks into a warm-up medley of cowboy songs. Western was Cash's support act and general road buddy during the hell-raising, pill-shovelling days of the early to mid-'60s, so this is something of a reunion. Between ballads, Western makes it his business to thank a large number of local dignitaries for making this event possible: the mayor, the police chief, the fire chief – and the mall's owners, natch. Seated on a stool at the side of the stage all the while is Cash himself, coughing and signing autographs for on-duty policemen.

At 8.15, Johnny Western does what he did for seven-odd years and gives his old boss the grand showbiz build-up: 'Here he is! The Man In Black! "I Walk The Line"! "Ring Of Fire"! "Folsom Prison Blues"! Put your hands together for . . . *Johnny Cash!!!*' And slowly Cash walks on to the familiar sight of thousands of hard-working, God-fearing middle Americans risen to their feet in mass homage. People swarm to the front with their cameras, crouching below Cash to capture his majesty on a home snap.

'It's windy tonight,' Cash's voice booms out of the PA. 'But it's a good wind, a *Kansas* wind. You can breathe it.'

He starts with 'Folsom Prison Blues', then slides into the vintage rockabilly shuffle of 'Get Rhythm', a song he wrote forty years ago for his Sun labelmate Elvis Presley. A sombre treatment of Kris Kristofferson's 'Sunday Morning Coming Down' seems to connect with everyone, even if it does feature the word 'stoned'.

'There's some country songs on my new album that I really hope you'll get to hear,' he announces, a veiled reference to the fact that 1994's Rick Rubin-produced *American Recordings* was comprehensively ignored by country radio. He sings the exquisite title track from the new album, and does it without a hint of sappiness. He tears up 'Country Boy', one of two old Sun rockers reprised for *Unchained*. And then, despite the pronounced absence of anything even resembling a teenager in this crowd, he introduces 'Rusty Cage'.

'It's a Soundgarden song,' he states, to deafening silence.

Cash's performance of Chris Cornell's song, both live and on the album, is a masterpiece of mythopoeic menace. 'I'm gonna break / I'm gonna break my / I'm gonna break my rusty cage and run,' he all but roars at the mall audience as the song hits its grungey climax. I stare out across the rows of farming families and wonder what they make of it. I see only blank incomprehension, and then huge relief as the band segues seamlessly into 'Ring Of Fire', its mariachi brass motif duplicated on a small synthesiser by pianist Earl Ball. A lady with a big Bob Dole badge rushes forward and waves her original copy of the *Ring Of Fire* album at Cash. The Man in Black doesn't notice.

The fact that he went ahead and did 'Rusty Cage' anyway says something about Johnny Cash. Not a lot, but something. It says that he doesn't really care whether this corn-shucking crowd objects to Soundgarden or not, just like he didn't care too much what God-fearing middle Americans in the '60s thought of his stands on issues like Vietnam, prison reform or the plight of American Indians. It says that he's not in the play-safe nostalgia business, that he needs to move forward as much as he needs to oblige diehard fans with songs he's been singing for forty years. It says, like almost everything he's done in his long career, that he is a law unto himself.

Right now, Johnny Cash is part-way into the third wind of his career, a new lease of life after the doldrum years of the '80s. And some wind it is turning out to be. His fellow Highwaymen (Willie Nelson, Waylon Jennings and Kris Kristofferson) may have recorded albums with Don Was, but Cash's knight in shining armour turned out to be a long-haired New Yorker best known for loosing Public Enemy and the Beastie Boys on the world. Just as Bob Dylan had cronied with Cash in the '60s – prompting a Columbia press statement that the Man in Black had 'finally been discovered by the underground' – so Cash's first album for Rick Rubin's American label has led to every two-bit grungester and supermodel wanting to bask in his formidable presence. The man has become a trans-generational icon, a godfather of American Gothic, a *tabula rasa* for people who prefer mythology to reality.

For *Unchained*, the follow-up to *American Recordings*, Cash has opted for a full-band sound (essentially Tom Petty and the Heartbreakers, with assorted guests) that almost recalls the raw twang of his Sun days. It's a more accessible album than its predecessor, which wasn't so much unplugged as unclothed. It also manages to span fifty years of music – from Jimmie Rodgers' 'The One Rose' to Beck's 'Rowboat' via Dean Martin's 'Memories Are Made Of This' – without anything sounding out of place. It is, in short, one of the year's best records.

'*American Recordings* was harder,' Cash tells me in his Wichita hotel room. 'There was nothing to hide behind, and that was scary. With this album I had more fun because I was with a bunch of people makin' music together. It's a more musical record. The sessions felt a lot like the Memphis days . . . that kind of freedom. Sitting around and talking: "Whaddya wanna do now?" No clock on the wall, no pressure. I'd been doing "Country Boy" in concert, so we got into that and, boy, it felt good. "Mean-Eyed Cat" was originally written forty years ago but never finished, so I wrote another verse about a year ago.'

I gather you were initially reluctant to cover the Beck and Soundgarden songs.

Well, if a song doesn't feel right, then it isn't communicating. That was the problem I had with 'Rusty Cage'. But Rick and Tom came up with an arrangement that was real comfortable for me, and I think it may be one of my favourite songs to perform now. 'Rowboat' was another one I turned down: as it was, it wasn't for me. I couldn't see a way that I could do it.

What did you make of Beck when he opened for you in LA last year?

My impression was that in a way he was a great hillbilly singer. He had that Appalachian music like he really felt it and loved it.

Would you say your success with the alternative rock crowd has cost you any country fans?

No, I have not turned my back on Nashville. I don't know if they turned their back on me. Doesn't really matter, I wasn't doing anything there anyway but going through the motions. I got totally down and out with Nashville when I realised that Mercury only pressed five hundred copies of the last album I did there. So why spin my wheels?

Last year you quit Branson, Missouri {country theme town where Nashville veterans perform for package tourists}, when you were only getting three hundred people in a three thousand-capacity theatre. I wondered if you felt the Heartland country fans had abandoned you.

Erm . . . you may be right. But Branson is kind of a whole other thing. Mel Tillis' theatre is full almost every show, but that's because, a year in advance, his people go out and sign up these tour bus companies. I didn't have that going for me in Branson. The whole situation for me was disappointing, because it was *not* what I wanted to do with my life. I wanted to go out and perform for people and do something new. I didn't desert anybody and I don't think anybody deserted me. But Branson didn't work out for me and I won't ever go back.

You also closed the House of Cash {tourist attraction near Cash's home in Hendersonville, Tennessee} last year.

Yes. I don't wanna be in the tourist business. It was a collection of antiques and paraphernalia that June and I have gathered over the years, and it was very interesting to me for people to go through them, but we got tired of that. My mother died, for one thing [in 1991], and she was kind of the boss there.

The phenomenal sales of country music have finally reached a plateau after ten years. Do you think people are thirsting for something a little more soulful from Nashville?

There's a greater selection of songs now, but I think there's a glut of records that sound overproduced. A few people are trying to stylise their own music rather than sounding like the same hat acts over and over, and I think it'll mellow out to being real country music again. Some of the stations are startin' to play the veterans again. People like Haggard. George Jones gets a lot of play. Possibly they might play a track or two off this new album of mine, because it's a real country record in a lot of ways. It's got a country classic by Jimmie Rodgers, and then there's the Don Gibson song ['Sea Of Heartbreak'] and 'I Never Picked Cotton' [a 1970 hit for Roy Clark].

You transcend category, in any case. American Recordings *was as much a folk album as a country album.*

I've always loved folk music. It's the backbone of country, or it used to be. It's where country came from, and I think if country ever looks again to its roots and draws on that tradition it'll be in good shape.

Do you relate to people like Steve Earle and Dwight Yoakam as Nashville rebels? Earle's recent prison gig inevitably recalled your Folsom Prison and San Quentin albums.

Those two are my favourite country singers at the moment. Dwight's my friend. He went in and really told Columbia what he thought when they dropped me [in 1986]. I did a session with Steve Earle a year ago: we did a song called 'In Your Mind' for *Dead Man Walking*. He's a lot like me back when I was younger. He wears his clothes from the inside out!

I heard that your next record with Rick Rubin will be a gospel album. It reminded me that when you first auditioned for Sam Phillips you described yourself as 'a gospel singer'.

Gospel music is so ingrained in my bones. I can't do a concert without singing a gospel song. It's the thing that inspired me as a child, growing up on a cotton farm where work was drudgery. When I was in the field I sang gospel songs all the time, because they lifted me up above that black dirt.

Are there any songs you simply know *you're going to have to do on the album?*

Several we've already got recorded with just me and my guitar, but if we do any with a band, we've already got an arrangement for 'Farther Along'. Mike Campbell [Heartbreakers guitarist] suggested that to me. There are others I love so much – some Sister Rosetta Tharpe songs. 'Strange Things Happening Every Day', I gotta record that. And maybe 'Didn't It Rain, Child'. Plus the old *country* gospel things, like 'How Beautiful Heaven Must Be'.

Did you ever talk about gospel with Elvis?

Oh yes. That's *all* we talked about . . . well, we talked about girls, too! Elvis and I, a lot of shows we would sing together in the dressing room, and invariably we'd go to black gospel. In Tupelo, that was what he heard, and I was in Arkansas about forty miles away. So we grew up on the same songs, everything from Bill Monroe to black gospel to the Chuck Wagon Gang. Elvis and Carl and I would sit in the dressing room before shows and sing those Blackwood Brothers gospel songs.

Some people would have it that when the 'Million Dollar Quartet' [Presley, Cash, Carl Perkins and Jerry Lee Lewis] fortuitously came together at Sun, you actually went out shopping.

That is a tale RCA or somebody tried to get authenticated with a couple of people in Memphis – I guess to keep from having to deal with me on royalties. But the fact is, it was Carl's session and I was the first one there with him. Then Elvis walks in with his girlfriend, so the session stops. Elvis sits down at the piano, and then Jerry Lee Lewis comes in. I was all the way down at the other end of the piano from that big RCA mic, so you don't hear me. And when you do, I'm singin' real high, because I couldn't find my harmony.

Do you think you could ever have been a preacher?

No. I think in my world of religion you're *called* to preach or you don't preach. I've never been ordained to preach the gospel.

What's your view of televangelists?

First of all, I don't know many of 'em, and I've made it a point not to know many of 'em. Because that kind of thing, if I was a preacher, that's definitely *not* what I would be doing. I would be preaching in a little country church somewhere, ministering to the spiritual needs of my little flock. And I don't think I would *ever* go on TV if I were a preacher. I'm not saying I don't condone that, but I don't support it. The only preacher who's been on TV that I like is Billy Graham, because I know him really well. His thing has never been money. We've sat together on the beach many an hour and he is what he appears to be.

Compared to someone like Jerry Lee, you seem to have done a little better at keeping the demons at bay.

I wish I had. I wish I had. They've eaten me alive a few times.

You've only been married twice, for one thing.

I never was one to change wives a lot. I love the one I've had now for the last twenty-eight years. Boy, we've had a good time. It's been a party.

You're a man of apparent contradictions. A man who can record an album [Bitter Tears, 1964] *about Native Americans on the one hand and a jingoistic anthem, 'Sold Out Of Flagpoles'* [1976], *on the other. Where does the truth lie?*

I guess Kristofferson summed it up in the song he wrote about me: 'He's a walking contradiction / Partly truth and partly fiction.' And Patrick Carr [music writer] wrote in a story about me that I'm the Indian in the white man's camp. Maybe that's it, or maybe I'm the white man in the Indian's camp. I don't know. I'm here to live an interesting life, I'm not here to hurt the country establishment or any such thing. I pressured my producer to record *Bitter Tears,* and he almost fainted. Right now, looking back over the years, I think it's one of my two favourite albums that I ever recorded; the other one would be *Ride This Train* [1960]. A lot of Indians come to my shows and they like to feel that somebody in that other establishment cares for them. I'm still glad I was able to be the voice for them, for a few minutes anyway. All I've sung and talked about are the things you can find in the treaties the white man made with them in the first place. The songs don't ask for anything more than what's right for them.

On the eve of the presidential elections {Clinton vs. Dole}, how optimistic are you about America's future?

I'm very optimistic. I wish we'd stop meddling in little wars, though, or stop starting them. That bothers me. That *really* bothers me. It always has. I think we're messin' around in parts of the world where we don't belong. I think we should kind of mind our own business, be a part of the UN but not try to jump ahead and lead it.

I have to ask this. Just how scared were you when you went into Folsom Prison in January 1968?

We weren't scared at all, but we went into a couple later that I was worried about getting out of. In 1980, we went to Vacaville in central California, and the concert was very coldly accepted. Afterwards we had to walk all the way across a field three or four hundred yards to get out. So I took June by the arm and we started to walk to the gate. And a bunch of convicts lined up across the entrance to the gate, as if to say, 'You're not gettin' out.' I thought, well, this is it, but I'm not gonna accept it till it happens. So I told June, just hold on and don't stop. And when I got right face to face with them, they backed off and let us through. I've only been to a couple of prisons since then.

How is the pain in your jaw these days?

It's pretty severe, almost all the time. Except when I'm onstage. I pray for that, and it works. It doesn't alter or hinder my performance. I don't take painkillers. I've got into trouble with them two or three times already.

How can you live with that pain?

After six, seven years you probably get to where you can handle it. Once I can get my face laid down on a soft pillow for about ten minutes, I can go off to sleep. I'm handling it. It's my pain. I'm not being brave – I'm not brave at all – but after what I've been through, I just know how to handle it.

You haven't sued? I thought everyone in America sued. [Cash's jaw was broken when a dental surgeon attempted to remove a cyst from it. Infection then set in, and 'the hell started'. He has so far had thirty-four surgical operations on his jaw.]

Everybody advised me to sue, but I wouldn't do it. I don't wanna do that with my life, I don't want that hassle.

The last song on Unchained, *'I've Been Everywhere', could be your life story. Do you need to tour so much and work so hard?*

For my soul, I do. My mother always told me that any talent is a gift from God and I always believed it. It's not that if you don't use it you lose it. I don't believe that. But if I quit, I would just live in front of the television and get fat and die. And I don't wanna do that.

There's an incredible work ethic in country music — people like Ernest Tubb touring till they drop.

Well, why not? People die in the workplace everywhere. You know, I just hope and pray I can die with my boots on — *really*. I've been in hospital beds, and I don't *wanna* end up there.

Do you never get tired of singing the same old songs?

Absolutely not. I got over that. I went through a period when I didn't wanna sing those old songs again, and I might have given 'em one or two in a show. But I finally decided that I was really cheatin' them *and* myself. And I started singin' all the old ones with *gusto* and *lust*, like I *love* them. And now, there's not a song they can ask me to do that I won't try, if I can remember the words to it. Those songs, they're part of me, an extension of me. When I get in front of a microphone, there's a part of me going through the mic to that audience, and they feel it and they know it if *I* feel it, and they'll turn it right back to me. And that's what performing is all about: sharing and communicating.

Do you see an American icon when you look in the mirror?

God, what a question! *Shit!* No. No. No. I see the pimples on my nose, and the fat jaw from the pain where it's swollen . . . thinning hair, whatever. Icon, no. Not in *my* mirror.

1996

'I Love You . . . You *Cunt*!' – Randy Newman Speaks

He doesn't look like a rock star, this pudgy, professorial man with big uncool glasses. He's wearing a white shirt and black pants like he's about to go play a bar mitzvah. Except that it's a bright Monday morning in London, and Randy Newman is wearing these clothes because they're the clothes he happened to pack.

Jetlagged as he is, there's a twinkly mirth in the creases of Newman's big kind mouth. His lips are thin, but his mouth is always half-smiling and his eyes are full of warmth. He has a portable electric keyboard near to hand, and it functions as both a prop and a security blanket. He likes to wander over to it and spill out a self-parodying sequence of chords. Even when you talk to Randy Newman on the phone, he'll impulsively break off from the conversation to play a couple of bars from a new composition.

He is a wonderful talker, droll and wise, possessed of the humility that comes only from seeing the world as faintly absurd. He enjoys talking, just as he enjoys spieling between songs during his ever-rarer concerts. He might be a standup comic if anyone could prise him away from his piano. But he is wedded to the keyboard, an extension of his body. Can one picture Randy Newman with a guitar?

You watch him tinkling his way through what he calls 'some useless shuffle' – his word for the loose, rolling style that forms the bedrock of many of his great songs. Newman isn't sure if he somehow soaked up the sound of New Orleans when he vacationed there as a boy, or if Fats Domino and Huey 'Piano' Smith simply sneaked under his skin when he was a teenager in Los Angeles. At some level he knows he is a captive of this easy, lazy rhythm and blues – too deeply rooted in it to write commercial pop music.

Then again, one senses that Newman feels slightly guilty for taking the easy money of Hollywood, for whipping up anodyne froth like 'I Love To See You Smile' (from *Parenthood*) and 'You've Got A Friend In Me' (from *Toy Story*). Not guilty because of the money, but because such commissioned work enables him to defer ever longer the writing and recording of a new Randy Newman album.

In the fall of 1998, ten years after he took us to the *Land of Dreams*, Newman will enter the studio to record his first album for DreamWorks, the label to which he's been signed by his boyhood friend Lenny Waronker. The album will be called *Bad Love*.

Waronker once tagged Randy 'King of the Suburban Blues Singers'. Folk singer Dave Van Ronk called him 'the Hoagy Carmichael of the '60s'. Other admirers know Randy Newman simply as the most acute and most subtly outrageous singer-songwriter America has produced in the rock era, a man whose work stands more properly alongside the songs of George Gershwin and Johnny Mercer than next to Paul Simon or Elton John or Billy Joel.

Indeed, Newman is really a kind of anti-singer-songwriter; a man who regards his songwriting as a profession rather than an excuse for self-absorption. 'You should be able to write anything to order,' he once said. 'Suburban' is probably right.

It says something about how far we've come from the craft and guile of the great Broadway and Tin Pan Alley writers that Newman's most recent work, the wildly playful 1995 treatment of Goethe's *Faust*, was greeted with resounding indifference by the world's music press. Just as we now seem to prefer pocket-size short stories to novels, so our attention spans have contracted to the point where we seem incapable of taking on board anything more ambitious than the most trite four-minute pop song. Yet spend a few hours with *Faust* and its riches soon become evident: there are songs here as savagely funny as 'Short People' or 'My Life Is Good'; as touchingly tender as 'Marie' or 'Texas Girl At The Funeral Of Her Father'. And its all-star cast (Don Henley, Bonnie Raitt, James Taylor et al.) clearly had a ball making it.

Newman is that rare thing, a native Angeleno, yet he spent a significant portion of his childhood in the Deep South, whence his mother hailed, and which inspired the masterful 1974 album *Good Old Boys*. In Los Angeles he followed in the footsteps of his highly successful movie-scoring uncles Alfred and Lionel by studying music at UCLA, then in 1962 became a staff writer at Metric Music, a West Coast version of New York's Brill Building. 'We were a kind of poor man's Carole King and Barry Mann and Neil Sedaka,' he has said of a group of songwriters that included David Gates, P.J. Proby and Jackie DeShannon.

Hits were thin on the ground before Alan Price cut 'Simon Smith And His Amazing Dancing Bear' in 1967, but Newman's songs were already intriguing enough to earn him a contract with Warner Brothers. Since signing to that label he has signally failed to record a single bad album. The best, arguably, are *12 Songs* (1970), the aforementioned *Good Old Boys* and *Little Criminals* (1977), which boasts his biggest (and most hilariously misunderstood) hit 'Short People'. You can't go wrong with any of the other seven.

All these albums include masterpieces whose deep compassion and startling ambiguities are unparalleled in pop: vignettes of small-town and big-city America stripped of sentimentality ('Baltimore', 'Birmingham'); exquisite love songs that refuse to flinch from naked need and selfishness ('Living Without You', 'Real Emotional Girl'); capsule studies of racism that pack more punch than any 'protest' song ('Sail Away', 'Roll With The Punches'); and many simple portraits of human beings in all their self-deluded splendour ('I'm Different', 'My Life Is Good'). The man is simply in a class of his own – the Elmore Leonard-meets-Raymond Carver of rock 'n' roll.

Newman has three grown-up sons, one of whom, Amos, works for Glen Ballard's Java label. He lives in the Hollywood hills and goes to work each morning in his living room. He still has the suburban blues.

Tell me about your childhood memories of the South.

I only lived there till I was three, but then we'd go back every summer till I was about eleven – New Orleans, Jackson, Mobile – because that's where my mother was from. There are still things that interest me about the South. It is different, and New Orleans is different from Earth. But I always think I'm done with writing about something and then I end up doing it again. I've written about racism about six times.

Do you ever go back?

I played there a couple of years ago, but my family's sort of dying off.

One still hears so much New Orleans in your music – that loose-rolling rhythm & blues piano.

I've no idea why. It must have come from Fats Domino or Ray Charles. It just is really what I like. When Prince sits down at the piano, the first thing that comes out of him is not some useless shuffle like the stuff that comes out of me. Sting or Elton John will start, I bet, at a more valuable and luckier pop level. What interests them is maybe closer to what interests the pop audience. I almost can't help it [*goes over to electric piano in the room and plays archetypal blues/ragtime chord sequence*] – I don't even know I'm doin' it. Maybe I could trace it back, you know – a lot of the records I liked were from New Orleans – 'Sea Cruise', 'Let The Good Times Roll' – although I didn't even know they were from New Orleans at the time. So maybe there was some kind of childhood osmosis going on. It's not like we were in the [French] Quarter all the time or even listening to that much stuff, so I don't know what it was.

Back in California, you studied at UCLA. You've said that you could have worked harder at things like composition – that you regret your idleness.

Studying would have made the movie stuff easier – not the songs. But I've reconciled myself to it, and I've done enough now to where I've learned a great deal – and gotten paid for it. I don't think I've ever really been lazy; I think it was a more complex fear of trying and not having it there. It was sort of burdensome having big guys in the family. I'd see my uncle Al and he'd be worried about the score for *The Greatest Story Ever Told*, and I was just a little guy – eight, ten years old – and I must have thought, if he's worried I'd better *really* worry. I think I'm different now, and when I have a job to do I do it. But I don't have a record of writing hit after hit, the way Billy Joel or Paul Simon has, or Stevie Wonder had – which I wish I had, but it isn't what I do. Even when I set out to try, it doesn't turn out that way. If I'd written 'Just The Way You Are', I'd have gone 'I love you just the way you are . . . *you cunt!*', or something. At the end I would have fucked it up. I'd get to somewhere that sorta resembled a hook, and then somewhere I'd just go completely off and do whatever the hell I did. And it wasn't because I wanted to foil my attempt at a hit, it's just where I thought it should go.

Would you say the influence of your uncles was detectable in your music?

Only in the way I write for orchestra when I'm doing an arrangement. I believe Alfred sort of liked the blues. Maybe he got it from Gershwin, where I got it more from Ray Charles or Fats Domino, but I think we both liked it and had some appreciation for, like, American music, whatever that is – and that's a real question, I don't know whether it's [Charles] Ives or what the hell it is. I don't mind three chords at all, they don't bother me. They bother me less than they bother Sting or Paul Simon, who get harmonically bored with triads. I like the basic moving around.

What was it like growing up as a teenager in southern California?

Twenty years later, you go to a reunion and talk to a person and you think, 'Jeez, they seemed to just glide through life'. And yet they're telling you, 'No, it wasn't like that, every day I woke up with that social pressure'. It's a difficult time: I've seen three boys through it, and they all took it in different ways. I remember one time, I went to *Cats* here in London, and I felt like I was back in high school. I used to play sports and stuff, but when I'd go to a high school football game and people were jumping up and down, I just didn't give a shit, really. And *Cats* was the same experience. I felt like I was from another galaxy, I just didn't get what they were liking up there, and it was that same kind of feeling. I still have it, apparently. I mean, my taste does not correlate with the taste of the general public, for the most part.

But don't you feel the people who like you care more about you than the people who like Elton John care about him?

Maybe. I don't know. It's possible to do both: there are people who've done good work *and* made hit records. I don't know, I don't think about it. It would help. Now – more than ever, apparently – you have to have something on the radio to sell records. There are a number of people who *love* my records, but there aren't enough of them to make it a booming industry. It's a very fringe kind of operation. I don't think I could make much of a living from my records; maybe a fair living. One of the reasons there's been such gaps between them is that there isn't, like, the impetus behind them. It isn't like Green Day: Jesus Christ, they sold four million and you wanna get another one out. I ain't had that happen but the one time, with 'Short People' and *Little Criminals*, and then I came back with an album pretty quick [*Born Again*] which was an enormous stiff, the least I ever sold on anything, except in Germany. It's really a strange album; it sounded very good but it presumed that people knew who I was, a presumption I'd never made before and have never made since. You almost had to know who I was in order to get some of the stuff.

But surely you've never been interested in being a pop star in the way Sting or Elton John are.

True, but I don't hold celebrity in disdain. I like getting recognised, I like signing autographs, and a little more of it wouldn't bother me. An enormous amount of it, of the kind people who are on television get, I wouldn't enjoy. When I had 'Short People' I didn't like the experience much. I've got no high ethical stance on this. I try to keep my work as clean as I can, in the sense that it's the best I can do. It's the one part of my life where I stay as honest as I can. Other things in my life get compromised, but with my writing I can feel proud and know that I did the best I could. It isn't saying very much. I mean, when I'm conducting an orchestra I say, 'Now, do your best, try your hardest', and it's such a stupid thing to say, because everyone is trying their hardest. I don't know, writing's real important, and it's how I judge myself. I'm willing to go to great lengths for it.

Are you fairly happy with most of the songs you've written?

Not necessarily with the way they turned out, but fairly happy with having written them.

Is 'God's Song' still the one you're proudest of?

It's hard to say. I'd rather *perform* things like 'The Same Girl' or 'Real Emotional Girl'. The best *record* I believe was 'Miami'. 'God's Song' was a good song, and 'Sail Away' and 'Rednecks' were good. 'Dixie Flyer' is a very good song. It's a strange thing, I was looking at a website dedicated to me and they held a poll of favourite songs of mine. And their favourites are atypical, like 'Marie', which is more solidly within some sort of pop tradition than most of the stuff I've done. And I think I should have done more of it, you know? I was perhaps too shy about being directly emotional, and it put me in this odd kind of third-person bag.

Do you think you'd be happy with the first album if you listened to it today?

I know that I wouldn't be happy with the singing and the execution. I'd be happy with the ambition of it and some of the sounds I made, like on 'Linda' and 'Davy The Fat Boy', some of the sounds from the orchestra. They're pretty good songs for a fairly young man. I was proud of the arrangements, though in some cases it was like building a mountain I couldn't climb. You know *Krapp's Last Tape*, by Beckett? Wouldn't it be great for an old rock guy to do something like that?

Some old drunk Rod Stewart guy rummaging through his old records and sayin', 'Oh Jesus, what was I *thinkin'* about?!'

How much of an impact did the Brill Building songwriters have on you when you were working at Metric?

With most of them I wasn't stunned by their greatness so much; they weren't intimidating to me. But Carole King sorta was, because I was trying to do the same things and I knew I wasn't doing them as well. I've never been absolutely stunned by anybody again much, except Stevie Wonder at a certain period of time, and Prince to some degree – things I *knew* I couldn't do.

Were you pleased with any of the versions of your songs at that time?

The best of the bunch was Cilla Black's 'I've Been Wrong Before'. And the Alan Price records. Mostly I was disappointed. You expect as a kid they'll do your songs better than you could, but it sometimes takes you thirty years to find that the more input you have in it yourself the better you'll like it. It still may be crap, but at least it's your *own* crap. The Cilla Black and the Price stuff were good, and the Harry Nilsson stuff [*Nilsson Sings Newman*] was good, too.

How did you come to record your own stuff in the first place?

People at A&M and Warners wanted to sign me. Lenny Waronker tried to exploit the fact that we'd been friends. I told him A&M were offering me $10,000 and he said, 'How can you do this to me? Don't you understand that money isn't important now? Bet on yourself!' I wasn't going to bet on myself – I'd have lost! So Warners matched A&M's offer, and I went with them.

And now you're following Lenny Waronker to DreamWorks.

Well, I've sent Warners an amusing letter of resignation, having been there more than thirty years, and I haven't heard anything. It's like trying to find a general to surrender to. I *think* I'm gone, y'know? And I signed with DreamWorks and I haven't heard from *them*! So the people I'm leaving don't give a shit that I'm leaving, and the people I'm going to don't give a shit that I'm coming.

Did Warners become a less friendly place for you?

Well, that hasn't been the case in the record business for a number of years. Lenny was artist-friendly, and the new head guy Russ Thyret is a good guy. But in my opinion an artist like me couldn't get started now in the business. There are few record companies now which would give you the time I was given to develop, to where *Sail Away* sold respectably, or who give you that long *afterwards*. I mean, it's never been a million records with me, it's never even been a consistent five hundred thousand. It's been two, three hundred thousand, and I don't know if that's economic for them or not.

It's funny, considering that a novel that sold two hundred thousand would be deemed a bestseller.

I know, and not only that, because in my opinion the Top 10 album list is, in my opinion, of higher quality than the Top 10 bestseller list. It isn't quite so putrid. The things that win the Booker Prize don't necessarily sell. I know Barry Unsworth won't sell as many books as Danielle Steel, and I know Richard Rayner's new book won't sell as many as the new Stephen King. In pop music, to some degree, what's sort of good gets rewarded a little bit better. There's usually something there, like Alanis Morissette, something of worth. It's a more alive form. There's more entertainment value coming out of the top ten records than out of the top ten movies, books, TV shows.

How much can you tell us about Bad Love?

Well, there are gonna be some historical songs on it. I've always been interested in history, though I haven't done it much – 'Sail Away', the songs about Huey Long on *Good Old Boys*. There's a song called 'The Great Nations Of Europe', which is about European imperialism from the fifteenth century onwards. [*Sings: 'Hide your wives and daughters, hide the groceries too / The great nations of Europe coming through . . .'*] There's a cheap joke about English food in there, but I may get rid of it. Another one, 'Shame', is kind of like that Steely Dan song 'Hey Nineteen'. It's about an older corrupt fellow trying to convince this young girl to come over and see him. Then there's 'Better Off Dead', which is about falling in love with a Woman Who Loves Too Much. And there's one called 'The World Isn't Fair'. [*Sings: 'When Karl Marx was a boy, he took a hard look around / He saw people were starving all over the place, while others were painting the town . . .'*]

For many years you agonised over writing for your own albums. How easily did these new songs come?

I would rather be making an album now than doing movie stuff. Because, irrespective of quality, I think it'll end up that when I'm dead in a couple of years that this was the main thing I did . . . you know, write songs. These ones weren't so bad. I'd talked so much about how assignments were so easy for me that I just sort of made up assignments for myself. It was slow coming. I wrote three or four songs that weren't any good before I got back to a decent level. There's some concern: I've always watched for signs of decline and decay. But I think this batch of songs is as good as the *Sail Away* batch.

What was the first song where Randy Newman's voice and persona really came through?

'Simon Smith And His Amazing Dancing Bear'. I had a different lyric – 'Susie, Susie' or some girl's name like that, and I couldn't stand it. And whatever happened in my mind, something clicked, snapped, broke, and I wrote 'Simon Smith'. And after that, that's what I liked doing best.

Do you prefer singing the songs with the more, shall we say, 'literary' lyrics?

Not necessarily. I'll enjoy 'I Think It's Going To Rain Today' because the audience gets absolutely quiet, but I'll notice as I'm going along that it's a little soft, that it's a young man's song: 'Tin can at my feet/ think I'll kick it down the street / That's the way to treat a friend.' With that, I don't see the picture too good.

Is that the criterion, then – seeing the picture?

In some ways. That and getting the voice right, the diction, the way the guy would talk. Neatness. I'm such a mess in general in my life that neatness is the criterion for me. 'Dixie Flyer''s pretty solid; maybe there's musical things wrong with it, I can't exactly remember. But as for performing, I don't care: it's whatever works. I enjoy 'I Think It's Going To Rain' plenty when I'm playing it.

Jimmy Webb says that young songwriters have lost their respect for craft. Do you share that feeling?

I'm not so sure it's true. The generation that grew up after 1954 isn't gonna know songs like [sings] 'All alone by the telephone . . .', but is that such a great tragedy? It's not like Bosnia. There are people like Oasis, who are sort of adventurous harmonically. There's this band Fastball, who are very fancy harmonically, they know how to get in and get out of things like the Beatles did. Even Megadeth are kind of fancy. It's not gone: songwriting talent is never connected with much learning. McCartney, Irving Berlin . . . it's got nothing to do with how much music you know. One thing about someone like Paul Simon, though, is that he still looks hard for an interesting change or an interesting way to do something. I'll do it less so. I like the old 'Louie, Louie' changes. I sing well to that kind of stuff! But when I'm working on something that requires it, I'll work at it.

Do you still belong in the world of rock 'n' roll?

The feeling I get sometimes may just be Old Croc-liness, but I was sorta there at the beginning of singer-songwriters, and you'd hear quotes from people like, 'I'm not gonna be doin' this when I'm thirty-five, I'm not gonna be doin' this when I'm forty' – and then no one's leavin' the stage. But now there are people gettin' *forced* to leave the stage. I think it's tough going in the United States. What I've been thinking about is that I'm not convinced that it's not the kinda business where people don't do their best work at a young age. I don't think it's so with me, but I'd be the last to know, y'know. It's like physics or chess, y'know, where people, once they're past thirty-two or thirty-three, it's sort of over. There are far more cases of people who do their best work and sort of decline than there are of people who're gettin' better and better. You can't think of hardly any. Clapton is maybe no worse than he was. Maybe Neil Young's *better* than he was. Billy Joel's so tough that he keeps bouncin' back. But it's a difficult thing.

Tell me what originally gave you the idea of putting outrageous sentiments into the mouths of your characters.

I've no idea. It sure is an odd thing to do with the form, isn't it? There hasn't been much precedent for it, and there hasn't really been anything that's come after it. Shyness? Or perhaps I'm a short-story writer who got stuck with being a musician. It just interested me more than *me*. I mean, I wanted to be able to be somebody whom we in the audience could listen to and then decide what to believe and what not to believe. I don't mind people judging my characters; they deserve it. The guy in 'My Life Is Good' is a shithead.

Do you ever laugh when you're singing 'My Life Is Good'?

Sometimes, if I really get into the part where he's lost for words and he's talking about Bruce Springsteen and the woodblock – it isn't much of a musical term but it's the best he can do at the time. There are times like that when my characters get trapped and just can't get the word right, when they're trying for dignity or *hauteur*. That's what I like best.

Were there any satirists or comedians who influenced you?

No. I mean, I can't think of what I'd read at the time. I hadn't read Jonathan Swift or any of the guys from that age. I don't know what the hell it was. Movies? If I thought about it, I'm sure I'd be able to think of something, because it's such a big deal, such a strange course to take. I think other people do it occasionally – maybe Prince, with that old lady voice he has sometimes.

You seemed to feel no desire to sing about your own feelings, when so many of your singer-songwriter contemporaries felt no shame about baring all.

Maybe, and yet when you meet 'em you're not so sure that's what they're writing about. I'm not sure you can't tell more about *me* from what I've written than you can tell about purportedly confessional songwriters. True, I'm more in the tradition of Irving Berlin and Harold Arlen and those guys who were just doing their job. I'm just doing the job, too, with my kind of characters. Sting is just doing the job and Paul Simon's just doing the job, too, although Paul seems to dig in pretty deep. He's genuinely telling you about himself in his stuff.

    It's funny, I was talking about this the other day, because the thing that rock 'n' roll used to do to you as a kid was make you sorta feel tough. The Rolling Stones sort of embody it, and yet you could blow Mick Jagger over with a feather. It isn't real: these people die when they start thinking it's real, like Cobain or like Snoop Doggy Dogg. How fuckin' stupid. Musicians aren't tough. It's artifice. It's like when you meet an actor, it's always a disappointment. This little guy is *Tom Cruise*?! There haven't been five tough musicians in history, and they're doing all this posturing and sneering and snarling. And that's fine, that's what you do. 'Street Fighting Man', 'Under My Thumb'. I mean, how long would it take you to get out from under Mick Jagger's thumb?!

One of your perennial themes is racism, from 'Sail Away' to 'Roll With The Punches'. Where did that start?

In New Orleans. One thing about my parents was that they had no sort of prejudice in them. My father hated almost everyone, but he didn't hate anyone on that basis! But in New Orleans, you'd see ice cream trucks and drinking fountains saying 'White' and 'Colored', and it just sort of . . . *hurt* me. I didn't get it, and as I grew older I thought, well, this is just so obviously unfair. Nowadays, if you say that, things are so polarised that it isn't even counted as good will, it's like you're being patronising. Well, all I can say is that if it's gonna be separate – as it appears now that it'll have to be – then it sure as fuck *should* be equal. There shouldn't be worse schools and worse housing for blacks. I don't buy the argument that it isn't racism that's holding people back; it *is* racism that's holding people back. And I've written about it enough times, and strangely enough nothing's changed, despite all my songs . . .

Do you ever get weary of preaching to the converted? Isn't that a basic problem with your music?

Well, at least I'm talking about these things, and nowadays that means something. It didn't take courage to come out against the Vietnam war, but some of the positions I've taken on, say, religion have been unpopular with the public.

In his chapter on you in Mystery Train, *Greil Marcus noted the transgressive effect of singing 'Underneath The Harlem Moon' to an audience of 'urbane, liberal rock 'n' roll fans'. Some people must have done a double take when they heard you sing it.*

They always do, and the more people who hear it, the more people get nervous. That certainly happened with both 'Short People' and 'Rednecks'. If *Faust* is widely successful it'll make plenty of people plenty nervous. In general the people who come to see me are already converted, but the people who came to see *Faust* at the La Jolla Playhouse were not, they were a different audience and an audience I couldn't have played for.

How did Faust *sell in America?*

It didn't sell much, and it was hard to find a scapegoat. You know, you had Elton John and Don Henley and Linda Ronstadt and Bonnie Raitt on it. There was only one negative involved: *me!*

It's sad that no one's got the time these days to sit down and listen to something like Faust.

It really does take a few listens; there's so much in it. Best album I've ever made, I believe, because I've put so much of what I know about orchestras and things like that in there, and I've written things that I myself couldn't sing because I had these voices at my disposal.

What prompted you to tackle the Faust legend in the first place?

I always loved the idea of heaven, with the main thing being the relationship between the Lord and the Devil, and the fact that they're old friends who know each other very well. The Devil made one little mistake and got sent down, and he wants to move back up there. And I liked the idea of moving it to the '90s, where the Lord and the Devil just don't understand people.

Is it true that some of the songs were as much as twelve years old?

'Gainesville' and 'How Great Our Lord' I think I had then, and the rest are all from the last two or three years.

Is there any chance of a one-off performance of Faust *with all the guest stars?*

You mean, are they gonna be onstage? Jesus, have you seen any of our videos? It would be *brutal*. It would be some of the worst acting since the last farewell tour of Sarah Bernhardt! I don't know, we might do a TV show, but it's hard gettin' everybody together. I think we'd all enjoy it, because everybody had fun doing the album.

Linda Ronstadt claims to have been shocked by how dark the vision of Faust *was.* ['What he's written is a satire of our callous and jaded culture that pulls so few punches, you could mistakenly think he's embracing those attitudes.']

Really? I don't think it's that savage a view. I believe I have a more benign view of mankind than she does. Much more so. I mean, she has less faith in human beings than I do, and she may be right. The people I've chosen to write about 80 per cent of the time are a hell of a lot worse than normal people: my people are exaggerations. Sure, people have their little traits – I've talked to people like the guy in 'My Life Is Good'; people who, no matter what their kid does to your house, are always like, 'No, that's fine, that's good, we never say no to little Sparky'. I've seen it all, but they're all exaggerations.

Given Faust, *I wondered what feelings you'd had about the failure of Paul Simon's* The Capeman.

It's a very different thing, but it's the same in the way that musicals are a very difficult world to operate in. What would really make a funny musical is a story about a guy like Paul, who is used to controlling every aspect of his environment, running into – on the one side – these business guys on Broadway, and on the other these creative people who put on things that Paul and I wouldn't understand. I mean, I've been to some Broadway shows, I don't even know what the hell they *liked* about them. It's like being on the moon. What would make a great musical is someone like Sting encountering these people.

You must have felt some sympathy for Simon.

Oh, sympathy, but also some recognition of the fact that the music is still infinitely better than most of the stuff you hear on Broadway. The record is a good Paul Simon record. Sympathy, though I would hope that he wouldn't take their valuation of him as an accurate one.

Are you happy with the ratio of Randy Newman albums to Randy Newman movie scores?

No. I haven't made enough albums. The last four or five years I've been working very, very hard, but it's been on movies. I wish I'd worked this hard fifteen years ago just on getting albums out. For a while it was like I just had to earn a living. Now I don't have that excuse exactly.

Is it hard work being you?

The only thing in my life that's really hard – in terms that people who have real jobs wouldn't sneer at – is writing a score for a movie. That's hard – every day, twelve hours from 7 a.m. to whatever at night. *Toy Story* was the hardest yet, but with all of them you don't have any time to do anything else. The next step up in hardness would be real work, like threading pipe or laying cement.

Do you still 'love LA'?

Yeah. That song was making fun of the city in a way that the city could understand. People know they're from LA; it's like coming from Slough or something.

Pardon?!

Well, you know you're not in Paris, put it like that.

1998

4

Kalifornia

Tycoon of Trash: The Life and Grimes of Kim Fowley

'Only the mice and the great ones are happy when I arrive . . .'

One starry night in America, you're cruising the airwaves. You've dragged your dial through Air Supply, Toto and Christopher Cross, passed Men At Work en route, and more or less come to the conclusion that the scene is dead. But you need that final assurance, a record that defies all hope, so you inch the pin a little further. Another couple of notches through the FM wasteland and *gluuuurp* . . . you've slid into a vat of syrup so glutinous it sucks you into a state of terminal teen nirvana.

The dial is stuck in a song so effortlessly crass, so archetypally anodyne, you'd swear some impish computer programmer had fused into one emollient melody Survivor's 'American Heartbeat', Chicago's 'Hard For Me To Say I'm Sorry' and Toto's 'Hold The Line'. The song is 'You Don't Want Me Anymore' and the group . . . but wait for it . . . the group is *Steel Breeze*. Ponder for a moment the ingenuity of this concept. It must be the very code name of blandness. Can you *imagine* a steel breeze? (Can you imagine a glimpse of nothingness?) The juxtaposing of Steel (read heavy) with Breeze (read Fogelberg and Foggins and Fedelman) falls only just short of divine inspiration.

It's sure a steel breeze that blows Kim Fowley. 'You Don't Want

Me Anymore' is the latest chart trick by that *éminence grise* of rock 'n' roll pimpdom. Having infiltrated every other nook and cranny in the bastion of hype, the reptile prince of Hollywood trash has finally pitched one into the stadiums and wormed his canny way into the heart of Foreignerland USA.

By all the rules of decency, Kim Fowley should be the most contemptible leech on the face of rock 'n' roll. Not once in his entire career have his commercial speculations given way to aesthetic judgement. Yet he pulls it off: his manipulations transcend cynicism and become their own source of delight. Fowley is the oldest pop pusher on the make because he's the only one doing it for its own sake. If, as he claims, he is the missing link between Orson Welles and Chuck Berry, he is also the man who in the story of pop music connects Colonel Tom Parker with Malcolm McLaren. Like Laurence Harvey in *Expresso Bongo*, he is a prototypal manipulator; like Phil Spector, a myth in his own lifetime.

Concentrated in the six feet and five inches of his gaunt frame is the ghost of showbiz itself, clinging like a vampire from outer space to the self-repeating rituals of wheeling and dealing which put records in the charts. Kim Fowley bleeds liquid vinyl.

One can do no more than hint at the way Fowley's presence pervades the history of pop. Countless records exist to which he has nothing but publishing rights. A track on a Joan Jett LP here, a one-hit monster in Holland there. The early successes are famous: the Hollywood Argyles ('Alley-Oop'), the Murmaids ('Popsicles and Icicles'), B. Bumble & the Stingers ('Nut Rocker'). The Runaways are infamous: they gave America Joan Jett. But the following are just some of the artists for whom Fowley's services have been more tangential: Paul Revere & the Raiders, P.J. Proby, the Seeds, the Seekers, Cat Stevens, Jonathan Richman & the Modern Lovers, Helen Reddy, Kiss, Leon Russell, and Herman Brood – and if you detect a single consistent stylistic thread in that bunch I'd like to hear from you.

Fowley is ubiquitous. He handclapped on Gram Parsons' *Grievous Angel*, cameo'd in Stigwood's *Sgt. Pepper*, and emceed *Live Peace In Toronto*. That's without counting magnificently trashy solo albums like *Animal God Off The Street* and *Sunset Boulevard*. He also writes poetry, and his latest and finest ode to himself is 'Hollywood Trash' on Harvey Kubernik's *Voices Of The Angels* compilation. (All subsequent connecting quotes are taken from this epic of egotism.)

'Where are the herpes virgins as I put on my lonely spurs?'

'When you came to look for Kim Fowley, what did you think you were gonna find? Some guy shooting heroin in a dirty back room? Huh? Well, I've outlasted everybody. Who else my age is having hits? Not Spector, not Bob Crewe, but Kim Fowley is. The point is that I'm not trendy. As David Bowie said, style transcends fashion. Kim Fowley is a for-hire killer. When bands bring me their dreams I don't criticise them, I just put them on tape.'

Meet Kim Fowley: Erich von Stroheim crossed with Andy Warhol, a misbegotten mogul and a quintessential part of the Hollywood tradition.

'I should have been a star, but if I were a star I'd be a burden to everybody. You see, I'm smarter than your average rock pig. My IQ is 164. This knowledge didn't come without pain. As in organised religion, sports, politics, there are rules – various moves according to a model of structure and procedure. There are no day jobs as rock immortals.'

Now you're dreaming, floating down Sunset Boulevard in Kim Fowley's white Cadillac, sharing the back seat with a green plaster frog that has a seven-inch penile erection. Every rock hustler starts life as a chauffeur. Fowley was Beach Boy mentor Nik Venet's; his own is a backwater bumpkin named Jo Jo Clark, 'an Elvis reborn in front of Creedence Clearwater Revival'. A tape of Clark bombards your neck from the back of the Cadillac, doing for America what Shakin' Stevens in England does for Home Counties rockabilly. This is Sunset Swamps, Inc., produced, with scrupulous fidelity to the boy's Everglades wildcatter roots, by Kim Fowley.

As Sunset flows past like an endless cartoon backdrop of American lowlife, you realise that Fowley's Hollywood Trash is for real. He is the lizard king of the independent Svengalis and a true scion of Tinseltown. His fare is the glittering garbage of Sunset Boulevard when the ghouls and goils come out to play. Kim kisses to make 'em stay. It's a twenty-four-hour hot pussy show, a Beverly Hills matron being raped in the doorway of Frederick's of Hollywood, a cherry bomb on the rock 'n' roll cheesecake. Jester of the damned, death ejaculates through his voice. The pop universe of Kim Fowley is Antonin Artaud's theatre of the plague – in a new prime-time slot.

But Fowley's done with mouthing obscenities at tonight's Sunset People. The electric window slides shut and you're pulled over to a House of Pancakes where a funk band, all gold bracelets and Tru-Curl perms, is bathing in buttermilk. They look like reformed LAPD officers.

In the half-light of the starch palace you begin to make out Fowley's features. His face is built around the jutting ridge of an almost dislocated chin, the upper row of teeth curved like a single piece of bone. His eyes are a dead marble blue, like those of an aristocratic drug addict. They focus and the brain starts to deposit information. Facts and opinions spill over the table. Fowley is his own subject. It engrosses him. When he pronounces his own name it's as though he was seeing himself on the other side of the room – and the doppelgänger is dining off a platinum disc.

Fowley makes sure your tape is running. For a Wednesday night this is a pretty good hustle. You play along. Those dead fish eyes might bore through the back of your brain if you say anything too smart. Tonight he's hustling the chance to get his half-Japanese heavy metal band Tsunami interviewed by an English 'rock writer' [sic] and you're just as much bait as they are. So after the final maple milkshake you clock into Sunset Sound, where these Bay Area stormtroopers are 'laying down' their first album.

Fowley sets to work. 'Come on, I want you to *think*! What makes you different from all the other heavy metal groups? Why are they going to love you in England?' From under a mass of Sammy Hagar curls a voice drawls out something about 'real' metal. Fowley squeals with pleasure and proceeds to give you the lowdown on the profound intercultural significance of Tsunami. One of the Japanese boys takes his cue. 'They're making sweeping statements now', yelps Fowley, 'the ones you put under their picture!'

Finally we listen to three songs: 'Fade To Black', 'Revenge' and 'Call Off The Dogs'. Hastily you exclaim that as far as you're concerned Tsunami would blow the Scorpions off the stage any day and pray your tracks are covered. It works, but as you walk away from the studio that gave the world Van Halen you sense that, behind his revelling in the game, this is a matter of Fowley's life and death. He grins anyway. 'See!' he says. 'Iggy Pop couldn't do a dissertation on Ernie K. Doe and Slim Whitman and then discuss isolated cultures. I can.'

'Stranded here in cuckooland, isolated in vast fast food landscapes, I am far from the kingdom of God'

Several days elapse before your next Fowley session. It takes that long to get over the queasy sense of somehow having time-travelled back to 1973. When you show up at the Fowley apartment on a balmy September afternoon, his current galaxy of stars – well, two groups anyway – are on hand for your private audience. It's what used to be known as an 'artist development' session: Kim Fowley and ten plastic teenagers. *Bon appétit*. Not quite the Leon Sylvers-lined Solar lottery, but here we go.

First up, Candy, Fowley's 'male Runaways'; actually a sort of exhumed Bay City Rollers. Candy showcases a medley of teenyglit lullabies with such promising titles as 'Cherry Cola', 'Weekend Boy' and 'Saturday Arcade'. Cross Hello with the Heartbreakers and you get 'Electric Angels'. 'I've found America and I want to be number one!' they croon with broad Listerine smiles.

Fowley leers. 'If Kim Wilde fucked Jimmy Savile, you'd be the sons, right?' But there's no time for banter. Here's Money Jungle, the Kim Fowley version of Buck's Fizz. Two cute girls and two cute boys, or the Archies come to life. Eric the keyboard kid has tunes worthy of a young Brian Wilson, but in the LA money jungle Joanie only loves Chachi if the ratings are high. Fowley directs the scene from a cross-legged guru position on the floor.

'What are you, Money Jungle?'

'We're technopop dance with a new-wave edge,' bleeps the answer.

'But you're more Mamas and Papas than Human League, aren't you?'

'Are we?'

'Yes, you *are!* And why will you be successful, Money Jungle?'

'That's easy! We're being executive-produced by Kim Fowley!'

'Right now, kids, let's see some smiles!'

You think aloud: 'This is like a toy Tamla Motown.'

'Yeah', says Fowley, 'but I'm too much Howard Hughes to be Berry Gordy.'

'What is the future of the future? Will it last?'

'I'm not decayed – the wrinkles are timeless.' As at the end of Thackeray's *Vanity Fair*, the puppets have been put away. Fowley is back to expatiating on his own legend. Jo Jo Clark is on hand to confirm the data on the Kim Fowley diet.

'Jo Jo, what do I eat?'

'Milk and toast, beef stew, tuna and cheese.'

'What about my drug intake?'

'Kim doesn't take any drugs apart from the ones he's prescribed.'

Fowley seems pleased to have cleared up the matter. 'You see, a successful behind-the-scenes person like me leads an isolated existence. This is a deceptively gruelling business in which you can only be true to yourself. I don't have ego, I just have skills. I feel out of place in the twentieth century, especially amid the cast of characters we call 'the rock world'. I would hope that by the twenty-third century more people will be multiple personalities like me. To paraphrase John Travolta, you are what you do. The guys at Throbbing Gristle couldn't do a Benny Hill album, but I could. I mean, you realise that Throbbing Gristle could have been as successful as the Nolan Sisters if they'd understood structure and procedure.

'However, the most innovative thing I'm doing at the moment is living. I'm an extreme individual in a mediocre world, and I'm still here. The reason I'm great is that I look at rock 'n' roll as a reflex. I have never owned a house and never had a job with a record company, yet I have a lifetime income from rock 'n' roll. For twenty-three years I've been making a living from songs that pay for themselves over and over again.'

What does he feel about the Go-Gos?

'They got it right, I admit it. The Runaways were too threatening.'

What about Hollywood?

'A waste of time unless you're Kim Fowley and can turn over deals. LA was great when if you were a lump of shit you could be put through a blender and come out a lump of gold. But it's always been a dirty place. The first movie was shot in 1911, the first heroin overdose was in 1912. A lot of people come here and don't cut it. Charlie Manson came, and John Hinckley and Mark Chapman came, and they didn't cut it.'

'End of an era – no more physics, pimples, young girls sweating old math . . .'

'After Elvis died, it was no longer rock 'n' roll. After John Lennon died, it was no longer rock. Now it's just show business. No record companies are hiring anybody, nothing is happening. Anything that's new or original or great or wonderful is not part of the programme. Most everywhere else is bullshit. My instinct would be to go to Australia, just like it was Italy's turn for the movies at a certain point in the '60s. In England you suffer from the Michael Caine syndrome, the class distinction. Whatever your accent is limits you. Here you just have to wait in line – and you see the mutilated bodies as they're brought in.'

Is LA still a cosmic cattle-market?

'It was. Now the memories are rotting in the street.'

Who influenced you?

'Howard Hughes, who said "Concepts don't betray me, humans do." And MacArthur, who said "Preparedness is the keynote to victory."'

What do you listen to?

'Indonesian gamelan music — imagine Phil Spector on angel dust. Plus a form of Haitian music called Tropicale. I'll be buying the next Asia album. When I fuck, I play the dub version of "Guilty" by Honey Bane, followed by the first Ramones album or "Cocaine In My Brain". "Blue Moon" and "Heartaches" by the Marcels are just awesome. Then of course "Friday On My Mind", "YMCA", "Judy In Disguise" . . .'

Why don't you write a book?

'I *am* a book. Actually, there's a lot of beat poetry down here, and I have two books of it published. Supposedly I am the heterosexual Rod McKuen.'

Regrets? Had a few?

'That I never found a real rock 'n' roll girlfriend. Jerry Hall is the ultimate rock 'n' roll girlfriend. She'd make a great manager. And I think Bob Geldof has a pretty good chick.'

Some would allege that you are a sexual chauvinist. Is that fair?

'I'm an aggressive male pig. I have to come a lot. But I'm only good for girls who want to be near greatness.'

What of your solo records, like the recent compilation *Son Of Frankenstein*?

'Jim Morrison said to me: "You're not a bad singer, and you're a good poet, but you'll only make a great record when you're in love." So I guess you'll have to wait till I've found my Linda McCartney. As far as being an artist is concerned, it's like Gram Parsons — I've got to be dead to be appreciated. As a matter of fact, I've already composed the music for my funeral. I have a see-through casket with a telephone. Be sure to come, it'll be real event. I hope somebody carries on where I leave off because it's been hard doing it all by myself. Believe it or not, I'm really rich, and my will provides that when I die a committee of my friends will vote once a month on the most desperate people with commercial ideas, and the foundation will give them money. In the meantime, Kim Fowley is still here — a necessary evil for the rock industry.'

What are Kim Fowley's greatest hits?

'1) When I produce David Bowie's comeback album. 2) When I produce Wilson Pickett's comeback album. 3) When I see Money Jungle at the top of the British and European charts. 4) When I mix *Live In*

Japan starring Candy. 5) When I finally get a chance to sing my folk music: *Kim Fowley As Kim Fowley, Vol. 1.* 6) My announcement of the Easybeats' reunion live on stage in Australia. 7) Having my voice on *Live Peace In Toronto* – my most successful album sexually. 8) *Kim Fowley In Philadelphia*, with the O'Jays singing my lyrics. 9) When I find my *Star Wars* rock band. 10) Kim Fowley producing the communist Beatles.'

For Kim Fowley, tycoon of trash, sultan of sleaze, there is neither fear nor loathing in this world. There is only the next deal.

1983

Combing the Wreckage: Variations on Tom Waits

Few of the patrons of the China Light diner in Santa Rosa glance up when Thomas Alan Waits shuffles through the door. Attired as he is in coarse indigo denim and clutching a bulky leather briefcase, to them he's merely another ambling eccentric off the street. Just as he blended effortlessly into the barfly *demi-monde* of sleazoid Hollywood in the days when he was barking out songs like 'The Piano Has Been Drinking', so now – despite living in rural near-bliss with a wife and three children – Waits can wander into a Chinese diner in northern California without causing much commotion.

Then again, when you're sat down with him and he's yanked a battered paperback called *The Ultimate Book of Oddities* out of the brief-case, Waits hardly looks like your average workaday Schmoe. Perhaps it's the little swatch of white-grey hair beneath his lower lip, or the nest of dark red locks scrunched under his old fedora. Is it the chunky silver rings that adorn his gnarled, grey-brown fingers? Maybe it's the deep, growling voice – pitched somewhere between Lord Buckley and Leonard Cohen – in which he holds forth on upcoming local attractions like the Banana Slug Festival.

'They're gelatinous gastropods ten inches long, and people cook with them,' he grunts. 'They're indigenous to this area. A nephew of mine asked me to capture and send him one. We did, and it was a big hit.'

The truth is, Waits doesn't much care for the interview ritual, even if this one is to promote his terrific new album *Mule Variations*. It might be different if he could talk about gelatinous gastropods all day, but the realities of the modern music industry behove him to address the many ramifications of his singular three-decade career. It's probably a good thing that he only comes out of hiding every few years.

Recorded in a small home-made studio in Cotati, near Waits' home, *Mule Variations* gives us the forty-nine-year-old singer in all his favoured (dis)guises, from Dada-esque bluesman to maudlin balladeer and back again. One minute his guttural groans suggest a dying Howlin' Wolf; the next he's at the parlour upright crooning gruffly to his wife and collaborator Kathleen Brennan. He's still singing about dogs and moons and shoes and ditches and trees, and he still sounds like a mutant throwback – a poetic madman singing with the debauched growl of Orson Welles in *A Touch of Evil*.

Less crazed than *Bone Machine* (1992) or *The Black Rider* (1993), the album has a rough-hewn feel that strongly intimates backwater contentment. If one excepts 'Blind Love', his 1985 collaboration with Keith Richards, it may be as close as Tom Waits ever comes to making a country record.

Mule Variations, moreover, is coming out at a time when Waits' musical influence has never been greater – when the Nick Caves and P.J. Harveys of the world are carving careers out of the man's crazed Bible-Belt imagery, and when everyone from Beck to Sparklehorse to Gomez is trafficking in his mangled country blues.

'With the digital revolution wound up and rattling, the deconstructionists are combing the wreckage of our age,' Waits wrote in his introduction to *Gravichords, Whirlies and Pyrophones*, Bart Hopkin's 1996 book about experimental instruments. 'They are cannibalising the marooned shuttle to send us on to a place that will sound like a roaring player piano left burning on the beach.'

Waits will be fifty in December, which makes 1999 a good year to look back on his work. For thirty years this weathered maverick has remained determinedly out of step with pop culture, or simply years ahead of it. When the British invaded America in the '60s, Waits played guitar in an R & B band called the Systems. When the world beat a path to Haight-Ashbury, he went back to the literature of the Beats and the jazz of the '40s and '50s. When the denim cowboys of southern California made pseudo-country rock records to snort cocaine by, Waits explored the Los Angeles of Raymond Chandler, penning sketches of downtrodden lowlifes cruising diners on rainy nights. And when '80s pop turned into a hideous parade of hairstyles and bogus soul, he offered up the surreal primitivism of *Swordfishtrombones* and *Rain Dogs*.

Two decades after *The Heart Of Saturday Night* (1974) and *Small Change* (1976), America has finally caught up with Waits. Suddenly one can't move for movies like *Pulp Fiction*, *Get Shorty*, *L.A. Confidential* and *The Big Lebowski*, all of them bustling with characters out of Waits songs. Where has Waits himself been? Apparently out of sight, though hardly out of mind: in a burst of energy in the first half of the decade, he scored Jarmusch's *Night On Earth*, collaborated with Robert Wilson and William Burroughs on a macabre musical called *The Black Rider*, and recorded the stark, demented, Grammy-garnering *Bone Machine*. (Wearing his thespian hat, he also appeared as Lily Tomlin's mate in Robert Altman's *Short Cuts*, yet another LA movie populated by Waitsian misfits and sleazeballs.) Now, thirty years after he first left the San Diego suburb of National City to try his luck in Hollywood Babylon, Waits is releasing his first album in six years.

Mule Variations is very different from his 1972 debut *Closing Time*, or any of the other albums that made Waits' name in the '70s. For then he played the part of a pie-eyed LA hipster who'd retreated into the pre-rock universe of Jack Kerouac and Thelonious Monk. And just how 'real' the Charles-Bukowski-sings-Mickey-Spillane persona of *The Heart Of Saturday Night* (1974) and *Nighthawks At The Diner* (1975) was remains a slightly sore point to this day.

'It's a ventriloquist act, everybody does one,' Waits says, a touch impatiently. 'People don't care whether you're telling the truth or not, they just want to be told something they don't already know.'

Whether it was 'true' or not, Waits, by the end of the '70s, had grown weary of his alcoholic-beatnik persona, and especially of the way his slurry ballads were being smothered by overly lush orchestrations. In 1982, following his superb soundtrack for Francis Ford Coppola's *One From the Heart*, he took an abrupt detour off Beatnik Boulevard. Producing himself for the first time, he enlisted a fresh group of musicians to help him forge a new sonic language: knotty, neo-primitivist, completely unlike anything that was being made in that soulless, upscale decade. Inspired by cult composer and instrument-builder Harry Partch's concept of 'corporeality' – of 'sound grounded in the body' – Waits brought off the astounding feat of self-reinvention that was *Swordfishtrombones*.

'I was trying to find some new channel or breakthrough for myself,' he says. 'It was like growing up and hitting the roof, because you have this image that other people have of you, based on what you've put out there so far and how they define you and what they want from you. It's difficult when you try to make some kind of a turn or a change in the weather for yourself.'

Even those Waitsians wedded to an image of their hero wallowing in a Hollywood gutter were stunned by the brilliant eclecticism of *Swordfishtrombones* and its successors. Listening again to the album – and to *Rain Dogs* (1985) and *Frank's Wild Years* (1987) – what continues to astonish is just how earthy and radically lo-fi they are. At a time when pop music was being buried under layers of studio gloss, Waits reduced his sound to a few antiquated keyboards, some makeshift percussion, and a guitarist, Marc Ribot, who seemed to play with a flagrant disregard for the correct notes.

'I wanted to find music that felt more like the people who were in the songs, rather than everybody being kind of dressed up in the same outfit,' he says. 'The people in my earlier songs might have had unique things to say and have come from diverse backgrounds, but they all looked the same.'

As he had always done, Waits sang of drifters and grifters, amiable losers like the bumbling trio in Jim Jarmusch's *Down By Law* (played by Waits, John Lurie and Roberto Benigni). How apt that Waits should have worked with Jarmusch, whose dry, low-key '80s comedies now look like black and white blueprints for every hip, quirky movie made in the ensuing decade. Back in 1987, the year of both *Down By Law* and *Frank's Wild Years*, pop culture was all about

Madonna and Michael Jackson, Stallone and Schwarzenegger. Twelve years later, the Waits/Jarmusch aesthetic is everywhere: in every Elmore Leonard movie adaptation and post-grunge album of skewed Americana.

For fifteen years, Waits has been a totemic figure for a generation of alternative acts who want their music to sound dirty, visceral, human. From the gothic swamp-rock of Cave and Harvey to the muddy grooves of the Beta Band and the stomping blues-punk of Jon Spencer, Waits is the hidden presence behind so much music that rages against mechanical blandness. Just as Waits himself fused Partch's fantastical ensembles with the Dada blues of Captain Beefheart and the acid schmaltz of Randy Newman, so these '90s acts have variously combined rock and hip hop with the sound of Waits' self-styled 'mutant dwarf orchestra'.

Perhaps what they love most about Waits is how resolutely he's refused to sell out. (It's a splendid irony that he's probably made more money suing companies for using or impersonating his music in ads than he would have made by allowing it to be used.) It is difficult to imagine Waits rubbing cummerbunds with Robbie Robertson and Ahmet Ertegun at a Rock and Roll Hall of Fame dinner. Just as Kerouac and Burroughs were waging guerrilla warfare against the cultural status quo, so Waits has refused to cosy up to the rock establishment, knowing how much it would compromise what he does. By his own admission, he's never been much of a joiner-in.

'I'm suspicious of large groups of people going anywhere together,' he says. 'I don't know why, I just always have been. If there's thirty thousand people going to see some event, I'm suspicious of it.'

Waits draws on the time-honoured Beat strategy of dissembling, bluff-calling, tall-tale-telling. He wriggles out of the media's grasp, refusing to be pinned down. For him, there is no 'essence' of Tom Waits, no message to be interpreted. Instead, he roots himself in a tradition of 'show business', exaggerating the very nature of 'performance'.

Tied in with this is his parallel life as a paterfamilias. Rickie Lee Jones, whom Waits squired when he lived in the '70s in West Hollywood's infamous Tropicana Motel, was wont to remark that behind the man's sozzled Skid Row exterior was an old bear who just wanted to settle down in a bungalow with a bunch of screaming kids. Give or take a couple of storeys, turns out she was right. The last time I met him, Waits was living in New York with his screenwriter wife Kathleen Brennan and young daughter Kelly. Fourteen years on, he and Brennan have added Casey and a second son, Sullivan, to their brood.

'You know,' he reflects as he drives, 'I didn't wanna be the guy who woke up when he was sixty-five and said, "Gee, I forgot to have kids." I mean, somebody took the time to have *us*, right?'

Being a proper dad, as opposed to an absentee rock 'n' roll sperm bank, is clearly high on Waits' priority list. He says that, even though he collaborates with Kathleen on most of his songs, there's precious little overlap between work and domesticity in their house. 'Mostly my kids are just looking for any way I can come in handy,' he says. 'Clothes, rides and money . . . that's about all I'm good for. But I think it's the way it's supposed to be.'

For the most part Waits is happy to answer questions about family life, but there's a wary, guarded side to him that takes exception to prying. 'Tom's a very contradictory character in that he's potentially violent if he thinks someone is fucking with him,' Jim Jarmusch has said. 'But he's gentle and kind, too. It sounds schizophrenic, but it makes perfect sense once you know him.'

Jarmusch's observation calls to mind an evening in the early '80s when Waits rounded on a hapless Ian Hislop during a glib chat on the TV show *Loose Talk*. 'Could you speak up a little?' Hislop innocently requested, unable to make out a word the gravel-toned Californian was saying. 'I'll speak any damn way I please,' was Waits' terse response to the future editor of *Private Eye*.

One of the tracks on *Mule Variations* is a comically spooky piece called 'What's He Building In There?', the monologue of a prying busybody obsessed with the unsavoury things his mysterious neighbour might be up to. ('I swear to God I heard someone moaning low / And I keep seeing the blue light of a TV show . . .') Aside from being hysterically funny, the track almost functions as an allegory of Waits' own nonconformity.

Like the man next door, Tom Waits keeps to himself, working in the spirit of someone tinkering in a greasy workshop. In an America where any solitary activity seems to make people suspect that there's a serial killer living next door, Waits, thank God, remains deeply private, an introvert doing his own thing while everyone around him tries to second-guess the next big trend.

'What's he building in there?' mutters the song's curiosity-maddened speaker. 'He never waves when he goes by. He's hiding something from the rest of us . . . he's all to himself.'

Not a bad way of putting it, really.

1999

Love the Ones You're With: Crosby, Stills, Nash . . . and Young

'We finally got 'em in the right order this time,' laughs Henry Diltz, the photographer who shot the fuzzy picture that adorns the back cover of Crosby, Stills, Nash and Young's *Looking Forward*. And sure enough, here they are, the four horsemen of the rock and roll counterculture, the self-styled 'Rat Pack of the Woodstock generation', lined up left to right: C, S, N and Y.

It's funny, though. Take a few seconds out to look at the picture properly and you can't help noticing that the Y of CSNY is, well, *set off* from the C and the S and the N. He's kinda tucked behind Nash's left shoulder, *there but not there*, implicitly excluded from the original trio that formed in 1968 as Crosby, Stills and Nash. And if you know anything at all about the Y of CSNY, you find yourself wondering if he didn't secretly pick this photo out. Just as he may have secretly picked out the photo on the cover of the 1969 Buffalo Springfield album *Last Time Around*, a sideways group portrait that showed him looking very pointedly in the opposite direction from Stephen Stills and the band's other members . . .

Two album covers, two studies in togetherness and separation. Both, in their way, summing up the stormy, on/off, love/hate relationship between Neil Young – brooding, epileptic, shaggy-haired, flannel-shirted, multimillionaire god of California rock – and rock and roll entities larger than himself.

'Before I joined Crosby, Stills and Nash I made it clear to both sides that I belong to myself,' Young told *Rolling Stone* in December 1969. Eight years later he was piping much the same tune: 'I enjoy being able to visit but I want to avoid people thinking, "Oh, there's Neil Young from CSNY."'

Three decades on from their second gig (an intimate little set in front of half a million people at Max Yasgur's farm), it seems it's still Crosby, Stills, Nash . . .

. . . and Neil.

Fans of CSNY got the news they wanted last October when it was announced, after months of rumour and denial, that rock's ultimate supergroup would be saddling up one more time and heading out on the wide open road that is America's arena circuit.

CSNY2K, as it was inevitably dubbed, kicked off in Detroit in late January and has already been doing brisk business. Extra dates have had to be added in cities like Boston and New York, as have a slew of appearances at European festivals in the summer. For the boomer devotees of *Déjà Vu* and *After The Gold Rush* who've hurried to reconnect with their spiritual leaders, CSNY are still the living embodiment of Woodstock consciousness, keepers of the flame that never quite goes out, frozen in time with their unkempt hair and patched denim jeans.

'We still have it,' Graham Nash declared last October, shortly after breaking both legs in a freak powerboat accident. 'We still mean it. It's not for the money. It never was. It's for the music.'

'They used to say we were speaking for our generation, and I think in a sense that's still true,' added David Crosby. 'You hear a lot of music these days about rage and frustration and anger, but not much about hope and love and forward motion. That's what we continue to stand up for.'

Even Neil Young put in his two-cents' worth on this hoary theme. 'CSNY reminds people of a certain feeling,' he averred. 'Our audience want to see it alive again because somehow it verifies the feeling that they're alive too.'

Released not long after the tour's announcement, *Looking Forward* taps in to all CSNY's old stances and motifs. Crosby reached back to his folkie protest past on the strident 'Stand and Be Counted' (also the title of a documentary film he's making about that past). Stills set woolly lyrics about making the world a better place to cod Latin grooves ('Faith In Me'). Nash warbled balmy ballads of love overcoming darkness ('Someday Soon'). And, just as he'd brought 'Helpless' to *Déjà Vu* all those years ago, Young imported a batch of songs from a projected solo album, the best of them a lovely rumination on ageing called 'Slowpoke'. *Looking Forward* wasn't *Looking Back*, but the album's overall flavour was one of autumnal resolution – with just enough rage and fervour to reassure us that they hadn't nodded off at the wheel.

The way the band was talking in the fall, you'd never have guessed that their thirty-five-year relationship has been fraught with rage, jealousy and chronic drug abuse. Or that Young in particular has frequently voiced his impatience with – and contempt for – the others. In 'Thrasher', a song on his 1979 album *Rust Never Sleeps*, he bemoaned CSN as 'just dead weight to me / Better down the road without that load'. After the 1988 release of the insipid CSNY reunion album *American Dream*, he remarked tersely that 'I've gone all over the place and they're still doing what they've always done.'

Mind you, CSN gave as good as they got. 'The best thing for me to think about Neil Young is: *later*,' Crosby told Cameron Crowe in April 1977; 'if he showed up right now he'd just weird it out'. Young, the Cros sneered, would rather 'clunk around' with Crazy Horse, 'that garbanzo band of his'. Ironic when you reflect that Young's music with the garbanzo boys – the churning, visceral sludge-rock of *Everybody Knows This Is Nowhere*, *Zuma* and other albums – was precisely what made him the pre-eminent singer-songwriter of the period.

So just why *has* Neil Young opted to team up once again with 'the lost companions' he decried in 'Thrasher'? What's in it for him? Could it just be the moolah?

'I think it's, "I'll help them out, and I'll help myself out at the same time,"' says the British writer and seasoned Young-watcher Nick Kent. 'I mean, "Slowpoke" is a total piece of autobiography about a guy who's becoming old and slow and has no problem with that. He's telling his audience, "Don't expect anything mercurial from me, cos

I'm going back out with these three old cunts." He's worked this thing to come out as Mr Benefactor, but he's really taking care of No. 1.'

When Young first became the Y of CSNY three decades ago, he'd already made it clear that he was a man who wanted simultaneously to be *a part of* and *apart from*. He'd joined Buffalo Springfield because he dug trading angry guitar lines onstage with Steve Stills, but had walked out on them just as they were about to appear on *The Tonight Show*. He'd made his debut solo album virtually without help, then persuaded a glorified bar band called the Rockets to become his personal Rolling Stones.

According to producer Jack Nitzsche, Young saw a gap in rock and roll waiting to be filled by someone who combined the Stones with Bob Dylan. Which is what he proceeded to do on a series of albums that veered schizophrenically between electric rage and acoustic calm, feedbacking violence and pastoral ease, burnout and fadeaway. As with Dylan, the main model for his career, the perpetual need for change was at the root of it all. 'My career is built around a pattern that just keeps repeating itself over and over again,' he told Nick Kent in 1994. 'My changes are as easy to predict as the sun coming up and going down.'

Young's decision to become an equal partner in the joint-stock company that was CSNY was attributed at the time to the thrill he got from playing with Stills, a man transparently less talented than Young himself. More plausible was the gamble that the foursome would provide more exposure for Young than he would garner by himself, particularly given that the group's career was in the hands of a young and ravenously ambitious David Geffen.

Crosby, Stills and Nash *sans* Young were already a big hit, of course. Like Young, Crosby and Stills were veterans of the early '60s folk scene, young bucks with instant protest songs waiting their turn to sing at clubs like the Troubadour on Santa Monica Boulevard. Crosby had sprung from the Byrds, the folk-rock band that single-handedly put the LA scene on the map, and he'd been at the epicentre of that fomenting scene.

'Crosby was like the young prince around town,' says Henry Diltz. 'He wore his *Borsalino* hat and he walked through the Troubadour handing out packets of rolling papers, and it was like the crowd would part.' Crosby, adds his long-time friend Carl Gottlieb with a chuckle, was 'an absolute hedonist brat'.

Inspired not a little by the Byrds' success, the Texan-born Stills had pitched up in LA looking to launch a similar folk-rock entity. Running into his Canadian friend Neil Young in a Sunset Strip traffic jam, he put together Buffalo Springfield as an outlet for his and Young's shared vision of psychedelic folk-country-blues. But this was also where their epic struggle for control began: live onstage, their searing guitar battles looked to many onlookers like a pair of stags rutting. Buffalo Springfield, it seemed, wasn't big enough for the both of them.

Booted out of the Byrds for his arrogance, Crosby bonded with the post-Springfield Stills. Enter Graham Nash, the Manchester-born Hollies singer who'd had enough of singing twee Britpop songs like 'Carrie Anne' and wanted in on the über-groovy scene coalescing around Crosby and Stills in LA's Laurel Canyon. Discovering a supernatural vocal blend when they sang together in Mama Cass Elliott's Canyon living room, the trio released the perfect post-acid FM album in the hazy summer of '69. Fey and escapist, layered and textured, *Crosby, Stills and Nash* sounded like Yes blended with Jefferson Airplane.

With Young came a whole extra dimension of danger and unpredictability — not to mention the epilepsy from which he intermittently suffered. 'People were always very afraid of Neil,' says his manager Elliot Roberts, who in partnership with Geffen snatched up the leading lights of the LA rock scene. 'He sort of glared at people and they'd freeze. He was so intense. Nothing was casual.'

Young's intensity was soon felt in the music he brought to CSNY, in the searing rock of 'Ohio' and the live 'Southern Man'. Onstage his piercing eyes and heavy brow made him look like a feral hybrid of Nick Cave and Herzog's Kaspar Hauser, while the unearthly fragility of his voice paradoxically lent it a strength and authority denied to Crosby, Stills or Nash. His guitar playing was unique: instinctual, primitive, spat out, his solos like seizures. 'He plays on the edge every single moment,' says Russ Kunkel, who drummed with the foursome in 1974. 'He's always taking a leap of faith, always stepping off the edge of the cliff.'

Like fellow Canadian Joni Mitchell, whose anthemic song 'Woodstock' CSNY made their own, Young knew exactly how good he was. 'He thinks he's the modern Shakespeare,' former Geffen-Roberts associate John Hartmann opined in Fred Goodman's 1997 book *The Mansion on the Hill*. 'He thinks he's better than everybody, more than even Dylan,' adds Nick Kent. 'He really thinks he's a superior entity.'

It wasn't long before Young's lofty assessment of his own talents got in the way of his collaborations with Messrs C, S and N. By the time it came to record *Déjà Vu*, the supergroup was in a tenuous, fractured state. 'Neil was always very self-contained,' says Henry Diltz, who shot hundreds of pictures of CSNY in their heyday. 'He didn't go for the hype, and he was always very definite in what he did and didn't want. He doesn't suffer fools lightly. He'd get a taste of something and enjoy the initial experience of playing with somebody, but then the bullshit would take over.'

Following the tour that produced the double live album *4 Way Street* (1971), Young split. 'All I knew was that things were happening really fast for me and that I had a lot of music I had to get out of me,' he said. He quickly scored No. 1 hits with 'Heart Of Gold' and with *Harvest*, the album that defined 'mellow' as aural comedown music for survivors of the long strange '60s trip.

For a while, the others fared almost as well as Young. Graham Nash charted with *Songs For Beginners*. Stills had a hit with the perennial 'Love The One You're With' and formed a new band called Manassas. Crosby, a man who'd morphed into a comical cross between a Furry Freak Brother and the Dennis Hopper of *Easy Rider*, released the surprisingly good *If I Could Only Remember My Name*.

Soon, though, it was clear that CS&N weren't in Y's league. Everyone knew it and no one could quite bring themselves to say it. Where Crosby, Stills and Nash rested on their laurels, Young surged restlessly into a new phase. In an oft-quoted liner-note scrawled on the sleeve of his 1977 anthology *Decade*, rock's lone wolf wrote that 'Heart Of Gold' had put him in 'the middle of the road', and that travelling there 'soon became a bore so I headed for the ditch — a rougher ride but I saw more interesting people there'.

A 1973 tour produced Young's first great volte-face, the mordant live album *Time Fades Away*. A dry run for the better-known, more cathartic *Tonight's The Night*, its frayed, jagged lo-fi rock and roll was heavily spiked with tequila and cocaine. Young's ditch years were in full swing. 'Neil was sort of dribbling out of the side of his mouth,' Elliot Roberts says of the infamous *Tonight's The Night* tours. 'He was getting booed off the stage on that tour, the mood was so down. He wasn't playing one hit, one song from *Gold Rush* or *Harvest* that you came to lay down your good poundage for.'

'The audiences were freaking out,' says Nils Lofgren, who played guitar on both the album and the tour. 'There were a couple of nights in England where the audience was so rude that Neil finally stormed offstage.' Ironically, *Tonight's The Night* has done more to ensure Young's lasting credibility than anything else in his career. 'I didn't need the money, I didn't need the fame,' he told Cameron Crowe. 'You gotta keep changing. Shirts, old ladies, whatever. I'd rather keep changing and lose a lot of people along the way.'

Perhaps it was too easy for Young to say this in August 1975. After all, the previous year he'd reunited with Crosby, Stills and Nash for the most lucrative tour in the history of rock to that point. 'The '74 tour was sort of scary,' Carl Gottlieb says. 'No one had ever imagined it could get that big.' Only Led Zeppelin was bigger at this stage in the decade.

'We've got to go out and say something we mean now,' Graham Nash declared before the tour began. 'Not what we meant then. It's going to be difficult, but I think we can pull it off.' A cynic would have pointed out that all four members of CSNY had seen drops in sales of their solo projects over the previous two years. Young described the 1974 tour as 'a huge money trip . . . the exact antithesis of what all those people are idealistically trying to see in their heads when they come to see us play'. Throughout, he travelled separately from the others, driving from stadium to stadium in a camper van while CSN plumped for the Lear Jet. 'Neil likes to be on the road,' explained Crosby. 'He loves driving down the old highway.' Added Nash, 'he doesn't trust a lot of people'.

Onstage, Young included a generous smattering of new solo work. When he ripped into *On The Beach*'s incendiary 'Revolution Blues' – a song skewering the smug community of which CSN were such a core part – Crosby politely suggested that he dispense with his 'dark shit numbers'. The 1974 tour, Young commented, 'was the swansong of CSNY for me'.

'What Young can't stand about those guys is the way they always pat each other on the back after every song they play,' says Nick Kent. 'Every fucking song, it's like they've just delivered a baby or something. Young comes there and he wants to move people, he doesn't want to stand around and jerk off for two hours.'

After the tour, Young was en route to join Crosby, Stills and Nash in an LA recording studio when he abruptly turned his car around and drove home. Once again, the others were dumbfounded, and would doubtless have concurred with the 1994 words of Mo Ostin, boss of Young's label: 'You're dealing with a true eccentric . . . whenever you'd think he'd go right, he'd make a left on you.' As it was, they merely muttered and grumbled about 'ego problems'.

In truth, Young was simply dealing in his own truculent way with the problems besetting every major band of the period. The constant friction of insecure, drug-damaged guys trying to keep things together had undone the Beatles and it would do for many other groups. 'It's not easy when you take someone who's basically right out of puberty and who becomes a millionaire responsible to no one,' says Carl Gottlieb. 'I mean, it's tough enough when you learn the lesson in middle age, but these guys got that experience very early on.'

'Somehow I feel like I've surfaced out of some kind of murk,' Young told Cameron Crowe at the time of 1975's *Zuma*, the album that contained the molten, incandescent 'Cortez The Killer'. (Was it mere coincidence that Crowe said Neil saw Cortez as 'the explorer with two sides, one benevolent, the other utterly ruthless'?)

Once again Young found himself being pulled back into the CSNY fold. 'Stills is one guy I *always* get off with,' Young declared when the two men were reunited in Miami in the spring of 1976. So good was the vibe that Crosby and Nash were invited to fly down and join them. Yet the moment Crosby's and Nash's backs were turned, Stills and Young junked their vocal tracks and opted to record the album instead as the Stills–Young Band. 'I just have to say I deeply resent David's and my vocals being wiped off the album,' said Nash. 'The fact that we deprive people of happiness by acting like children really bothers me sometimes.'

'To this day there's two factions there,' points out Henry Diltz. 'There's Graham and David, and there's Neil and Stephen. David and Graham are a little bit more men of the world. They're more social, they have social graces. There's a twinkle in David's eye, and you don't really get that from Stephen or Neil. They don't kid around, they know what they want. They're both more driven and less accessible than Graham or David.'

Three shows into a Stills–Young Band tour in the summer of 1976, Young bailed out. 'Dear Stephen,' he wrote in a note to his erstwhile musical *confrère*, 'funny how some things that start spontaneously end that way. Eat a peach, Neil.' Joe Vitale, who drummed on that tour, remembers Young's sudden departure as baffling: 'It's like when you look at a happy marriage and everything just seems peachy-cream, and then suddenly there's a divorce.'

The following year, Young decided to sit in with a Bay Area bar band called the Ducks, yet another entity that – in his words – 'presented me with a perfect vehicle for playing in a band without being the leader'. But once again he simply disappeared one day, leaving the poor Ducks reeling. 'It's almost hard to comprehend it ever happened,' admitted guitarist Jeff Blackburn. 'I guess we were in the fairy tale and unable to see out of it.'

A hallmark of the greatest artists has always been the ability to shift with the times. Young's embrace of punk rock in the late '70s made him the honorary exception to that music's blanket dismissal of rock dinosaurs. One of the neatest symmetries of the period was Young name-checking Johnny Rotten on 'Hey Hey My My' at a time when Rotten himself – to the great displeasure of Sex Pistols manager Malcolm McLaren – was playing Neil Young songs on *Desert Island Discs* on BBC Radio 4.

Half-acoustic and half 'punk rock', 1979's *Rust Never Sleeps* was a fitting climax to Young's '70s. (Both *Rolling Stone* and the *Village Voice* named him Artist of the Decade.) Fittingly, too, it included the barely veiled swipe at Crosby, Stills and Nash that was 'Thrasher'. For Young, indeed, his 'lost companions' were the very definition of rust.

Young, it must be said, fought the corrosion in some odd ways during the '80s. As Bruce Springsteen took up the slack and became the decade's defining rock hero, Neil moved from the awkward vocoder-rock of *Trans* to the trad country of *Old Ways* to the '50s retro-rock 'n' roll of *Everybody's Rockin'* to . . . well, you get the point. 'That was a period when I was just changing palettes, doing different shades,' he claimed. 'You just look at them and figure out what it is or ignore them completely. It doesn't matter.'

The lost companions, meanwhile, were turning into a pure nostalgia act – with the interesting twist that Crosby, the Walrus of Brotherly Love, was now a chronic freebaser of cocaine. Unlike Jerry Garcia's, Crosby's addiction spilled out all over the place. In a Dallas court in June 1983 he dozed off and snored loudly throughout the proceedings. Edward Kiersh, in a 1985 *Spin* piece respectfully entitled 'The Death of David Crosby', observed that 'the spiritual leader of the Woodstock generation' was now 'a vision of decay'.

Perhaps rashly, Young told Crosby that if he cleaned up his act he would help to reactivate CSNY. When, against all the odds, the Cros did just that, the desperately bland 1988 album *American Dream* was pieced together at Young's Broken Arrow ranch in northern California. In *Hit Men*, his riveting 1990 study of the music biz, Fredric Dannen reported a phone conversation in which David Geffen told Atlantic's Ahmet Ertegun that 'Crosby, Stills and Nash are *old fat farts*! The only one with any *talent* is Neil Young!'

Once again, the reunion fizzled out. 'It only lasted a while, then it was over,' Young remarked. 'Coming back together wasn't as easy as I thought it would be.' The reason Young opted not to tour with CSN was that *Stills* had now got heavily into freebasing. 'Do I think cocaine destroyed CSNY?' Neil said. 'Absolutely. Cocaine and ego.'

Significantly, the release of the widely panned *American Dream* coincided with Young's sudden rebirth as a rock god. In two short years he released the anti-corporate-sponsorship single 'This Note's For You', the vicious, stripped-down *Eldorado* EP and an album of blazingly impassioned rock and roll called *Freedom*. 'Rockin' in the Free World' made Young both the elder statesman of rock rebellion and the godfather of the new punk rock – grunge.

Veering between squalling broadsides and serene ruminations – between the full-tilt fuzz of *Ragged Glory* and the woodsy murmurings of *Harvest Moon* – Young kicked serious ass. Playing live with Pearl Jam, he lurched across the world's stages like a Jurassic fusion of Angus Young and Meat Loaf; solo and acoustic he was a lumberjack sage, still singing in that sweetly mournful, almost feminine voice. Meanwhile Crosby, Stills and Nash slipped ever deeper into Farthood, their insipid songs (e.g. 'After The Storm') increasingly consisting of nothing but empty meteorological metaphors.

By the mid-'90s, even Young had gone off the boil. The two most recent Crazy Horse albums, *Broken Arrow* and *Year Of The Horse*, are water-treading exercises at best. Which is perhaps why some people have dared to suggest that CSNY2K is as much a career resuscitation for the untouchable Young as it is for his old *compadres*. 'Crazy Horse isn't sparking anything new at the moment,' argues Nick Kent. 'He's holding back and he's wondering.'

Young's motives aside, the thirty-four-date tour certainly comes as a boon to the other three. The blunt truth of the matter is that, having been dropped by Atlantic Records after all those years and millions of records, CSN might never have got a major label deal without Young's participation. None of them is exactly struggling to make ends meet, but they could all do with a few extra million in the bank.

'Undeniably the four of them together is a geometric leap in terms of bookings,' concedes the loyal Carl Gottlieb. 'Clearly the tour is going to make them a lot of money [a guarantee said to be in the vicinity of $500,000 a date . . .]. But I think the aphorism is: *Just because you're rich doesn't mean you don't need money!*'

Perhaps the man who has come through it all best is Crosby, whose absorbing autobiography *Long Time Gone* Gottlieb co-authored. Having survived not only freebase hell but a 1994 liver transplant, the Cros has emerged as happy, grateful and rather wise – not to mention the father of a four-year-old boy. 'David, among the four of them, has travelled the rockiest road and gone further out than any of them,' says Gottlieb. 'Some of them grew up ahead of David, and then I think David grew up very quickly and has probably now passed them in terms of wisdom.'

'Graham has never been a problem,' says Henry Diltz. 'He's the consummate gentleman. Mostly David was the bad boy, but he's progressed past that stage now and he's finally grown up. I think almost dying gave him a new lease of life. And Stephen too has progressed a lot from the days of being a bad boy. He's recently remarried and he has a great little boy. So I think it's just a matter of getting over those rocky years and mellowing a bit. Neil has always been the dark horse. If he stays with them they've got something better going, so of course they acquiesce to him a bit. I think it's a little bit like the old days, when Stephen and Neil were both a little more in charge.'

Carl Gottlieb was in the studio with CSNY as they worked on the very mixed bag that is *Looking Forward*. For him, the four men have made their peace with each other, healed by what Young in 1994 called 'the soothing balm of forgiveness'.

'I don't think the guys worry too much about being compared to each other anymore,' Gottlieb says. 'They worry about the practicalities of getting themselves into a studio at the same time. The tour is the result of different people making different levels of concessions, but all of them have shown the same willingness. I mean, Neil might think it's a total drag to work with three guys that he needs to explain everything to, but he's undertaken it because he knows the result is going to be worth the effort.'

'I'm still living the dream we had / For me it's not over,' Young sang on *Broken Arrow*'s 'Big Time'. With CSNY2K under way and pulling the boomers in by the thousands, 'the dream' is clearly alive and well.

David Crosby was asked in October what he hoped the fans at the shows would come away with. 'Smiles,' he replied with a sly grin. 'And merchandise.'

Hey hey, my my. Rock and roll will never die.

2000

Back to Monomania:
The Legend of Phil Spector

Word is that Cameron Crowe and Tom Cruise are set to make a movie about Phillip Harvey Spector, the greatest record producer in the fifty-year history of pop music. If we're lucky it'll be as good as *Citizen Kane*, the film Phil used to watch repeatedly in the early '70s in the sepulchral gloom of his Beverly Hills mansion. If we're unlucky it'll be another specious slice of celluloid nostalgia, full of faithful detail, devoid of credible characters.

That the producer of the Ronettes and the Righteous Brothers returned so compulsively to Orson Welles' thinly veiled biopic of press magnate William Randolph Hearst says a lot about how this paranoid, self-obsessed man saw himself in his early thirties. Six years after the shattering failure of Ike & Tina Turner's stupendous 'River Deep, Mountain High' pushed him into near-retirement at the ripe young age of twenty-five, Phil Spector was already consecrating his own legend. If he wasn't watching *Citizen Kane*, he was blasting Wagner's bombastic *Ride of the Valkyries* through the corridors of his secluded Xanadu.

And just how a spindly Jewish kid born in the Bronx came to worship the notoriously anti-Semitic composer of the Ring Cycle is another story altogether . . .

'I think Phil became a replica of what he read about himself,' Ronnie Spector, successively his *protégée*, muse and victim, told me in 1991.

'If they said he was a genius, he became a genius. If they said he was a *mad* genius, that's what he became. I actually think he's quite sane.' Asked why she put up with the virtual incarceration that was her marriage to Phil, Ronnie was disarmingly honest: 'I put up with him for that long because I was fearful and I didn't know any different. I didn't know how to say, "I don't *want* to watch *Citizen Kane* tonight."'

Ronnie broke free of her tyrannical, demonically possessive husband in 1972, by which time she was a frazzled, frightened alcoholic. Twenty years later she told her story in *Be My Baby*, at which point her former husband was more of a recluse than ever — a man who turned up (usually drunk) at Rock and Roll Hall of Fame dinners but otherwise hid away in his new compound in Pasadena.

A decade on from the publication of *Be My Baby*, the Spector legend remains as potent as ever, not least because the figure of the *auteur* — the Svengali-as-genius — seems all but extinct in the prefab-pop era of Pete Waterman and Lou Pearlman. (True, there are still a few sonic visionaries at large — Richard 'Aphex Twin' James, Spiritualized's Jason Pierce, and arguably even Max Martin, who's said to have spent two hundred hours remixing Britney Spears' 'Oops, I Did It Again' — but few of them have taken things quite as far as Uncle Phil did.)

When we listen to the great Spector records, from 'He's A Rebel' through 'River Deep' to the Ramones' *End of the Century*, what we're hearing is pop music on a massive, Herculean scale: the sound of megalomania writ large, a glorious neo-Wagnerian cacophony. As Evan Eisenberg wrote in his marvellous book *The Recording Angel*, 'in its urgent solipsism, its perfectionism, its mad *bricollage*, Spector's work was perhaps the first fully self-conscious phonography in the popular field'.

As much as he was an aural solipsist, Phil Spector was a cultural nonconformist — implicitly the Rebel of the Crystals' great 1962 hit. Except that this wasn't a Marlon Brando/Jimmy Dean rebel; this was the outcast-as-outlaw, a nerd who dressed like a Carnaby Street mod in a world of Malibu surf Nazis. Spector's is the ultimate story of the little guy taking revenge on a butch world — in Nik Cohn's words 'a saga of self-invention: a demonstration, on heroic scale, of the possible'.

*   *   *

Spector is sixty now, and all but retired from the business of 'phonography'. Periodically rumours surface that he's going back into the studio – a recent one involves Sean Lennon, offspring of a man with whom Phil worked both happily and tempestuously in the early to mid-'70s – but too many people have read the stories about him imprisoning artists in his houses (and pulling guns on hapless studio engineers) to enlist his services.

The famously chinless face is still recognisable beneath the cascading heavy-metal hairpieces Phil favours these days. It's the visage of a lower-middle-class boy born in the Bronx to a rage-aholic mother and a depressed father – a scrawny schlemiel who, after his dad's suicide in 1949, moved to the Fairfax district of Los Angeles and there grew into his unhappy early teens.

Music was Spector's salvation from as early as he knew. Striking up a friendship at Fairfax High with the buff, handsome Marshall Lieb – 'I was really his first bodyguard,' Lieb told Marc Ribowsky, author of the excellent biography *He's a Rebel* (1989) – Phil co-wrote teen-dream doo-wop songs and took lessons with Howard Roberts, a guitarist who would later strum on his pupil's famous sessions.

Spector and Lieb began playing bar mitzvahs as a trio with pianist Michael Spencer, all the while soaking up the new teenage culture at hangouts like Canter's on Fairfax Avenue. By 1957 Phil was hanging out at Gold Star, the studio where many of the key early LA pop hits – including Eddie Cochran's immortal 'Summertime Blues' – were crafted.

The following year he penned the funereal lullaby 'To Know Him Is To Love Him', inspired by the inscription on his father's tombstone at Beth David Cemetery back in Elmont, Long Island. It was basic '50s teen dreck, but – as sung by Phil's girlfriend Annette Kleinbard – it packed a winsome sincerity that instantly connected with America's youth and took it all the way to No. 1. 'You never saw such a complete change in a little fuckin' Jewish kid,' muttered the crusty Lew Bedell – co-owner of the label which released the Teddy Bears smash – of Phil's ballooning egomania.

In early 1959 Spector went to see Lester Sill, then in partnership with Lee Hazlewood, the Texas-born, Arizona-based producer of Duane

Eddy. Spector was intrigued by the sound Hazlewood was getting on Eddy records like 'Rebel Rouser', and particularly by his use of echo and reverb. With Sill's blessing he went down to Ramco Recorders in Phoenix to learn from the lugubrious Texan.

At the risk of glibness, one could argue that the legendary Wall of Sound = Lee Hazlewood + Leiber & Stoller x Richard Wagner. Certainly the brilliant duo of Jerry Leiber and Mike Stoller, to whose New York office Lester Sill despatched Phil in May 1960, were as decisive an influence on the young pop gunslinger as Hazlewood had been. The authors of 'Hound Dog' and 'Jailhouse Rock' were amused by Phil's chutzpah but recognised talent when they heard it and even hired him to play guitar on the Drifters' 'On Broadway'. More important, Spector got to collaborate with Leiber on Ben E. King's liltingly lovely 'Spanish Harlem', a useful notch on his belt that led in turn to his producing artists such as Gene Pitney, whose 'Every Breath I Take' (1961) was a $14,000 dry run for the Wall of Sound.

When Sill summoned Phil back to LA to produce the Paris Sisters' silkily seductive 'I Love How You Love Me' – a Top 5 hit in 1961 – Spector seized his chance and proposed the formation of a new label, Philles. Tired of being patronised by old-school New York sessionmen who thought him a jumped-up brat, he decided to settle on the West Coast and work instead with a gang of younger, hipper pickers who dug his flamboyant grandiosity. Playing on the Crystals' 'He's A Rebel' and Bob B. Soxx and the Blue Jeans' 'Zip-A-Dee Doo-Dah' at Gold Star were such future linchpins of Spector's famous 'Wrecking Crew' as Hal Blaine (drums), Ray Pohlman and Jimmy Bond (basses), Al DeLory (piano), Steve Douglas (tenor sax) and Tommy Tedesco (guitar).

The Disney song 'Zip-A-Dee Doo-Dah' was just one of a string of Philles hits Spector produced between 1962 and 1966, four years which saw him redefine the role of the producer and become a cult hero to everyone from Brian Wilson to the Beatles to the young Bruce Springsteen. (These are the years that dominate the 1991 box set *Back To Mono*.) Assisted by a battery of Wrecking Crew members that expanded to include Leon Russell (keyboards), Glen Campbell (guitar), and Carol Kaye (bass); by his brilliant arranger Jack 'Specs' Nitzsche; by his Italian-American lieutenants Sonny Bono and Nino Tempo;

and by the cream of the his'n'hers songwriting teams from the New York Brill Building school, Spector created his 'little symphonies for the kids', elevating teen anguish to the level of *Liebestod* and turning trite ephemera like the Ronettes' 'Be My Baby' into swirling mini-operettas.

In the Ronettes' Veronica, Spector found his true muse, a Hispanic vixen with a trashy streetcorner vibrato. The open secret of the Phil-Ronnie affair put paid to his first marriage in 1965, by which time the Ronettes' hit streak was already over and Spector had reached a new peak with the Righteous Brothers' cavernous, harrowing 'You've Lost That Lovin' Feelin'' – the greatest three minutes fifty seconds of blue-eyed soul in the pop canon and a No. 1 at the tail end of 1964.

In his cashmere and waistcoats and fob chains, the twenty-three-year-old Spector was now officially a legend in his own lunch break – 'the first tycoon of teen', in Tom Wolfe's famous phrase. Meanwhile for Howard Roberts, who'd given him guitar lessons a decade earlier, Phil had 'slipped into that Never-Never land of Hollywood success and really strange weirdness' – a man believing the press he was getting from the likes of Wolfe.

Flaunting his success was certainly never a problem for Phil: his twenty-one-room Italianate mansion at 1200 La Collina Drive, formerly part of the Woolworth family estate, was stuffed with Louis XV antiques, and he was chauffeured around Hollywood in a $100,000 white Rolls. If he got bored, he had Minnesota Fats and Willie Mosconi come by the house to play billiards. (The producer's big-spending past recently caught up with him when he sued the mother of his friend Donna O'Hara for selling, without permission, a 1964 Cobra Daytona coupe he'd bought from racing legend Carrol Shelby. The car went for a cool $4 million.)

And yet by early 1965 he had a problem, which was that – thanks in great part to his new best friends the Stones and the Beatles – his fabled sound was going out of fashion. Mop-topped Brits with guitars were writing their own songs and asserting themselves in ways Spector's pliable vocal groups had never managed.

At first, Spector tried to put his seal on the post-Beatlemania spate

of guitar/harmony bands: he courted the Young Rascals and the Lovin'
Spoonful, and even signed an LA band with the desperately unhip
moniker of the Modern Folk Quartet. But finally, in a spectacular roll
of the pop dice that bordered on hubris, Spector signed Ike & Tina
Turner to Philles and set to work constructing what for many is the
greatest pop record of all time, the apex of the Wall of Sound: the
storming, orgasmic 'River Deep, Mountain High', rendered in a cord-
shredding howl of a performance by a sweat-soaked Mrs Turner. Cut
at Gold Star in March 1966, 'River Deep' spat in the face of LA's new
jingle-jangle Byrdsworld, a $22,000 production that took Wagnerian
intensity to the limit of overkill.

'River Deep' – rag doll, puppy and all – should have shot to the
top of the singles chart. But Spector, believing himself to be bigger
than the record industry, was cruising for a bruising. DJs who hadn't
had their palms greased effectively boycotted the record. Even Jeff Barry
(who co-wrote the song with his ex-wife Ellie Greenwich) thought
'River Deep' nothing more than the sound of Phil's ego projected into
the cosmos. 'To me,' he told Richard Williams in the latter's fine study
Out of His Head: The Sound of Phil Spector (1974), 'what he's saying is,
"It is *not* the song I wrote with Jeff and Ellie . . . it's *me . . .*"'

For Barry, as for many others, Phil Spector was being punished for
his megalomania. Not even the championing of 'River Deep' by Stones
manager Andrew Loog Oldham and friends – championing that helped
the single rise to No. 3 in Britain – compensated for its failure in the
US, where it climbed no higher than No. 88. Phil never recovered
from the humiliation.

Spector spent the remainder of the '60s in virtual hiding. After making
a cause out of Lenny Bruce in the final squalid months before the
comedian's death in August 1966, Phil nursed his wounds on La
Collina Drive while Ronnie went quietly insane. (On the rare occasions when she was allowed to go out by herself, Spector installed a
Phil-lookalike dummy in the passenger seat so that other men wouldn't
hit on her in traffic.)

He emerged in 1969 via a new production deal with Herb Alpert
at A&M – a solitary hit came in the shape of Sonny Charles & the

Checkmates' 'Black Pearl' — and a cameo role as a coke dealer in his buddy Dennis Hopper's *Easy Rider*. But a much bigger prize came in the form of the Beatles, then in their death throes. Avid Spector fanatics both, John Lennon and George Harrison sought the maestro's services on key solo recordings: 'Instant Karma', 'My Sweet Lord', *Plastic Ono Band*, *All Things Must Pass*. Spector may have screwed up the feeble farewell that was *Let It Be* — he was famously lambasted by Paul McCartney for the slushy strings on 'The Long And Winding Road' — but he did some of his greatest work on *Ono Band* and *All Things*. Harrison's exhilarating 'Awaiting On You All', sublimely remastered on a two-CD reissue, showed the Wall of Sound was alive and well.

'There's no selling Phil short,' former Philles aide Danny Davis told Richard Williams, 'but the feeling around the industry is that until the Beatles gave him a second chance, he'd just about had it.'

That wasn't quite the way Spector saw it. In 1976, he told the *NME*'s Roy Carr that 'there wasn't a day, an hour, a moment when they were in the recording studio . . . that I didn't influence the Beatles, that I didn't work for them, that I didn't aid them, love them and give my all to them.' (To Carr's astonishment, he insinuated that he was paid handsomely to keep his mouth shut about just how much he'd had to do with Beatles albums going all the way back to *Rubber Soul*.)

By then, however, Spector had fallen out with Lennon, who, during his 'lost weekend' of the mid-'70s, was even more out of control than Spector. (The two men had been ejected from A&M studios when the sessions for Lennon's 1975 *Rock 'n' Roll* album — a nostalgic revisiting of '50s and '60s chestnuts whose outtakes included 'Be My Baby' — degenerated into drunken violence.)

There were other troubling incidents during this period. A car accident in February 1974 supposedly left Spector with multiple burns and head injuries: when he emerged from hospital he was wearing frizzy wigs sprayed with silver and gold, not to mention a giant cross around his neck, apparently the result of seeing *The* (Jack Nitzsche-scored) *Exorcist*.

A new boutique label set up by Mo Ostin at Warner Brothers temporarily resurrected Phil's waning career. But the Warner-Spector deal yielded no hits, and Dion's 1975 album *Born To Be*

With You – hailed today as a cult classic by the likes of Jason Pierce and Bobby Gillespie – was never even released in America. When Bruce Springsteen dropped in on the Dion sessions at Gold Star (the young Boss was on the covers of *Time* and *Newsweek* that very week), Phil felt upstaged rather than flattered. On another occasion Phil punched an uppity David Geffen, who at the time – in a fleeting heterosexual phase – was squiring Warner-Spector artiste Cher.

When Roy Carr came to do his interview in early 1976, Spector greeted him with a loaded gun jammed into his waistband. At one point during their conversation, Phil left the room and returned, stripped to the waist, playing serenades on an accordion. Calling himself the Silver-Haired Fox, he announced that he was challenging Richard Perry and Todd Rundgren to a contest. 'I'm the Champ and I feel that I'm the very best there is at what I do,' he announced. He told Carr that Richard Wagner lived in his mind.

Was this just Phil playing Norma Desmond, griping that it was the *music* that got small? When he blacked out the windows of the La Collina Drive fortress, it was hard not to see it that way. And when he did emerge, it was for yet another stormy recording – Leonard Cohen's dark *Death Of A Ladies' Man* (1978). 'Phil couldn't resist annihilating me,' Cohen recalled of the album. 'I don't think he can tolerate any other shadows in his own darkness.'

A rather different clientele showed up in the form of the Ramones, whom Spector was taken to see at the Whisky-A-Go-Go. Ironically, fifteen years after the Modern Folk Quartet, here was Phil working with an actual self-contained band. And if he couldn't stop himself turning Joey Ramone into a bizarre version of the long-lost Veronica – manipulating him into singing 'Baby, I Love You', no less – *End Of The Century* was a terrific record. The sessions, again at Gold Star (and again with Larry Levine at the controls), were the polar opposite of any da brudders had previously experienced. Dee Dee remembered them as 'a crazy Chinese water torture' of numbing repetition, and had the inevitable gun pointed at him when he protested.

After the murder of John Lennon, Spector produced half of Yoko Ono's *Season Of Glass*. But the rest of the '80s were hardly glory years for Phil: there were rumours that he beat his adopted children, and there was a night in 1986 when he kept LaToya Jackson (of all people) an overnight prisoner on La Collina Drive. An invitation from Depeche Mode for Spector to remix some tracks in 1987 resulted in such a long delay that the band gave up on him. That year, to everyone's surprise, he showed up his thirty-year reunion at Fairfax High. But when his old Teddy Bears partner Marshall Lieb approached him, Phil – flanked by bodyguards – was remote and incoherent.

Eighteen years before, Spector had shown Nik Cohn a picture of his teenage self at that same high school. Cohn described the photo thus: 'Half a dozen kids in a loose semi-circle, crewcut, golden-fleshed, archetypal Californians: they slouch and chew gum, take their ease, while Phil peeks out, half-hidden, from behind a silver surfer.'

For Cohn, this was the real Phil Spector, with his 'white flesh in a world of tan'. This was the melancholy misfit, the genius-wimp who got beaten up (and urinated on) by a group of jocks after a Teddy Bears show.

Remarkably, Spector is still a pop presence, and one should not bet against him making another comeback. Even if he never makes another record in his life, the seismic reverberations of 'Spectoresque' pop can be traced all the way from *Pet Sounds* through *Born To Run* to McAlmont & Butler's epic 'Yes' and Spiritualized's *Let It Come Down*. And if Crowe and Cruise get to make their Spector biopic it will further enshrine the legend of the man who built the Wall of Sound.

Perhaps fellow *auteur* Bert Berns said it best. 'Phil Spector,' the writer-producer of 'Piece Of My Heart' opined before his death in 1967, 'is a holocaust.'

2001

POSTSCRIPT

For the seasoned Hollywood Babylonian, it was irresistible: life imitating celluloid all over again.

The shooting of B-movie actress Lana Clarkson in legendary producer Phil Spector's 33-room Los Angeles château in February carried more than a faint echo of Billy Wilder's withering *Sunset Boulevard*. If you listened closely you could even hear the diminutive, bewigged Spector yelling at some hapless valet: 'It was the *records* that got small, not me!'

Sorry to sound so callous, but wasn't it always going to end this way? Maybe I'm too attuned to the arc of LA dementia – when I heard about the shooting I was still reeling from a British TV documentary about Michael Jackson, a portrait that horribly demonstrated the effects of childhood trauma intersecting with LA fame. But I still say there's a peculiarly Californian teleology to this tale.

Granted, Spector wasn't Jackson, but he has nonetheless spent his life enacting a personal version of Hollywood psychosis, trapped in an occluded Xanadu fantasy of Norma Desmond/Citizen Kane recluse-hood.

Friends attested that Phil was happier, healthier than he'd been in years. Sober and relatively socialised, he'd been venturing out to awards shows, hanging with bands, easing back into production. But that couldn't change his history of megalomaniac control and abusive behaviour: abusing wives and children, pulling guns on people, incarcerating artists in various *Sunset Boulevard*-style mansions. Not to mention the fact that he'd started drinking again: when he took Lana Clarkson home from the House of Blues at four in the morning, he was drunk as a lord

Like Michael Jackson, Spector – the son of a father who killed himself and a violently rage-aholic mother – had never properly resolved the loss and abuse he suffered as a child, only displaced it and misdirected it at others.

February 2003

5

Urban Studies

The Alternative Metallica

They make the oddest of rock couples, James Hetfield and Lars Ulrich. Watching them at work in Manhattan's Right Track studios, it's hard to imagine how they ever found enough common ground to work together.

Hetfield, the band's principal singer-songwriter and rhythm guitarist, is big and bearded, his feet planted squarely on the carpet in chunky black Caterpillar boots. A heavy key chain loops down from his belt into the pocket of his black jeans. Though he's wearing a Tom Jones T-shirt ('I saw him two months ago in California – really good!'), he looks like a biker on a permanent hair trigger – Thor crossed with a Montana Freeman. His voice, when he deigns to speak, is slow and deep.

Drummer Ulrich, by contrast, is a skinny little thing in a vest, hunched over the SSL 9000 mixing desk as he tries to select the best of the backing vocal parts Hetfield has just recorded for the song 'Ronny', an everyday tale of a smalltown mass murderer. Lars almost never stops talking, his voice at least an octave higher than Hetfield's. But it is these two who came together as poodle-headed teenagers on the Los Angeles hard rock scene of 1981 and formed the band that became the biggest, thrashingest metal monsta in the world.

Moments later, Ulrich decides they've got the vocal part they need. 'We got a part without Bob!' he shouts, referring to producer Bob

Rock, who has unexpectedly had to fly home to Vancouver on family business. 'I wonder if we're doing it right . . .'

'Who's gonna tell us?' grunts Hetfield.

'Maybe we should just send everybody away, James . . .'

'Like real rock stars . . .'

You don't have to hang around Right Track for long to realise that Metallica are cutting things fine. Their new album *Load*, the follow-up to the brutally exciting, fourteen million-shifting *Metallica* (aka the 'black album'), is due in record stores the world over on Tuesday 4 June. It is now Wednesday 24 April.

Because of the pressure, Right Track has become a kind of Metallica factory, doubling as mixing studio and interview suite. I have the giddy sensation of being a tiny cog in the Metallica machine, doing my bit to push an album that isn't even finished yet. Although no one is saying it outright, the expectations being placed on *Load* are immense. Because *Metallica* (1991) did spectacularly better than anyone could have predicted, its successor is being seen as nothing less than the very saviour of the genus Heavy Metal.

There is a slight problem with this. For if Metallica are expected to 'save' the endangered species that is metal, then by the same token their association with metal (hard to avoid, given their nomenclature) could be the very thing that drags them down to an ignominious place called Flopsville.

'I hope people aren't expecting us to, uh, save the world of metal,' says James Hetfield. 'We're out to play Metallica '96. There's absolutely no other plan, and there can't be.'

'I don't think we're gonna save heavy metal whatsoever,' says Lars Ulrich. 'I do believe we've kinda hovered in our own space for the last few years, and it really has not that much to do with where heavy metal as an art form is going.'

'If metal comes back as a result of our success, fine,' says lead guitarist Kirk Hammett, 'but it's not a major concern.'

'I'd rather say we're not only the best heavy metal band, but we're also in contention for being just the best popular rock band,' says bassist Jason Newsted.

So there you have it. Metallica are standard-bearers for no one but Metallica.

The band knows only too well that *Load* is being released into a very different musical climate from the one in which *Metallica* thrived so profitably.

'When we put out the "black album", nobody knew who Kurt Cobain was,' says Lars Ulrich, squeezing in a chat betwixt mixes. (His accent is Copenhagen-via-the-Bay-Area, in the same way that footballer Peter Schmeichel's is Copenhagen-via-Cheadle Hulme.) 'It's mind-boggling.'

Of the four members of Metallica, Ulrich is the one most aware of rock's ever-changing landscape. He is the chief strategist of the band, the one who all along possessed the vision and the belief to make it work. He is also the member of Metallica most open to new trends, most curious about fresh developments in rock. Lars' passion for Oasis is only the latest in a series of rock 'n' roll crushes.

'I'm the one who will go and find out what goes on in Oasis-land or Guns'N' Roses-land or Alice In Chains-land,' he says. 'I'm so curious to see how other bands do things. It's fun to sit down with Liam Gallagher and talk complete and utter nonsense about music.'

It is no coincidence, either, that Ulrich is the member of Metallica most aware of the crossroads they've reached in their career. He knows the risks they're running in their attempts to somehow transcend metal. Six weeks before *Load*'s release, various Metallica websites are buzzing with rumours that the band is sloughing off the worn and rusty shell of HM.

'It's funny to think that people can be so caught up in something. But then, I do understand that to a lot of people Metallica is much more than fuckin' four guys playing music,' says Lars. 'There's all these little chit-chat forums on the net and sometimes it's fun to go in and see what lies they're talking about you this week – like, "Oh, Metallica are going all Alternative!"'

Ah, the dreaded A-word. All across America, metal diehards have been working themselves into a frenzy at the notion that Metallica have sold out to the nipple-ringed Hydra of Alternative Rock. (In America, the Alternative has become the new Mainstream – anyone with a shred of nous is busy foraging for an 'alternative' to Alternative.) Chief among their concerns is the band's new image, particularly their woeful lack of manes.

Ulrich groans: 'I think people have this vision that we booked this group appointment at the barber or something! It's like, I'm thirty-two years old, I've had hair down to my fucking bellybutton since I was seventeen. There's nothing more to it than that I woke up one morning last summer and I was really bored with it.'

'When someone says "Metallica", they think heavy metal, thunder and lightning, long hair, drunk kids,' says Kirk Hammett. 'But times have changed and the kind of person who listens to metal doesn't necessarily look like that. And why should we? Why should we conform to some stereotype that's been set way before we ever came into the picture?'

The fact that Hammett currently looks a good deal less like the satanic Carlos Santana of old and a good deal more like Dave Navarro – tattoos, mascara, pierced flesh et al. – goes some way to explaining the defensiveness of his tone. And the fact that Metallica are about to start touring as headliners of Lollapalooza – the original Moveable Feast of '90s Alternative Rock – may explain why they've moved several inches closer to the visual style of the Red Hot Chili Peppers.

Jason Newsted sits cradling one of several new basses he may be using during Lollapalooza. 'It doesn't matter how short my hair is, how many times Kirk modifies himself,' he snaps. 'What matters is what's comin' out on tape and how we're able to back it up. All the political crap, the record company shit, the hoopla, the anticipation, the expectation, it doesn't mean anything.'

Of course, he's right. The question should be whether Metallica can deliver anything as shudderingly awesome as 'Enter Sandman' or 'Sad But True' on the 'black album'.

The consensus seems to be that *Load* is a very different beast from *Metallica*, but that what it lacks in tunnel vision it more than makes up for in breadth and feel. Culled from more than twenty-five tracks the band began recording last year, the album is anchored in metal but is considerably looser in its approach to the business of hard rock.

In contrast to the relentless black fury of its predecessor, it's packed with surprises: stomping boogie rhythms suggestive of nothing so much as vintage Southern rock; a track that pays homage to the influence of Bob Mould's Hüsker Dü; even a 'country song' dating from James Hetfield's early '90s infatuation with the 'outlaws' of the '70s. (One of Metallica's guests in a revolving slot on Lollapalooza will be Waylon Jennings.) After the densely monolithic textures and stacked staccato guitars of *Metallica* (and of earlier albums like *Kill 'Em All*, *Master Of Puppets*, and ... *And Justice For All*), *Load* positively swings. Slide guitars, pedal-steel-style 'B-benders', a little Hammond B3 organ: all these and more feature in a soundscape closer to classic 'hard rock' than to thrash metal as we knew it.

'The vibe was to make it less rigid, less tight,' says Kirk Hammett. 'To loosen it up a bit and show people we have some groove in us, and that we can take some other styles and integrate them into our sound.' It's no coincidence that it is Hammett who talks in these terms about the record. A crucial stage in *Load*'s recording came when the fanatically proprietorial James Hetfield went off on one of his fabled hunting trips and the others indulged in a little experimentation.

'To his dying day James will think this was planned,' says Lars Ulrich, 'but I can tell you it wasn't, because I was there. Me and Bob Rock were doing some solos with Kirk and – just totally off the cuff – I said, "Why don't you try and play the rhythm track on the right-hand side and see what that would do?" And he played it, and it instantly opened up the music to different nuances, even though the riffing was the same.

'So we did it with a couple more songs, and when James comes back from the Wyoming wilderness he hears Kirk's solos, and he stood there and went, *"What the fuck?!?"* But two or three days later he loved it.'

Hetfield gives me an evil snigger: 'I knew it wasn't a conspiracy, but it felt like one the more I heard. Initially I hated it, and when I heard Lars singing, that was it – I snapped! But he got it out of his system, and it's not on this record, so that's OK. There's some stuff that freaks me out because it's not as tight as I'm used to, but a lot of good things came out of it.'

'I can lay it all down for you pretty simply,' says Jason Newsted. 'After the black album, we finally found some grounding and some stability. James and Lars brought down the guard that they'd wrapped so tightly around the thing they held dearest; they finally opened up and realised that four heads are better than two.'

Newsted becomes quite emotional as he talks about finally earning a little respect from the duo once dubbed The Lars'n'James Show: 'A huge thing that's been within me – very personal, actually – was always having to try extra hard as "the new guy" – always eating myself inside out. For the first eight and a half years in this band! And this album was the first time Lars and James left me in the studio with Bob and Randy [Staub, chief engineer] to play my bass parts however I want to. The green light has been given!'

The adjective Metallica are using most frequently to describe *Load* is 'greasy'; others are even going so far as to call it 'bluesy'. Yet for all the stomping swagger of 'Ain't My Bitch', '2x4' and 'Dusty', for all the added dynamics of the intertwined, cross-cutting guitars, the group would have to get a whole lot looser to approach true filth. Metal fans can rest assured that this beast is still a fairly hardcore entity, still a ways off from the libidinous raunch of AC/DC or Aerosmith.

'The thing I'm happiest about is that this will not be the black album part two,' says Lars Ulrich. 'I don't think it's gonna do as well as the last record, partly because I don't think you can make those kind of records back to back. But what we wanted was a record that sounded more like a group instead of The Hetfield–Ulrich Project. And I think we've accomplished that. Now you got U2 and R.E.M. . . . and Metallica.

'In America, these borders just don't exist any more. After Cobain came along, everything became so blurred. Nowadays, bands are just bands: some are harder, some are softer, but heavy metal and pop and this and that . . . it's all just one big fuckin' soup.'

1996

Manhattan Misfits: Blondie

And you don't stop / Do the punk rock . . .

I'm bumping down Manhattan's Seventh Avenue in a taxi, staring through the window in amazement at a ginormous Levi's ad in the garment district. The thing consists simply of a vast image of the Sex Pistols, with a slogan running vertically alongside it. The slogan reads *'Our models can beat up their models.'* A quarter-century after the halcyon days of CBGBs, I decide that this slick slice of corporate co-opting provides a fitting millennial epitaph for punk rock.

An hour later, sitting in the cavernous Space photo studio down in Chelsea, I mention the billboard to Debbie Harry and Chris Stein and we all agree that it's, huh, *mighty ironic*. It probably isn't ironic at all, but it *is* eloquent testimony to American capitalism's ability to subsume and tame just about anything it wants to – an indication of how far we've come from the days when the entertainment industry wouldn't touch the Sex Pistols (or Blondie) with Brobdingnagian bargepoles.

Stein: *'Everything is so tightly worked out now. It used to be like, Gee, let's just go on a TV show!'*

Harry: *'The industry's changed a lot. There really are no surprises. Everything is so carefully routed.'*

It may be that Blondie are more sensitive to the wholesale changes in the music business than most of their fellow CBGBs legends – those, at any rate, who are still alive. For unlike Patti Smith, who recently returned to recording after years of domestic hibernation, or Television's Tom Verlaine, who produced many of the tracks on Jeff Buckley's posthumous *Sketches (For My Sweetheart The Drunk)*, Blondie happened to have sold millions of records, helping to transform punk into the much more palatable 'new wave' music of the late '70s and early '80s. Keyboard player Jimmy Destri could well be speaking for all four members of the reformed original Blondie when he confesses that there was 'a certain amount of guilt involved' in the group's success.

'Blondie weren't *ever* geared up to be the stadium-rock type of band that they became,' says the amiable Craig Leon, who co-produced the band's first album in 1976 and then returned twenty-two years later to pilot their new *No Exit*. 'You've got to realise that they went from being The Band Least Likely To Succeed to signing to Chrysalis, probably the best record label of that era, and having big-time LA management. Anybody who said they knew Blondie were gonna be as big as they became would be full of crap. Blondie were not sitting around thinking, We're gonna have six No. 1 singles. If Clem got his picture in a magazine, he would have been the happiest guy in the world, and that was about it.'

The same could almost be said of New Jersey boy Burke twenty years later. Of the four original band members, Blondie's drummer seems the least damaged by the saga of the band's rise and implosion. Slender as a rake and looking nary a day older than he did in 1977, Burke remains the enthusiastic heart of Blondie, a true fan. Craig Leon says that when the group recently dropped in on a session he was producing at Abbey Road, Burke instantly became an unofficial tour guide, pointing out the piano John Lennon had played and showing them where Ringo's drums had been set up.

Just as Burke had much to do with urging the demoralised Blondie of late 1974 to keep going, so it was he who pressed for the reunited band of the late '90s to do this thing right. 'The whole criterion was that it was important for us to become a band again before we tried to do any of this stuff,' he says. 'And that's what we've been doing over the past two years really.'

Burke is seated on a sofa next to Jimmy Destri, the former hospital orderly and sometime Milk And Cookies tinkler whose Farfisa keyboard chords added the crucial musical touch that set Blondie on their trashy peroxide-pop course. The Italian pretty boy of 1977 has aged less well than Burke, but the endearing Brooklyn street charm hasn't deserted him. Occasionally, as the two men speak and interrupt each other, there are flashes of good-humoured friction that recall the volatility of the old days.

Destri: 'You know, I think I'm part Chris Stein and part Clem Burke.'

Burke: 'Man, that sounds horrible. How d'you live with yourself?!'

With a fine regard for hierarchical etiquette, Destri and Burke have arrived at Space a half-hour before Harry and Stein. Dressed all in black, they're readjusting to the business of being pop stars, although one senses that both men are well aware of the risks the group is taking in bringing Blondie back to life. The good thing, they say, is that this time around they've been able to enjoy the various processes of writing, recording and rehearsing.

Burke: 'We keep using the analogy of us being a dysfunctional family, but I think it's still very apropos. It's like any relationship you go back to, be it an old friend or an old lover – you bring a lot of emotional baggage back with you. Sometimes that can work to your advantage. We've all been in therapy over the years, so that's a big help . . .'

Destri: 'I think we look at each other in a lot funnier light now. We don't take each other as seriously.'

Burke: 'Plus we're more aware of the business aspects. I mean, we were always pretty much business-sussed, but as someone once said, it's the price of an education. It's just to get to the other end of it, is the thing. It's not unusual to get ripped off in the music business, and I don't know if we have more or less of that than other people, except now people are smarter—'

*Destri: 'We have a bigger background of getting reamed, so therefore we come
with a little more cynicism. And that cynicism does breed a humour of like,
Oh, don't tell me that! It puts a sorta lump in your throat and paints you
a little green with envy when an artist that sells half the records you do is
living in a mansion in Highgate. But then some kids my age went to Vietnam
and didn't come home, y'know?'*

Later, after a respectful interlude, Clem Burke will sit in on my conversation with Debbie Harry and Chris Stein. It's almost as though he
wants to monitor how well the interview is going.

'Someone asked me if we anticipated great success with this record,'
he interjects after Harry's told me how much she hates rehearsing.
'And I said that, for me, success was that we'd made the record. I
mean that sincerely. That we actually got back together and made the
record. So we already are a success.'

The quiet dignity with which he says this contrasts with Harry
herself, who on this grey autumn afternoon seems strangely anxious
and distant. Perhaps it's the unwelcome pressure of a photo session
that will undoubtedly focus on her, triggering uneasy memories of
her status as one of pop's major pin-ups. 'She's not very relaxed when
she's approaching photo sessions,' says Victor Bockris, the confidant
whose 1982 collaboration with Harry and Stein, *Making Tracks: The
Rise of Blondie*, has been reissued in the US by Da Capo. 'When they
do these Blondie things, so much more is on her shoulders than anyone
else's. Because she is Blondie, she is the person everyone really wants
to talk to.'

While Stein, droll and laconic, slouches droopily at his end of the
sofa, Harry sits tensely at the other, her mind apparently elsewhere.
She doesn't say much, and defers often to her ex-partner.

I ask the pair if the fame that suddenly swept Blondie away from
their Lower East Side roots after the 1979 disco-pop No. 1 'Heart Of
Glass' had in any way isolated them – from their friends, from their
musical peers, from the rest of the band.

*Harry: 'I felt kind of cut off, yeah. And then of course the scene had changed
so much, and it happened rather quickly. So I really had no place to go where*

I was just little me with my little friends. That had evaporated in the time that I had gone out.'

Stein: 'I'm more isolated now, I'll tell you, than I ever was in those days.'

Harry: 'Are you?'

Stein: 'Yeah! What the fuck is there to do in fuckin' New York now?'

Harry: 'Yeah, that is true. People really have gone their separate ways. I think what I really felt isolated about was that I had no anonymity, in that I couldn't just slink around the streets being my own usual cruddy self.'

Stein: 'But then you have to consider the inverse, which is not getting anywhere.'

Harry: 'I don't know if that's true. I think that you can adapt to anything, and if you aren't successful and you don't get big popularity, you can find happiness doing other things. I mean, this is not the only thing in life that's gonna make you or me or Joey Schmoe happy. You can hold on to your artistic integrity. Those things are kinda precious, and you compromise constantly when you're reaching out or you're getting bigger.'

For a moment it's as if the idealistic hippie-chick who warbled away in '60s folk-rock troupe Wind In The Willows had suddenly blotted out any trace of the trashy street Venus who fronted Blondie and loudly proclaimed to the world that she was 'no debutante'. It also reminds me that – according to received wisdom – Harry sacrificed any real chance of solo stardom in order to nurse a dangerously ill Stein back to health in the mid-'80s. Debbie Harry is nothing if not diffident when it comes to the matter of her celebrity.

'She wasn't like one of these ambitious people who kill to get to the top,' says David Johansen, who became a close friend of Harry's after the demise of the New York Dolls. 'I think she's an artist, essentially. One of the great things about her stage persona in Blondie was that you could see her nerves. That to me made the show more interesting, instead of saying, *I'm just this indomitable spirit*. She was like, I'm doing this, but it's not easy. She's ultimately an intellectual. The whole Marilyn Monroe thing was just like a Jungian archetype. Sure, she turned herself into that archetype, but she did it as an art project.'

'I think Debbie always had this great sense of irony,' says writer and Blondie acolyte Glenn O'Brien. 'I think she always was completely aware of the difference between your intentions and how you're perceived. She could play off of being the Marilyn Monroe figure, but actually she was kind of Arthur Miller and Marilyn Monroe wrapped up into one.'

Could the story of Blondie, then, be of an 'art project' which parodied and ironised stardom but miraculously metastasized into bona fide megafame? Start with the dressing-up-box dreams of a pretty adopted girl in Hawthorne, New Jersey; add the morose attitude of a skinny Jewish black-magic-dabbler from Brooklyn; work in the whole background of Andy Warhol's glitzy decadence; and lo, what of all things you wind up with is a quintessential New York pop band whose sassy snap and '60s referencing legitimately catches fire on a global scale.

'Blondie were sort of the exception to the CBGBs rule in that they were actually a very good-looking group,' says Marty Thau, who signed the band to his Instant Records production company in 1976. 'They were young and they were happy and positive, and their songs were loaded with hooks. They were really the pop dream.'

When Chris Stein first clapped eyes on the pert platinum blonde singing with a girl-trio-fronted band called the Stilettoes, the New York underground was moving to embrace the trash aesthetic at the heart of pop. Five years younger than Harry and a roadie for Eric Emerson's Magic Tramps, Stein swiftly finessed his way into the Stilettoes.

'Chris was always a weird guy,' says the group's prime mover, Elda Gentile, who'd recruited Harry after running into her at Max's. 'When you went into his apartment there was nothing but black magic memorabilia all over the place. When he saw Debbie, he had the hots for her, like, unbelievably. Let's just say that he was very, very smart the way he handled her. I knew he wanted her body, soul, and spirit, but he played it very cool to get her. He nurtured all her insecurities. See, everybody loved Debbie because she had this Marilyn-Monroe-in-the-gutter quality, but she was very insecure, and a little bit paranoid.'

(Harry's early '70s flirtation with drugs, including heroin, stemmed from this insecurity.)

The Stilettoes' *Rock Follies*-meets-Riot Grrrl pop took the form of camp covers (Labelle's 'Lady Marmalade', the Shangri-Las' 'Out In The Streets', the latter reprised on *No Exit*) and became briefly hip among those in the know: Bowie and Iggy checked them, and Keith Moon swung by a legendary lesbian dive called Club 82 to gawp. Harry was funky-but-chic, Stein a platform-stacked glitter boy. The couple fell so deeply in love that they were once discovered *in flagrante* in CBGBs' notoriously revolting bathroom. 'That's true love, making it in the toilet at CBs,' chuckles Joey Ramone, whose band was rooted in the same customised teen-pop tradition as Blondie.

When the Stilettoes broke up in August 1974, Harry and Stein took the remnants of the band with them, playing their first CBGBs shows as Angel & the Snake. Within a couple of months Blondie was born, evolving through a series of unstable line-ups over the ensuing year. Even as she sung lines like 'I wanna be a platinum blonde / Just like all the sexy stars', Harry, alone in the spotlight for the first time, looked nervous and uncertain.

'The weak part about them, as I recall, was that Debbie was not that confident,' says Victor Bockris. 'She would try to do things and then kind of look to the audience to see if it was right.'

Tiny and incestuous though it was, the CBGBs scene scorned Blondie as lightweights. Next to Patti Smith's Rimbaud readings or Television's tense jamming, Blondie's ditsy *True Confessions* pop sounded lame. 'Patti absolutely looked down on us,' says Stein, a trace of hurt in his voice even after all this time. Concurs Harry, 'she was very competitive'.

'There were a lot of little cliques in those days, and probably still are,' says Craig Leon. 'These were all people running around thinking they were French Symbolists, and here comes Blondie, who are really like true punks and actually much more the mass-media future band than any of the others. In a way, some of those CBGBs bands might have been the dead end of progressive rock 'n' roll. Not a lot of people really see that.'

Pretty much everyone who saw the early Blondie at CBGBs or

elsewhere agrees that they stunk live. Even the late Alan Betrock, who included the group in the first issue of his pioneering *New York Rocker* in January 1975 and financed a primitive Blondie demo, admitted the shows were completely chaotic. 'They never had it together onstage,' he told me not long before his death. 'The guitar would break, and they'd have problems. That's why I thought their métier would be to record, and why we went and did this demo in Queens in some guy's basement.'

One night in May 1975, Clement Burke made his debut on drums and bassist Fred Smith quit to join Television – a departure so devastating to Harry and Stein that they almost threw in the towel there and then. (Harry still blames Patti Smith, then Tom Verlaine's paramour, for Fred's defection.) Burke rallied them, and brought in an old school friend named Gary Valentine to play bass. Come the fall, James Destri and his trusty Farfisa were on board and Blondie were being re-evaluated by the CBGBs crowd. 'I remember going to see Debbie at CBs at this time,' says Elda Gentile. 'I think she'd discovered that Blondie identity and was able to run with her.'

When Craig Leon at Sire Records got wind of the nascent scene down on the Bowery, he convinced '60s pop veteran Richard Gottehrer (Angels, Strangeloves) to come down and check out the bands. During a series of recordings for a *Live at CBGBs* album, Debbie Harry charmed Gottehrer into producing a single by Blondie.

'I remember going to a rehearsal and watching them play and grinning from ear to ear,' says Gottehrer. 'These were people that had great songs and were playing arrangements almost beyond their means. The execution wasn't perfect, but it had so much spirit. So that got me interested.'

'Sex Offender', written by Harry and Valentine and based on the latter's traumatic experience of knocking up his underage girlfriend, was recorded at the comparatively plush midtown studio Plaza Sound and sounded killer. Retitled 'X-Offender', it shocked many of Blondie's detractors into a begrudging respect. Perhaps most bizarrely of all, it was released on Private Stock, a label known principally for Frankie Valli's 1975 No. 1 hit 'My Eyes Adored You'.

'We ended up on Private Stock because everyone else passed on

Blondie,' says Marty Thau, who shopped the single around town. 'There were a number of good-sized companies who came to see them, but even those in A&R circles who knew what was going on downtown were hesitant because they didn't believe in the so-called punk atmosphere.'

According to Thau, most of the work on 'X-Offender' and the first Blondie album was done by Craig Leon. 'Richard Gottehrer was in the studio and thought he was in charge,' he says, 'but it was really Craig who was the backbone of the whole thing.'

Leon himself is self-effacing as to the accreditation; perhaps producing the Ramones and Richard Hell's seminal 'Blank Generation' was enough for him. But he'll concede that he had more than a little to do with 'shaping the sound that Blondie carried through all the way until they got really experimental with disco and rap'.

'They were shambolic,' he adds, 'but through that you'd start hearing this great kind of recreation of the Shangri-Las mentality, mutated with all these other things.'

For Leon, *Blondie*, initially released on Private Stock in February 1977, bridged the group's very different camps: Stein's and Harry's arty humour and Warholesque subversion, Burke's *Tiger Beat* Anglophilia and Hal Blaine-meets-Keith Moon playing style, Destri's Rascals-nurtured New York pop smarts. In the delectable 'In The Flesh' – inspired by a crush Harry had had on David Johansen and featuring Brill Building queen Ellie Greenwich on backing vocals – it also boasted Blondie's first hit (No. 2 in Australia).

'Clem's influence was the perfect counter-punch to Chris' artier side, and that was really a driving force,' says Destri. 'It was actually part of the thing that kept *me* there.'

'I always knew the songs were pretty well sussed,' says Burke. 'There was a nucleus of maybe fifteen, sixteen at the time, and there was also the taste we all had in cover songs. I didn't know too many people in my group of friends who really liked the Shangri-Las or the Velvet Underground. They were all in their bedrooms trying to be the next Jimmy Page.'

As Blondie's sound crystallised, so the band's '60s thrift-store mod look came together. 'The reason we got these clothes is because they were what we could afford at first,' Debbie Harry recalled in 1979. (A key influence on the band's skinny-tie, narrow-collar image was that of designer Stephen Sprouse, who lived for a while in a Bowery loft with Harry and Stein.)

From a British perspective, Blondie were a knowing power-pop antidote to the splenetic rage of punk – a retro dream for the Phil Spector fan in all of us. We loved the nod to *West Side Story* in 'A Shark In Jet's Clothing', the surf-pop homage that was 'In The Sun', the B-movie goofing of 'Kung Fu Girls' and 'Attack Of The Giant Ants'. Not to mention the sheer gleeful trashiness of 'Rip Her To Shreds'. (An infamous early Chrysalis ad featured a pic of Debbie and read WOULDN'T YOU LIKE TO RIP HER TO SHREDS? Countless spotty young onanists wanted to do exactly that: in the delicate words of a boy interviewed for Fred and Judy Vermorel's marvellous *Starlust*, 'I'd like to screw the heart off Blondie, and I said heart not arse'.)

In May 1977, we got to see Debbie in the flesh when Blondie came to England to support critics' darlings Television, and nine months later we made their gender-reversing adaptation of Randy & the Rainbows' 1963 hit 'Denis(e)' a No. 2 smash.

Watching Blondie at the Hammersmith Odeon on that tour, did I honestly think they were better than Television, whose brilliant *Marquee Moon* had just come out? Of course not. But when I walked out of the gig I realised Blondie had been a lot more fun than Verlaine's navel-gazing quartet. Amusing, then, to hear from Blondie twenty-one years later how miserable Television (and 'Patti's clan') made life for their support act.

'We were pretty much at the bottom rung of the totem pole in the CBGBs scene,' says Destri. 'I think the only reason we went to England with Television was that we had a label and they were willing to put support on the tour. So we went out, and the audience reaction was great for us. And that was the first indication that maybe somebody else gets this.'

As good to Blondie as London was Los Angeles, where – following February 1977 gigs at the Whisky-A-Go-Go – the band was quickly embraced by a burgeoning new wave scene and welcomed with open arms by scenesters like KROQ jock Rodney Bingenheimer. 'LA was pretty inspirational for us,' attests Burke. 'It was certainly a much less jaded type of audience, more open to the kind of trash aesthetic we were putting forward. It was a different sorta demographic.'

Away from the CBGBs in-crowd, Blondie were starting to cross over. With the 1978 release of *Plastic Letters* – a darker collection of power-pop which nonetheless included 'Denis' and its fine follow-up Brit hit '(I'm Always Touched By Your) Presence Dear' – Debbie Harry became a star, a pop permutation of the luscious dumb blonde blueprinted by Monroe and filtered through the likes of Jayne Mansfield and Mamie Van Doren. 'She looked like a corn-fed Polish girl,' recalled Ritty Dodge, who'd worked alongside Harry as a Playboy bunny.

'Debbie and Chris come out of the beatnik tradition, and those people did not see themselves as entertainers,' says Victor Bockris. 'On the other hand, she once showed me how she would transform herself from Debbie Harry into Blondie: the different layers of make-up she used, and how she got dressed. And I must say, it was quite fasci-nating, because as she was doing it, by the time she was finished, I was very turned on. It was like, Now I'm Blondie, a sort of pouty cartoon character.'

'Both Marty Thau and Richard Gottehrer said to me that the way I performed and sang and the way I wrote was so different from the person they knew socially,' Harry says. 'They just couldn't put those two personalities into one person.'

It should be said that Harry's elevation to sex-symbol status was always tempered by the knowledge that she and Chris Stein were lovers – a unit unto themselves within Blondie. Indeed, the band's manager Peter Leeds was so concerned about the detrimental effect of Harry somehow being sexually unavailable to the world that he suggested she and Stein split up.

Harry: *'We always operated as a couple, and that's how it sort of went. Although I was very decisive or instigating a lot of stuff, Chris would have to sort of be the one to tell people—'*

Stein: *'Nobody now realises how much criticism Debbie got for being overtly sexual and doing the stuff that was commonplace among male performers.'*

Harry: 'For the times I guess I was sort of shocking, but compared to today's standards it was nothing. There weren't very many girls around, and the ones that were were pretty strong-willed. Lydia Lunch was around a little bit later on. There was Tina Weymouth. Of course women's lib was in the press at that time, and all that stuff was going on. At that time I really did not want to do stuff that victimised women. That was clearly a motive.'

Again and again in the Blondie story one comes back to a central conundrum: how a besotted bohemian couple came to front one of the biggest pop acts in the world, and how they did (or didn't) handle it. Plus, as an adjunct to that, how they were royally fucked over by almost everyone along the path to success.

Perhaps the biggest turning point in that path was Blondie's signing to Chrysalis, whose English boss Terry Ellis was as smitten with La Harry as the callowest of schoolboys. 'She'd be screaming and throwing things and screaming at everybody backstage,' he remembered in a recent VH1 *Behind the Music* special. 'It was that kind of friction and energy that made them exciting and made them wonderful.'

'After the Pistols, so many bands just got eaten up,' says Elda Gentile. 'The real good thing that happened for Blondie was that Chrysalis were very smart. They *developed* Blondie over three or four albums – they *worked* them, which is an unheard-of thing in this day and age.'

Catalyst for this development was Australian producer Mike Chapman, half of the great Chinnichap glam-rock team which had churned out early '70s hits for the Sweet, Mud and Suzi Quatro. 'Mike Chapman actually inherited a lot of the efforts of what we did way back then,' says Craig Leon. 'But I don't want to slight him, because in my opinion he is probably the greatest producer of the '70s pop era. And he *really* made Blondie into something commercial and world-wide when he got a hold of it.'

Swanning into New York's Power Station studio in his aviator shades, a cigarette jammed into a naff white holder, Chapman announced that he was going to make a masterpiece. What he actually produced, in the summer of 1978, was a crossover album par excellence – what Lester Bangs in *Blondie* called 'New Wave for that great mythic Ozzie and Harriet audience out there in the heartland'.

'*Parallel Lines* is good tight listening,' Chapman later reflected. 'That's what Blondie's all about . . . I didn't make a punk album or a new wave album with Blondie. I made a pop album. If the radio stations would only forget this evil word "punk". It's modern rock 'n' roll.'

'Modern rock 'n' roll', in Chapman's definition, included 'Heart Of Glass', a *bête noire* for the band's hardcore fans but an American No. 1 hit in March 1979. How ironic that a song recorded almost as a novelty – a perverse New York nose-thumbing to the Disco Sucks crowd – should have been the one to propel Blondie into the big time. But propel them it – and *Parallel Lines* – did, in the process fostering an entire American wave of lame noowave skinny-tie bands.

Parallel Lines introduced a new Blondie line-up, with Gary Valentine replaced by ex-Silverhead Brit bassist Nigel Harrison and the guitar sound bolstered by a runty-looking guy called Frank 'The Freak' Infante.

In Britain, where they were bigger than ever, *Lines* spawned four hits, including two No. 1s in 'Heart Of Glass' and 'Sunday Girl'. 'Blondiemania' was no exaggeration for what the band experienced at events like in-store signings. Suddenly, says Debbie Harry, 'everyone was *at you, at you, at you* . . .'

Back in Manhattan, a mixture of local pride in their success and resentful envy served to cocoon the band still further in a strange bubble of fame. 'When we started getting attention, it was such a weird thing,' says Chris Stein. 'Everybody was just a bunch of fucked-up maniacs on the streets, and it seemed like a fluke, I think, all around. And that this attention was almost unreal and we'd better all jump on it. As a result, everybody got very competitive.'

'Of course everyone was jealous,' says Craig Leon. 'None of the other bands had hits, apart from Patti with "Because The Night". Blondie were the only ones where you could actually point to a chart and say, Here is one of the CBGBs bands and they're up there with David Soul!'

'One of the things people really forget is the fact that Debbie and

Chris *wrote* most of these hits,' says Alan Betrock. 'I mean, Patti Smith's hit was written by Bruce Springsteen. Debbie and Chris were writing all these songs, and they were worldwide hits that sold millions of records. None of the other New York bands could match that.'

With manager Peter Leeds putting them on nonstop worldwide tours, the inevitable happened – only it was exacerbated by a uniquely New York surliness and recalcitrance. First the band weren't talking to each other, and soon they couldn't stand to be in the same room. Barrels of laughs all round.

'Everybody would always disagree about everything,' Stein says. 'Debbie and I would disagree with each other, the band would disagree with us, the band would disagree among themselves. The whole thing was turmoil.'

'They went through the same thing a lot of groups go through, where there's success and then everybody's ego gets inflated,' says Glenn O'Brien. 'All of a sudden Frankie Infante thinks it's a democracy. And I think that democracy and successful bands is just something that's never been resolved.'

Peter Leeds failed to mollify the growing friction. Nor did the cash flow run smoothly. O'Brien: 'People don't realise that Debbie and Chris would be calling up Chrysalis and saying, "Where's the money?", and Chrysalis would say, It's in the pipeline. There was a big lag between the time they got famous and when they actually earned anything.'

'Leeds gave birth to Blondie, in a sense,' says Victor Bockris. 'He put them on their first world tour, and he played a few tricks with them and got them a higher profile. But he also planted the negative seeds in the very basis of their career. Debbie and Chris were very straightforward about things, and expected to be treated straightforwardly. And they weren't.'

With the release of 1979's *Eat To The Beat*, Blondie switched their management to LA bigshot Shep Gordon. But Gordon wasn't ideal for them either. 'Shep was a real game-player, and he was operating on a lot of different levels,' says Bockris. 'I don't think Blondie was the most important thing in the world to him.'

This didn't stop *Eat To The Beat* continuing the group's meteoric rise, featuring as it did 'Dreaming', 'Union City Blue' and the glorious 'Atomic', Blondie's third British No. 1. Much of the record, though, sounded cold and antiseptic, making an odd contrast to the sexuality ostensibly projected by Harry.

When the touring stopped, Harry and Stein retreated to a townhouse they'd bought on East 72nd Street, hiding away from the glare of cameras. In his splendid 'oral history of punk', *Please Kill Me!*, former punk figurehead Legs McNeil notes that at some point he actually began to feel sorry for Harry. The former fun-loving scenester, he said, 'just seemed so lonely'.

'The Debbie who really likes to have a good time tended to get less available, and in a sense less wanted,' says Victor Bockris. 'Because when she was Blondie, so many people wanted a bit of her that the only time she could get away from all that was when she and Chris would hole up in their apartment and not see anyone. We think it's ridiculous for rock stars to complain when they're making so much money, but the fact is that it is really painfully isolating in a way that very few people understand.'

To an impartial observer, the onset of Blondie's demise must have been obvious. Asked about the band's unravelling, Chris Stein replies simply that 'it was never *ravelled* . . . the band exploded and then I exploded'.

Clem Burke says that between 1980 and 1982 he saw no one in Blondie socially. Which only makes 1980's *Autoamerican* more remarkable for its stylistic range, not to mention the huge success of the pointedly un-Blondie-ish singles 'The Tide Is High' and 'Rapture', the first a cover of the Paragons' reggae classic, the second the first real example – five years before Run DMC's 'Walk This Way' – of white pop interfacing with black hip hop.

Unfortunately, the same could not be said of 1982's *The Hunter*, the disastrous last album by Blondie Mk 1. In six years, Blondie had gone from being one of the most vibrant pop bands of the '70s to being mere MTV fodder. Stein, in any case, was becoming visibly ill, wasting away and becoming worryingly pale. I assumed he was a junkie; his friends thought he must have contracted a scary new virus then beginning to ravage America's gay communities.

'Nobody knew what was wrong,' says Glenn O'Brien. 'We thought, maybe he had AIDS but how did he get AIDS because he didn't do any of the things you're supposed to do to get AIDS. You could see he was like a skeleton.' Stein's disease was eventually diagnosed as the rare and potentially fatal skin condition *pemphigus vulgaris*.

With Harry and Stein all but disappearing from view, Blondie quietly dissolved, the band's other members scattering to find gainful employment. Clem Burke played with the Eurythmics, and then with the Romantics and various other power-pop-rooted entities. Jimmy Destri released an unheralded 1982 solo album, *Heart On A Wall*, bounced around Europe, and eventually settled for life back in Brooklyn as a contractor. Nigel Harrison played with Burke and ex-Pistol Steve Jones in Chequered Past, then wound up working in A&R for Capitol and Interscope.

Harry and Stein finally re-emerged in the mid-'80s, with Stein apparently on the mend. 'I can remember Chris coming over to my apartment to meet William Burroughs,' says Victor Bockris. 'It was amazing to see him because he was a completely different person — so turned on, and so funny, just talking and talking.'

Harry, whose solo career had started rockily with 1981's much-ridiculed, Chic-produced *Koo Koo*, returned to make *Rockbird* (1986) and hit with the inane 'French Kissing In The USA'. She also continued the movie career she'd begun with *Union City* (1979) and David Cronenberg's *Videodrome* (1982), appearing as Sonny Bono's wife in the John Waters romp *Hairspray* (1988).

'Of course I was kind of lost after Blondie,' she says, 'but I kept on trying to figure it out. And then I wanted to make more records. I guess the best thing that I know now is what it really takes to be creative and to hold on to my artistic soul. And I guess I really didn't know that, I didn't know how to activate it. I think one of the reasons that I was so attracted to Chris is that he is so naturally adept at expressing that constantly. And it's taken a while just to become habitually in touch with that, and just to live my life like that.'

'Many women going through what she went through might easily have fallen apart and become very dispirited or very bitter,' says Victor Bockris. 'Debbie maintained a pretty good attitude towards all this stuff. I never saw her go through periods of long depression. She's a person who basically got up and tried again.'

Although they split up at the end of the '80s, Harry and Stein remained close friends and continued to work together – on *Def, Dumb And Blonde* (1989) and *Debravation* (1993), neither very captivating. 'I Want That Man' was another overproduced piece of late '80s schlock, and another hit. Who really cared? Meanwhile Blondie's influence peeped through only in the underwhelming form of the Primitives, Transvision Vamp and Kim Wilde. Of course, there was that Madonna broad . . .

More cred-boosting by far was Harry's work with the Jazz Passengers, a loose-knit New York bop ensemble who may have heard her initial (and very credible) stabs at jazz singing on *Autoamerican*. 'It's much more about real singing, which is definitely what I'm more adept at,' Harry says. 'I work very hard to be a good singer and I study, and I've kept working. I really work to be a musician, and I contribute to the arrangements as much as I'm capable of doing. And that's what I love. I get joy from that.'

'I think the Jazz Passengers thing was really good for Debbie,' says Glenn O'Brien. 'It enabled her to make music and even improve her skills while taking the spotlight off her and just being one of the boys in the band. And I think she's more one of the boys in Blondie now than she was in the beginning. She's not playing up the glamour part so much as just being a great entertainer and kind of a freak.'

'In a weird way Debbie has become a lot better than she was,' says Craig Leon. 'All of them have grown up, but she has gone off into a completely different area and done very well creatively in it.'

Leon says that trying to incorporate the new, jazz-oriented Harry into a reactivated Blondie sound was 'probably the biggest challenge for her and for me and the band as well'. While *No Exit* kicks off with a supercharged blast of vintage Blondie pop ('Maria') and returns to the band's Shadow Morton girl-group roots ('Out In The Streets'), it also takes in a slew of very different genres, each bringing out a new element in Harry's voice. There's the slinky hepcat jazz of 'Boom Boom In The Zoom Zoom Room', the stomping ska-pop of 'Screaming Skin', the gothic hip hop of the title track, the hyper-sequenced, *très*

'80s 'Forgive And Forget', and a lovely, sensuous reverie called 'Night Wind Sent'. If anything, *No Exit* is too eclectic for its own good.

'Getting herself comfortable with even singing in a pop style again was hard,' says Leon. 'It's just totally different to what she's been doing for the past few years, and it's probably musically a little less interesting than the avant-garde things she's recorded.'

All of which begs the question of just how keen Harry is to re-enter the arena of Anglo-American pop culture as 'Blondie'. At fifty-three, she may have a rough ride at the hands of ageist commentators. 'I truly hope this Blondie thing is a wonderful success for her, because she really deserves it,' says Elda Gentile. 'People look at a person like Debbie and think, Oh, she lives such a glamorous life, but I don't think that's really true. I think she works *hard* to live up to the image of Blondie, and the pressure on her must be enormous right now.'

'She's probably old enough to be the mother of a lot of people in her audience, but she's still like a wild thing,' says Glenn O'Brien. 'I've been saying, Look, you should come out there looking like June Cleaver. She thinks she should look like Marilyn Manson, but what's more surprising than coming out looking like a Serial Mom?!'

The best news for the moment is that the group's reunion has been, for the most part, a happy experience. With the trusted Leon at the controls and the powerful Left Bank management team behind them, Blondie have found a renewed zest for life as a band. Even the arguing has been fun this time around.

'There's always this melting pot of ideas on the same song,' says Craig Leon. 'It can still get pretty violent with everybody fighting for their ideas: Chris wanting it one way, Jimmy wanting something here, Clem wanting something there, and Debbie kind of serenely sitting back and saying, When you guys get it together, I'm going to give you the hit melody and vocal. It's all just because they all have a fabulous sense of pop history.'

'They always quarrel, but now they have more informed and amusing quarrels than they used to,' says Glenn O'Brien. 'During the recording sessions they were having a lot of fun kind of goofing on each other. It's almost like they never broke up.'

Sitting with Blondie at Space, on the eve of their first tour in over fifteen years, the band appear cheerful enough about their prospects.

'As it goes along week by week,' says Chris Stein, 'I think everybody's getting much more positive about the whole thing. The last tour Debbie and me did, what'd we do? Two of the fuckin' hit songs, maybe. Five years ago I wouldn't have wanted to do the old songs, but now I feel real positive and real emotional about doing them. And unless we get heavily bombarded by tomatoes and beer cans, I think it's going to be fine.'

There are no tomatoes in evidence when, six weeks later, Blondie take the stage at Poole's Arts Centre for the penultimate gig of their European tour. Instead the Saturday night crowd gives the band the rapturous welcome that's become routine on the tour – a welcome born of equal parts nostalgia and curiosity. At the Arts Centre you can spot the punk vets who've hung up their safety pins and joined the mortgage set, but you can also see Debbie-ettes who were still in nappies when Blondiemania reigned.

For a few numbers the performance looks tired and uninspired. Harry, wearing a '40s hourglass suit, seems tentative as she tackles the sequenced rock-pop of 'Forgive And Forget'. Meanwhile the others look like LA musos. Lee Fox, black jacket sleeves rolled up to his elbows, has the temerity to play a bass solo on 'Atomic'. From the Shangri-Las to . . . Spyro Gyra! Is it meant to be ironic?

But as the show goes on, Harry, her voice huskier and more Joni Mitchell-ish than it used to be, loosens up and starts to enjoy herself. When the Poole boomers bob as one to 'Sunday Girl', clapping along on the bridges with Harry, the band goes with the flow. 'Oh baaaybeh . . . my sweet baaaybeh,' Harry coos, and for a second we're transported back to girl-group heaven – Brooklyn, summer '64. By the time the band reach 'Rip Her To Shreds', via 'In The Flesh', everybody's happy.

'NO ONE CAN SAY WE DIDN'T HOLD OUT FOR 15 MINUTES' reads the back of the Blondie tour T-shirt, the quote daftly attributed to Sartre (author, lest we forget, of a play called *No Exit*). It's not as if the band don't realise how sad these reunions can be.

After obligatory encores of 'Denis', 'The Tide Is High' and 'Heart Of Glass', Blondie shuffle off and leave us with our warm memories of picture discs and *Top of the Pops*.

'And you don't stop . . .'

'Personally for me it's been very stress-free as a result of so much acceptance,' says Chris Stein *après le* gig. 'I think Debbie's the most worn out, because I get to sort of phase out, whereas Debbie's level of focus is a lot higher.'

Stein says the tour's first date in Stockholm was 'dismal' but that almost every subsequent show has been a blast. The previous weekend's pair of dates at London's Lyceum had brought out everyone from gnarled war heroes like Rat Scabies to Blondie-inspired Britpop bands like theaudience. 'I'm more familiar with the faces from the old punk days,' says Stein, 'but Clem is up on the new breed.'

Burke: 'Speaking of old punks, take a look at my lucky Carnaby Street punk bracelet. Only three pounds, man.'

Stein: 'We went to fuckin' Hermès and they had them for three hundred pounds.'

Burke: 'So we were inspired to buy the ones for three pounds. Although I did get my girlfriend a punk necklace from Vivienne Westwood for seventy quid.'

Stein: 'A mere drop in the bucket.'

Burke tells me it's 'getting boring saying how good everything's been going'. Only an hilarious incident in Lugano, Italy, where Blondie were being presented with a highfalutin' cultural award – previous recipients: Fellini, Callas, Nureyev – provided any hiccup along the way.

'It was this black-tie fuckin' situation,' says Stein. 'Polanski was there with some eleven-year-old dancer, I don't know if it was his date. And Clem got progressively drunker and drunker and tried to leap over his drums, and he fell on Paul and Lee in front of this whole crowd of bejewelled courtesans. It was a disaster, but at the same time it was a major existential moment.'

'I had completely forgotten that I had drunk three bottles of champagne, and also that I had my Anello & Davide Cuban-heel Beatle boots on,' says Burke. 'So I go over the drums and next thing I know I'm on the floor on top of Lee, and then the drums come crashing down in a chain reaction, and all you hear is five hundred people going, *Oh my God* . . . in Italian, of course.'

Stein: 'By the way, the award was a really beautiful thing with a marble base and silver shit and a fuckin' gold mask, whereas our fuckin' Q award must have cost all of four dollars—'

Clem: 'But the Q award means a lot—'

Destri {piping up in the background}: 'Fuck the meaning! It's cheap!'

Burke: 'But let's face it, what are Fellini and Maria Callas compared to Weller and Massive Attack?'

I turn around and see that Debbie Harry has emerged from her dressing room to pose for pictures with a pair of peroxide blonde girls, each wearing the 'Vultures' T-shirt Harry used to model back in '77. Pop's sometime Marilyn Monroe looks glazed but happy.

1999

Wiggaz with Attitude:
The Beastie Boys

I can still remember the morning, way back in the sweaty London summer of 1983, when three skinny New York wiseasses burst into the old *New Musical Express* office on Carnaby Street brandishing the Ratcage 12-inch of their single 'Cooky Puss'/'Beastie Revolution'.

I don't recall if we knew anything about the Boys at *NME*, but I do remember that esteemed scribe Richard Cook reviewed the record in his singles column the following week, appraising it in a wryly amused tone that summed up what most of us thought of these snotty Manhattan pranksters. (For his trouble, he was subsequently nicknamed – you guessed it – Cooky Puss.) The record chimed in perfectly with what hardcore punk bands like Flipper and the Angry Samoans were doing out on the West Coast, and what the even more gratuitously scatological likes of the Meatmen were doing elsewhere in America.

I still have that Ratcage single in my prized collection of 12-inch platters from the early '80s. Listening to 'Cooky Puss' now, and to the doltish dub skank of 'Beastie Revolution', I am suitably impressed by the distance Mike Diamond and Adams Yauch and Horowitz have travelled in the intervening fifteen years. *NME* certainly didn't see them as anything more than privileged brats killing time before going to law school or dentistry college. At least, not till the paper put them on the cover three years later as Beastiemania burst wide open with the release of the seminal *Licensed To Ill*.

What's amusing in 1998 is listening to the Boys wax nostalgic about their early Manhattan days, to realise that so much of what they do is still root-down in the stupid fun they were having when they recorded 'Cooky Puss'. To hear Ad-Rock (Horowitz) tell it, the days when the group hung out in the East Village, idling the hours away at the Ratcage store on East 9th Street, and then nipping across the road to play Breakout in the local video-game joint, were halcyon days of innocence and wonder, days that the group is still trying to capture in its music.

'I'm trapped in the past,' Ad-Rock has said. 'You know, I just get nostalgic. The changing times and stuff. I get nostalgic for Atari. You know what I'm saying? For a cheeseburger.' All the Beasties' records, he claims, go back to playing video games and smoking joints.

Does it sound odd to hear a Beastie Boy talk of nostalgia? Hip hop is supposed to be the sound of *now*, an aural response to life in the manic, hyperreal metropolis. (Much of it stems from growing up in New York City and contending with what Mike D calls 'the over-whelming input that defines your existence from the day your parents bring you outside the apartment in a stroller'.) Above all, hip hop is a music that regards the past merely as raw material for dismember-ment, snipping up pieces of history and inserting them into a future muzik of restlessness and unease. (Random Beastie examples: the stab-bing strings of Bernard Hermann's *Psycho* shower scene laid over a Sly & the Family Stone drum loop on 'Egg Man'; 'Funky Boss' jumping from Barrington Levy into Pere Ubu; Eugene McDaniels' '70s-soul voice crying out in the middle of Q-Tip's rap on 'Get It Together'.) As a group perched on the cutting edge of music technology – and of fashion, business, politics, general societal shifts – the Beasties have been anything but sentimental.

Yet there's another way of hearing Beasties music, one that accords more closely with an idea of nostalgia, of being 'trapped in the past'. That's to see them as hunters and collectors, gatherers and recyclers – as *fans*. For, in a sense, all Beasties tracks involve gathering pieces of bric-a-brac and assembling newfangled structures from them. Even when they were merely (hi)jacking off old Led Zeppelin and AC/DC riffs – with metalhead Rick Rubin egging them on from the console

– the Beasties were doing the retro shuffle (with a giant smirk on their faces).

The Beasties' recycling aesthetic is obvious not only from the production on albums such as the brilliant *Paul's Boutique* – a loop-layered samplefest that works like a hip-hop yard sale – but from the deep immersion in pop-culture debris suggested by their fantastically discursive lyrics. Long before Quentin Tarantino made a fetish of '70s kitsch, the Beasties were writing about pulp America like Beat poets, spewing impressionistic shorthand that revelled in blaxploitation minutiae and effortlessly parodied rap slanguage.

The aesthetic is obvious, too, from the group's *Grand Royal* magazine, a publication that effortlessly straddles the divide between oh-so-hipness and hopeless unfashionability in its fearless investigations of Bruce Lee, Lee Perry, mullet hairstyles and demolition derbies. The spirit of the Beasties' recycling is one entrenched in the humour that's kept them sane through their roller-coaster career – an 'appreciative, compassionate' laughter that's deepened and matured as the slack's been taken up by idiot jesters like the Jerky Boys and the Insane Clown Posse. ('The Beasties are the fucking Bugs Bunny of hip hop,' quoth Q-Tip in Alan Light's recent oral history of the band in *Spin*.)

'I appreciate their willingness to explore and not take themselves too seriously,' says Beck, whose *Odelay* was constructed with the aid of the Dust Brothers (and hailed by Mike D as the album that 'legitimised hip hop as the folk music the '90s'). 'On the other hand, everybody else takes them seriously. They're an inspiration. I like the way they're able to straddle the line of complete pastiche, but also to do it so committedly so that it never disintegrates into triviality.'

So seriously do people take the Beasties' serious fun these days that a recent hand-wringing *Spin* piece about whites and hip hop referred to the group as 'father figures'. With the phenomenal success of this year's *Hello Nasty*, it does seem as if Ad-Rock, Mike D and MCA have been invested with a kind of sacred elder statesmanship. Holy token honkies of b-boy culture, they've used hip hop as a blank slate on which to scrawl their many obsessions, happy to serve as style mentors and champion obscure heroes from the worlds of music, sport fashion, martial arts and other cultural strata.

Perhaps most significantly, the Beasties have managed to transcend the issue that's dogged so many of their Caucasian colleagues in hip hop – though there are those who would take strong issue with such a claim. For *Spin*'s Charles Aaron the trio's reluctance to 'explore their relationships with African Americans' is tantamount to 'an enormous denial', one made no more excusable by the kudos afforded them by many black hip-hop artists. And in a curious *New Yorker* piece in October – one hailing Polly Harvey over Lauryn Hill as 'the soul-music diva of the new age' – the African-American critic Hilton Als challenged the right of both the Beastie Boys and Beck 'to parody a certain fraction of black culture because [they] felt a part of it'. (Given the unsavoury Five Percent anti-Semitism of some of the artists 'parodied', the fact that Horowitz, Yauch and Diamond are all Jewish is especially ironic in this context. Still, Sire has just released the first album by described 'Hebe-hoppers' M.O.T, so we must be making *some* progress in this area.) Aaron at least concedes that the Beasties 'aren't hyped about being martyrs'. Fifteen years into their career, one could argue that that deserves to be discussed outside the parameters of black/white miscegenation.

Certainly, the Beastie Boys have never done blackface – or pulled a *Bulworth*, for that matter. They still sound just as petulantly white and suburban as they did in 1986. Being Jewish already puts them at one remove from the white-bread values of America's goyim, giving them the edge Jewish comic satirists always have had in American culture. True, part of their father-figure appeal is the way they've grown up and thrown themselves into causes like freedom for Tibet. And let's face it, none of them is likely to end up like Tupac or Biggie. But their music never gets po-faced – not even when they're putting shame in the Prodigy's game, requesting that the English rave-yobs drop 'Smack My Bitch Up' from a recent festival set. *Hello Nasty* proves the Beastie Boys' sense of humour is perfectly intact.

That album may be the best made this year. While pandering to our collective attention deficit disorder, as all hip hop does, it still manages to process disposable moments into a brilliantly cohesive montage that one can experience in one sitting without fidgeting. As such, it returns us to what the Beasties do best: *Check Your Head* may have been an admirable swerve away from the sample-saturated *Paul's Boutique*, but to these ears the Beasties copping old Crusaders and Malo licks on their own instruments just wasn't as groove-y as the sampled stuff on *Boutique*.

With *Ill Communication*, the band achieved a happier blend of samples and performance, going easier on the lounge-R & B jams and 'Groove' Holmes organ pastiches. (Spike Jonze's 'Sabotage' video, of course, raised their *Starsky and Hutch*-via-Monty Python schtick to a point of high art.) Now *Hello Nasty*, featuring their first rhymes written in partnership since *Paul's Boutique*, updates that album's unprecedented playfulness and diversity, grafting ancient hip-hop and reggae and Latin-rock samples on to busy break beats, dropping gospel eminence 'Professor' Alex Bradford and husky soulstress Barbara Lynn into the bouillabaisse, and even finding room – on 'Electrify' – for snippets of Igor Stravinsky and Stephen Sondheim.

Much has been made of *Hello Nasty*'s relocation of the Beasties back to New York City. And yes, there are lots of old-school gestures and scratches on the record; for the nostalgic Ad-Rock, the album is clearly intended as a reaffirmation of the band's b-boy roots. But *Nasty* also transcends the tropes of hip hop in the way Lee 'Scratch' Perry's deranged dub mixes transcended reggae in the '70s. Like Perry's, the Beasties' music is all about deconstructing/reconstructing beats and melodies – making the old new again. (For them, as for him, songs are loose, lateral artefacts, not sacred texts.) It couldn't be more fitting, therefore, that Perry is one of the guests making a cameo appearance on *Hello Nasty*.

'This is a living dream, from the beastly brothers and the beastly boys, with their beastly toys . . . they give you some beastly joys.'

So intones the Scratchmeister on 'Dr Lee, PhD', the makeshift track that he sings on. As a description of the album it'll do very nicely, thank you.

1998

The Great White Hope:
Eminem

First came Elvis – America's worst nightmare, the white-trash negro. Then came Mick Jagger and Marilyn Manson, Johnny Rotten and Kurt Cobain, Tupac Shakur and Snoop Doggy Dogg. America is always waiting for the next musical menace to society.

Yet nothing quite prepared the God-fearin' US of A for Marshall Bruce Mathers III, a sulky-faced, bleach-blond, trailer-park nobody in dungarees going by the *nom de rap* of Eminem. And nobody could have predicted that this creature would become the biggest pop star on the planet – the indisputable ruler of AD 2000.

This was no black demon rising up from the ghetto, Uzi in hand. This was no goth-glam alien androgyne for the trenchcoat tribe. This was a true punk, the archetypal Ritalin-stoked attention-deficient über-brat become tabloid superstar. This was blue-collar white America in revolt, a rebel with a brain, an anti-hero messing violently with his country's Mickey Mouse fantasia.

A writhing knot of contradictions, Eminem wasn't even just Eminem. On his first EP and album, he was for much of the time Slim Shady, the implicitly black alter ego who recalled the legend of the ruthlessly amoral Stagger Lee. Slim was Em's id, 'sent to piss the world off', revelling in outrage and gross out. Slim was the devil on Marshall Mathers' left shoulder.

The stats talk loud. This year's *Marshall Mathers LP* sold 1.76

million copies in its first week of release and 6.5 million in its first month. At nine million and counting, it's well on its way to being the biggest hip-hop album of the genre's twenty-year history. In Britain – a country for which Mathers professes no great love – the album has sat tight in the Top 10 ever since its release.

Trouble is, no one quite knows what to think of Eminem, or least-ways how to articulate the confusing responses his music provokes as it walks its fine-line tightrope between cartoon and nightmare, *South Park* and *The Texas Chainsaw Massacre*. As a verbal swordsman the boy's as good as any African-American practitioner of the hip-hop art. As a repository of – and vent for – vile views towards women and homosexuals he's utterly abhorrent.

'Anyone who understands what MC'ing means, you can't front on him,' says Posdnuos of De La Soul. 'There's a lot of things that Eminem can say that I don't personally agree with, but he's an MC. He's beyond just someone getting caught up in the hype of him being a Caucasian MC.'

And it's not just Em's African American peers in the hip-hop world who've saluted him. If the Gay and Lesbian Alliance Against Defamation have described the twenty-six-year-old's songs as 'the most blatant, homophobic lyrics we've seen in a long time', ultradiva Elton John claims that when he put *The Marshall Mathers LP* on in his car the first time it felt a 'nuclear bomb' had hit.

'I just could not believe how brilliant it was,' quoth Elton. 'On the surface it seems so politically incorrect. Rap records are often full of shit, and this is really hardcore stuff, but it's intelligent hardcore stuff – it's funny, it's clever, it's poetry.' Tell that to Timothy White, the professional *Billboard* editor who wrote an outraged diatribe when Eminem's first album, *The Slim Shady LP*, came out last year.

'I murder a rhyme, one word at a time,' Eminem raps on 'I'm Back'. 'You never heard of a mind as perverted as mine.' The boy's skills as an MC are of a piece with the portraits of him on the cover of *The Marshall Mathers LP*, pen and pad in hand, thoughtful look on face. For all the controversy he's courted, Eminem wants to be taken seri-ously as a phrase-shaper. A big part of the Eminem story is the legwork he put into his art back in the days when he lived in Detroit's crack neighourhoods and sat for hours writing lyrics in the local Burger King.

Mathers was the first white MC to use hip hop as a voice for the dispossessed white urban poor. 'He was doing something radical, claiming white poverty was equal to black poverty,' says William Shaw, the author of a bracing study of LA gangs and rappers called *Westsiders*. 'He brought white people into the ghetto.' Something that's never fully acknowledged in America is that there *is* no white music for the white urban poor: hip hop and R & B speak a great deal louder to their experience than rock or country music, both essentially suburban genres.

Mathers grew up in dirt-poor Detroit, neglected and badly bullied, with a mother who he claims took more drugs than he did. (His father split when the boy was six months old, never to be seen again.) Both his albums are strewn with contemptuous digs at the woman who sired him; the biggest bee in his bonnet concerns the parents of kids like the dysfunctional duo who went on the killing spree at Colorado's Columbine High School in 1999. 'They just didn't pay attention to their fucking kids,' he says.

Doubtless this explains the very big deal Mathers makes about being a good father to his five-year-old daughter Hailie; perhaps he's even re-parenting his own inner child through his devotion to her. 'The *only one thing* I'm scared of is being taken away from my little girl,' he professed to *The Face*. Along with the occasional outbursts of grief and sorrow on his records, his love for Hailie is one of the few things that makes him endearing as a human being. On the other hand, bringing the then-three-year-old child into the studio to add her gurgles to the macabre "97 Bonnie and Clyde' – a hideous fantasy about driving with Hailie to dump her dead mother's corpse in a nearby lake – might not be construed as model parenting.

After dropping out of school at fifteen and working a succession of dead-end jobs in Detroit, Eminem braved it out on the city's hip-hop circuit, gradually earning begrudging respect and then a contract with the local Web Entertainment label. His first album *Infinite* tanked, and the resulting despair can be heard on *The Slim Shady LP*'s 'Rock Bottom'. Yet a month later he came to the attention of the legendary

Dr Dre, the former Nigga With Attitude who'd loosed Snoop Doggy Dogg on the world in the early '90s. Dre assumed Em was black.

'We clicked,' Em recalled of the meeting with the Doc arranged by Interscope mogul Jimmy Iovine. 'First day in the studio we knocked off three songs.' One of those was the emphatic, unanswerable 'My Name Is', first track on *The Slim Shady LP*. He adds: 'I do believe that [Dre and I] will help break down the fuckin' barriers of stereotypes.'

If Dre initially caught flak for working with a white rapper, Mathers seems to have won over America's hip-hop arbiters: his was the first white face to appear on the cover of rap bible *The Source* in the magazine's twelve-year history. 'Eminem gets attention because he's dope – regardless of what colour his skin is,' says Missy Elliott, who featured him on her superb *Da Real World*. 'I love him cos he's white and he knows he's white. He's just him, and whatever he raps about is whatever he's going through, and I ain't mad at that.'

Like the Beastie Boys – products of a far more privileged background than Mathers – Eminem has earned kudos by not trying to come on like some Vanilla Ice fly guy. The 'wigga' syndrome that cursed Ice, trips up Tim Westwood and gets lampooned by Ali G simply doesn't apply to a boy who was listening to 2 Live Crew when he was eleven. (The biggest tragedy of Mathers' life was the 1993 suicide of the man who turned him on to hip hop, his uncle Ronnie.) Eminem still surrounds himself with boyz from his old hood, most notably his (black) childhood sidekick Proof. Mathers *looks* like a guy who should be as racist as he is sexist and homophobic, but he's blacker than Elvis ever was.

But is Eminem really just Elvis all over again? Or is he merely a Jerry Springer version of Tupac Shakur? You can look at it two ways: he *is* Elvis all over again, a white kid pilfering from black style and making more loot than any black rapper ever did. Or he's a white kid paying legitimate tribute to the harder edge and way-cooler style of African-American music. 'I don't do black music, I don't do white music,' Eminem declaims on 'Who Knew'. 'I make fight music . . .'

However you look at him, Eminem is keeping it as real as Tupac or Biggie ever did, blurring the fine line between act and reality. As with 'pac and Snoop Dogg, DMX and Ol' Dirty Bastard, the kid's Slim Shady persona constantly spills over into reality. Back in June, in the space of two days, he brandished a gun in the face of an employee of hated Motor City rivals Insane Clown Posse and pistol-whipped a man he thought was kissing his wife Kim.

A month later, after a series of shows in which he brought a blow-up sex doll onstage and referred to it as his wife, Kim attempted suicide at their house. In August, his mother filed a $1 million lawsuit against him, claiming his comments about her original $10 million slander suit were themselves defamatory, and Kim sued for another $10 million on grounds of 'intentional infliction of emotional distress'. Yes, folks, it *is* a real-live *Jerry Springer Show*.

Mathers is himself only too painfully aware of the irony of his success: how he set out on this road so he could afford presents for his daughter, only to run the risk now of not being able to see her. Indeed, *The Marshall Mathers LP* is almost exclusively about the lie of fame: how success and riches have only made Eminem more enraged and frustrated. 'I'm so sick of bein' admired that I wish I would just die or get fired,' he rails on 'The Way I Am'. As his manager Paul Rosenberg acknowledges, 'the media and public just give him more stuff to be pissed off about'.

Here again there are maddening contradictions: Eminem doesn't buy into the ego-stroking bullshit of celebrity culture, yet the whole album is a relentless emission of neurotic megalomania – an entire record about himself and how (he thinks) the world sees him. 'I just wanted to make fans, regular people, feel more in touch with me,' he has claimed. 'Like I was a real person . . .' But that sense of proximity carries a hefty price tag, as he himself is coming to realise: 'My life . . . story, my life, is, like, for the public to view now. And that shit don't make me happy.'

The ultimate expression of this, of course, is 'Stan', the story of a crazed Mark Chapman-type who worships Eminem and then turns against him when his letters get no response. Musically the tenderest, most moving song on the record, 'Stan' is a fragmented epistle laid over sweet-sad guitar chords and punctuated by an airy vocal couplet by British singer Dido. It's also, in the words of *NME*'s Stephen Dalton, 'a fearsome dissection of the psychotic love/hate triangle between star, audience and the media'.

How will the Eminem drama play out? Will he mellow out? Will he get shot? More to the point, has the bullied boy become the bullying braggart? And are all of us armchair B-boys in this post-PC pop culture just sucking up to the playground bully because they're too cool to disapprove?

2000

6

World's
Forgotten Boys

Evan Dando: The Smoker You Drink, the Player You Get

Driving through the sheeting rain from the miniature airport that serves Martha's Vineyard, the guy at the wheel informs me that we're heading towards the 'way-coolest' part of the island. The part in question is the south-western tip of this squillionaires' summer playground, and it's called Gay Head.

Big Gay Heart, Big Gay Head . . .

'Gay Head is the last, like, funky part of the island,' the driver tells me. Moments later he narrowly avoids forcing a jogging squillionaire into the ditch. The guy shouts 'Asshole!' at him.

'I'll get that motherfucker on my way back,' the driver grunts.

After another twenty-five minutes in the car – passing, en route, such Vineyard landmarks as John Belushi's grave and the old Jackie O estate – we turn down a rain-sodden track and approach a house that could just about pass for 'funky'. Evan Dando's family has been coming to the island for most of his life, but this summer he's renting his own crash pad. In the heavy rain, Gay Head looks not unlike Cornwall.

As I make a desperate and drenching dash from car to crash pad, I can hear what sounds like Nick Cave's voice issuing through the window. My first thought is that Cave himself must be a houseguest, but as I push open the screen door I see Dando hunched over an acoustic guitar in the middle of the room, barefoot and unshaven and droning his way through a discordant medley of Saint Nick's favourite

murder ballads – all to the hoarse-throated mirth of a tattooed and
goatee-bearded party animal who rocks from side to side on a battered
sofa. Between the two figures is a table crammed with crushed cans
and upended bottles.

Welcome to the world of the reformed head Lemonhead, mid-
August 1996.

Evan Dando has been holed up and holding court here since 14 July,
when he finally finished work on *Car Button Cloth*, the first Lemonheads
album since he began an infamous near-three-year 'lost weekend' in
late 1993. He says he feels less exposed to temptation on Martha's
Vineyard than he does in the city, able to stick to booze and pot and
to steer clear of the more perilous substances. He does not say what
is pretty obvious, which is that the place has become the party house
of choice for a select group of Gay Head slackers.

'I come here, and there's not much urge when it's nice, hangin' out
with really cool people, havin' a beer, swimming, playing guitar. I'm
not a city kid, I'm really not – it never agreed with me. It makes me
destroy myself. There's too much commotion and it's too loud. Come
to think of it, that's why I started really taking heroin a lot when I
was twenty years old or something. It was just cos of all the screeching
noises in Boston, which isn't even that loud. I just wanted to cushion
it all somehow.'

Later he will concede that the partying can get a little out of hand.
'You gotta watch it cos sometimes your drunk crazy friends become
just too annoying to deal with. I mean, I never have parties here,
right? But sometimes they just . . . happen?'

As if on cue, four more Gay Headers pour in from the rain. They're
planning their daily run to the West Tisbury dump, a trash site wherein
rich people casually dispose of things that you or I would spend months
saving for. I may be wrong, but it seems to me that most of these
kids are younger than Dando. One of them, fittingly enough, turns
out to be James Taylor's nephew – fittingly because, like Dando, James
Taylor was a heroin addict and a habitué of the psychiatric wards of
Boston.

One of the songs on *Car Button Cloth* is called 'Hospital'. It's a sinisterly pretty ditty about 'a disease going around' and about 'green leaves falling from the trees'. It was written at Silver Hill Hospital in Boston after Dando had suffered an acid-triggered breakdown in Sydney and been flown back to America by his family.

'I went crazy and forgot that I was addicted to heroin, and I started doing all these other drugs down in Australia. I hadn't slept, and then I took a hit of acid and fuckin' lost it. I was imagining laser gun sights on my face, and I was feeding coins into grates, thinking I was going to – *poof!* – go back to America. Cos it said "In God We Trust" on the dollar bill.'

The only thing that cheered Dando up was learning that Edie Sedgwick had once been committed to Silver Hill. 'When I started to feel better, I'd start strumming "Just Like A Woman", trying to conjure up the spirit of Edie!'

The fact that Dando can talk so lightly of his breakdown is either amusing or alarming, depending on your perspective. His combination of pretty-boy amiability and hopeless self-destructiveness suggests a cross between Keanu Reeves and Gram Parsons, one of his great heroes. It even suggests a latterday Montgomery Clift, another upper-middle-class American beauty who disguised his torment with goofiness.

None of this would matter that much if Dando wasn't such a gifted songwriter and musician – if he hadn't recorded the almost perfect *It's A Shame About Ray* (1992) and its underrated follow-up *Come On Feel The Lemonheads* (1993); if, indeed, he hadn't recently defied all the odds by releasing the excellent *Car Button Cloth*. In a post-grunge world of sub-Cobain mediocrities, the guy still stands out as one of the most distinctive talents in American rock.

Car Button Cloth should astound anyone who'd written Dando off as a lost cause. It's very different from *Ray* or *Come On Feel* – there are virtually no acoustic guitars on the record, for starters – and it's also considerably more varied: *The Many Mood Swings Of Evan Dando* might be a more appropriate title. (Ev's explanation of the actual title: 'In second grade we were told to go home and fill up our tub and put things in it and see what floated and what sank. I had a racing car, a button and a piece of cloth. They all sank.') Moving in the space of minutes from affable drollery ('The Outdoor Type') to hoarse desperation ('Something's Missing'), from churning Ramonarama ('Six') to sweet, sleepy soulfulness ('C'mon Daddy'), it is an album of resilience and even a certain repentance.

Three tracks in particular make much of Dando's previous work sound almost frothy. Taking up where 'Style' (on *Come On Feel*) left off, these are the album's real killers. 'Break Me' is as beautiful as *Ray*'s 'Rudderless' but five times as intense. The slurred Largactyl vocals and slashed guitars of 'Losing Your Mind' make for a harrowing account of mental instability. And the closing 'Tenderfoot', a track co-written by Adam Young and Tom Morgan (Dando's collaborator on a handful of songs on *Ray* and *Come On Feel*), is a searing song of contrition that recalls vintage Hüsker Dü at their frenzied best. On all three of these, Dando overcomes his instinctive dopiness and gives us a real sense of what he's been through in the last three years. 'Just can't decide if I should lie or tell the truth and try to hide,' he sings on 'Losing Your Mind'. Here, at the very least, he's come out of hiding.

'This is the first record I've worked really, really hard on,' he says. 'Every time I've finished a record before I've just split for Australia, but this time I even went to the mastering. I had this really pompous idea that I wanted to make some lasting contribution to music as a whole, so I really went for it. I'm actually really serious about the work, which is why I have to get so silly in interviews and stuff. It's so hard to talk seriously about music, because actually music and talking don't have that much to do with each other. For the person making the music, they'd rather not do it, really, so why not completely bullshit your way through interviews? That's why I created the force field of the idiot dope fiend around me, saying "Yeah, cool, man" all the time. That was just my way of shielding it.

'The whole persona that people saw me in, where I was all optimistic and stuff, was always slightly ironic. I was just trying to play it up to the hilt for the sheer perversity of it. The dark shit was always underneath there, but it definitely came out on this record. It's funny, we were on tour in Spain at the same time as the Bad Seeds, and Nick Cave told our bass player that we weren't dark enough! We had a good laugh, but actually it was good advice. In fact, we were gonna call the new record that – *The Lemonheads Aren't Dark Enough*!'

Does he think *Car Button Cloth* will restore the credibility he's lost?

'If I'd cared what people thought about me, I never would have been daring enough to go forth and try and make a career in some kind of creativity. Of course, there must be something wrong with me that makes me seek approval on a mass scale – something to do with my parents getting split up and all that bullshit people talk about in interviews – but it doesn't matter what people think of you if you're having fun making the music. The people that, like, vilify me – whoever the hell they are – they don't know me, and if they do I probably hate them back just as much. I don't care!'

Looking back over Dando's protracted 'lost weekend', one could date the first signs of trouble to the late summer of 1993, when he was holed up in LA's Chateau Marmont in druggy emulation of Gram Parsons. As it turns out, the problems had started years before, while he was growing up as a privileged wild child on the streets of Boston.

'I was a horrific, horrible demon vandal child when I was ten. I mean, my goal was to break as many windows as possible, and that's probably why I got on a peace kick for a while – I just felt so bad about all the stuff I did when I was a kid. I was the typical really bad little kid. It was always, "No TV or skateboarding for a month!" And I think drugs sublimated all my destructive urges – I got to destroy my brain instead. I did so much acid in ninth grade they made me do it twice, and that's why the Lemonheads exist, because I was put into a cooler grade with the two guys [Jesse Peretz and Ben Deily] who were gonna be in the band. Every day after school we'd get together and jam out on acid.'

Formed as the Whelps in 1985, when Dando was eighteen, the Lemonheads were just one of the innumerable bands who emerged from the quagmire that was alternative American rock between 1985 and 1990 – between hardcore and grunge.

'We started out wanting to be a horror-rock punk band, cos our favourite bands were, like, the Misfits and the Angry Samoans. The Samoans gave us our first break in show business. We got to support them on a couple of East Coast dates because we baked them a cake and brought it to their hotel room.' (Dando says he still steals lines – 'The brown acid's kicking in!' and 'My goal in life is to die at the Ozzy concert!' – from former Samoans frontman Metal Mike Saunders.)

With vague leanings towards the sound of Hüsker Dü and the Replacements, the Lemonheads changed personnel several times and made dismal albums like *Creator* (1988) and *Lick* (1989). Their 1990 Atlantic debut *Lovey* showed some of the distinctive touches that would blossom on *It's A Shame About Ray* but was otherwise headed towards the same bargain bins as all the other sub-Mudhoney albums pouring out of college-town America at the turn of the decade.

'I find the earlier records very erratic and variable in quality now, but there are bursts of something that I could make it through listening to still today: "Mallo Cup", "Circle Of One", "Die Right Now" . . . a few things that we're gonna do on the tour. I'm kinda glad that we didn't get big quickly, cos I never was complacent. The fact that we survived at all was down to our lawyer [former *NME* Big Apple correspondent Richard Grabel], who got us a "Two Firm" clause on our contract, meaning they had to put out two records, and had the "Commercially Viable" clause struck from it.'

It's A Shame About Ray, assisted by the UK hit cover of Simon & Garfunkel's 'Mrs Robinson', made Dando a golden-haired poster boy for what some dubbed 'bubblegrunge'. Its twelve short tracks included timelessly tuneful songs like 'Confetti', 'The Turnpike Down' and 'My Drug Buddy', as well as harder-rocking numbers like 'Rockin' Stroll' and 'Alison's Starting To Happen'. The crisp, assured sound was like an electro-acoustic Ramones fronted by a feckless Mark Eitzel, veering from pining heartache to slacker irony.

Come On Feel The Lemonheads was only slightly less satisfying, including as it did the fine single 'Into Your Arms' and the divine 'Big Gay Heart', the ravaged 'Style' and the Tom Morgan country charmer 'Being Around'. After the last of several exhausting tours, the most durable of the band's many line-ups (seventeen to date) dissolved. David Ryan is currently playing drums in Fuzzy and writing screenplays, Nic Dalton running his Half A Cow record label. 'The last line-up was very successful, but it definitely came to its fruition and stopped being as fun for everybody. No one could do anything anymore, so I had to get new people.'

Seasoned Dando-watchers will tell you that things started rolling downhill when the singer opted to stay in England after the *Come On Feel* tour ended. The spectacle of the lanky Yank jumping onstage to rattle a tambourine on Oasis' UK tour of 1994 is indelibly etched in the mind of anyone who cares anything about dignity in rock 'n' roll. 'That was when I said, Hey, these guys look like they're on to something. I think I'll hang around and help lug equipment and stuff and see what goes down.'

What actually went down is that Dando became progressively more wasted and ridiculous as the tour rolled on. A Britpop backlash against him culminated in his ill-judged decision to play, two hours late, to an impatient crowd of Portishead fans at the 1995 Glastonbury Festival. Unceremoniously booed offstage, it looked as though the former press darling and 'alternahunk' had hit the nadir of his career. It now looks, moreover, as though the one thing he had to show for all his cronying with the 'sis – a throwaway Dando/Gallagher song that would not be out of place as third track on an Oasis CD single (and that was intended to be the first UK single from *Car Button Cloth*) – will never see the light of day.

'"Purple Parallelogram" came about when we were running around Amsterdam in 1994 trying to scare people and stuff, and we bought all this terrible *not-coke*, you know, just white powder that burned and made you feel like you wanted to die. And we almost got in some kind of tussle with some guy in a bar, and we got home and I went, "Wait a minute, guys, I've got some *real* drugs, *legal* drugs, in my knapsack upstairs!" And they were these pills that a doctor had prescribed me, which looked like purple parallelograms. And next morning we all sort of woke up singing the song.'

How does Dando look back on the last three years?

'It's been like a gradual defoliation, getting to the core of the real me, which I had gotten so far away from. My last statement to the press before I didn't do any more interviews was, "I'm just gonna get in my dune buggy with my gun and my girlfriend and drive to the next town and kill everyone who isn't beautiful!" And that was one of the reasons why I freaked out, cos after that I went out on tour with Oasis and went to Australia and had my nervous breakdown. Part of the nervous breakdown was, Woah, what a fucked-up thing to say! That I had that much anger in me . . .'

Back in America, Dando had a brief respite from his drug use when he was cast alongside Liv Tyler in a movie about small-town life in upstate New York.

'*Heavy* damn near saved me. It stopped me doing drugs for a while, cos I didn't *need* to do drugs hanging out with this amazingly cool sixteen-year-old girl all day. The main thing was that I was away from rock, doing something productive, with some really cool people like Debbie Harry and Shelley Winters.'

By the spring of 1996, Dando had gathered enough songs – and was in good enough shape – to end his long silence. Going into Dreamland studios in West Hurley, New York, with producer Bryce Goggin (Pavement, Breeders et al.) and a cracking band comprising ex-Dinosaur Jr drummer Murphy and Aussie guitarist/bassist Bill Gibson, he spent six weeks tracking and two mixing the record at nearby Bearsville studios. The record sounds very fresh, helped by great arrangements and some incidental extras – whistling solos, off-the-cuff percussion, a few Moogs and mellotrons – that lend it a raw, rough-hewn feel.

'The sessions went pretty well. I mean, I only had to go to the hospital once, and that was only because I started hyperventilating after doing the vocal for "C'mon Daddy" while lying under the recording console. It wasn't easy, cos I was real excited about making the record and couldn't sleep and stuff. There are no acoustic guitars on it apart from one noodly acoustic part on "Tenderfoot", and that was just because we didn't wanna be totally dogmatic about it.'

With a first single in the infectious and hummable 'If I Could Talk I'd Tell You' (written after doing lines of coke on Napoleon's draughting table, an item belonging to 'a very, very rich and famous family whose name you know and which I probably shouldn't say') and a creditable cover of the Louvin Brothers' Appalachian murder ballad 'Knoxville Girl' (Nick Cave eat your heart out), *Car Button Cloth* may not quite be *It's A Shame About Ray*, but it's a damn sight better than anyone had any right to expect. Dando says he's looking forward to touring again, with the *Car Button Cloth* band fleshed out by returning Lemonheads veteran John Strohm. 'I thrive on something to do,' he adds. 'I don't really get that bad a drug problem when I'm working.'

How does he feel about the devastation that heroin is once again causing in the rock fraternity?

'I don't know, it's beyond me. I have no idea and it's very sad. But knock on wood, man, I can't, I don't wanna go out like that. I got more important things to do. Like, I'm a godfather now [to the daughter of Keith Richards' son Marlon]. I really care about this kid, and I wanna have a real relationship with her. I wanna send her post-cards.'

Dando's pals return with a present from the dump: an absurd blue pyjama suit several sizes too small into which he somehow manages to squeeze himself. A girl named Meadow giggles and puts her arms round his shoulders like he's her big brother. The local store is about to deliver the evening's supply of alcohol.

From the basement beneath us comes the crashing sound of a drum kit.

'Woah, that's my friend Jet Craze,' guffaws Dando. 'We've recorded this really horrible loud jazz-rock album with Tarka Cordell [son of the late Denny], and I'm gonna release it on my new label Breath Of Salt Water! I'll play you a tape of it!'

Evan jumps up and puts on a tape that sounds like three very stoned sixteen-year-olds assing about in their parents' garage.

'This is a song called "Mr Creepy"!'

As I listen to the tuneless and rhythmless din, I'm wondering when the real Evan Dando is going to stand up. Is this him, or is it the guy who wrote 'Break Me' and 'Losing Your Mind'?

'Hey, look at me in my house,' giggles Evan Dando. 'I'm like a suburban housewife, taking the occasional Valium, getting a little upset about my record, doing the dishes, putting on my *Texas Chainsaw Massacre* video, going to the dump, listening to *Murder Ballads* . . .

'You know, it's my intention just to stick to the booze, and a little pot, maybe. I toy with the idea of completely, y'know . . . I take breaks from drinking, and I take breaks from smoking cigarettes, but when I really get clean I think I'm gonna stop playing rock. Really. I think I'd rather spare everybody the gory details of me getting clean on record, making an album without anything to, like, release the demons. I don't know what all that stuff does, but it works, I think. Rock 'n' roll and alcohol and drugs go weally rell together . . . I mean, really well together! Oh no, I'm damaged! I'm damaged goods!'

He grabs a can of beer and gets back to work.

1996

The Wizardry and True Stardom of Todd Rundgren

Hello, it's him.

Standing in the doorway of a two-storey industrial structure on the edge of San Francisco's Mission District, clad only in a pair of green plaid shorts, is the star-spangled wizard – the sometime rabbit-toothed runt – who goes by the name of Todd Rundgren. Tanned and lean and exuding the rude health one might expect in a man who recently upped and moved lock, stock, barrel and children to Kauai, northernmost of the Hawaiian islands, Rundgren beckons me inside and leads me up some stairs to the loft he keeps as his Bay Area pied-à-terre.

The loft is full of detritus, a combination dressing room and antique store. A row of multicoloured stage costumes sits atop a long shelf. A pulpit sits in a corner. And bang in the middle of the room, winking at me, is the inevitable Apple Powerbook, from which my arrival has dragged Todd away. Turns out he's making changes to his website, primary vehicle these days for communicating with his legion of fans.

Though I myself have never been a fully-fledged Toddist (or Todd-is-Goddist), I count myself among the sizeable number of Rundgren devotees who think the man should – and could – have been the biggest rock star of the '70s. As I sit watching him tap away at his keyboard, I think back to a mind-blowing show at the Hammersmith Odeon in October 1975 when Todd and the second edition of Utopia took me on a psychedelic glam-prog journey that changed the face of rock music for me forever.

'Todd could have been the biggest and most important artist of the era,' Paul Fishkin, former general manager of Rundgren's '70s label Bearsville, will tell me a few days later. 'If he had taken a little more time to work with me and whoever else saw that potential in him, there's no question in my mind that we could have had it all. Todd's whole thing was, he was who he was at any given moment and everyone else be damned. The egomaniacal part of that is that he expected everyone to go along with it.'

Rundgren is still tapping at the Powerbook as his long-serving, long-suffering road manager Mary Lou Arnold drives us north on 101 to Petaluma, the small town in which 'The Total Individualist' will play a one-man gig tonight in a quaint establishment called the Mystic Theater. When Todd jokes that he has 'a back-up band' in case the computer fails, I realise that much of the music we'll be hearing tonight is contained inside that small metal box.

Mary Lou interrupts to check on the route to Petaluma. A nervous driver at the best of times, she awaits Rundgren's orders with mild trepidation. Time was when he used to bark directions at her through a megaphone: twenty years of driving through America together has made them a hilarious double act.

'Follow the force, Mary Lou,' is all Rundgren will say at this juncture.

Friends say that Todd was into computers as early as 1965, when he was a lanky, long-faced sixteen-year-old growing up in the Philadelphia suburb of Upper Darby. By then he was certainly already a precocious specimen, albeit the product of a typically dysfunctional middle-class family.

'My family was not close knit,' he says. 'Everyone was sort of competing with each other. We never said "I love you", we never hugged each other. My dad got into a thing with me that was nearly abusive, not physically but psychologically. As a result everyone in my family [dad Harry, mother Ruth, sisters June and Lynette, and baby brother Robin] turned out to have some psychological problem.'

Rundgren says a major part of his karmic journey has been breaking 'the lineage of bad fathers' whence he sprung: his commitment to his own children Rex, Randy and Rebop (as well as to the actress Liv

Tyler, who grew up as his daughter) comes, he claims, before anything else in his life.

'Before I ever knew what karma meant,' he says, 'I swore to myself that I was not going to be my dad, that I was gonna want to have any kid that I had. I feel so bad for my father that he never experienced what I do.' For someone who is emotionally more remote than he perhaps realises, Rundgren seems close to tears as he says this.

One thing Harry Rundgren did give Todd was an exposure to a range of music that broadened the boy's palette beyond mere pop music. If Todd's first group was a covers band called Money, his own tastes inclined as much to classical music and Broadway show tunes as they did towards the British Invasion hits and soul records of the mid-'60s. As a 'weedy and undersized' would-be class clown, he was never into rock 'n' roll per se.

'I didn't particularly like Elvis Presley. He looked like the greasers who beat me up all the time. I thought the whole rock milieu was kinda silly. I listened to anything from Debussy to Richard Rodgers.'

After school was out, Rundgren — the boy the kids teased as 'Runt Green' — would sit at the piano in the empty auditorium and tinker with major sevenths and 'cool progressions'. He says many of his trademark changes were worked out during these late afternoon sessions.

Debussy notwithstanding, the teenage Rundgren did in time become a rabid guitar fanatic, styling himself, like a thousand other American boys, after the Eric Clapton he heard on Bluesbreakers and Yardbirds records. On 23 June 1966, the day after his eighteenth birthday, he packed everything he owned into a case and split for Ocean City, one of the umpteen seaside towns dotted along the New Jersey shoreline.

Not long after, he caught a show in nearby Wildwood headlined by the Byrds: bottom of the bill that night was a Philadelphia band called Woody's Truck Stop, 'who'd sort of modelled themselves after the Butterfield Blues Band and were blowing everyone's minds'. Within a couple of months, Rundgren had joined Woody's Truck Stop as its resident slide-guitar maestro. 'I became the Elvin Bishop of the group' is how he remembers it.

'Todd was completely different from everyone else,' says Paul

Fishkin, who'd assumed managerial duties for the group. 'First of all, everyone else was taking drugs, and he took nothing. People just couldn't believe it. Also, he was very ambitious – all he wanted to do was play.'

Fishkin maintains that Rundgren was actually fired from Woody's Truck Stop for not taking drugs. Rundgren himself says it was simply a difference of emphasis that led to his departure: 'Influenced by the San Francisco scene, the band decided they wanted to take acid and get it together in the country. I had to draw the line when the lifestyle became more important than the music.'

Leaving shortly after Rundgren was bassist Carson Van Osten, a Philadelphia College of Art graduate with whom he proceeded to form Nazz, a name that came from Lord Buckley via the Yardbirds' 'The Nazz Are Blue'. Recruiting drummer Thom Mooney and singer/keyboardist Robert 'Stewkey' Antoni from rival Philly bands, Rundgren was unequivocal about his Anglophile goals. 'We wanted to combine the Beatles' genius in the studio with the heavy-duty show business of the Who onstage,' he states simply today.

The Nazz story was one of such failed promise and twisted internal politics that it almost derailed Rundgren's career. An energetic, good-looking group that wowed crowds at psychedelic dungeons like Trauma and the Electric Factory, they were adopted by Mamas and Papas publicist John Kurland after they saw the Who support the Mamas at a show in early '67.

Kurland was a closet homosexual whose idol was Brian Epstein, and his Beatle-esque gameplan was for Nazz to have their cake and eat it too: they would slay the teenagers and enjoy critical credibility. Quick to recognise Rundgren's prodigious gifts, Kurland sequestered them in a house in Great Neck, Long Island, and groomed them to be America's next pop sensation.

'Todd was certainly the leader, and by far the most talented,' says Michael Friedman, Kurland's assistant when Nazz signed their management contract at the beginning of September 1967. 'But Kurland overpromoted the teenage aspect of the band, and their credibility was affected by that. He sort of led them in the direction of,

"You're gonna make it through records", which is always the wrong strategy.' Kurland kept them cooped up in the Great Neck house, the resulting cabin fever leading to predictable squabbles and resentments. The group didn't play its first official show till January 1968.

When the debut Nazz single 'Hello, It's Me'/'Open My Eyes' was released on Atlantic affiliate SGC (Screen-Gems-Columbia) in the summer of 1968, it instantly signalled that here was a pop genius who could do blistering hard rock, heavenly chord changes and lilting pop ballads – and do them all equally well. The parameters were clear just within 'Open My Eyes', a psych-pop classic and Top 50 hit subsequently included on Lenny Kaye's immortal *Nuggets* compilation: it starts like the Who's 'Can't Explain', features a screaming guitar solo and some outrageous 'Itchycoo Park' phasing, yet still finds room for a meltingly gorgeous Brian Wilson middle eight.

Then there was 'Hello, It's Me', putative A-side and massive hit for the solo Rundgren when rearranged and released as a single from *Something/Anything?* in 1973. The only catch was that Rundgren didn't sing lead vocals on either of these Nazz songs, or on almost any Nazz song. Instead vocals were handled by the blandly uninteresting Stewkey, who had the gall to be rude about Todd's supposedly thin voice.

Nazz, recorded in Los Angeles with an old-school hack of a producer named Bill Traut, made Rundgren's talents even more clear. Moving from the Cream-style power-trio blues of 'She's Goin' Down' to the Jimmy Webb orch-pop balladry of 'If That's The Way You Feel' (string arrangement: Todd) was diverse and then some.

'The eclecticism was part of the Beatles formula,' says Rundgren. 'They weren't self-conscious about experimenting and nor were we, even if other people might have thought, What's this with the Beach Boys and the heavy metal in the same song?'

Kurland's hyping of *Nazz* made little appreciable difference to the album's fate, for all the money splashed out on mod togs and haircuts. Released in August 1968, the LP never rose any higher than No. 118. At the end of the year, the band flew to London to start work on their second album, ambitiously planned as a double with the title *Fungo Bat*. After the completion of just one song ('Christopher

Columbus', subsequently included on *Nazz III*), the Musicians' Union learned that the group played instruments as well as sang and swiftly terminated the session.

Returning to New York, the Nazz quickly began to splinter, the retitled *Nazz Nazz* (1969) fomenting the envy and jealousy within the band. Rundgren's deep immersion in the music of Laura Nyro – most evident on the closing, eleven-minute 'A Beautiful Song' – particularly rankled with Stewkey and 'Moody' Thom Mooney.

'I was starting to find myself as a songwriter, which they didn't like,' says Rundgren. 'I pretty much took over the production and the spokesmanship, because whenever Stewkey opened his mouth everyone started laughing.'

It didn't help that John Kurland began playing the members off against each other. 'Kurland had a very sick dynamic going,' says Paul Fishkin, who kept up with Todd during the Nazz period. 'Ultimately he wasn't a manager at all. He was just a publicist and he thought like a publicist.'

Rundgren recalls that the scales only fell from his eyes after Kurland's wife died and he announced that he wanted to give Todd his wife's wedding ring. Supposedly, Kurland wrote a novel about the rise and fall of Nazz, in which (according to the famed rock encyclopaedist Lillian Roxon) Rundgren 'emerges as a sort of anti-hero . . . someone incapable of feeling real love . . . [who is] quite cold and ruthless'. Several years later, tragically, Kurland would commit suicide.

By the time *Nazz III* (made up of tracks from the *Fungo Bat/Nazz Nazz* sessions) appeared in 1970, Rundgren had long fled the coop, moving out of the Great Neck house into a Manhattan apartment owned by the Screen-Gems music publishing company. Profoundly disillusioned by the Nazz experience, he decided to set his sights on producing.

'Todd came out of the Nazz tremendously embittered that it had failed,' says Paul Fishkin. 'He would get people telling him how great he was, and yet he was pretty much broke. It wasn't like he quit music, although from time to time he threatened to quit and become a computer programmer – that was his other choice.'

Falling in with the Greenwich Village fashion crowd, Rundgren hung out with the proprietors of Stone The Crows, a sister store to London's Granny Takes A Trip – 'I got into a much more cooperative lifestyle . . . girls who were real nice to me!'

He decided he was never going to be in a band again.

Rundgren is still wearing his green plaid shorts as he takes the stage in Petaluma. The small theatre is packed for what Todd isn't shy about describing as 'a warm-up show for my imminent appearances in Japan and Shanghai'. Kicking off the gig with a selection of one-man-and-his-axe back pages, he howls his way through 'Hammer In My Heart' and 'Mystified', segueing from the latter into the *faux*-ZZ Top of 'Broke Down And Busted'. 'I'm just in a *manly mood* tonight,' he confides after singing himself ragged.

A significant portion of the show is given over to material from the interactive *No World Order* and the recent *The Individualist*, with Rundgren singing over backing tracks played by the Powerbook. When the disk malfunctions and Todd is obliged to run it again, the thought occurs that a) he is being hoist by his own petard, and b) there might be more dignified ways to earn a living.

A kind of 'shut up n' play yer guitar' mood is detectable in the audience, who breathe an audible sigh of relief when Rundgren shuts down the computer and seats himself behind the piano for an extended suite of eighty-eight-key classics. From a fluffed 'Fidelity' to a Freddie Mercury-esque 'Song Of The Viking', the guy almost gets away with his Victor Borge of Rock act – but not quite.

After another Powerbook karaoke sequence that includes the propulsively danceable 'Family Values', Rundgren – always an entertainingly cynical raconteur onstage – muses on the making of *With A Twist*, a new album of what he terms 'personal standards' rerecorded in a loungecore/bossa nova style in Hawaii. The album is actually a treasure, serving more than anything to remind us just how great Todd's 'greatest hits' ('I Saw The Light', 'Can We Still Be Friends', 'A Dream Goes On Forever' et al.) really are, and to rekindle interest in such overlooked pearls as 'Influenza', 'Fidelity' and 'Love Is The Answer'. Onstage tonight he treats us to his bossa nova version of 'Saw The Light', and to the album's serene reading of Marvin Gaye's 'I Want You'.

And then he sings what may be my favourite Todd Rundgren song of all: 'Cliché'. I am jetlagged but delirious.

Sally Grossman pokes at a plate of Chinese food in the Little Bear, one of the restaurants founded by her late husband Albert in Bearsville, the tiny hamlet that serves as a satellite to the more famous town of Woodstock, New York. Sitting a stone's throw from the disused video studio Albert built for Todd in 1980 – 'the big white elephant building', as she puts it – she is remembering the goofy prodigy who first surfaced in Grossman's New York office in the late summer of 1969.

'Todd was this boy wonder,' she says. 'To be such a renaissance man as he was at the age of twenty-one was very striking. We were spoiled, of course, because we were so used to brilliant people – Dylan, Janis, Butterfield, The Band. But he was like all of them, his talent was already full-blown. It wasn't like you heard him and thought, Gee, with the right songs and the right producer . . .'

In the late summer of 1969, Rundgren was at large in Manhattan. Days were spent girlwatching with Paul Fishkin on St Mark's Place; nights were devoted to scoping rock's *beau monde* at Steve Paul's The Scene. But Todd Rundgren's wastrel days were numbered, since it turned out that he had a major champion in John Kurland's old partner Michael Friedman, by now working as right-hand man to none other than Albert Grossman.

'Albert at that point was spending large chunks of time up in Woodstock, so I ended up being up to my ears,' says Friedman. 'Initially he didn't like Todd or think he was talented, but Todd was with me and I basically presented him as a producer. Even at that point, he was brilliant in the studio.'

'I knew Albert was supposed to be this Allen Klein kind of guy,' says Rundgren. 'It wasn't too long before he started to see something in me, and to give me engineering and production jobs on a trial basis. Very early on, he put me with Libby Titus, who was Levon Helm's girlfriend. And then I went up to Toronto with Robbie Robertson to produce Jesse Winchester's first album. They were pretty happy with the results, so they made me the titular sound guy on The Band's *Stage Fright*.'

It was possibly during the sessions for *Stage Fright*, recorded with a mobile truck at the Woodstock Playhouse in 1970, that Rundgren first acquired a reputation for brattish arrogance – a rep which has accompanied him throughout his career as a producer.

'He stood out like a sore thumb among the Woodstock crowd,' says Mike Friedman. 'He was wearing red velvet pants and had green hair, and he was never accepted socially in that context. He should have been in London or Los Angeles, because he had no use for most of that scene and he thought The Band were a bunch of old farts.'

Friedman told Fred Goodman, author of *The Mansion on the Hill* (which includes a fascinating chapter on Grossman), that he once witnessed Levon Helm chasing Rundgren around the studio 'trying to kill him because he'd made these nasty remarks about Garth Hudson being an old man'.

While he alleges that *Stage Fright* was 'one of the more maddening experiences I had as a sound guy', Rundgren admits somewhat ruefully that he was 'not quite fully fleshed out in terms of socio-political skills'. There would, he says, 'be friction in the studio because of my inexperience and lack of wisdom in dealing with people'.

Yet in a sense the arrogance was endemic to Woodstock and the Grossman stable. Grossman certainly didn't help when he told Rundgren he was going to make him 'the highest-paid producer in the world', and then proceeded to do it. When Rundgren took over the production of Badfinger's *Straight Up* from George Harrison (then busy with the Concert for Bangladesh), Grossman demanded an unheard-of fee for his wunderkind. 'He asked for a shitload of money, more than any producer had ever been paid,' says Rundgren. 'And they paid it because it was Albert Grossman.'

Recalled Badfinger's Joey Molland of the experience: 'Todd was unbelievably rude. He would insult us. He'd say we couldn't play, we couldn't write and couldn't sing and couldn't do anything. I don't know where he got off.' The list of Rundgren clients who would concur with such grievances is long and impressive. 'Nobody ever used him twice,' says Mike Friedman. 'He was just so self-involved. And there was never a thank you – Albert would never have given him those projects if it hadn't been for me.'

A point came, inevitably, when Rundgren thought it might be nice to cut his own album. 'They figured, "Let the kid make a record",' he remembers. He moved out to LA, hired former Electric Prune Jim Lowe to engineer the session, and set to work on his debut album *Runt*. It was very close to brilliant.

'We'd already met him and jammed with him in New York,' says Tony Sales, who with his drummer brother Hunt formed the album's rhythm section. 'But we'd thought he was just this guitar player who sounded like Eric Clapton. We had no idea what he could really do.'

Here was the runt of the rock litter proving, straight off the bat, that he could do it all: the jubilant pop of 'We've Gotta Get You A Woman', a Top 20 hit in November 1970; the Brian Wilson balladry of 'Believe In Me'; the throwaway Big Star trash-rock of 'Who's That Man?'; and the heavenly 'Once Burned', recorded back in New York with Levon Helm and Rick Danko. Here were all the blueprints for Rundgren's styles, stirred into a pot by an impish, Disney-esque wizard not unlike the one pictured on the album's back cover.

'I finished the record and Bearsville were, like, floored by the range and variety of it,' says Rundgren. 'They were even more floored when "We Gotta Get You A Woman" became a hit.' Unfortunately, the song also ran aground on the perilous shore of early '70s feminism. 'The line about women – "they may be stupid, but they sure are fun" – caused a lot of problems when a key female music director in Detroit took exception to it,' chuckles Paul Fishkin, on whose lack of success with the ladies the song was based, and who by this time was himself working for Bearsville. 'And then a women's dorm in Connecticut threatened to blow up the campus radio station if they continued to play the record.'

A group of women who made rather less fuss about the song were the groupies who glommed on to Todd in California – especially Miss Christine, one of the Girls Together Outrageously who'd recorded for Frank Zappa's Straight label. 'Christine was really strange, but Todd liked the adulation he was getting from her,' says Tony Sales, himself stepping out with Miss Pamela (later Des Barres).

Rundgren's adventures in Tinseltown continued with the recording of 1971's *The Ballad Of Todd Rundgren*, another smorgasbord of effortlessly accomplished pop songs and ballads. Rundgren had by this time started smoking pot, and the results, he says, were 'immediate in terms of the refinement of a style'.

'I didn't take any kind of drugs until after the first album. Why? I never do anything because it's a fad. I do it because I need to do it. Pot made me aware of my own thought processes. The symbology of language took on new meaning for me, rather than just reflexive meaning. I didn't look at the drug as recreational or escapist. It was always about going to something.'

What stuck out most of all on *Ballad* were the dazzling tunes, most of them on ballads or mid-tempo tracks written on the piano – songs by the callow troubadour he now slightly dismisses as 'the amateur singer, the amateur piano player, the funk-free boy doing his little song'. Funk-free they may be; unmemorable 'Wailing Wall', 'The Range War' and 'The Ballad (Denny And Jean)' are not. This was Todd tipping his hat to Laura Nyro and Carole King, for sure, but doing it superbly. The album sold a lot less than *Runt* but elicited excellent reviews, including one in *Rock Magazine* from Patti Smith, the proto-punk New York poetess with whom Rundgren had a brief affair and began a lasting friendship.

'We became friends because we were both sort of alien, misfit-type people,' says Smith. 'We were wiry, skinny, hard-working people who didn't quite fit in. Neither one of us was involved with drugs or anything at the time, and it was a relief just to meet somebody to talk to where you didn't have that kind of drug-culture peer pressure to worry about. He was very interested in firecrackers and computers and writing music.'

More important, *The Ballad Of Todd Rundgren* led seamlessly to the breathtaking *Something/Anything?*, in the estimation of many Todd Rundgren's finest achievement. Recorded again in LA, *Something* was never meant to be a double album – a record that now sounds like the missing link between the *White Album* and *Sign O The Times*.

'*Something* was pretty much gonna follow along the lines of *Ballad*,' says Rundgren. 'But it just went and went and went, fuelled by pot and Ritalin. I'd record for eight hours during the day, but I'd also rented an eight-track machine and some synths for other ideas I didn't wanna burn studio time on. So at night I'd take Ritalin and finish writing a couple of songs, then go over to record some more till four or five in the morning. The first three sides of the album were done in three weeks. I was, like, Mr Music.'

No less crammed with treasures than its predecessors, *Something* was also a conscious display of tricks, flaunted with the chutzpah of a rock 'n' roll jester. Seven years before Prince recorded his first album *tout seul*, Rundgren turned the studio into a solipsistic laboratory. One minute he was the guitar-toting hard-rocker of the slow, mesmerising 'Black Maria', the next the power-pop god of the chiming 'Couldn't I Just Tell You', the next the epic balladeer of the ecstatic 'Sweeter Memories'.

'Song Of The Viking' drew on his boyhood love of Gilbert and Sullivan; 'Marlene' – about his pert seventeen-year-old girlfriend Marlene Pinkard – was the most delicately pretty thing he'd ever written. The synth instrumental 'Breathless' anticipated the symphonic interludes of *A Wizard, A True Star*, and 'I Saw The Light' could have been Badfinger in George Harrison mode.

'Go ahead, ignore me,' challenged the ads in the music press, which showed an unhinged Rundgren clutching a stick of dynamite. (In a *Rolling Stone* profile in April 1972, he told Ed McCormack that he envisioned himself becoming 'the Elvis Presley of the '70s'. In the same piece, Patti Smith is quoted as saying that Todd 'has absolutely no heroes'.)

He wasn't ignored for long. 'I Saw The Light' climbed to No. 16 in May '72 and by the summer the album was in the Top 30. Tours supporting Jeff Beck and Alice Cooper gave him important live exposure. At this point, Rundgren met Bebe Buell, a young Virginia-born model on the books of the Eileen Ford agency. 'He rang me up and asked me on a date,' Buell recalls. 'We went to Max's, but we didn't sit in the famous back room because I don't think he thought he would fit in.' Over the course of the next three years, Bebe made sure that she and Todd 'fit in' wherever they damn well pleased. 'I became his social director,' she says. 'A lot of the fun he had, he had because I dragged him by his multicoloured mop of hair. He was always an abstract little buddha, always preferred to be thinking rather than drinking.'

Creem described Todd and Bebe as 'the prettiest stars on the New York turntable'. 'I guess that's what we were,' says Bebe. 'We didn't do the uptown, I'm-too-prissy-to-go-to-Max's act like Mick and David.' For Buell, Rundgren was close to being a father-figure: her own dad had died when she was very young. For Rundgren, Buell was the conduit to a hipper-than-thou scene than he might never have embraced of his own volition. It was Bebe who insisted he see the New York Dolls at the Mercer Arts Center, who marched him up to Mick Jagger at Max's, who first turned him on to magic mushrooms. Which brings us neatly to the tale of Todd Rundgren's radical left turn into the stream-of-consciousness sphere of psychedelia.

'Psychedelics brought me to an awareness of myself that I'd no comprehension of previously,' Rundgren says of his first trips. 'The pot gave me a window into my thinking process, but that's just the process. You don't know your "You" until you've had your ego stripped away, and you realise you're all that stuff. For most people, I think it's a good thing to realise there's an essential part of you that's really sort of alone but that's also very universal. You begin to see your ego elements as these weird, goofy, aberrational appendages.'

Rundgren claims it was surrendering to 'this sort of flow of stuff' that made him question his musical procedures. 'So much musical product is just a function of habit and ego, in that you wanna come off a certain way. It's almost like putting on clothes or make-up. So rarely is the music honest. So many people use music as obfuscation, as a wall between them and the audience.'

A Wizard, A True Star, recorded in late 1972 in Rundgren's new Secret Sound studio on Manhattan's West 24th Street, was Todd 'just mapping my head right on to a record . . . battling against any sort of filtering process'. It was also a gloriously unpunctuated rollercoaster ride through the various musics Rundgren had colonised – a voyage through the cosmos garnished with synthesisers that twinkled like stars, nineteen tracks that leaked into each other or tripped on each other's heels, jumping from the fuzztone metal of 'Rock And Roll Pussy' to the surreal ephemera of 'Dogfight Giggle', from the nonsense of 'Just Another Onionhead' to the anthemic rush of 'When The Shit Hits The Fan', and even finding room for a soul medley that paid homage to Curtis Mayfield, Smokey Robinson and Thom Bell. For some, myself included, *Wizard* was – and is – the most awesomely ambitious rock record ever made.

'I remember an epiphanal moment in the subway one Sunday afternoon when it was real quiet,' says Rundgren. 'I suddenly heard this noise, and I realised it was in my head, and it started freaking me out. It wasn't tinnitus, it was that I'd gotten aware enough of my internal environment that I had reached the noise floor in my head. I could actually hear the hum of my own nervous system.'

'Rock and Roll for the Skull,' raved Patti Smith in her *Circus* review of *Wizard* when it came out in March 1973. Sadly, the record never rose any higher than No. 86, and it baffled many listeners, including the good folks at Bearsville Records.

There was an added complication when the new version of 'Hello, It's Me' mysteriously took off on radio and started making fast for the Top 10. When this relatively straightforward rock'n'soul ballad hit No. 5, *A Wizard, A True Star* started, in comparison, to sound even more wildly offbeat.

'There was bad luck with timing,' says Paul Fishkin, by now in charge of Bearsville. 'We didn't put out "Hello" right away, which was my mistake. Meanwhile Todd was off on his psychedelic adventure, and then a year later "Hello" becomes a hit. At which point we're up against Todd in a completely different mindspace. With five more potential hits on *Something*, he says, No fucking way am I releasing anything else off that album. And the culmination of all the madness is the *Midnight Special* appearance where he gets on the piano singing "Hello, It's Me" and looking like a fucking drag queen.'

'I called it the Man-Eating Peacock outfit,' laughs Bebe Buell. 'I mean, you look back now and it was no nuttier than Peter Gabriel dressed as a sunflower. But we were all so upset. It wasn't self-sabotage; I think Todd thought everyone would like it. But [make-up artist] Nicky Nichols was not only highly creative and highly gay but he was stoned out of his mind with unlimited access to paint and feathers!'

'At this point, Todd was into a sort of existential use-me-as-a-piece-of-art kick, and he let Nicky do whatever he wanted,' recalls Fishkin.

'Todd had iron fucking balls, I will say that about him, but the *Midnight Special* appearance was for me the moment when it all came crashing down. This is his chance to be Elton John and the Beatles and more, and he goes on TV singing this beautiful loping smash-hit ballad and Nicky has made him up with wings and painted his eyes as multicoloured teardrops! The world is watching, and this is the Todd they see!'

Whether or not this was the moment at which Todd Rundgren's career 'came crashing down', it was certainly symbolic of the man's refusal to march to any drum but his own. 'Todd wouldn't take any advice, not even from Albert,' says Mike Friedman. 'He was just so impossible to deal with, you had no influence at all. Todd knew everything, and he always wanted to be five miles down the road from where he was. The bottom line was that the public didn't buy it. He wasn't Stevie Wonder, who was another guy who could do it all but who knew how to make commercial records.'

The first signs that Rundgren was wilfully turning his back on pop success was the 1973 tour with the band that was eventually christened Utopia. Assembling a line-up that included the Sales brothers, keyboard players David Mason and Moogy Klingman, and a demented, Eno-esque synth twiddler named Jean-Yves 'Frog' Labat, Rundgren developed what he remembers as 'an expensive, high-concept, technically complicated show' that featured an eight-foot geodesic dome and exploding flashbulbs. It was not a resounding success.

'Frog was inside the dome, and Hunt sat on top of it,' recalls Tony Sales. 'Hunt was so high up he'd get a one-second delay before he heard the guitars! All of our hair was different colours. Mine was fuchsia-pink and blond, Hunt had a skunk hairdo with a fuckin' tail coming off it. Frog was green, and Todd's just looked like vomit. I remember we spent a shitload of money, but we only did eight gigs.'

'We delivered one memorable show in Cleveland,' says Rundgren. 'But we had a disastrous gig in Philadelphia when this big elaborate intro built to a point of thunderous loudness and then the flashbulbs didn't go off, there was no sound coming out of the guitar amps, and we were just standing there with our thumbs up our asses.'

This Tap-esque fiasco was not enough to deter Todd from pushing the prog-rock envelope still further. A second incarnation of Utopia was unashamedly inspired by the flashy virtuosity of Yes and the Mahavishnu Orchestra.

'Todd was constantly milling over his fucking Yes albums,' remembers Bebe Buell. 'He would wake up every morning and put freaking "Roundabout" on, and it just used to make me insane! Even when I did finally get him to see the New York Dolls, he just thought they were funny. He sat there on the couch as they did a showcase for us, and I just remember him laughing hysterically from beginning to end. The psychedelic experience really did change him, it opened up that third eye. Utopia was a concept he really believed in, musically but also as a potential way of life.'

With the intermittently brilliant double album *Todd* (1974), and then with *Initiation* (1975), Rundgren's music increasingly began to reflect the arcane ideas and theories he was picking up from books on mysticism and Eastern philosophy.

'I hadn't done much dabbling around in the mystical at all,' he says, 'but I was looking at these books and they were explaining some of the phenomena I was experiencing. I started devouring these Eastern philosophies, never buying any of them whole but following the thread of anything that was consonant with what I was experiencing.'

The Utopia theme, which had been tentatively introduced on *Wizard*'s 'International Feel', was officially unveiled on 1974's *Todd Rundgren's Utopia*, complete with all thirty minutes and twenty-two seconds of 'The Ikon'. 'City in my head / Utopia / Heaven in my body / Utopia / It's time for me / For me to go' went the opening track, recorded live in Atlanta. Looking back from our current vantage point, much of the music on the record wasn't bad at all: if we're going to rehabilitate Pomp Rock and posit Radiohead as neo-prog gods, then the least we owe Utopia is a bit of a look-in. Unfortunately, that doesn't change the fact that many people – including those at Bearsville – looked on Utopia with distaste that bordered on alarm.

'Albert was more tolerant of Todd's eclectic tastes than a lot of people,' says Bebe Buell, 'but from a business point of view he decided this just wasn't marketable. Music was getting simpler and Todd Rundgren was getting more complicated.'

The climax of Todd's technocratic madness was undoubtedly the bombastic *Ra* (1977), the first album credited simply to Utopia and the first to feature the trimmed-down four-piece line-up (Rundgren, keyboardist Roger Powell, bassist Kasim Sulton and drummer Willie Wilcox) that would stay together for almost a decade. At a point when the '70s pomp rock of Pink Floyd was being overturned by hoards of scabby punks, Rundgren chose to go on the road with a beyond-*Spinal Tap* stage set built around a twenty-five-foot pyramid and a giant gold sphinx that shot laser beams out of its forehead.

Having witnessed the tour twice in 1977, I can myself vouch for the fact that the *Ra* shows deeply divided Rundgren's audience between prog fiends who dug the laser beams and solo Todd fanatics who wanted to hear songs like 'Couldn't I Just Tell You' – who clung as though their lives depended on it to the fact that the solo album *Faithful* (1976) boasted such nuggets of pop genius as 'Cliché', 'The "Verb To Love"' and 'Love Of The Common Man'.

'There was a whole period where I continued to make Todd Rundgren records but only toured with Utopia,' concedes Rundgren. 'So it became this double life where Utopia was the live thing and drew giant crowds. There was a split in the audience.'

Ironically, even the twenty-year-old Kasim Sulton was bemused by material like the histrionic seven-minute 'Hiroshima'. 'I felt like most people,' he says. 'I really wanted to do the singer-songwriter stuff because that's where I came from. It was difficult for me to reconcile myself to this high-concept tour: I thought, why can't we just do things like 'Couldn't I Just Tell You' for two hours? Wouldn't that be a lot easier and more fun?'

Perhaps it was no surprise that Rundgren began to retreat from the music scene. Although he continued to work as a producer, most notably on Meat Loaf's multimillion-selling *Bat Out Of Hell* (1977), he began to spend increasing amounts of time in the house he'd bought in Mink Hollow, near Woodstock.

'I don't enjoy rock 'n' roll anymore,' Todd told *Creem* in October 1975, three months after the move to Mink Hollow. 'I have to say honestly that I don't enjoy the scene. And I seriously wonder if I was meant to make myself deaf in front of a bunch of people, just playing this super-loud frantic music.' One of the tracks on *Initiation* was a bitter tirade entitled 'The Death Of Rock 'n' Roll'.

'Todd felt under duress,' says Bebe Buell, who lived with him at Mink Hollow. 'I noticed that his boyishness began to diminish and he became harder. I saw him toughen up and lose a lot of his sensitivity. He became an angry young man.'

Exactly how much Rundgren's anger was a result of Bebe's infidelity with Aerosmith's Steven Tyler – the result being the birth of '90s screen starlet Liv Tyler in July 1977 – is something Buell herself doesn't care to consider. When the issue of Liv's paternity finally became public in 1991, it led to a complete cessation of relations between Rundgren and Buell, who'd split up a year after Liv's birth in 1978.

March 1978 brought the release of the aptly-titled *Hermit Of Mink Hollow*, a splendid return to solo melodiousness that included a smattering of classic break-up songs ('Too Far Gone', 'Hurting For You', the oft-covered 'Can We Still Be Friends'). Entirely performed and recorded by Rundgren in the new Utopia Sound studio he'd built at Mink Hollow, *Hermit* should have been a much bigger hit than it was. Following on its heels that year was *Back To The Bars*, a double live album of Rundgren's best-loved songs recorded – as a kind of anthology – at the suggestion of Paul Fishkin.

Meanwhile, Utopia did a volte-face from the pomp of *Ra*, releasing the decidedly poppier *Oops! Wrong Planet* (1977), an album summarised by Roger Powell as 'an Armageddon-ish earth-on-the-skids opera' and by *Goldmine* as 'power pop meets *Blade Runner*'. The inimitable Rundgren melodies were still there in abundance, but so were the new sounds of Powell, Sulton and Wilcox: Todd made a point of stressing that the group was a democracy. By 1980, on the moderately successful *Adventures In Utopia*, the band had climbed aboard the new wave bandwagon and were busy in the studio with the burgeoning technology of '80s pop: the result was sub-par, even if 'Set Me Free' actually managed to dent the Top 30.

'With that whole Utopia thing, he lost not only me but hundreds of thousands of people,' says Sally Grossman. 'The whole misguided notion that they were doing it all together, when in retrospect all they did was drag Todd down . . . in my candid opinion.'

Rundgren himself felt that Utopia were never given a fair chance by Bearsville: 'We never sold records commensurate with the size of the crowds we drew – mostly because, whatever the fans thought, Bearsville did not take the records seriously.'

Another person who thinks Utopia were hindered from making it is Chris Andersen, who became Rundgren's principal sound engineer in 1977. 'Albert never thought Utopia was very good,' Andersen says, talking at his Nevessa studio in Woodstock. 'There was a love-hate relationship with Albert all the time.'

An alternative explanation, Andersen concedes, is that Rundgren was and is 'a completely unmanageable personality', someone who, when presented with an opportunity to have success, shunned it. 'When *Adventures* did well, instead of buckling down and capitalising on it, he went off in another direction . . . on purpose, I think. In some ways he's afraid of success.'

Kasim Sulton concurs with this: 'Todd never did anything to please anybody else. After *Adventures*, the most successful record we had, we wanted to follow up with another record like it. So what does Todd do? He announces that we're gonna do a Beatles parody record [*Deface The Music*]. And John Lennon was killed a month after the album came out.'

Rundgren's attention, in any case, was being diverted towards toys other than Utopia. '*Bat Out Of Hell* became a giant cash cow for me,' he says, 'and it created an incredible amount of money that I found all kinds of ways to squander.'

Squander it he did, first and foremost on the new video studio he and Grossman built at Bearsville. Ever the techno-pioneer, Todd had first merged video images with computer-generated electronic music on the first Utopia tour in 1974. Now he was again ahead of the curve, producing videos that composited live action with computer graphics. ('Time Heals' would become the second video ever to be played on MTV, after Buggles' 'Video Killed The Radio Star'.)

'Rundgren by 1980 was a town industry,' wrote P. Smart in his book *Rock and Woodstock*. 'He hired dozens of people to do studio dates, to put together a body of video work. Employees came and went, complaining about his ever-increasing ego, unprofessional ways, shrewishness and miserliness.'

'Todd's lack of communication skills became a real problem,' says Chris Andersen. 'I mean, you can make records by yourself, and write a computer graphics programme by yourself, but when you try to do video it requires clear communication of the idea and of what all the jobs are.'

Other people think Rundgren was simply too far ahead of his time. 'I wouldn't say Todd was exactly squandering money,' says Kasim Sulton. 'But things could maybe have been done a little differently. When they were putting the video studio together, Todd would say we were gonna get all kinds of production work up there – and this was when MTV hadn't even started!'

On 13 August 1980, four masked men broke into the Mink Hollow house, bound and gagged Rundgren and his new girlfriend Karen 'Bean' Darvin, and loaded up a truck with various items of studio equipment. 'One of the stories I heard was that one of them was actually whistling some of his songs while they were going round the house,' says Chris Andersen. The intruders were never apprehended, and Rundgren was badly shaken by the experience.

Almost as traumatic was the fact that just a few days before he shot John Lennon in December 1980, Mark Chapman made a trip up to Woodstock to look for Rundgren. It turned out that Rundgren had replaced Lennon in his obsessive affections.

The connection is particularly ironic when one considers Lennon's 'Open Lettuce to Sodd Runtwhistle', published in *Melody Maker* in September 1974 after Rundgren had slagged off the music of the ex-Beatles. 'I think the real reason you're mad at me is 'cause I didn't know who you were at the Rainbow in LA,' Lennon wrote. 'When I found out later, I was cursing 'cause I wanted to tell you how good you were.'

The entirely DIY album *Healing* (1981) was written and recorded partly as therapy after these dreadful events. Primarily using synthesisers, Rundgren used the record to make a moving plea for compassion in an increasingly brutal world. As the '80s progressed, moreover, Rundgren's writing began to address society's ills head-on, not least on the 1982 Utopia release *Swing To The Right*.

A new contract with Al Khoury's Network label brought *Utopia* (1982), an album of new wave power-pop in a style redolent of XTC, themselves soon to be produced by Rundgren. By the time the band had turned in the last of three very listenable electro-rock albums for Passport [*Oblivion*, *P.O.V.* and *Trivia*], band morale had hit an all-time low.

'We saw less money upfront, and the tours were winding down,' says Kasim Sulton. 'We weren't expanding our fan base. Willie wanted to do a record one way, and Todd wanted to do it another way. Roger and I were sort of caught in the middle. Willie and Todd really butted heads after *Oblivion*. I think *P.O.V.* is one of the better Utopia records, but it was a nightmare to make. People yelling and screaming at each other, Willie with drum machines breaking down on him and Todd saying he could just as well do this by himself.'

In effect, that is what Rundgren did do. With Utopia taking an indefinite sabbatical, Todd recorded *A Capella*, a bold album composed entirely of solo vocal tracks that also marked the end of Todd's relationship with Bearsville, leading eventually to a deal with Warner Brothers and to his move to San Francisco.

'Albert connived that *A Capella* was not acceptable,' he says. 'I'd worked really hard on the record and thought I'd achieved as complete a concept as I'd ever visualised, and yet he refused to accept it.' As it turned out, Grossman died in 1986 on a plane to London.

For a while, Rundgren virtually commuted between Woodstock and San Francisco, continuing to produce acts at Utopia Sound while at the same time cultivating a new circle of acquaintances among what he calls 'the artsy counter-cultural elite' of the Bay Area. More often than not, his bread-and-butter cashflow came from work as a studio gun-for-hire.

'His own projects were the joy of his life,' recalls Chris Andersen. 'He liked to work on the floor, and there'd be keyboards all over the floor, wires everywhere. In contrast to that were the production projects. There were some artists he was really interested in working with, like Patti Smith, the Psychedelic Furs, the Tubes and Cheap Trick. With others it was just a job, and he wasn't good at pretending he wasn't interested. He'd sit on a bed at the back of a studio reading computer magazines while I engineered.'

Ironically, says Andersen, one of the projects to which Rundgren genuinely did commit himself was XTC's superb *Skylarking* (1986) – ironically, because the band's Andy Partridge and Colin Moulding expended a great deal of energy slagging Todd off after the record was finished. 'It may be one of the best records he's ever made, and yet he got such shit from the band in the press,' says Andersen. 'That had to hurt quite a bit. They complained about everything, from the grittiness of the toilet paper to Todd smoking pot in the studio.'

Bebe Buell thinks that Partridge was 'as much a control freak and as diversely brilliant as Todd was', and that putting two such scientists in one laboratory was always going to be a disaster.

Chris Andersen says the most stressful part of any Rundgren production was always the mixdown stage: 'Todd developed a technique of basically ramming the mix down the artist's throat. He wouldn't allow the artist in the studio – the band would be sequestered down in the guest house. Then I'd call down and tell them to come up and listen, whereupon Todd would turn the volume up to a hundred and thirty decibels, pin their ears against the back of the wall, and say, Well, whaddya think?'

Another act in whom Rundgren took at least a putative interest was the Pursuit of Happiness, a Canadian band led by Todd disciple Moe Berg. Berg's songs took their cue directly from Todd, many of them sounding not unlike tracks from such Utopia albums as *Oblivion* and *P.O.V.*

'When I hear about people not getting along with Todd in the studio, it's totally understandable to me,' says Berg, who vividly remembers the *Love Junk* sessions at Mink Hollow in the summer of 1988. 'Fortunately I sort of got off on all his antics. Like, he'd read while you were doing a take. I'd look up and see him reading a magazine with his feet up on the console. Every once in a while he'd stop you and say, You sped up!, and that was it. When he found out that 'Survival' [on 1990's *One-Sided Story*] was gonna be five minutes long, he went, Oh my God, I better get a *book*! The whole idea was that you were boring him to tears.'

On the other hand, Berg says that Rundgren was an invaluable help at the preproduction stage. 'With "Walking In The Woods" [*Love*

Junk], for example, he said the music was too happy for the subject matter, so I rewrote the chorus and it became a lot darker.'

At the tail end of the '80s, Rundgren recorded one of the greatest albums of his career. *Nearly Human* (1989) had its inception in three things: Warner Brothers' request for commercially viable music, Todd's desire to get back to live, full-band sound and a new immersion in the black soul music of his youth.

'It was the first time I had built soul generally into the concept,' he reflects. 'What really inspired me was Terence Trent D'Arby. When I first saw him perform, I was knocked out by the intense dynamics, the fact that he sung like a motherfucker, and the fact that he was on this quest as well. And I went back and listened to a lot of Marvin Gaye.'

Bolstering the soulfulness of the album was Bobby Womack, who sang alongside Rundgren on 'The Want Of A Nail', and a large gospel-style chorus of backing vocalists. Suffice to say that there was barely a duff track on the record, and that songs like 'Fidelity', 'Parallel Games' and 'The Waiting Game' must count among the most euphoric and uplifting music of Rundgren's *œuvre*.

'I thought *Nearly Human* was brilliant,' says Sally Grossman, who threw parties for Todd in New York and LA when the album was released. 'But people were not interested, and are still not interested. Anybody I got to go to those shows raved about them, but I couldn't get many people to go. It's like this complete perception problem. Albert used to say, We know you're capable of making commercial records, and Michael Ostin at Warners would say the same thing. The line must have gone down and become institutionalised: Todd, we know you can do something that appeals to more people. I mean, it gets scary when you can't sell a hundred thousand records.'

By the early '90s, Rundgren was back to being a cult artist without a major-label deal. Not that it affected the man's prodigious output, or the quality of his music. The fifteen songs he wrote for the off-Broadway musical version of Joe Orton's Beatles screenplay *Up Against It* brilliantly utilised Todd's early love of show tunes, veering from the influence of Gilbert and Sullivan to that of Brecht and Weill. The minor hoopla surrounding his interactive *No World Order* CD (1992) obscured the fact that it contained some charged techno-rap diatribes; the same goes for 1994's *The Individualist*.

Yet it was difficult not to feel that, for all the vaunted Rundgren rhetoric about 'aggressive personal evolution', he had become a desperately marginalised figure, of interest only to the legion of Todd obsessives with whom he communicated via his websites. The culmination of the whole process was his decision to give up on record companies and sell his music directly to his fans through the net – hardly radical now, but (as always with Rundgren) too far ahead of its time.

'He's his own worst enemy, commercially,' says Sally Grossman. 'By doing this to himself, he cannot fulfil the visions he has because he has to do everything on the cheap. It steadily gets more myopic. In the last few years of going to shows he hasn't got a new audience, partially because if you went to a show it was so fucking insular. It's not good for him or the music.'

How insular does it feel this Saturday night at Slim's, the San Francisco club founded by Boz Scaggs back in 1988? Actually, not very: there's a nicely diverse mix of people crammed into this spacious, revamped restaurant, testament to the esteem in which Rundgren is still held in the city that was his adopted home for over a decade. From the moment he breaks into the sludgy fuzz-rock of *Todd*'s No. 1 'Lowest Common Denominator', Todd – attired in a fetching turquoise sarong – sounds considerably more together than he was in Petaluma.

But the same sense of slight unease descends on the spectators when Todd fires up the Powerbook and runs through 'Temporary Sanity' and 'Beloved Infidel' from *The Individualist*. A singer with the support act had cheekily remarked that Todd was 'gonna do some karaoke and home movies for you tonight', and the swipe wasn't so wide of the mark. Despite calls for 'The Last Ride' and 'Just One Victory', Rundgren concentrates on lesser-known material like 'Compassion' and 'Free, Male And 21'. He sings 'I Saw The Light' in its new Astrud Gilberto incarnation – 'we've been lounging since before lounge was hip' – and he returns to the interminable one-man jam of 'Mystified', torturing his vocal cords and parodying the figure of the blues-rock guitar god.

As I watch him, alone on the stage, it strikes me that there's a splendid isolation about the guy that's also a little sad. It's as if he's painted himself into a corner from which there's no way back to the musical mainstream. Should that matter? Does he care?

'I started changing when I realised that, when you get to my age, there's no way to make a comeback,' he says to me as we wind up a four-hour conversation in his San Francisco loft. 'Especially if you haven't gone that far away to start with. I could still make a healthy living just off my musical output if I was a little looser about producing people I don't really want to produce. There are any amount of compromises I could take on, and even if I don't my family can live fairly comfortably. I'm not particularly smart about money, and when I get a big chunk of it from Meat Loaf, what do I do? Blow it all on a video studio.

'At certain points you have to make decisions: to continue on your current path or make necessary changes. I made personal changes that are nobody's business but mine, but I also assessed my position in the scheme of musical things and came up with what to me were completely logical conclusions. The problem was, I had to redefine myself one way or another. I could have decided to redefine musically, take the Neil Young route and redeem myself with the kids and squeeze I don't know how many more years out of my career. But I realised it wasn't just about the style of music, it was about deconstructing the whole musical process – including the delivery medium.'

'He's always been the Davy Crockett of rock 'n' roll,' says Bebe Buell. 'He thinks of all these things before everyone else, beats the door down and then gets none of the money or credit. The pioneers are always the people who either have to die or take the flak. Has Prince ever uttered Todd's name? I met Prince when he was sixteen, when Todd played Minneapolis in 1974 – this tiny little person with huge hair standing backstage who wanted to meet Todd. And Todd did his usual "Oh, hi, kid" number, and Prince was like, "I play everything and I'm real talented . . ."

'Todd should never be under financial duress. A lot of multiplatinum artists were born from the little eclectic buddha called Todd Rundgren, and not one of them has admitted it. Now I just think of him as the lonely wayward genius. He doesn't realise how many people still love him. There's a kindness and goodness inside of him. He's like a wounded creature who's been hurt so much that outsiders probably don't notice these gestures of his as much as I do.'

'He has always been a very kind and personable friend,' says Patti Smith. 'He's very supportive, and he's a good father. He was very kind to my children after my husband passed away. See, stardom and fame are fleeting things, they're totally relative. The fact that Todd did exactly what he wanted to and didn't bend to trends is admirable to me. When you look back on your life, wouldn't you rather have been a pioneer than a rich person who cashed in?'

'Todd was more of a specialist thing than, say, Bowie or even Iggy,' says Tony Sales, who's played with both those men. 'It's almost the way my father [cult comic Soupy Sales] was: a unique talent to be appreciated by the people who understand the joke. With Todd, you had to understand the joke.'

'Todd thought that eventually everyone would get it,' says his old friend Paul Fishkin. 'By the time he got the credibility, all it did was reinforce the cult even more. And yes, he did have continual problems getting along with people, because his defensiveness caused him to be arrogant. It made for a tumultuous time: the juxtaposition of the people around him who knew he could be huge and the fanatics who would have done anything for him. And I think the saddest part of all this is that, underneath it all, he was very disappointed.'

'The things I'm involved in, and the ideas that I have, are as accessible and as fascinating as anyone's music,' Todd Rundgren told *NME*'s Paul Morley fifteen years ago. 'It's not my loss if no one discovers it. I'm living it all the time. I have more important priorities. By the time people discover where I am, if they ever do, I'll be someplace else anyway.'

Catch you there in the next millennium.

1998

Wayward Son: The Ballad of Alex Chilton

The sun is going down on Memphis, site of rock 'n' roll's immaculate conception and explosive birth. On a warm spring evening, the Mississippi's purplish-brown waters are swirling and eddying beside me. In the distance loom the empty towers of the city's devastated downtown centre. People drift into a performance area demarcated as 'The Budweiser Stage', one of several set up for this weekend's annual 'Memphis in May' festival.

A few feet from where I'm sitting backstage, a shaven-headed streak-of-piss in a mustard-yellow shirt and black winkle-pickers is pacing restlessly about. This will be the largest gathering Alex Chilton has played to in many a month, and it may also be the strangest one. For tonight the retooled Big Star, returning to their home town for a rare appearance, are playing third on the bill beneath jam band Rusted Root and redoubtable hard rocker Sammy Hagar.

After several minutes Chilton comes over and perches beside me. When he says nothing I try to break the ice with a facile quip about Sammy H joining him onstage for a duet of 'September Gurls'. Chilton grunts blankly in response. Directly in front of us is a vast, gleaming-red eighteen-wheeler unloading Hagar's equipment for his headline set.

Emerging from Big Star's trailer at this point is Jody Stephens, the drummer who first played with Chilton twenty-eight years ago. Wearing black gloves, he's warming up his wrists and confessing to a mild attack of nerves. After just one two-hour rehearsal and a brace of shows – played as usual with guitarist Jon Auer and bassist Ken Stringfellow of Seattle power-popsters the Posies – Big Star are about to plunge into the deep end.

Jennifer, a DJ from Memphis station Rock 103, extends a big thank you to 'all our sponsors, and of course Budweiser'. To her left, Alex Chilton is raking his fingers over his guitar strings and sizing up the sparse crowd. 'You guys ready for some o' that homegrown stuff?' squeaks Ms 103. ''Cause we got an old Memphis favourite here for ya!!'

When Chilton fires up the intro riff to 'In The Street', that timeless anthem of youthful ennui and bored cool from Big Star's 1972 debut #1 Record, people suddenly swarm towards the stage. 'Hangin' out, down the street / The same old thing we did last week . . .' How great to hear a song that so epitomises the musical tension which made Big Star's such a sharp sound in the flabby quagmire of early '70s American rock. Rifferama and melody, danger and beauty, power and pop: in these conjunctions lies all of Big Star's angry-sweet genius.

'Big Star sounded like someone was speaking to me,' says Chris Stamey, who played with Chilton in the late '70s. 'Where I grew up in North Carolina, everything was the Allman Brothers and it didn't have anything to do with the way I felt. The Big Star records were invigorating and exuberant and they contrasted with how draggy music had become at that point.'

'We were all pretty absorbed with the Move and Wishbone Ash, and along comes this band that's playing this beautiful, clean, twinkey, crazed pop from Memphis of all places,' says Peter Holsapple, Stamey's partner in the dBs. 'We clung to those Big Star records as oases of melody and short songs and concise harmonies and interesting production.'

By the late '80s, the group's influence had extended still further. R.E.M.'s Peter Buck claimed Big Star 'served as a Rosetta stone for a whole generation'. The Replacements recorded a song called, simply, 'Alex Chilton'. The Bangles covered 'September Gurls'. The dark Big Star Third became a totemic record for a new generation of Chilton devotees: This Mortal Coil did 'Holocaust' and Jeff Buckley sang 'Kanga Roo' in live performances. The most clearcut influence was on

Teenage Fanclub, who went so far as to name their second album *Thirteen* after Chilton's shimmering ode to teenage lust on *#1 Record*.

'I think we were struck most by the clean sparkle and Byrdsiness of the sound, and by the way the guitars had been produced,' says the Fannies' Norman Blake. 'On those Big Star records, the chords are really brilliant against the melodies.'

'I love the way they sang,' says Elliott Smith, who regularly covers 'Thirteen' onstage. 'It was just really cool to hear Americans singing that way, because at the time it was all gravelly-voiced guys.'

The strange twist to this tale is that Alex Chilton himself has always had mixed feelings about the music he made with Big Star. While he's happy to sing the lighter, poppier songs at Memphis in May, he delegates the darker, more passionate material to his hired guns. It's Jon Auer who sings the aching 'Back Of A Car', Ken Stringfellow who gamely tackles the glacial 'Daisy Glaze'.

Later that night, according to volunteers working at the festival, Alex Chilton will, in a fit of post-gig pique, return to the band's trailer dressing room and trash it. 'When Alex comes back to town, the demons come back,' says *Third* producer and Memphis legend Jim Dickinson. 'Those demons are still alive.'

Dickinson, legendary veteran of landmark sessions from the Stones' 'Wild Horses' to Dylan's *Time Out Of Mind*, is one of the seminal figures of Memphis rock'n'soul. He also happens to have known Alex Chilton since he was nothing more than 'a little towheaded, bare-footed kid'.

'He was kind of an art brat,' Dickinson recalls of the boy who was born on 28 December 1950, and grew up in an unusually hip home in midtown Memphis. 'Alex's father Sidney kind of hung out with musicians, and his mother ran a little art gallery. The first time I saw Alex, he couldn't have been more than ten or eleven. William Eggleston [the photographer whose famous lightbulb shot graces the cover of *Radio City*] had given him peyote, and his eyes were like that scene in *The Wind in the Willows* where Mr Toad's eyes distended.'

Dickinson also knew another Memphis kid who was just two weeks younger than Chilton. The son of a successful restaurateur, Christopher

Bell came from a rather different part of town, the privileged enclave of Germantown. There was little or no music in the Bell mansion, a fact that didn't stop the moody and introverted Christopher, born 12 January 1951, becoming besotted with the Beatles and their British Invasion contemporaries.

'Chris was a dreamer,' adds Bill Cunningham, who played with Bell in a band called the Jynx. 'He felt that we were going to do the same thing the Beatles had done. All our songs were all based around the Beatles and the Kinks. And Alex would always be in the audiences at the places we played.'

Bands like the Jynx and the Jokers were the white, East Memphis counterpart to the funkier South Memphis sound of Stax. 'The people who made the rock 'n' roll records and the soul records were from south of the tracks or out in redneckville,' says Richard Rosebrough, who drummed in teenage bands with Bell. 'Our scene was Memphis prep: snotty-nosed, spoiled-brat Germantown kids.'

'Whenever anybody talks about Memphis, it's not long before they start using terms like "melting pot",' says John Fry, the Ardent studio owner whose engineering had so much to do with the Big Star albums. 'You couldn't grow up around here without being in the middle of soul music culture, but we were real English music fans too.'

Like Chris Bell, Alex Chilton was too young to appreciate the redneck god that was '50s Elvis. 'I didn't get really caught up in the rock scene until the Beatles came along,' he told Robert Gordon in the latter's absorbing book *It Came From Memphis*. 'The rock 'n' roll that first really captured me was mid-'60s British pop music.'

Not that Alex Chilton was averse to soul, or to black culture in general. When he would occasionally make a guest appearance with the Jynx, more often than not he'd sing an R & B or soul song. Indeed, it was Chilton's gruff rendition of Bobby Hebb's hit 1966 'Sunny' at the school's talent show that convinced Central High band the Devilles that they'd finally found their new frontman.

It is ten days since Big Star played Memphis, and tonight Alex Chilton is fronting a very different act in a dank Manhattan bodega on St Mark's Place. The Sunday night crowd is a mix of downtown Chilton diehards and outer-borough oldies nuts who remember when the Box Tops were the hottest thing on *American Bandstand*.

Sheathed in a thrift-store sharkskin jacket with thin lapels and sporting a still thinner tie, Chilton twirls his microphone and puts on his best soul-man moves for 'Cry Like A Baby', a single which reached No. 2 in the spring of 1968. It's hard to equate the man who sang 'Holocaust' with the amiable guy who horses around onstage with bassist Bill Cunningham.

When the skinny sixteen-year-old Chilton showed up at the Devilles' audition in late '66, he had holes in his jeans and wore a black T-shirt – a foretaste of wardrobes to come. By the end of the year the Chilton-fronted Devilles had renamed themselves the Box Tops.

One morning in January 1967 the quintet found themselves in Memphis' red-hot American Recording studio. For the Tops' first session, producer Dan Penn had earmarked a slice of chugging white soul called 'The Letter'. It was the start of a relationship between producer and singer in which Chilton would be little more than Penn's puppet: as anyone familiar with Penn's own voice will attest, Chilton's throaty Roy Head-meets-Roger Chapman style was uncannily close to that of his mentor.

'I first met Alex when Dan would come into Ardent and overdub stuff on Box Tops things,' says John Fry. 'Alex would usually just sit there on the floor and not say anything. It was almost like he was sort of an onlooker rather than a participant.' But if the Box Tops were a southern Rascals, Chilton was an American Stevie Winwood. Like Winwood, he would soon tire of Top 40 pop and aspire to something altogether hipper.

The Tops' 'bubble-soul' formula gave them a grand total of seven hits, but for Chilton it was a blunt initiation into the realities of pop exploitation. By 1969 he was starting to assert himself as a songwriter. The band's fourth and final album, *Dimensions*, included Chilton songs like the stately 'Together' and the bare-bones blues song 'I Must Be The Devil'.

'It was obvious that Alex was very talented and that he was going to continue in music,' says Bill Cunningham. Following 'Soul Deep', which snuck into the American Top 20 in the autumn of 1969, Chilton announced to the others that he was quitting.

'The first time I really talked to Alex, the Box Tops were careening to a close,' recalls Jim Dickinson. 'He had been so obviously exploited that I may well have been the first person who ever talked to him sympathetically about his production ideas.'

Early in 1970, Chilton went into Ardent and recorded a number of tracks for a projected solo album. More than they anticipate Big Star itself, the boogiefied blues-rock songs – later released as *1970* – prefigure the music Chilton would make after Big Star had disbanded.

Chilton's rejection of Box Tops pop not only returned him to an early love for Bob Dylan but led him to embrace bands like the Velvet Underground – the dark antithesis of the Tops' cheery pop-soul. So much so, indeed, that in mid-1970 he left Memphis and made his way up to New York.

'The first time I met Alex, we both lived on the same block in the heart of the Village,' says Bud Scoppa, a rock writer who had published a book on the Byrds. 'He seemed mysterious and enigmatic even then, and I couldn't connect him with the guy who'd sung in the Box Tops.'

It was in New York that Chilton picked up an old Blind Willie McTell riff from Keith Sykes, a folkie friend from Memphis. The riff metamorphosed into 'In The Street', one of several songs Chilton would bring to Big Star when he returned home. Perhaps the most striking thing about his new material was that he was singing it in a completely different voice.

'Something happened when he was in New York,' says Jim Dickinson. 'And in defence of Alex against people complaining that he won't do that old Box Tops voice anymore, he can't. I've heard him try.'

John Fry is standing in Ardent's Studio A – the big room where *#1 Record* was finished and *Radio City* and *Big Star Third* recorded in their entirety – and talking about the Big Star years.

Fry is an unlikely figure in the band's story, an avuncular, conservative-looking man who looks more like the manager of a plastics factory than the exceptional engineer/producer he is. (Like many of the people who work for him at Ardent – including Jody Stephens – he is a born-again Christian.)

As Fry tells it, the story of Big Star began when a group of young musicians began hanging around the original Ardent studio on National Street and were gradually pressed into doing something useful. One of the apprentices in question was Chris Bell, who was still trying to put together his ideal neo-Beatles band with high school friend and bass player Andy Hummel.

In 1970, Hummel recommended a drummer he knew who was then playing in the Memphis State University production of *Hair*. 'Andy came to see *Hair* and said they were putting a band together and was I interested in coming and jamming,' says Jody Stephens, born 4 October 1952. By the time Alex Chilton came to see Chris Bell's band play at a local Veterans of Foreign Wars hall, the group was called either Ice Water or Rock City: no one seems to remember which.

'Knowing both Chris and Alex individually as I did, I knew that they both had something to offer one another,' says Richard Rosebrough. 'They were hanging out together, trading off ideas. And being in the confines of Ardent studios made it all work, because it was a permissive environment.' To Jody Stephens, moreover, the contrast in the two men's personalities instantly suggested a Lennon–McCartney dialectic, with Chilton as John and Bell as Paul.

During early rehearsals at Ardent, the band would often cross the street for hamburgers and milkshakes at Sweden Kream. Next door to the little eaterie, which stands there to this day, was one of a chain of Memphis supermarkets called Big Star. In a moment of tongue-in-cheek hubris, Bell and Chilton decided this was a fitting name for their band. 'I think John Fry must have felt we could be stars,' says Jody Stephens. 'You can't go into a project like that with as much heart and diligence as he did without really believing in it.'

Recording at Ardent through the winter of 1971–2, Big Star were like any young male band, high on the adrenalin of creativity and camaraderie. 'When they were making *#1 Record*, everybody seemed to get along fine,' says Fry. Yet Chilton has said that Chris Bell – unofficially the band's leader – 'didn't really want the rest of us fooling around in the studio, [that] that was his business'.

Were Big Star ever a real band? Jim Dickinson calls them a 'hybrid studio group', a description borne out by Jody Stephens: 'None of us really kind of hung out together. At the end of the day, I think we were all kind of ready to be with our girlfriends.'

While the question of authorship within Big Star has never been exactly clear, the high spots on *#1 Record* – there was still more wry hubris in the album's title – would seem to be Chilton's. The man himself has described songs like 'Thirteen' and 'The Ballad of El Goodo' as 'groping around', but their diaphanous melodicism has endured better than the strained hard rock of Bell's 'Feel' and 'Don't Lie To Me'.

Big Star barely played in support of *#1 Record*'s release: a couple of shows in Memphis and one each in New Orleans and Oxford, Mississippi. 'We thought we were the Beatles, and the Beatles weren't touring anymore,' is the way Chilton has told it. 'Chris was too high and mighty to bother with gigs.' Chilton makes it plain that Big Star were never popular in their own home town: 'People who sounded like Led Zeppelin and Ten Years After and all these fledgling heavy metal bands – that's what people wanted to hear.'

The more fundamental point is that Big Star, stranded in a town that had zero interest in their music, badly lacked the machinery that might have propelled them into the big time. 'I think they probably would have toured and played more had anybody wanted them to,' says John Fry. 'But it's also true that there wasn't any management except for whatever we could do here.' Even more of a handicap was the fact that Ardent had entered into a distribution agreement with Stax, a label that was a) rooted in black soul music and had little understanding of the white pop market, and b) in dire financial straits.

Big Star Mark 1 quickly started to implode. Not even glowing reviews of *#1 Record* made up for the disappointment felt, especially by Chris Bell. Indeed, Bell's pain was exacerbated by the fact that what press the band received focused almost exclusively on Alex Chilton. 'I think he was really dissatisfied with living in Alex's shadow,' says Jody Stephens. 'The press we were getting was spotlighting Alex because Alex was a bridge to the reader.'

Couple this with Chilton's more aggressive personality and it was inevitable that Bell would at some point lose control of his own group. But the truth may be more complex than that scenario suggests. 'Chris was moody a lot of the time, and you never really knew what he was thinking or what was going on,' says Richard Rosebrough.

In fact, Bell was virtually at war with himself. Leaning heavily towards Christianity even at this early stage, he felt terrible guilt over his use of drink and drugs. There was also the small matter of his homosexuality.

'People look at Big Star in terms of, "They knew chords like the Beatles knew chords",' says Chris Stamey, 'but it's the Christianity and the homosexuality which provided the friction behind that spark. There's really no way around that.'

'Chris was tormented about his sexuality and his drug addiction,' says Jon Tiven, a rock writer turned producer who worked with both Bell and Chilton. 'He was completely gay and fighting it. I mean, he would go around with the Bible all the time and try to live his life by it. And it was very difficult for him, because he loved drugs – particularly Dilaudid – and he was gay.'

By late 1972, Bell was almost suicidally depressed. In addition to Chilton's usurping him as the focal point of Big Star, he'd learned some unsavoury things about Stax's business practices that only further disillusioned him.

At the end of 1972 Bell quit the group, a departure which Alex Chilton has perhaps disingenuously claimed 'was always mysterious to me . . . all I knew is one day he kind of blew up and was gone'. For a while it looked as though Big Star was over too.

Chilton, on a creative roll, put together a new group with Richard Rosebrough on drums and Danny Jones on bass. The trio only ever played one show, but Chilton and Rosebrough started going into Ardent in the early hours of the morning. Both 'Mod Lang' and 'She's A Mover', rough'n'ready homages to English rock, were recorded during these drug-fuelled marathons; both wound up on *Radio City* alongside 'What's Goin' Ahn', a dread-filled ballad graced by weeping guitars and a scared, chilling vocal.

'When I listen back to "What's Goin' Ahn", I know that it has a dark feeling to it,' says Rosebrough. 'Feelings were hurt and friendships were becoming fragmented. Alex had taken control and was starting to get wild and crazy. And nobody knew how to react, so they just followed him and did what he said.'

The song's darkness may be what has made Chilton all but disown it. 'It's like they're not really rock 'n' roll songs,' he remarked of 'What's Goin' Ahn' and 'You Get What You Deserve'. 'I don't know what they are. They're some kind of psychodramatic tunes about something that doesn't have any particular place in music.'

For Chilton, the cult of Big Star is all about sad geeks who like to wallow in musical pain — in his words, 'confused twenty-year-old college students'. But the music's strange, troubled mood and phrasing speak volumes louder than his covers of Dean Martin's 'Volare' or Brenton Wood's 'Oogum Boogum Song'.

'There was a lot that went down in those days that none of us wants to live again,' says Richard Rosebrough. 'A lot of people have theorised that he was disappointed that Big Star didn't work out, but I can see him sitting here right now saying I put out this 45 two years ago and it's just the best song I ever wrote. And what do you say?'

The joke goes like this: if everyone who heard the Velvet Underground in the '60s went on to form a band, then everyone who heard Big Star in the early '70s went on to become a rock critic. Exactly how much this had to do with the 'Rock Writers of the World' convention staged in Memphis in the spring of 1973 by Ardent publicist John King is a matter of conjecture.

'*Everybody* was there,' recalls Bud Scoppa. 'I remember Cameron Crowe walking around barefoot. Lester Bangs and Richard Meltzer. We just all loved this band. They played the set as a three-piece and we thought they were the godhead.'

Jon Tiven, who helped to compile the list of invited critics, says the twenty-three-year-old Alex Chilton was 'so enthused at the reception that he decided to convert his solo record into a second Big Star record'. Regrouping at Ardent, the band sifted through a new batch of songs, some of them left over from the Chris Bell days. (Some say that 'O My Soul', *Radio City*'s blazingly funky opener, was entirely Bell's work, and that 'Back Of A Car' was also his in great part.)

Whatever the truth behind the writing credits, the *Radio City* songs were sublime. 'Back Of A Car' was a brilliant Byrds/Beatles amalgam, a desperate ode to teenage heartache and aimlessness. 'September Gurls', with its misspelt nod to the Beach Boys, was an instant power pop classic rooted in Chilton's obsession with astrology. 'Daisy Glaze' and 'Life Is White' were uncategorisable slices of 'musical psychodrama' – songs about fucked-up relationships sung and arranged as statements of dread and ennui.

Stephens' drumming was inspired throughout, not least on 'O My Soul', a hybrid of Anglophile pop and Memphis funk. 'It's hard to play music here and not have some sort of element of Memphis in your sound,' Jody says. 'To that extent we were a soul band, we just had edgy, melodic guitars. It was maybe a coming together of a soul band and a British pop band.'

There's a Southern truculence to Big Star that consistently tempers the Badfinger/Raspberries power-pop elements. 'Though they are ostensibly a pop band, there's an underlying menace to Big Star's work,' Robert Gordon notes in *It Came From Memphis*. 'They meld the winsome with the twisted.' Jim Dickinson concurs with this: 'If Big Star was anything it was dangerous – in an almost imperceptible way, yet you knew it was there, like a switchblade ready to pop.'

Not the least of the factors that make *Radio City* a masterpiece is its sound, which is at once meaty and sparkling. 'We had a variety of guitar sounds that played against each other in a kind of pleasing, almost orchestral way,' John Fry told Robert Gordon. 'We also featured drums a lot more prominently than it was fashionable to do at the time.'

Once again there was precious little follow-up, let alone airplay of the kind at which the album's title so ironically hinted. After a handful of gigs, Andy Hummel decided he'd had enough of the Big Star life. 'Andy was easier-going than Chris or Alex, and he was also just a bit more practical,' says Jody Stephens. 'He left thinking, This isn't working out, I need to go back to school.'

Stepping into Hummel's shoes for the series of 1974 shows that produced Rykodisc's *Big Star Live* album was Chilton's friend John Lightman. Gigging as a three-piece, Chilton did well to fill space with a deft combination of lead and rhythm while Lightman held the songs down with busy bass lines.

Stephens says he remembers coming off the tour in a resigned state of mind: 'I'm sure I was disappointed, but I don't think my expectations were real high.'

For Alex Chilton, meanwhile, it was just the beginning of a perilous slide into oblivion.

In his sleevenotes to *I Am The Cosmos*, David Bell recalls the night in the summer of 1974 when he walked in on his younger brother 'pulling with his teeth on a rubber tourniquet, a syringe in his hand'. Chris Bell had now been out of Big Star for eighteen months and was floundering badly.

It wasn't as though Bell's talent had dried up. If anything, the songs he'd recorded at the little eight-track Shoe studio in Memphis – especially 'I Am The Cosmos', a surging cry of double-bind hopelessness – were better than his material on *#1 Record*. Also recorded at this time was the limpid acoustic ballad 'You And Your Sister', the occasion of a rare reunion between Bell and Chilton.

'After the split between those two guys, they eventually made up and decided they were still gonna be distant friends,' says Richard Rosebrough. 'Alex thought "You And Your Sister" was just beautiful, and he was so sweet to Chris – like, I feel so bad that all this has gone down between us, but listen to this beautiful voice. It was like two angels holding Jesus.'

By the late summer of '74, Bell's depression was such that his brother urged him to get away from Memphis and join him in Europe. 'David Bell wanted to save his younger brother from killing himself,' says Rosebrough, who in September flew to Rome with Chris. 'We were all real worried about him.'

David Bell's ploy was to dangle the prospect of recording at the famous Chateau d'Hierouville studios outside Paris. 'I somehow had to make him feel like a star, like someone on the verge of discovery,' he wrote in his *Cosmos* sleevenotes.

Among the tracks recorded at the Chateau were fervent Christian songs like 'Better Save Yourself', beefed-up rockers like 'Get Away' and pained ballads like 'Speed Of Sound'. Rooted in Beatle-esque pop-rock, the *Cosmos* songs bear the imprint of a soul in profound torment.

Still more of a thrill for Bell were the mixing sessions with famed Beatles engineer Geoff Emerick at Air in London. The downside was that Bell kept returning to remix the songs. 'The funny thing about *Cosmos* is that it got so blurred because the tape got so worn,' says Chris Stamey, who released 'I Am The Cosmos'/'You And Your Sister' as a single on his Car label in 1978.

The fact that there was no record deal at the end of all this hard work was devastating. When Max Bell interviewed him for *NME* in the early summer of 1975, Chris seemed desperately insecure. 'He was a real Southern disaster area, like something out of a Carson McCullers novel,' says Bell. 'I've got some very depressing letters from him where he talks about Big Star a lot. The impression I got from Chris was that he had some kind of moral code going on there which had nothing to do with being in a rock 'n' roll group with somebody like Chilton.'

'I think [Chris] might have been angry with the people at Ardent and I think he was angry with me too,' Chilton later told *New Music News*. 'He left [Big Star] in kind of a huff and then I assume he came to England and told Max Bell a bunch of dirty stories about me. But if you ask me it was totally his paranoia. He was taking very heavy drugs and then he got into Jesus . . .'

'Chris was kind of looking for something, and the search went on for a long time,' says Jody Stephens. 'He found Christ, but I'm not sure how comforting that was to him. At the end of the day, I think he was just looking to be a musician.'

It says something about Chris Bell's desperation that, when he returned to Memphis at the end of July 1975, he actually contacted Alex Chilton and suggested working together again. 'The idea was quickly abandoned,' noted David Bell, 'as the two not only had musical differences but had gone vastly different routes in their personal lives.'

Chilton's 'vastly different' route was all too clear from the extraordinary album he recorded at Ardent studios in the fall of 1974. Originally entitled *Beale Street Green*, then dubbed *Big Star Third*, and finally released by Rykodisc in 1992 as *Third/Sister Lovers*, the album was a wild departure from the jewelled guitars and harmonies of *Radio*

City – and one that had at least something to do with the prodigious quantity of drugs Chilton was ingesting. (Particularly ubiquitous on the Memphis scene at this time were quaaludes, downers that caused people to melt into blissed-out blobs of uninhibitedness.)

'I was getting pretty crazy and into some pretty rotten drugs and drinking a lot,' Chilton has admitted. 'And I just wasn't thinking in any practical terms at all after having the first two Big Star albums go pretty much unsought . . .'

'Alex was way out there by *Third*,' says Richard Rosebrough. 'He was getting out past left field fast, and I started to want to back away from it. A lot of drugs, a lot of alcohol, a lot of crazy girlfriends and bar scenes and some of the damnedest stories you've ever heard.'

Partnering Chilton in his escapades was his girlfriend Lesa Aldredge. 'There were a lot of ladies in Alex's life, but all of the stories are about Alex and Lesa,' says Rosebrough. 'They were always together and it was always heavy and there were always fights – in my living room and my front yard.'

'Lesa is what *Third* is all about,' says Jim Dickinson. 'Lesa brought punk rock to Memphis. She formed a band called the Klitz, who were like the Shaggs on downers, and she really stirred things up.' Making things even more interesting was the fact that Jody Stephens was simultaneously dating Lesa's sister Holliday (hence *Sister Lovers*).

It was Lesa who sang the back-up part on *Third*'s version of 'Femme Fatale'; Lesa who hurled a bottle of gin at Alex, only for it to smash on top of the mixing console. And it wasn't just Lesa tearing it up with him, either: Chilton had by this time acquired a motley entourage of hangers-on. 'There were many strange people coming around and hanging around the sessions,' remembers John Fry, who still winces when talking about the album.

Jim Dickinson, however, is keen to dispel the myth of *Third*'s controlled chaos. 'Alex was in pretty good shape,' he says. 'It took a long time to do the record, and he was healthier at some times than he was at others. But the idea that it was totally debauched the whole way through is not correct, because Fry wouldn't have tolerated it.'

Dickinson says that most of *Third* was cut with just guitar and drums, and everything else overdubbed. To Jody Stephens, whose drumming magnificently anchors the always-about-to-fragment music, Chilton's new material came as something of a shock: 'To hear him in the studio, you were thinking, That's just bizarre, who would ever have thought to make that sound? But twenty-five years later, you realise that Alex was pretty brilliant at capturing what he was going through.'

One of the misconceptions about *Third* is that it's a bleak master-work in the vein of *Berlin* or *Tonight's The Night*. Doubtless that's because the tracks people remember best on the album are wallowing, barbiturated death-wish songs like 'Holocaust', 'Kanga Roo' and 'Big Black Car'.

At least a third of the album, though, consists of febrile, full-blown rockers like 'Kizza Me', 'O Dana' and the revealingly titled 'You Can't Have Me'. It's as though Chilton, like the Neil Young of *Tonight's The Night*, is torn between sinking into a pit of self-loathing and burning out in a riot of musical madness. 'In a way I look back on all those songs from *Third* and I don't remember much about writing any of them,' he has said. 'I think the whole process was just kind of auto-matic, free association . . . I was just spewing things out.'

To Jim Dickinson, *Third* is a kind of aural soap opera. 'What I figured out recently about the album is that it's literally about midtown Memphis,' he says. 'Every one of those songs has a geographic location: Alex's mother's home, the Holiday Inn, Lesa's house, Holliday's house.'

'A Dickinson session was always a long session,' says Richard Rosebrough. 'A lot of fun, a lot of smoke in the air, and the craziest people you'd ever want to meet. Jim doesn't necessarily want to get the best performance or the best sound, he wants to get it when it's really the most interesting. And then he does all kinds of wild post-production to it.'

The post-production may be what gave *Third* its edge, yet also what made it so hard for record companies to understand when Dickinson and Fry shopped it around in 1975. 'No one would even accept it as a "demo" these days,' Dickinson maintains. 'Yet it's been more respon-sible for my so-called career than anything else. I've had people tell me it saved their lives.'

When *Third* – belatedly released on the PVC label in 1978 – failed to garner any record company interest, it simply confirmed for Alex Chilton that he might as well give in to his ever-stronger impulse towards sabotage.

For much of 1975 he ran around in the company of one Danny Graflund, a big tearaway of a man hired during the *Third* sessions as Alex's personal bodyguard. Danny's speciality was metamorphosing into 'Other Man', a psychotic brute who, on a signal from Chilton, would provoke fights and upend tables wherever Alex and his cronies went in Memphis.

Behind the mayhem, though, Graflund detected in Chilton a thoughtful guy who'd been hurt. 'There's a group of people in Memphis who, when they hurt, you don't realise how *deeply* they hurt,' Graflund says. 'So they become where you *can't* hurt 'em. We did a lot of partying. It was like, "Let's go get invisible! Let's be like Jerry Lee Lewis! Let's eat some pills and drink some whiskey!"'

For Jody Stephens, Chilton quickly crossed the line between acceptable hedonism and unforgivable lack of concern for others. 'I don't know that I was concerned about his drug use so much as about his behaviour,' Stephens says. 'There was a group of people who followed Alex around, and he did something incredibly mean to one of them and this person didn't turn around and leave. And I thought, That's sick. I'm outta here.' Stephens and Chilton would not speak again for what Stephens remembers as 'years and years'.

'Those people in Memphis could be pretty cruel,' says Peter Holsapple, who came to Memphis in quest of Chilton some time later. 'Some of Alex's acolytes seemed to wear their reform-school institutionalisation on their sleeves as a badge of honour.'

One person who found himself on the receiving end of the sadism was Jon Tiven, who came to Memphis to produce Chilton in September 1975. With Richard Rosebrough drumming and engineering, a session was booked at Ardent and a bunch of ramshackle, slaphappy songs auditioned. Gone was the darkness of *Big Star Third*, in its place a loose, vaguely Stonesy sound crawling towards the off-the-cuff chaos of *Like Flies On Sherbert*.

'The first night I had this really strange feeling, like there were demons running around,' says Tiven. 'It seemed like Alex was intent on anarchy without any kind of point. We'd go through the songs and Danny Graflund would step up to the microphone and say: "I don't care if you're Mott The Hoople out there, who gives a shit!"'

'This is music performed with some of the most callous abandon ever to have been allowed in a recording studio,' Chilton would later write in some unpublished sleevenotes for *Bach's Bottom*. He noted of Tiven that 'the young producer was appalled and failed to see the beauty of letting the music happen in a manner so obviously out of control . . .'

Dickinson says he remembers walking with Chilton into Huey's, a popular Memphis restaurant, after the sessions were over. 'Tiven was standing at the bar, and Alex noticed him and said, Excuse me a minute. And he stood up and walked over to Tiven and spat in his face.'

'My mistake was trying to make a pop record with Alex,' Tiven says in conclusion. 'If he ever really tried to make a record that conveyed the blackness and wretchedness of his soul, he could give Marilyn Manson a run for his money.'

The concept of 'letting the music happen in a manner so obviously out of control' would become the guiding principle of Chilton's music for the remainder of the '70s.

Chilton has said that something 'clicked' in his head in 1975 with the writing of 'My Rival', a song that wound up on *Like Flies On Sherbert*. 'The whole way through I knew what the words said and I knew what it meant,' Chilton recalled. 'Before that I'd write things that were an ethereal nebulous string of words that really didn't mean anything.'

This is the point at which Chilton kisses goodbye to Big Star – jettisons the Byrdsy, Beatle-esque riffs and dumps the echoey haunt-edness of 'Holocaust' and 'Big Black Car'. In their place comes a twisted, derailed version of roots rock.

Nineteen seventy-six was a lost year for Chilton. 'People bothered him,' remembers Graflund. 'They'd wanna talk and siddown and be his buddy. And I think Alex was telling people, "Look, I don't wanna fuck with you. I'm over here drunk throwing up on this table, why don't you stay over *there?*"'

The bibulous existentialism came to a temporary halt with the belated release in early 1977 of the *Singer Not The Song* EP. When a deal was done with Ork, the New York label that had put out the first single by Television, owners Terry Ork and Charles Ball brought Chilton to New York. 'Alex didn't have any kind of standing in anybody's universe until he came to New York,' says Tiven. 'I told Charles Ball I'd been working with Chilton in Memphis and I made him a tape. They saw the punk attitude was there.'

When Terry Ork scouted around for musicians to play with Chilton, an obvious choice was Chris Stamey, whose Chapel Hill band Sneakers had put out a nervy, Big Star-ish EP the previous year. With Stamey playing bass, Chilton played a number of shows and even recorded some demos for Elektra.

When Elektra's interest came to naught, Chilton was virtually on the skids – and drinking heavily to boot. The fact that pictures of him in New York from this period make him look like Richard Hell was simply down to the fact that he couldn't afford to buy clothes or shoes.

As Chilton's optimism faded, so his music became more anarchic. A major turning point for him was seeing the Cramps for the first time at CBGBs. For Chilton, the band's Z-movie trasharama and voodoobilly racket were the ultimate release from the rigours of composition and arrangement, a crazed return to the days before pop became self-conscious.

In October 1977, the Cramps journeyed to Memphis to work with Chilton at Ardent. The band soon learned that he'd made many enemies in Memphis, principally among men he'd cuckolded.

'There were guys with guns, man . . . all sorts of crazy things,' Lux Interior told Nick Kent in *NME*. 'He's a real Southern boy is Alex. He believes in the Lord and the Lord sure as hell takes care of him.' One of the best-loved pieces of Chilton apocrypha from this time has him marching into the vocal booth at Ardent and jamming a gun against Lux's temple. His alleged words? 'Sing it right.'

Working with the Cramps pushed Chilton still further towards the musical abandon of *Like Flies On Sherbert*. Back in New York in 1978, he cut the frazzled psychobilly single 'Bangkok' with Chris Stamey. 'Songs like "Bangkok" were not romantic,' Stamey says with impeccable understatement. 'There was a famous quote – "tuning is such a European concept" – which I heard from Peter Holsapple.'

If working with Chilton was disillusioning for both Stamey and Holsapple, the two men defend him to this day. 'We did try to keep the effusive thrill we had about working with Alex,' says Holsapple. 'In some ways it was a healthy thing for me to meet somebody as . . . I don't wanna say *difficult* . . . but somebody who was standoffish and arms-length, for his own protection and mental wellbeing.'

'My life was on the skids, and *Like Flies On Sherbert* was a summation of that period,' Chilton told Robert Gordon in *It Came From Memphis*. 'I like that record a lot. It's crazy but it's a positive statement about a period in my life that wasn't positive.'

Once again it was Jim Dickinson to whom Chilton turned when he needed a producer. Moreover, it was Dickinson's part-time band Mud Boy & the Neutrons that Alex wanted to play on *Flies*. Setting a precedent for his future career, half the album's tracks were covers: country songs like 'No More The Moon Shines On Lorena' and Ernest Tubb's 'Waltz Across Texas', together with Roy Orbison's 'I've Had It' and KC & the Sunshine Band's 'Boogie Shoes'.

Not that any of these is remotely respectful: Chilton's take on the Carter Family may be the most extreme statement of musical nihilism Alex ever put on tape. '*Flies* has always been a tedious exercise for me to get through,' admits Peter Holsapple. 'Some of it has just been so underwritten and underperformed that I'm like, How I wish this could have been more than it was.'

So aggressively sloppy is the album's sound that if anything it is now heard as a forerunner to '90s lo-fi. 'The mix still really frustrates me, but it served its purpose,' recalls Dickinson. 'And all these new deconstructionalist guys just hold it up as some kind of anthemesque, truth-and-beauty document.'

Video footage of the *Flies* sessions gives some indication as to just how fucked-up the sessions were. Hunkered down at the Sam C. Phillips International studio over three nights, Chilton and chums are clearly doing their best to unlearn any knowledge they've ever acquired about music. With Dickinson torturing a dilapidated synthesiser and a wrecked, acne'd Chilton playing guitar like somebody who'd never picked up the instrument, this is dissipation as avant-garde art. In the midst of it all, Alex holds court with the evil smirk of a child preparing to lay waste to a sandcastle.

'*Flies* nearly killed us,' the late Memphis artist Randall Lyon told Robert Gordon. 'It was a horrible experience from beginning to end.'

Heavier still was the news Alex Chilton received on the eve of his twenty-eighth birthday in December 1978: Chris Bell had just been killed in a car crash.

'I was around Alex when Chris died, and it definitely affected him,' says Jim Dickinson. 'Of course you couldn't help but think it could just as easily have been *him* driving the car. A lot of people think Chris committed suicide. I don't know what to say about that. He was more of a mystery in that way than Alex is.'

Chris Bell's run of bad luck had continued with a series of disheartening pub and folk club gigs in Europe. Returning with his brother David to Memphis in December 1975, he decided to throw in the towel and take a sanity-preserving job as the manager of one of his father's restaurants. Which was where Peter Holsapple found him two and a half years later during a pilgrimage he made to Memphis.

'Chris struck me as being on that road to religion from which some people never come back,' says Holsapple. 'It didn't make me feel real good to know that a guy of that talent was having to schlep burgers around, but he was a charming host and he took us around.' Surprisingly, one of the places Bell took the trio of North Carolinians was the Phillips studio, where the *Flies* sessions were in full swing. 'Alex and Chris were kind of cordial,' recalls Holsapple.

Bell hadn't completely given up hope of achieving rock 'n' roll glory. He was still intermittently going into the studio with Richard Rosebrough. There were even rumours of a reunion tour by Big Star, whose first two albums had been reissued in Britain as a two-for-one by EMI.

On the night of 26 December 1978, Bell was rehearsing with Big

Star disciple Tommy Hoehn. 'Chris basically needed someone to align himself with because he wasn't getting anywhere on his own,' says Jon Tiven. 'There was another guitar player there named Gene Nunez, and Chris was really pissed off about it. He took a bunch of downers, poured his beer in Gene's amplifier head, and sped off in his Triumph TR-6 sports car.'

Bell was driving fast along Poplar Avenue in the early hours of 27 December when his white Triumph careered into a telephone pole near Perkins Road. The impact killed him almost instantly.

'I don't know that Chris killed himself on purpose, but when he went off in that car I think basically it was a big Fuck-You,' says Tiven. 'I think his death was just a result of hitting the walls for the last time.'

For Tiven and other Chilton nay-sayers, Bell was the real talent – the unacknowledged genius – in Big Star. 'The reason Alex wouldn't perform any of the Big Star songs for so long is because he legitimately recognised that his contributions were not the driving force behind the records,' Tiven says. 'He knows that what people are revering him for is Chris Bell.'

These are strong words, and it should be noted that Tiven is seen by many as harbouring vengeful feelings towards Chilton. There are also those who simply disagree with the assessment that Bell was a genius. 'Chris was a mimic and I think Alex goes way beyond that,' says Jim Dickinson. 'People who say the opposite are just obsessed with the mystery of Big Star.'

At the risk of identifying myself as one of the obsessed, I would say that even a cursory comparison between *I Am The Cosmos* and *Like Flies On Sherbert* at the very least suggests that Bell stayed truer than Chilton to a vision of rock music as a vehicle for spiritual transcendence.

'I don't think I know anyone on earth that I really consider understands me as a human being whatsoever,' says Alex Chilton. 'A lot of people do their best and still completely misunderstand everything about me.'

Chilton is explaining to me on the phone why he's changed his mind about talking to me for this piece. Why, while he has nothing against me personally, 'for you to write about me would be the *best* way for me to begin to have something against you'. It's Chilton saying again, as he's said in so many different ways for so many years, You Can't Have Me.

'The reason he won't talk to you is that he's probably afraid you'll see a glimpse of his dark soul and it'll come out in the article and maybe he won't get laid as much,' says Jon Tiven. 'The reason he disliked me so much is because I eventually saw him to be the vacant mooch that he is.'

'Alex can be as warm and charming a person as anybody could hope for, and he can also put a thirty-foot distance between you,' says Peter Holsapple. 'Recently I did a show with him in New Orleans, and I put a message through and said I'd love it if he would come up and play "Soul Deep" with us. And he was, like, Okay. And then I saw him at soundcheck and it was like Bartleby the Scrivener. I said, Are we still gonna do "Soul Deep"? And he took a long pause and said, "I would prefer not to." And that was the end of it.'

I would prefer not to: how Herman Melville's famous phrase sums up a man who's spent the last twenty years not doing the things his fans want him to: not being friendly, not playing Big Star songs, not pursuing fame and glory. Ironically, moreover, this refusal to play to his legend has coincided not with further self-abuse but with a measure of what one could call 'recovery'.

'Alex has a method to his life that he has adopted and that he follows,' says Richard Rosebrough. 'There's no question that he grew and evolved.'

'Alex told me about hitting bottom and then making the decision that he was going to survive and pull it back together,' says Bud Scoppa, who A&R'd *Columbia*, the live Big Star reunion album recorded at Missouri University in April 1993. 'He talked about doing the most menial things to bring his sense of himself back into some kind of fundamental place. And he doesn't need much. He lives in a little ramshackle shanty in a funky part of New Orleans surrounded by junk, and it doesn't bother him.'

Stories of Chilton washing dishes in New Orleans, where he moved in 1984, were legion in the mid-'80s. Supposedly when the Replacements' Paul Westerberg walked into Tipitina's and asked for his hero, the doorman pointed towards a scrawny figure sweeping the floor. By the early '80s, when he became a floating member of Tav Falco's manic swamp-a-billy band Panther Burns, Chilton had begun to find the peace of mind which eluded him the previous decade.

Post-Panther Burns, Chilton has taken the re-interpretative approach of *Flies* to its logical conclusion while dispensing with that album's anarchic lo-fi distortion. Releases such as the EP *Feudalist Tarts* and the album *A Man Called Destruction* have been oddly respectful, and oddly devoid of any personal stamp. Cover-heavy, they're sung in a thin tenor, with Chilton presenting himself as a lovably ironic lounge act. Certainly Alex knows his R & B and soul music. But whether this makes his versions of Carla Thomas' 'B-A-B-Y' or Slim Harpo's 'Tee Ni Nee Ni Noo' as valid as his best Big Star music is hard to argue.

More mystifying still is Chilton's professed belief that the few songs he *has* bothered to write in the two decades are far superior to all that Big Star music. (He told the late Epic Soundtracks that 'Thing For You', a piece of throwaway fluff from 1987's *High Priest*, was the best song he'd ever written.) Peter Holsapple thinks Chilton 'really delights in confounding people – it's a far easier row to hoe to make it so that people aren't gonna be guessing his next move.'

'The uncynical, utterly simple pop song is the zen state for him,' says Bud Scoppa. 'To some people his manifestations of that are maddening rather than sublime. But I really do think it bespeaks his complete rejection of all the things that people love him for.'

'Why Alex won't write anything serious I don't know,' says Jim Dickinson. 'I don't think I've ever seen Alex afraid, so it's not about fear. I think he's just reluctant and extremely pissed off. It's just, "How bad do you want it?"'

'I think the whole thing about people revering Big Star is annoying to him because no one was really interested at the time,' says Norman Blake. 'And I do think that he's continued to write good songs, although maybe not as frequently as he did during Big Star. Something like "Guantanamerika" is a really great song, but different to Big Star in the sense that Big Star weren't ever really lyric-driven.'

Jody Stephens admits he was 'shocked' when Chilton agreed to play a one-off Big Star reunion date with a couple of Alex Chilton devotees from the Posies. When I ask him if Chilton seemed older and wiser after all the years in which the two men hadn't spoken, he pauses for a good ten seconds.

'He wasn't doing drugs or drinking, but there was still an arm's length between us,' Stephens eventually says. 'I think Alex sees relationships differently than I do. For me, the wonderful thing about being in Big Star is that I get to meet people that I might not otherwise get to meet, whether it's Mike Mills or Golden Smog. I don't think Alex ever saw it as that.'

'That people want to write about me is probably good in some kind of promotional regard,' Chilton tells me with a yawn. 'I've come to the belief that it almost doesn't matter what they say as long as they spell the name right.'

As a small concession to the fact that I've been researching this piece for months – and making dozens of unreturned calls to him after he'd intially agreed to be interviewed – he adds that a new Alex Chilton album is due for imminent release.

'It's all covers, there are no original tunes on it and I think it's the best record yet,' he says in a blank, matter-of-fact tone. 'In Europe the title is *Loose Shoes And Tight Pussy*, but the American market may not be ready for that title.' Race you to the Megastore, fellow Chiltonheads!

'I think there's a danger that Alex gets cast as this incredibly prickly, mood-swinging villain, and I didn't think that was entirely the case,' says Max Bell. 'I mean, I always enjoyed meeting him, even if he was very blunt and candid. And I mean, witness Lou Reed. You certainly don't have to be a nice guy to take part in something that means a lot.'

Let's leave the last word on LX to the guy's old bodyguard.

'I think he's just holding himself in a place where he is mentally,' says Danny Graflund. 'Any time he wants to, Alex could step out and just go, All right, guys, here's what we're gonna do. I think he's a genius, and I think he's playing out whatever it is he wants to do. And the time might come and it might not ever come.'

1999

Pavement Goes Overground

Nobody could accuse Pavement of being rock archetypes. Take the group's frontman Stephen Malkmus, who spends much of his spare time flyfishing virgin rivers and scaling 18,000-foot mountains in America's Pacific North-west. Or guitarist Scott 'Spiral Stairs' Kannberg, who, when he isn't tending his meticulously manicured garden in Berkeley, California, is usually to be found on one of the Bay Area's many golf courses.

How about drummer Steve West, a heavily-bearded man in Blundstone boots who breeds dachshunds (forty of them, at latest head count) on his eight-acre property in rural Virginia. Or bassist Mark Ibold, who resides in Manhattan and – in indie-rock circles, at least – is a chef of legendary repute.

Not oddball enough for you? Then meet utility player Bob Nastanovich, the band's second drummer, Moog synthesist, and crowd-stirring MC. Bob, it transpires, is a bloke who devotes the major part of his non-Pavement life – a part threatening to overtake Pavement itself – to a pair of racehorses he owns in Louisville, Kentucky.

'Actually, we co-own one of them,' interjects Steve Malkmus. 'He's called Speedy Service. He won his first race last week in Ohio.'

Could Slash and Axl have claimed as much? Could Duff McKagan have whipped up an *omelette aux fines herbes*, or Izzy Stradlin nurtured a nasturtium? Did Matt Sorum race thoroughbreds at Saratoga Springs?

But what, you ask, does any of this have to do with Pavement's being The Last Great American Indie Band, heirs to the noble tradition of lo-fidelity art-rock established three decades ago by the Velvet Underground?

More, perhaps, than you'd think. At least a part of the point of Pavement is that its members – not counting original drummer Gary Young, a fortysomething Yes freak whose alcoholic antics led to his early departure – have never fallen foul of rock's insidious mythologies. They've never worn leather trousers or been habitual drug abusers. They've tended to look outside the group, as well as inside it, for artistic inspiration. They've maintained their working relationship while living thousands of miles apart from each other. And they've made some remarkable rock 'n' roll records that completely transcend – as well as critique – rock 'n' roll.

For ten years, Pavement have trodden their own whimsical path, part of the indie world but also apart from it. From their scratchy turn-of-the-decade EPs on Treble Kicker and Drag City to 1997's playfully mellow *Brighten The Corners*, the quintet have made messy, ironic records shot through with something more biting and poignant. Clever-clogs popsters who mask the aching beauty of their songs with half-assed arrangements, they've been a beacon of ironic intelligence in a sea of self-deluded '90s exhibitionists.

The one thing that's held Pavement back all this time is a certain stubborn unwillingness to make their Lou-Reed-meets-the-Fall sound a mite friendlier to the world at large. And that's where a certain young producer *du jour* enters the frame.

East 12th Street, New York City, November 1998. In the dim, reddish-brown light of the RPM recording studio, one can just make out the slender figure of Steve Malkmus, bent over a red Gibson guitar and drawling such extemporaneous lines as 'I wear Spandex pants cos my girlfriend says they make me look a fox' and 'architecture students are the worst people to party with'. Something about Malkmus suggests that the Spandex claim is a bare-faced lie, or at least an ironic reference to a rock demographic that has yet to embrace his music.

.Peer a little harder into the room's womb-like interior and other figures begin to emerge. Tucked away at the back is Steve West. To one side of his drum kit sit Mark Ibold and Scott Kannberg. None of these men betrays much emotion at the laconic non sequiturs of Malkmus' guide vocals: this is how he has always worked in the studio, allowing unedited thoughts and images to flow from his consciousness:

'Do not fuck with Indians when you have killed their forefathers too . . .'

'Hey, gonzo journalism went out with the wheel, I know it did . . .'

The track Pavement are working on this afternoon is called 'The Hexx', and it's a big, slow-building epic, a song with which they opened many of the shows on their last tour. Set to be a centrepiece of *Terror Twilight*, the band's fifth album proper, it's unlike anything they've recorded before – a song full of a sense of dread that belies Malkmus' off-the-cuff lyrics.

This may or may not have anything to do with the young man presently resting his legs on the mixing desk and urging the band not to 'get too Cars' on the song's bridge. In an earlier rock era, Nigel Godrich might have been a spotty engineer in faded denim, serving his apprenticeship under a Mutt Lange or a Roy Thomas Baker. In the late 1990s, however, he is *the* hot producer, a hip wunderBrit in trainers with a CV that already boasts Radiohead's *OK Computer* and Beck's *Mutations* among its stellar credits. A long-time Pavement admirer, Godrich expressed interest in producing the indie-rock icons after running into Lawrence Bell, major-domo of the band's British label Domino, at a Sonic Youth gig.

'I got a message from Lawrence saying Nigel was a big fan,' Malkmus will tell me later. 'And then I found out that Beck, my one rock star friend besides Justine Frischmann, was doing a record with him. And it was just this weird thing where Beck said, "You'd really like Nigel, he does a really good job, and he's fast and all this." And so it just sort of grew from that.'

Godrich is listening hard to 'The Hexx's' mournful circular riff, searching for ways to tighten the Pavement sound and coax out the band's strengths. When Malkmus goes off on an absurd tangent about beer and cheese and LA's Belage Hotel, Godrich stops the track. Malkmus reminds Godrich that he'll finish the lyrics properly when they mix the album in London.

'Isn't it a bit too fucking much, though?' asks Godrich, who is worried that Malkmus' meandering ad-libs will affect what the others are playing.

With the maturity of the musician who has now turned thirty, Malkmus agrees that it probably is a bit too fucking much.

'We'd never had a producer really, you know, pushing us or anything,' says Scott Kannberg, the quiet guitarist who formed Pavement a decade ago with Malkmus (and who has also managed the group since its inception). 'Nigel will kind of say, "That's not very good." Bryce Goggin did that a little bit on *Crooked Rain, Crooked Rain* and *Wowee Zowee*, where he'd say, "That doesn't sound in tune" or whatever, but Mitch Easter on *Brighten The Corners* just recorded us. With Nigel we were like, Yeah, okay, whatever. He's pretty cool. I think he's a little overworked these days. He was getting phone calls from, like, U2 and Red Hot Chili Peppers while he was in the studio with us.'

Kannberg says the group often ribs Godrich about Natalie Imbruglia, the doe-eyed Oz pop minx with whom the producer was romantically linked after he'd worked on her multiplatinum *Left Of The Middle*. There's also the little matter of the hideous 1979 Nigel Olsson album sleeve that's propped up on the mixing desk, defaced with Fall-esque graffiti like 'GLAM RAQUET' and 'POSH THE SECRET WEAPON'.

Teasing aside, however, Pavement's decision to work with the Radiohead kid – and to record in the pricey RPM studio, where Godrich mixed seven tracks on R.E.M.'s *Up* – is a gauge of the seriousness with which they're taking this album. (Rumours have been circulating that *Terror Twilight* may be Pavement's last.)

'It was kind of a last-moment thing,' says Malkmus in a blank, affectless tone that sounds like MTV's Butthead crossed with a Whit Stillman character. 'We didn't really know what we were going to do, as usual. We tried to make the record at Sonic Youth's home studio, but for us it was just too hard to get used to. And Nigel wanted to get into a proper studio, so we were like, OK, it's a little expensive for us, but if you want it, it's cool. There'll be some *OK Computer* tricks on the record, probably. No matter what, Nigel wants to make a good album and, like, he wants to keep a good track record. Obviously he's doing pretty good with the Beck record and Radiohead and Natalie Imbruglia. He listens back to, like, *Wowee Zowee* and he's really into that record, and he's like, fuck, what am I doing, are we doing as good as that? He's worried about that himself.'

It's difficult to tell how Malkmus is feeling about the album at this stage. The man once described by Courtney Love as 'the Grace Kelly of rock', and by others as 'the American Jarvis Cocker', is a dry, circumspect chap at the best of times. A flannel-shirted intellectual whose Unlikely Sex Symbol™ status was confirmed once and for all by rumours of an affair with Elastica's Justine Frischmann, he looks mildly stressed by the tight deadline Pavement have set themselves to finish recording at RPM.

'I mean, it's all gonna work,' he says, slightly unconvincingly. 'This week it'll all be done. I think it's normal that it takes a band this long to do its tracks.'

'One of the biggest misconceptions about Pavement is that we resist popularity,' Bob Nastanovich said when *Brighten The Corners* came out two years ago. 'And that's just not true. Stephen's just a worrier – he spends too much time obsessing over the imperfections.'

Given the shambling and amateurish quality of much Pavement music, some would say that perfection was the last thing on Stephen Malkmus' mind.

Avatars of the American 'lo-fi' sound that blossomed in the early '90s, Pavement – along with Sebadoh, Guided By Voices et al. – were a nerdy, too-smart-for-their-own-good riposte to the beefy bluster of Pearl Jam, Smashing Pumpkins and Stone Temple Pilots, at each of whom Malkmus has taken good-natured swipes in his time.

For Pavement, grunge – like too much rock music – was predicated on bad faith, a kind of *bogus primalism*, something Malkmus' ironic, unheroic songs actively sought to undermine. Listening to the group's first three albums (1992's *Slanted And Enchanted*, 1994's *Crooked Rain, Crooked Rain*, 1995's *Wowee Zowee*), it was clear they were simply too bright to buy into rock's posturing, a band who made no bones about being wimpy suburban intellectuals but whose droll intelligence transformed their songs into radical deconstructions of rock tropes.

'We came out of indie rock and we're always gonna be on that path,' says Malkmus. 'I mean, whatever soul you have being a suburban kid like us, what can you do that's right that way? Because we're not Black Sabbath, we're not working-class heroes and we can't get away with that. Luckily we're not hanging out at Met Bar, either – we're not New York City hipsters or anything – so that's our earthiness.'

The surprising thing about Pavement's music is that, for all its knowing, sardonic archness, there's plenty of pain and sadness in it too. Indeed, the key to the beauty of songs like 'Here' (*Slanted And Enchanted*), 'Silence Kid' (*Crooked Rain, Crooked Rain*), 'Father To A Sister Of Thought' (*Wowee Zowee*), and 'Type Slowly' (*Brighten The Corners*) lies precisely in their playful tussle between feeling and cleverness.

Pavement's blend of high IQ and fuzzy guitars shares a certain detached quality with Beck and even vintage De La Soul. Like Beck, Malkmus conveys emotion in the very way he cuts through rock's chest-beating bravado. Thin and unmusical as it is, his Bernard Sumner-goes-slacker voice is one of the defining signatures of Amerindie pop.

'Just after *Crooked Rain*, there was kind of this irony thing that was getting thrown our way, and that was the way that we dealt with it, I guess,' Malkmus says. 'And, like, British people really appreciate irony in a certain way. Cheekiness is cool in England somehow. Robbie Williams is all right for a pop star – he's cheeky or just having a laugh or something. I think British people relate to that in our music: they like that we try to be honest about things and we're not full of shit.'

To what extent does Malkmus think people pick up on his humour, or on the cultural references with which he peppers his lyrics?

'I don't mind if they don't,' he says. 'I've never been much of a lyric man, to tell you the truth. I listen to the music first, and if some lyrics are good, well, that's OK. It's first of all the cadences that are most important, and if you're not talking about pop culture in a dumb way or being too like the Verve or something that's too pretentious, then it's cool with me. And if people misunderstand the lyrics, that's good too, I guess. [*Adopts hilariously fey English accent*] "We want people to make their own meanings . . ."'

Given that Pavement are so different from Radiohead, could Malkmus ever imagine himself singing like Thom Yorke?

'Well, it's not really in that sphere. I mean, that's the way he does it: he feels his emotions that way. Our thing is not really vocally driven until the last moment. I mean, I like singing, it's kinda fun, but I have to be in the right mood. We have a style of singing that's sort of unique. I hear hints of it in some Beck songs. I'm sure he's listened to us. It comes around, but you can't really copy it, and I'm glad about that.'

Does he feel an affinity with Beck?

'Yeah, at least on the spectrum of, like, where we fit in. I would say that that would be someone who does cool stuff, and that I would root for in the pop sweepstakes. He's kind of on a roll now, and he's really great. As Justine says, he's got the muse right now, and it's all going really pretty excellently.'

St John's Wood, London, December 1998: the world-famous RAK studios, its corridors haunted by the piteous ghosts of '80s pop (Johnny Hates Jazz, the Thompson Twins, Curiosity Killed The Cat). In the waiting room, an unassuming gent in a blue suit flips through the *Sun* and occasionally glances at Sky Sports News on the telly in the corner. It takes a little while before it registers that the man is in fact RAK owner and pop legend Mickie Most.

Upstairs in Studio 2, Pavement are hunkered down in a cramped control room with Nigel Godrich and Radiohead's Jonny Greenwood, the latter having shown up on this damp grey afternoon to add some bluesy harmonica to two tracks (working titles: 'Billie' and 'Ground Beef Heart', the latter subsequently renamed 'Platform Blues'). Things aren't going as fast as planned: the band were supposed to have finished all recording by this point, and now Jonny and Nigel are taking off for Camden Town's Rock Shop to buy a better harmonica . . .

Turns out that Malkmus, his slim torso covered by a monstrous Holsten Export T-shirt ('I ran out of clothes'), hasn't even recorded his vocals yet. 'We started taking some passes through things,' he says of his tracks. 'It looks like we'll still have to mix some tunes in January. We did twelve days in New York, and that went as it did, and now we're kind of here, and it's going a little bit slower than we imagined.'

The previous day I'd met up with Malkmus, Kannberg and Ibold in a café in Notting Hill Gate. 'We were a little stressed, but now we're mellow,' Malkmus said by way of greeting. He and Ibold had been buying food for a big Thanksgiving dinner at Justine Frischmann's flat. (Malkmus has always maintained that his friendship with the Elastica beauty is strictly Platonic, and his story hasn't changed.) As he laid into a *croque monsieur*, I asked him what difference the whole Blur/Elastica endorsement of Pavement made to them three years ago.

'Maybe in England it made a little difference or something. Maybe some people that wouldn't normally listen to our band . . . maybe it made it slightly more fashionable. In America, people don't really care about that. I don't think it really got mentioned that often. It just kind of went by the wayside. Anyway, I'm sure Blur's on to new influences on their new record.'

Brighten The Corners was a lot more open and accessible than the dense, obtuse *Wowee Zowee*. How different is the new album likely to sound?

Malkmus: 'Hard to say. It's got some really weird moments that are like heavy rock. I had some pop tunes – like, our version of pop tunes, that probably are too weird to be really pop – that didn't really go right in New York. And so we're kind of doing that now, trying to fill in a gap. The idea was to sort of do four hard rock tunes: y'know, bring back hard rock, or things like the Groundhogs and Captain Beefheart, show that that's a valid thing that people should listen to. And then, like, four standard mellow tunes that we can do in our sleep that sound pretty. And then four pop tunes, which are not my best forte, or something that I have trouble with. It's like different versions of "AT+T" [*Wowee Zowee*] or "Box Elder" [*Slay Tracks* EP] or that kind of thing. They're just kind of nice.'

Ibold: 'There are some tunes where the tunefulness comes in hidden pockets, and then there's like a couple where the tunefulness is . . . sort of a messenger bag or something!'

Malkmus: 'It's a different sonic imprint, though it's the same people writing the songs. I don't know, no matter how hard we try to be different, it comes out sounding like Pavement. It's just less grungey-sounding, somehow. There's a modern psychedelic sound to some of the things. One of the things we wanted to do was riff, or at least do our riff-style thing. But riffs are tough: they're all there or they're not. You can get judgemental about it – like, are we boogieing or are we too wimpy to boogie? There's this song "Folk Jam" that sounds sorta like an electrified version of Pentangle's "Sweet Child". Then there's "Billie", which originally was going to be just a straightahead pop tune but has become acoustic and weird. And "Ground Beef Heart", which we consider a hybrid of, like, *Split*-era Groundhogs and *Lick My Decals*-era Beefheart. And that's pretty rocking.'

Kannberg: 'I think the album is more Pink Floyd than Radiohead. That's what I call this record: a Pink Floyd record. Just because of Nigel. And every time I say that, he gets really happy.'

Ibold: 'It's *Slanted And Enchanted*, but after somebody played Black Sabbath. The thing is, *Slanted* always sounded weird next to anything else on the radio, whereas the songs on this record . . . well, they'll still sound different to songs on the radio, but they're not going to have the problem of sounding like they're coming out of a different stereo system.'

Gimme dat Harp Boy! Jonny Greenwood has finally returned from Camden and is blowing up a storm at RAK for 'Ground Beef Heart/Platform Blues'. Bent over, his flared jeans slung low around his snakey hips, he is completely wrapped up in the track, which starts out like Led Zeppelin's 'Baby, I'm Gonna Leave You' and then cranks up into a full '70s rock blowout.

'He's blowin' the Oxford blues, man!' shouts Mark Ibold, staring down at Greenwood from the elevated control room.

Another spectator is a son of the South by the name of Robert Bingham – or 'Bingo', as the Pavement boys know him. This debauched-looking fellow has dropped by the studio out of the blue to say hello. A novelist and a Southern aristocrat who reputedly owns half of Louisville, Kentucky – home to Pavement's Nastanovich, who returned there after the New York sessions – 'Bingo' has struck up a sufficiently close friendship with the band for them to call his Tribeca loft their Manhattan pied-à-terre. Sipping from a hip flask of Scotch, Bingham tells Malkmus about the party from which he is recovering. 'I saw Bernardo Bertolucci and I went over and forced him to listen to *Wowee Zowee*,' he chuckles.

On 'Billie', Jonny Greenwood plays a repetitive, 'Three Blind Mice'-style phrase that requires several retakes. 'I hope he doesn't get bummed out about doing this,' mutters Mark Ibold, aware that it's not every day you get a bona fide genius to make a guest appearance on your album. Pavement needn't worry, though. 'I'd do anything for this band,' the Radiohead prodigy tells me when he's done.

'I kind of want to have that kind of *OK Computer* sound,' Scott Kannberg tells me afterwards. 'Not the same exact sound, but the idea of just a lot of weird sounds going on. This record will be better sounding, because the studio was a lot better, the instruments were a lot better, the takes were a lot better.'

'I think it's cool that Nigel worked on the Beck record, just because of all that stuff happening on it,' adds Ibold. 'We definitely had the idea of going in and doing this and coming up with extra parts or overdubs.'

How much is the band looking forward to playing the new songs live?

Malkmus: 'One thing that I feel – and that I know bands like Sonic Youth have felt once they've been in a career state of mind – is that having to go play old songs like "Summer Babe" or "Grounded" right now seems so irrelevant and so fake. When it's old songs, it just seems really dated to me. Maybe in twenty years' time, with a dwindling bank account, I might reconsider that.'

Why do we hear rumours that this will be Pavement's last album?

Ibold: 'Because Steve did a show with [Geraldine Fibbers guitarist] Nels Cline and mentioned something in *Rolling Stone* about people in the band wanting to have babies. He said that if that was what they wanted to do then we could stop playing. And since the internet is sort of like Chinese whispers, it gets passed along. I've had people come up to me and say, I hear you guys are breaking up.'

Malkmus: 'I admit to being pretty fried after the *Brighten The Corners* tour. That could easily have gone to hanging out after that. Touring that much makes you really depressed. We're old enough that we don't have to do that. We've put in our hard days, and if we're going to keep going it can't be like that.'

Is it hard to stay in touch when the band is so scattered across America – Malkmus in Portland, Kannberg in Berkeley, Ibold in New York, West and Nastanovich in the South?

Kannberg: 'We all have pagers.'

Ibold: 'I think I talk to pretty much everyone, maybe every two months.'

Malkmus: 'The good side of it is probably that we look forward to seeing each other. The bad side is that bands that live together are always working on stuff together and probably get good at creating songs, like, off the cuff. The separation just puts a delay on every-thing you do, but maybe that makes it fresher because you don't get tired of things.'

Why does 'rock music' appear to be dying?

Malkmus: 'I think the players aren't as good. The stakes aren't as high. People aren't shooting for as much. Seems like no one has the time to raise the level on each new record. I guess maybe Trent Reznor thinks he's doing that right now. Maybe it's just because I'm old that I don't like the new stuff as much. There are so many records coming out that you can't really focus on one person for very long. U2 tried creating an event for *Pop*, and they're like a big band and it didn't really wash, did it?'

Five months later, *Terror Twilight* is finished and mastered, ready to swim or sink in pop's unforgiving currents. It is, moreover, the album you always knew – or at least prayed – that Pavement had up their sleeves. Hiring Nigel Godrich to shepherd it may have been a calcu-lated risk, but it has enabled Malkmus and his sidekicks to make a record that's genuinely accessible without for a moment sacrificing their many idiosyncrasies. For anyone who ever doubted they'd find themselves walking around with Pavement songs on the brain, *Terror Twilight* defies you to leave 'Carrot Rope' or 'Major Leagues' or 'Spit On A Stranger' unhummed. This is pop music at its most direct and adorable.

'We're pretty pleased with the record,' Malkmus tells me in early April. 'Because I had this little digital four-track mixing thing at my house, I had things a lot more planned out, and if you combine that with Nigel and his meticulous ways, that was a good thing to go together because we're pretty slack musically. But he couldn't get us *too* uptightly tight.'

Are Pavement too wimpy to boogie? Not if 'Platform Blues' is anything to go by. Can they rock out and still retain their indie-cred? 'Cream Of Gold' says an emphatic yes. Can they do sad, sincere, pretty? Try 'Ann Don't Cry'. You want Radiohead-moody? 'The Hexx' is there in all its chiming magnificence.

Terror Twilight is a late-flowering masterwork.

Flashback to November '98: Steve Malkmus hunched over his red Gibson guitar, trying out lines for 'The Hexx'.

'I just love being in a band / Can't wait to go out on the road / I love riders, love beer, love cheese . . .'

Hell, what can a smart boy do, 'cept to sing for a rock 'n' roll band?

1999

Epilogue

The Last Star: Kurt Cobain and the Death of Rock 'n' Roll

The dads don't know, but the little boys understand.

Watch them pour out of the playground at teatime, all bony torsos and flapping T-shirts emblazoned with the names of today's top 'nu metal' bands – Papa Roach, Puddle of Mudd and their kind. Absurdly wide-bottomed jeans drag along the pavement as Harry and Sam scurry home to toast and homework.

In among the Roaches and Puddles there's always one black tee that spells out, in bright yellow letters, the legend of 'NIRVANA'. These middle-class urchins probably couldn't tell you what 'nirvana' means. The youngest weren't even *born* when, in early April 1994, the lead singer of Nirvana stuck a loaded shotgun in his mouth and pulled the trigger. But for them the late Kurt Cobain is sort of what Jimi Hendrix or John Lennon or Bob Marley are to their fathers: an icon, a martyr, a patron saint.

The ten-year-olds seem intuitively to grasp that Kurt Cobain was *the perfect rock star*: a good-looking misfit, a rebel without a cause, a man-boy with a voice like howling sandpaper.

Like James Dean – and like Dean's great disciple Elvis Presley – Kurt was a smalltown punk trashing American values, refusing to conform. Like every other significant rock performer, his act was anchored in dysfunctionality. And like all the true immortals, he had the nous to *burn out* rather than *fade away* – the words, copped from Neil Young, that he used to conclude his histrionic suicide note.

But perhaps the little boys also understand, at some level, that Kurt Cobain was the last real star rock and roll produced. Sure, the *NME* still valiantly hyperventilates every time some cocky Kurt-a-like comes along – the Vines' wildly overrated Craig Nicholls is only the latest such wunderbrat to have the mantle laid on his shoulders – but the rest of us have ceased believing that a new guitar hero will save us from the nightmare teleparade of identikit pop idols. We've lost our faith in transcendence through riffology.

'There's something wrong with that boy,' noted William Burroughs when, in 1993, Kurt Cobain dropped in to pay his respects in Lawrence, Kansas. 'He frowns for no good reason.'

The godfather of junk was right that something was wrong with Cobain, but wrong that the 'boy' frowned for no good reason. Kurt frowned because he was an intensely depressed, chronically drug-addicted young man in a harrowing state of crisis.

At that point he was also the biggest rock star on the planet – a scrawny logging town loser whom fate had transfigured into a messiah of misery, a poster boy for the punk-metal hybrid known onomatopoe-ically as 'grunge'. Nirvana, a power trio who sat somewhere on the Richter scale between Hüsker Dü and the Jimi Hendrix Experience, had broken through with the incendiary anthem 'Smells Like Teen Spirit' two years before. The album whence it came, *Nevermind*, had sold gazillions.

On 'Lithium' and 'Come As You Are', Kurt's agonising voice – always straining, always sore – seemed to embody the impotent rage of an American generation. Half-Sid Vicious, half-Jeff Buckley, this dark angel was the dream of punk writ large – the thrilling riposte to the testosterone bullshit of mainstream hard rock. 'The kid has heart,' Bob Dylan remarked after hearing *Nevermind*'s chilling 'Polly'.

Kurt was the flannel-shirted Eminem of *Twin Peaks* country, a petu-lant poet wracked by the void of his loveless childhood. (At thirteen he saw Jonathan Kaplan's seminal disturbed-teens movie *Over The Edge*, remembering it later as 'a story of troubled youth, vandalism, parental negligence, and most importantly real estate development dysfunc-tional families . . .') He was America's archetypal latchkey sociopath, his true siblings the high-school killers that dominate the hysterical history of what he called 'suburban subdivision hell . . .'

I'm so ugly, but that's OK 'cause so are you . . .

Kurt never anticipated the scale and resonance of his success, and it swiftly overwhelmed him. In the end, the double bind that was *punk superstardom* finally made his existence untenable. Charles Cross' dense biography, *Heavier Than Heaven*, already told us as much. Now the singer's 'journals', to which Cross had full access, make it still clearer just how confused and ambivalent he felt about his fame – and how jaded he felt about rock and roll itself.

'I feel there is a universal sense amongst our generation that everything has been said and done,' Cobain writes early in the journals, summing up the ennui of the analysed-to-death Generation X. A little later on he adds: 'God I'm so sick of Rock Trivia, big deal, it's like what am I gonna do when I'm old if I already know everything about Rock n Roll by the time I'm 19?' (In one of his first interviews, in February 1989, Kurt referred to the burgeoning Seattle 'grunge' scene as being simultaneously 'the last wave of rock music' and 'the ultimate rehash'.)

Kurt's journals take us from the jejune, self-consciously angsty entries of an adolescent ('My penmanship seems scatological because of my lack of personality, or excess of personality') through muted self-aggrandisement ('Nirvana can't decide whether they want to be punk or REM . . .') and eclectic lists for mix tapes (Leadbelly, NWA, Patsy Cline, Flipper, Beat Happening) to rabid rants about local rednecks ('Aberdeen's population consists of highly bigoted . . . deer-shooting, faggot-killing logger types').

'I've never been a very prolific person so when creativity flows, it flows,' Kurt writes. 'I find myself scribbling on little note pads and pieces of loose paper which results in a very small portion of my writings to ever show up in true form.'

In their raw struggle to articulate messy feelings, Kurt's journals comprise the textbook testaments of an angry, anguished and – above all – ambitious addict. Cobain on paper is a mass of contradictions: one moment touchingly vulnerable, the next splenetically sarcastic. 'Cobain ricochets between opposites,' wrote the *New York Times*' Jon

Pareles after interviewing Kurt in 1993. 'He is wary and unguarded, sincere and sarcastic, thin-skinned and insensitive, aware of his popularity and trying to ignore it.'

But what makes Cobain's journals especially riveting from a rock-historical point of view is his desperate effort to extract meaning from – or impose it upon – the moribund pop culture around him. His starting point is the awareness that the '60s dream failed.

'I like,' he writes, 'to blame my parents' generation for coming so close to social change, then giving up after a few successful efforts by the media and government to deface the moment by using the Mansons and other hippie representatives as propaganda examples . . .' He adds that if 'Jimmi [sic] Hendrix' were alive today he'd be sporting a mullet and 'sequin threads'.

Here we are now, entertain us . . .

Cobain knows that punk rock was/is a rejection of nostalgic classic-rock cliché, but he knows that punk, too, is guilty of bad faith. Caught between the desire to shake America with his songs and a despairing acceptance of the futility of that desire, Cobain writes in a caustic press release that 'we want to cash in and suck butt up to the big wigs in hopes that we too can get high and fuck wax figure hot babes . . .' Always the subtext in the journals is: How can we keep rock and roll alive as something *real*? With the implicit rejoinder: *Maybe we can't.*

The biggest difficulty Kurt faced was the misfit between his passionate politics and his skyrocketing celebrity. As someone who could write that 'I am going to fucking destroy your macho, sadistic, right wing, religiously abusive opinions . . .', Cobain was consumed with guilt about the way fate singled out Nirvana above all the other grunge contenders of the Pacific North-west. 'I feel so incredibly GUILTY for abandoning my true comrades who were the ones who were devoted to us a few years ago . . .'

'For some reason I've been blessed with loads of neat stuff within the past year,' he adds in the late summer of 1992, 'and I don't really think these baubles and gifts have been acquired by the fact that I'm a critically-acclaimed, internationally-beloved teen idol demi-God-like blonde front man.'

Yet the contrition runs deeper still: 'I like to be with my friends. I like to be by myself. I like to feel guilty for being a white, American male.'

Over and over again in the journals, what we hear is the sound of self-loathing – of the descent into abjection. (The original title for 1993's mordant, anti-commercial *In Utero* was *I Hate Myself And I Want To Die*.) Kurt describes himself at thirteen as 'a rodent-like, underdeveloped, hyperactive spaz who could fit his entire torsoe [sic] in one leg of his bell-bottomed jeans'. Desperate to be admired, but lacking innate belief in himself, he at one point offers 'a disclaimer . . . for my lack of education, for my loss of inspiration, for my unnerving quest for affection and my perfunctory shamefulness towards many who are of my relative age'. He is 'obsessed with the fact that I am skinny and stupid'.

On the one hand, Cobain detested machismo, on the other he was mortified by what he felt to be his physical inadequacy. This carried all the way through to his heroin-blighted decline in 1993–4, when he railed against the media's depiction of him as 'a notoriously fucked up Heroine [sic] addict, alcoholic, self-destructive, yet overtly sensitive, frail, fragile, soft spoken, narcoleptic, neurotic, little piss ant who at any minute is going to OD . . .'

Towards the end of his short life, Kurt's journal entries degenerate into bilious, smack-addled rage at the world – and particularly at the music press. Like many rock stars, he developed a pathological relationship with writers, biting hands that had fed him when Nirvana first hit the scene. He is, he says, 'not able to trust the majority of the incestually [sic] competitive english journalists . . . they're enemic [sic], clammy, physically deformed, gnome-like . . .'

Scorning the 'second-rate freudian evaluations' of his lyrics that he found in most analyses of *Nevermind* and *In Utero*, Kurt concludes one diatribe with the outburst 'Leave me alone!' – surely an ironic statement of solidarity with the similarly harassed Michael Jackson.

It's worth noting that Cobain's partner in addiction, Courtney Love – that inflammable mix of Yoko Ono and Nancy Spungen – was also his partner in rage. But Courtney was both smarter and feistier than Kurt, further underscoring his inadequacies even as he hid behind her.

'He worked out some of his aggression through her,' commented Carolyn Rue, drummer with Love's band Hole, in *Heavier Than Heaven*. 'He got off on it, vicariously, because he didn't have the courage to do it himself.'

'Bi-polar opposites attract,' Kurt sang in *In Utero*'s cynical, whingeing 'Radio Friendly Unit Shifter'. 'I love you for what I am not.' As fucked-up as she was, Courtney represented maternal strength to her husband: 'Throw down your umbilical noose,' he sang on *In Utero*'s great love song 'Heart-Shaped Box', 'so I can climb right back.' When she gave birth in August 1992 to their daughter Frances Bean, Courtney found herself comforting *Kurt* during her contractions: 'I'm holding *his* hand and rubbing *his* stomach while the baby's coming out of me.'

In the autumn of 2002, Love finally settled with Kurt's bandmates Dave Grohl and Krist Novoselic, granting permission for such unreleased Nirvana songs as the superb, surging 'You Know You're Right' to be released. The Kurt Cobain industry was finally back on track.

If rock has failed to produce a single truly totemic figure since Kurt Cobain's demise, it may be at least partly because of the violence of the death itself. The lesson seems to be: believe in music that fiercely – that uncompromisingly – and look what happens. Better to treat music as frothy ritual or disposable lifestyle appendage.

'Hey hey, my my,' wailed Neil Young at the start of the song Kurt quoted in his suicide note, 'rock and roll will never die.' But from our vantage point in 2002, Kurt's death looks like the last gasp of rock 'n' roll conviction in our flattening, hyper-mediated society. Who needs a 'leper messiah' in the age of stage school pop idols – or of endless 'last' Stones tours?

'There was no use in pretending,' sings Tom Petty on 'Money Becomes King', an angry track on his new album *The Last D.J.*, 'No magic left to hear / All the music gave me / Was a craving for lite beer.'

'Rock and roll is just an anomaly,' concluded Michael Wolff in a bracing piece in *New York* magazine earlier this year. 'While for a generation or two it created a go-go industry – the youthquake – it is unreasonable to expect that anything so transforming can remain a permanent condition. To a large degree, the music industry is, then, a fluke. A bubble. Finally the bubble burst.'

RIP Kurt. RIP rock 'n' roll.

2002

Index